Excel® 2019 For Dummies®

Published by: **John Wiley & Sons, Inc.,** 111 River Street, Hoboken, NJ 07030-5774, www.wiley.com

Copyright © 2018 by John Wiley & Sons, Inc., Hoboken, New Jersey

Published simultaneously in Canada

For general information on our other products and services, please contact our Customer Care Department within the U.S. at 877-762-2974, outside the U.S. at 317-572-3993, or fax 317-572-4002. For technical support, please visit https://hub.wiley.com/community/support/dummies.

Wiley publishes in a variety of print and electronic formats and by print-on-demand. Some material included with standard print versions of this book may not be included in e-books or in print-on-demand. If this book refers to media such as a CD or DVD that is not included in the version you purchased, you may download this material at http://booksupport.wiley.com. For more information about Wiley products, visit www.wiley.com.

Library of Congress Control Number: 2018954127

ISBN 978-1-119-51332-2 (pbk); ISBN 978-1-119-51333-9 (ebk); ISBN 978-1-119-51334-6 (ebk)

Manufactured in the United States of America

C10004151_082918

andard
erthyr
85 7262

Excel 2019

by Greg Ha   PhD

for
dummies®
A Wiley Brand

Contents at a Glance

Table of Contents

Introduction

'm very proud to present you with *Excel 2019 For Dummies,* the latest version of everybody's favorite book on Microsoft Office Excel for readers with no intention whatsoever of becoming spreadsheet gurus.

Excel 2019 For Dummies covers all the fundamental techniques you need to know in order to create, edit, format, and print your own worksheets. In addition to showing you around the worksheet, this book also exposes you to the basics of charting, creating data lists, and performing data analysis. Keep in mind, though, that this book just touches on the easiest ways to get a few things done with these features — I don't attempt to cover charting, data lists, or data analysis in the same definitive way as spreadsheets: This book concentrates on spreadsheets because spreadsheets are what most regular folks create with Excel.

About This Book

This book isn't meant to be read cover to cover. Although its chapters are loosely organized in a logical order (progressing as you might when studying Excel in a classroom situation), each topic covered in a chapter is really meant to stand on its own.

Each discussion of a topic briefly addresses the question of what a particular feature is good for before launching into how to use it. In Excel, as with most other sophisticated programs, you usually have more than one way to do a task. For the sake of your sanity, I have purposely limited the choices by usually giving you only the most efficient ways to do a particular task. Later, if you're so tempted, you can experiment with alternative ways of doing a task. For now, just concentrate on performing the task as I describe.

As much as possible, I've tried to make it unnecessary for you to remember anything covered in another section of the book. From time to time, however, you will come across a cross-reference to another section or chapter in the book. For the most part, such cross-references are meant to help you get more complete information on a subject, should you have the time and interest. If you have neither, no problem. Just ignore the cross-references as if they never existed.

How to Use This Book

This book is similar to a reference book. You can start by looking up the topic you need information about (in either the Table of Contents or the index) and then refer directly to the section of interest. I explain most topics conversationally (as though you were sitting in the back of a classroom where you can safely nap). Sometimes, however, my regiment-commander mentality takes over, and I list the steps you need to take to accomplish a particular task in a particular section.

What You Can Safely Ignore

When you come across a section that contains the steps you take to get something done, you can safely ignore all text accompanying the steps (the text that isn't in bold) if you have neither the time nor the inclination to wade through more material.

Whenever possible, I have also tried to separate background or footnote-type information from the essential facts by exiling this kind of junk to a sidebar (look for blocks of text on a gray background). Often, these sections are flagged with icons that let you know what type of information you will encounter there. You can easily disregard text marked this way. (I'll scoop you on the icons I use in this book a little later.)

Foolish Assumptions

I'm only going to make one foolish assumption about you, and that is that you have some need to use Microsoft Excel 2019 in your work or studies. If pushed, I further guess that you aren't particularly interested in knowing Excel at an expert level but are terribly motivated to find out how to do the stuff you need to get done. If that's the case, this is definitely the book for you. Fortunately, even if you happen to be one of those newcomers who's highly motivated to become the company's resident spreadsheet guru, you've still come to the right place.

As far as your hardware and software goes, I'm assuming that you already have Excel 2019 (usually as part of Microsoft Office 2019) installed on your computing device, using a standard home or business installation running under Windows 10 (this is the first version of Excel that is not supported by earlier versions of Windows, such as the infamous Window 8 or the ever-popular Windows 7). I'm not assuming, however, that when you're using Excel 2019, you are sitting in front of a large screen monitor and making cell entries and command selections with a physical keyboard or connected mouse. With the introduction of Microsoft's Surface 4 tablets and the support for a whole slew of different Windows tablets, you may well be entering data and selecting commands with your finger or stylus using the Windows Touch keyboard.

TIP

To deal with the differences between using Excel 2019 on a standard desktop or laptop computer with access only to a physical keyboard and mouse and a touch-screen tablet or smartphone environment with access only to the virtual Touch keyboard, I've outlined the touchscreen equivalents to common commands you find throughout the text such as "click," "double-click," "drag," and so forth in Chapter 1.

WARNING

This book is intended *only* for users of Microsoft Office Excel 2019! Because of the diversity of the devices that Excel 2019 runs on and the places where its files can be saved and used, if you're using Excel 2007 or Excel 2010 for Windows, much of the file-related information in this book may only confuse and confound you. If you're still using a version prior to Excel 2007, which introduced the Ribbon interface, this edition will be of no use to you as your version of the program works nothing like the 2019 version this book describes.

How This Book Is Organized

This book is organized in six parts with each part containing two or more chapters (to keep the editors happy) that more or less go together (to keep you happy). Each chapter is divided further into loosely related sections that cover the basics of the topic at hand. However, don't get hung up on following the structure of the book; ultimately, it doesn't matter whether you find out how to edit the worksheet before you learn how to format it, or whether you figure out printing before you learn editing. The important thing is that you find the information — and understand it when you find it — when you need to perform a particular task.

In case you're interested, a synopsis of what you find in each part follows.

Part 1: Getting Started with Excel 2019

As the name implies, this part covers such fundamentals as how to start the program, identify the parts of the screen, enter information in the worksheet, save a document, and so on. If you're starting with absolutely no background in using spreadsheets, you definitely want to glance at the information in Chapter 1 to discover the secrets of the Ribbon interface before you move on to how to create new worksheets in Chapter 2.

Part 2: Editing Without Tears

In this part, I show you how to edit spreadsheets to make them look good, including how to make major editing changes without courting disaster. Peruse Chapter 3 when you need information on formatting the data to improve the way it appears in the worksheet. See Chapter 4 for rearranging, deleting, or inserting new information in the worksheet. Read Chapter 5 for the skinny on printing your finished product.

Part 3: Getting Organized and Staying That Way

Here I give you all kinds of information on how to stay on top of the data that you've entered into your spreadsheets. Chapter 6 is full of good ideas on how to keep track of and organize the data in a single worksheet. Chapter 7 gives you the ins and outs of working with data in different worksheets in the same workbook and gives you information on transferring data between the sheets of different workbooks.

Part 4: Digging Data Analysis

This part consists of two chapters. Chapter 8 introduces performing various types of what-if analysis in Excel, including setting up data tables with one and two inputs, performing goal seeking, and creating different cases with Scenario Manager. Chapter 9 introduces Excel's powerful pivot table and pivot chart capabilities that enable you to summarize and filter vast amounts of data in a worksheet table or data list in a compact tabular or chart format.

Part 5: Life Beyond the Spreadsheet

In Part 5, I explore some of the other aspects of Excel besides the spreadsheet. In Chapter 10, you find out just how ridiculously easy it is to create a chart using the data in a worksheet. In Chapter 11, you discover just how useful Excel's data list capabilities can be when you have to track and organize a large amount of information. In Chapter 12, you find out about using add-in programs to enhance Excel's built-in features, adding hyperlinks to jump to new places in a worksheet, to new documents, and even to web pages, as well as how to record macros to automate your work.

Part 6: The Part of Tens

As is the tradition in *For Dummies* books, the last part contains lists of the top ten most useful facts, tips, and suggestions. In this part, you find four chapters. Chapter 13 provides you with the top ten beginner basics you need to know as you start using this program. Chapter 14 gives you the King James Version of the Ten Commandments of Excel 2019. With this chapter under your belt, how canst thou goest astray? Chapter 15 talks about the top ten features for managing and maintaining loads of data in Excel 2019, while Chapter 16 examines the top ten features for identifying trends and vital indicators in your Excel data.

Conventions Used in This Book

The following information gives you the lowdown on how things look in this book. Publishers call these items the book's *conventions* (no campaigning, flag-waving, name-calling, or finger-pointing is involved, however).

Selecting Ribbon commands

Throughout the book, you'll find Ribbon command sequences (the name on the tab on the Ribbon and the command button you select) separated by a command arrow, as in

HOME ⇨ Copy

This shorthand is the Ribbon command that copies whatever cells or graphics are currently selected to the Windows Clipboard. It means that you click the Home tab on the Ribbon (if it isn't displayed already) and then click the Copy button (that sports the traditional side-by-side page icon).

Some of the Ribbon command sequences involve not only selecting a command button on a tab but then also selecting an item on a drop-down menu. In this case, the drop-down menu command follows the name of the tab and command button, all separated by command arrows, as in

Formulas ⇨ Calculation Options ⇨ Manual

This shorthand is the Ribbon command sequence that turns on manual recalculation in Excel. It says that you click the Formulas tab (if it isn't displayed already) and then click the Calculation Options button followed by the Manual drop-down menu option.

The book occasionally encourages you to type something specific into a specific cell in the worksheet. When I tell you to enter a specific function, the part you should type generally appears in **bold** type. For example, **=SUM(A2:B2)** means that you should type exactly what you see: an equal sign, the word **SUM**, a left parenthesis, the text **A2:B2** (complete with a colon between the letter-number combos), and a right parenthesis. You then, of course, have to press Enter to make the entry stick.

Occasionally, I give you a *hot key combination* that you can press in order to choose a command from the keyboard rather than clicking buttons on the Ribbon with the mouse. Hot key combinations are written like this: Alt+FS or Ctrl+S (both of these hot key combos save workbook changes).

With the Alt key combos on a physical keyboard, you press the Alt key until the hot key letters appear in little squares all along the Ribbon. At that point, you can release the Alt key and start typing the hot key letters (by the way, you type all low-ercase hot key letters — I only put them in caps to make them stand out in the text).

Hot key combos that use the Ctrl key are of an older vintage and work a little bit differently. On physical keyboards you have to hold down the Ctrl key while you type the hot key letter (though again, type only lowercase letters unless you see the Shift key in the sequence, as in Ctrl+Shift+C).

Excel 2019 uses only one pull-down menu (File) and one toolbar (the Quick Access toolbar). You open the File pull-down menu by clicking the File tab or pressing Alt+F to access the Excel Backstage. The Quick Access toolbar with its four buttons appears to the immediate right of the File tab.

Finally, if you're really observant, you may notice a discrepancy in how the names of dialog box options (such as headings, option buttons, and check boxes) appear in the text and how they actually appear in Excel on your computer screen. I inten-tionally use the convention of capitalizing the initial letters of all the main words of a dialog box option to help you differentiate the name of the option from the rest of the text describing its use.

Icons Used in This Book

The following icons are placed in the margins to point out stuff you may or may not want to read.

TECHNICAL STUFF

This icon alerts you to nerdy discussions that you may well want to skip (or read when no one else is around).

This icon alerts you to shortcuts or other valuable hints related to the topic at hand.

This icon alerts you to information to keep in mind if you want to meet with a modicum of success.

This icon alerts you to information to keep in mind if you want to avert complete disaster.

Beyond the Book

In addition to what you're reading right now, this product also comes with a free access-anywhere Cheat Sheet that's full of pointers on how to make your way through Excel's command menus and immediately start using its features to create great-looking spreadsheets and charts. To get this Cheat Sheet, simply go to www.dummies.com and search for "Excel 2019 For Dummies Cheat Sheet" in the Search box.

Where to Go from Here

If you've never worked with a computer spreadsheet, I suggest that you first go to Chapter 1 and find out what you're dealing with. Then, as specific needs arise (such as, "How do I copy a formula?" or "How do I print just a particular section of my worksheet?"), you can go to the Table of Contents or the index to find the appropriate section and go right to that section for answers.

1

Getting Started with Excel 2019

Explore the Excel user interface and the Ribbon.

Make sense of the most commonly used tabs and command buttons.

Customize the Quick Access toolbar.

Start (and stop) Excel 2019.

Get online help with the Help tab and with the Tell Me feature in Excel 2019.

Become familiar with the prominent buttons and boxes for entering spreadsheet data.

Save your work and recover a lost workbook if disaster strikes.

Visit www.dummies.com for more great Dummies content online.

IN THIS CHAPTER

» Getting familiar with the Excel 2019 program window and Backstage view

» Selecting commands from the Ribbon

» Customizing the Quick Access toolbar

» Starting Excel 2019

» Surfing an Excel 2019 worksheet and workbook

» Getting things done with the Tell Me feature

Chapter **1**

The Excel 2019 User Experience

E xcel 2019, like Excel 2016, 2013, 2010, and 2007 before it, relies upon a single strip at the top of the worksheet called the Ribbon that puts the bulk of the Excel commands you use at your fingertips at all times.

Add to the Ribbon a File tab and a Quick Access toolbar — along with a few remaining task panes (Help, Clipboard, Clip Art, and Research, to name a few) — and you end up with the handiest way to crunch your numbers, produce and print polished financial reports, as well as organize and chart your data. In other words, to do all the wonderful things for which you rely on Excel.

Best of all, the Excel 2019 user interface includes all sorts of graphical elements that make working on spreadsheets a lot faster and a great deal easier. Foremost is Live Preview, which shows you how your actual worksheet data would appear in a particular font, table formatting, and so on before you actually select it. This Live Preview extends to the new Quick Analysis and Recommended PivotTables and Recommended Charts commands to enable you to preview your data in various formats before you apply them.

Additionally, Excel 2019 supports a Page Layout View that displays rulers and margins along with headers and footers for every worksheet with a Zoom slider at the bottom of the screen that enables you to zoom in and out on the spreadsheet data instantly. Finally, Excel 2019 is full of pop-up galleries that make spreadsheet formatting and charting a real breeze, especially in tandem with Live Preview.

Excel's Ribbon User Interface

When you launch Excel 2019, the Start screen similar to the one shown in Figure 1-1 opens. Here you can start a new blank workbook by clicking the Blank workbook template, or you can select any of the other templates shown as the basis for your new spreadsheet. If none of the templates shown in the Start screen suits your needs, you can search for templates online. After you've worked with Excel for some time, the Start screen also displays a list of recently opened workbooks that you can reopen for further editing or printing.

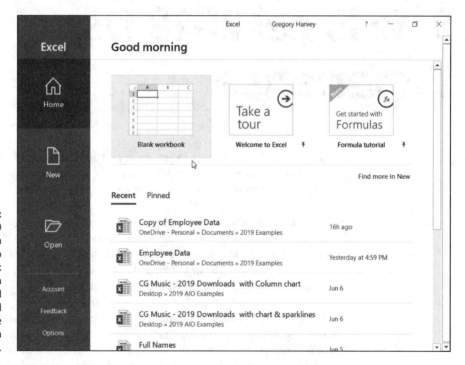

FIGURE 1-1:
The Excel 2019 Start screen enables you to open a new blank workbook or a recently opened workbook, or find a template to use as the basis for a new workbook.

When you select the Blank workbook template from the Excel 2019 Start screen, the program opens an initial worksheet (named Sheet1) in a new workbook file (named Book1) inside a program window like the one shown in Figure 1-2.

FIGURE 1-2:
The Excel 2019
program window
that appears
immediately after
selecting the
Blank Workbook
template in the
opening screen.

The Excel program window containing this worksheet of the workbook contains the following components:

>> **File** button that when clicked opens the Backstage view — a menu on the left that contains all the document- and file-related commands, including Info, New, Open (selected by default when you first launch Excel), Save, Save As, Print, Share, Export, Publish, and Close. Additionally, at the bottom, there's an Account option with User and Product information and an Options item that enables you to change many of Excel's default settings. Note that you can press Esc to exit the Backstage view and return to the normal worksheet view.

>> Customizable **Quick Access toolbar** that contains buttons you can click to perform common tasks, such as manually saving your work and undoing and redoing edits. This toolbar is on the left side and begins with the Save button in a new worksheet. The deactivated AutoSave button to its immediate left is automatically turned on after you manually save a workbook file in the cloud on OneDrive or a SharePoint website.

>> **Ribbon** that consists of a series of tabs, ranging from Home through Help. The tabs on the Ribbon contains the bulk of the Excel.

>> **Formula bar** that displays the address of the current cell along with the contents of that cell.

>> **Worksheet area** that contains the cells of the worksheet identified by column headings using letters along the top and row headings using numbers along the left edge; tabs for switching to a new worksheet; a horizontal scroll bar to move left and right through the sheet; and a vertical scroll bar to move up and down through the sheet.

>> **Status bar** that keeps you informed of the program's current mode and any special keys you engage and enables you to select a new worksheet view and to zoom in and out on the worksheet.

Going Backstage

To the immediate left of the Home tab on the Ribbon right below the AutoSave button and Quick Access toolbar, you find the File button.

When you select File, the Backstage view opens. This view contains a menu similar to the one shown in Figure 1-3. When you open the Backstage view with the Info option selected (Alt+FI), Excel displays at-a-glance stats about the workbook file you have open and active in the program.

FIGURE 1-3: Open Backstage view to get at-a-glance information about the current file, access all file-related commands, and modify the program options.

This information panel is divided into two panes. The pane on the left contains large buttons that enable you to modify the workbook's protection status, check the document before publishing, manage its versions, and determine which worksheets in the file are shown when the Excel workbook file is viewed in a web browser. The pane on the right contains a list of fields detailing the workbook's various document Properties, some of which you can change (such as Title, Tags, Categories, Author, and Last Modified By), and many of which you can't (such as Size, Last Modified, Created, and so forth).

Below the Info option, you find the commands (New, Open, Save, Save As, Save as Adobe PDF, Print, Share, Export, Publish, and Close) that you commonly need for working with Excel workbook files. Near the bottom, the File tab contains an Account option that, when selected, displays an Account panel in the Backstage view. This panel displays user, connection, and Microsoft Office account information. Below the Account menu item, you find options to give Microsoft feedback about Excel 2019 as well as options that you can select to change the program's many default settings.

TIP

Select the Open option to open an Excel workbook you've previously worked on for more editing. When you select Open, Excel displays a panel with a list of all the workbook files recently opened in the program. To re-open a particular file for editing, all you do is click its filename in this list.

REMEMBER

To close the Backstage view and return to the normal worksheet view, you select the Back button at the very top of the menu or simply press Esc on your keyboard.

Using the Excel Ribbon

The Ribbon (shown in Figure 1-4) groups the most commonly used options needed to perform particular types of Excel tasks.

FIGURE 1-4:
Excel's Ribbon consists of a series of tabs containing command buttons arranged into different groups.

To do this, the Ribbon uses the following components:

>> **Tabs** for each of Excel's main tasks that bring together and display all the commands commonly needed to perform that core task.

>> **Groups** that organize related command buttons into subtasks normally performed as part of the tab's larger core task.

>> **Command buttons** within each group that you select to perform a particular action or to open a gallery from which you can click a particular thumbnail. *Note:* Many command buttons on certain tabs of the Ribbon are organized into mini-toolbars with related settings.

>> **Dialog Box launcher** in the lower-right corner of certain groups that opens a dialog box containing a bunch of additional options you can select. (Note that you can mouse over this button to display a preview of the dialog box.)

TIP

To display more of the Worksheet area in the program window, collapse the Ribbon so that only the names of its tabs are displayed by simply clicking the Collapse the Ribbon button on the right side above the vertical scroll bar. You can also double-click (or double-tap on a touchscreen) any one of the Ribbon's tabs, or press Ctrl+F1 on your keyboard. To once again pin the Ribbon in place so that all the command buttons on each of its tabs are always displayed in the program window, double-click (or double-tap) any one of the tabs, or press Ctrl+F1 a second time. You can also do this by selecting the Pin the Ribbon button (whose icon looks just like a pin) that replaces the Unpin the Ribbon button and appears whenever you temporarily activate a tab to use its command buttons.

REMEMBER

When you work in Excel with the Ribbon collapsed, the Ribbon expands each time you activate one of its tabs to show its command buttons, but that tab stays open only until you select one of the command buttons or select an element in the worksheet. The moment you select a command button, Excel immediately minimizes the Ribbon again and just displays its tabs. Note that you can also use the Show Tabs and Show Tabs and Commands options on the Ribbon Display Options button's drop-down menu to switch between collapsing the Ribbon to its tabs and restoring its commands again.

TIP

If you really want to maximize the Worksheet area in Excel 2019, you can use its Auto-Hide Ribbon command to remove the display of the Quick Access toolbar plus the names of the Ribbon's tabs and commands. To do this, click or tap the Ribbon Display Options button (to the immediate left of the Minimize button in the upper-right corner of the screen) and select Auto-Hide Ribbon command at the top of the drop-down menu. With this mode turned on, you simply need to click or tap anywhere in the blank area of the screen above the Formula bar to display the tab names and their commands.

Keeping tabs on the Ribbon

The first time you launch a new workbook in Excel 2019, its Ribbon contains the following tabs from left to right:

» **Home** tab with the command buttons normally used when creating, formatting, and editing a spreadsheet, arranged into the Clipboard, Font, Alignment, Number, Styles, Cells, and Editing groups.

» **Insert** tab with the command buttons normally used when adding particular elements (including graphics, PivotTables, charts, hyperlinks, and headers and footers) to a spreadsheet, arranged into the Tables, Illustrations, Add-ins, Charts, Tours, Sparklines, Filter, Links, Text, and Symbols groups.

» **Draw tab** with commands for changing various pen and ink options, arranged in Touch, Pens, Convert, and Replay groups when running Excel 2019 on a Windows 10 tablet or computer equipped with a touchscreen or digital ink pad.

» **Page Layout** tab with the command buttons normally used when preparing a spreadsheet for printing or re-ordering graphics on the sheet, arranged into the Themes, Page Setup, Scale to Fit, Sheet Options, and Arrange groups.

» **Formulas** tab with the command buttons normally used when adding formulas and functions to a spreadsheet or checking a worksheet for formula errors, arranged into the Function Library, Defined Names, Formula Auditing, and Calculation groups. *Note:* This tab also contains a Solutions group when you activate certain add-in programs, such as Analysis ToolPak and Euro Currency Tools. See Chapter 12 for more on using Excel add-in programs.

» **Data** tab with the command buttons normally used when importing, querying, outlining, and subtotaling the data placed into a worksheet's data list, arranged into the Get & Transform Data, Queries & Connections, Sort & Filter, Data Tools, Forecast, and Outline groups. *Note:* This tab also contains an Analysis group when you activate add-ins, such as Analysis ToolPak and Solver. See Chapter 12 for more on Excel add-ins.

» **Review** tab with the command buttons normally used when proofing, protecting, and marking up a spreadsheet for review by others, arranged into the Proofing, Accessiblity, Insights, Language, Comments, and Protect groups. *Note:* This tab also contains an Ink group with a sole Hide Ink button when you're running Office 2019 on a device with a touchscreen, such as a tablet or a computer equipped with a digital ink tablet.

» **View** tab with the command buttons normally used when changing the display of the Worksheet area and the data it contains, arranged into the Workbook Views, Show, Zoom, Window, and Macros groups.

» **Help** tab with commands for getting online help or support using Excel 2019 or to give you feedback, arranged into a Help & Support and Community group.

REMEMBER

In addition to these standard tabs, Excel has an optional Developer tab that you can add to the Ribbon if you do a lot of work with macros and XML files. See Chapter 12 for more on the Developer tab. If you are running a version of Excel 2019 with the Inquire and PowerPivot COM Add-ins installed, an Inquire and Power Pivot tab appears near the end of the Ribbon.

Although these standard tabs are the ones you always see on the Ribbon when it's displayed in Excel, they aren't the only things that can appear in this area. Excel can display contextual tools when you're working with a particular object that you select in the worksheet, such as a graphic image you've added or a chart or Pivot-Table you've created. The name of the contextual tool for the selected object appears immediately above the tab or tabs associated with the tools.

For example, Figure 1-5 shows a worksheet after you click the embedded chart to select it. As you can see, doing this adds the contextual tool called Chart Tools to the very end of the Ribbon. The Chart Tools contextual tool has its two tabs: Design (selected) and Format. Note, too, that the command buttons on the Design tab are arranged into the groups Chart Layouts, Chart Styles, Data, Type, and Location.

Chart Tools contextual tab

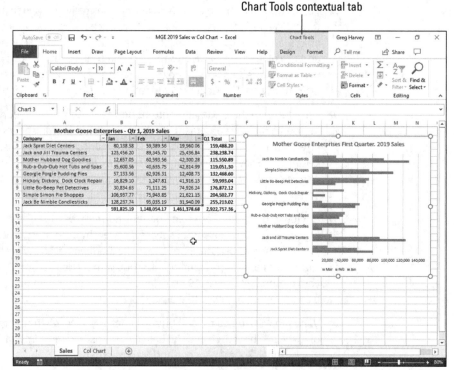

FIGURE 1-5:
When you select certain objects in the worksheet, Excel adds contextual tools to the Ribbon with their own tabs, groups, and command buttons.

The moment you deselect the object (usually by clicking somewhere outside the object's boundaries), the contextual tool for that object and all its tabs immediately disappear from the Ribbon, leaving only the regular tabs — Home, Insert, Page Layout, Formulas, Data, Review, View, and Help — displayed.

Selecting commands with mouse and keyboard

Because Excel 2019 runs on many different types of devices from desktop computer to touchscreen tablets, the most efficient means of selecting Ribbon commands depends not only on the device on which you're running the program, but also on the way that device is equipped.

For example, when I run Excel 2019 on my Microsoft Surface Book 2 in desktop mode, I select commands from the Excel Ribbon more or less the same way I do when running Excel on my Windows desktop computer equipped with a stand-alone physical keyboard and mouse or laptop computer with its built-in physical keyboard and trackpad.

However, when I run Excel 2019 on my Surface Book 2 in tablet mode, I normally select Ribbon commands directly on the touchscreen with my finger or stylus.

The most direct method for selecting Ribbon commands on a device equipped with a physical keyboard and mouse is to click the tab that contains the command button you want and then click that button in its group. For example, to insert an online image into your spreadsheet, you click the Insert tab and then click the Illustrations button followed by the Pictures button to open the Insert Pictures dialog box.

The easiest method for selecting commands on the Ribbon — if you know your keyboard at all well — is to press the keyboard's Alt key and then type the letter of the hot key that appears on the tab you want to select. Excel then displays all the command button hot keys next to their buttons, along with the hot keys for the Dialog Box launchers in any group on that tab. To select a command button or Dialog Box launcher, simply type its hot key letter.

If you know the old Excel shortcut keys from versions prior to Excel 2007, you can still use them. For example, instead of going through the rigmarole of pressing Alt+HCC to copy a cell selection to the Windows Clipboard and then Alt+HVP to paste it elsewhere in the sheet, you can still press Ctrl+C to copy the selection and then press Ctrl+V when you're ready to paste it.

Selecting commands by touch

Before trying to select Excel Ribbon commands by touch, however, you definitely want to turn on Touch mode in Excel 2019. In Touch mode, Excel spreads out the command buttons on the Ribbon tabs by putting more space around them, making it more likely you'll actually select the command button you're tapping with your finger (or stylus) instead of one right next to it. (This is a particular problem with the command buttons in the Font group on the Home tab that enable you to add different attributes to cell entries, such as bold, italic, or underlining: They are so close together when Touch mode is off that they are almost impossible to correctly select by touch.)

To do this, simply tap the Customize Quick Access Toolbar button followed by the Touch/Mouse Mode option on its drop-down menu. Excel adds a Touch/Mouse Mode button that now appears near the end of the Quick Access toolbar sandwiched between the Redo and Customize Quick Access Toolbar buttons. When you tap this button a drop-down menu with two options, Mouse and Touch, appears. Tap the Touch option to put your touchscreen tablet or laptop into Touch mode.

WHAT CLICK AND DRAG MEANS ON YOUR DEVICE

Given all the different choices for selecting stuff in Excel, you need to be aware of a few click-and-drag conventions used throughout this book. When I say *click* something (a command button, cell, or whatever), this means click the primary mouse button (the left one unless you change it) on a physical mouse or tap with your finger or a stylus on a touchscreen. When I say *double-click* something, this means click the primary button twice in rapid succession on a physical mouse and double-tap the object with your finger or stylus. When I say *right-click,* this means click with the secondary button (the right-hand button unless you change it) on a physical mouse or tap the object and keep your finger or stylus on the touchscreen until the context menu or pop-up gallery or whatever appears. If you're using a Microsoft Pen with your Surface device, you hold down the pen's side button as you tap the object with pen tip. Finally, when I say *drag* through a cell selection, with a physical mouse this means click the cell and then hold down the primary mouse button as you swipe and then release the button when the selection is made. On a touchscreen, you tap the cell to make the selection handles appear (the circles that appear at the upper-left and lower-right corners of the cell) and then use your finger or stylus to drag the selection handle through the cells.

Customizing the Quick Access toolbar

When you start using Excel 2019, the Quick Access toolbar contains only the following few buttons:

>> **AutoSave** that automatically saves your work as you make additional changes to an Excel workbook file that you've manually saved at least one time (see Save, the next item in this list) on your OneDrive or SharePoint Online storage in the cloud. To disable this feature, click the On button to the immediate right of AutoSave to change it to Off, in which case all saving all future Excel edits is strictly up to you.

>> **Save** to save any changes made to the current workbook using the same filename, file format, and location

>> **Undo** to undo the last editing, formatting, or layout change you made

>> **Redo** to reapply the previous editing, formatting, or layout change that you just removed with the Undo button

The Quick Access toolbar is very customizable because Excel makes it easy to add any Ribbon command to it. Moreover, you're not restricted to adding buttons for just the commands on the Ribbon; you can add any Excel command you want to the toolbar, even the obscure ones that don't rate an appearance on any of its tabs.

TIP

By default, the Quick Access toolbar appears above the Ribbon tabs. To display the toolbar beneath the Ribbon immediately above the Formula bar, click the Customize Quick Access Toolbar button (the drop-down button to the right of the toolbar with a horizontal bar above a down-pointing triangle) and then click Show Below the Ribbon on its drop-down menu. You will definitely want to make this change if you start adding more than just a few extra buttons to the toolbar. That way, the growing Quick Access toolbar doesn't start crowding the name of the current workbook that appears to the toolbar's right.

Adding Customize Quick Access Toolbar's menu commands

When you click the Customize Quick Access Toolbar button, a drop-down menu appears containing the following commands:

>> **Automatically Save** to add or remove the AutoSave button for automatically saving changes workbook edits to your OneDrive or SharePoint drive

>> **New** to open a new workbook

>> **Open** to display the Open dialog box for opening an existing workbook

- **»** **Save** to save changes to your current workbook

- **»** **E-mail** to open your mail

- **»** **Quick Print** to send the current worksheet to your default printer

- **»** **Print Preview and Print** to open the Print panel in Backstage view with a preview of the current worksheet in the right pane

- **»** **Spelling** to check the current worksheet for spelling errors

- **»** **Undo** to undo your latest worksheet edit

- **»** **Redo** to reapply the last edit that you removed with Undo

- **»** **Sort Ascending** to sort the current cell selection or column in A to Z alphabetical order, lowest to highest numerical order, or oldest to newest date order

- **»** **Sort Descending** to sort the current cell selection or column in Z to A alphabetical order, highest to lowest numerical order, or newest to oldest date order

- **»** **Touch /Mouse Mode** to switch in and out of Touch mode that adds extra space around the command buttons on the individual Ribbon tabs to make them easier to select on a touchscreen device regardless of whether you tap with your finger or a stylus

- **»** **More Commands** to open the Excel Options dialog box where you can add almost any other Excel command that you routinely use

- **»** **Show Below the Ribbon** to move the Quick Access toolbar down so that it appears on its own row immediately below the Excel Ribbon

When you open this menu, only the Automatically Save, Save, Undo, and Redo are the ones selected (indicated by the check marks); therefore, these buttons are the only buttons to appear on the Quick Access toolbar. To add any of the other commands on this menu to the toolbar, you simply click the option on the drop-down menu. Excel then adds a button for that command to the end of the Quick Access toolbar (and a check mark to its option on the drop-down menu).

To remove a command button that you add to the Quick Access toolbar in this manner, click the option a second time on the Customize Quick Access Toolbar button's drop-down menu. Excel removes its command button from the toolbar and the check mark from its option on the drop-down menu.

Adding Ribbon commands

To add a Ribbon command to the Quick Access toolbar, open the command button's shortcut menu (right-click with a mouse or tap and hold on a touchscreen) and then select the Add to Quick Access Toolbar menu item. Excel then immediately adds the selected Ribbon command button to the very end of the Quick Access toolbar, immediately in front of the Customize Quick Access Toolbar button.

If you want to move the command button to a new location on the Quick Access toolbar or group it with other buttons on the toolbar, select the Customize Quick Access Toolbar button followed by the More Commands option near the bottom of its drop-down menu.

Excel then opens the Excel Options dialog box with the Quick Access Toolbar tab selected (similar to the one shown in Figure 1-6). On the right side of the dialog box, Excel shows all the buttons added to the Quick Access toolbar. The order in which they appear from left to right on the toolbar corresponds to the top-down order in the list box.

FIGURE 1-6:
Use the buttons
on the Quick
Access Toolbar
tab of the Excel
Options dialog
box to customize
the appearance
of the Quick
Access toolbar.

To reposition a particular button on the toolbar, select it in the list box on the right and then select either the Move Up button (the one with the black triangle pointing upward) or the Move Down button (the one with the black triangle pointing downward) until the button is promoted or demoted to the desired position on the toolbar.

TIP

You can add a pair of vertical separators to the toolbar to group related buttons. To do this, select the <Separator> option in the list box on the left followed by the Add button. Then, select the Move Up or Move Down button to position one of the two separators at the beginning of the group and the other at the end.

When you finish adding and positioning your command buttons, select OK in the Excel Options dialog box to return to the Excel screen with the new buttons displayed on the Quick Access toolbar. To later remove a button you've added, open the Quick Access toolbar's shortcut menu (right-click or tap and hold on a touchscreen) and then select the Remove from Quick Access Toolbar option.

Adding non-Ribbon commands to the Quick Access toolbar

You can also use the options on the Quick Access Toolbar tab of the Excel Options dialog box (refer to Figure 1-6) to add a button for any Excel command even if it isn't one of those displayed on the tabs of the Ribbon:

1. **Select the type of command you want to add to the Quick Access toolbar in the Choose Commands From drop-down list box.**

   The types of commands include the Popular Commands pull-down menu (the default) as well as each of the tabs that appear on the Ribbon. To display only the commands that are not displayed on the Ribbon, select Commands Not in the Ribbon near the top of the drop-down list. To display a complete list of the Excel commands, select All Commands near the top of the drop-down list.

2. **Select the command button you want to add to the Quick Access toolbar in the list box on the left.**

3. **Click the Add button to add the command button to the bottom of the list box on the right.**

4. **(Optional) To reposition the newly added command button so that it isn't the last one on the toolbar, click the Move Up button until it's in the desired position.**

5. **Click OK to close the Excel Options dialog box.**

TIP

If you've created favorite macros (see Chapter 12) that you routinely use and want to be able to run directly from the Quick Access toolbar, select Macros in the Choose Commands From drop-down list box in the Excel Options dialog box and then select the name of the macro to add followed by the Add button.

Having fun with the Formula bar

The Formula bar displays the cell address (determined by a column letter[s] followed by a row number) and the contents of the current cell. For example, cell A1 is the first cell of each worksheet at the intersection of column A and row 1; cell

XFD1048576 is the last cell of each worksheet at the intersection of column XFD and row 1048576. The type of entry you make determines the contents of the current cell: text or numbers, for example, if you enter a heading or particular value, or the details of a formula, if you enter a calculation.

The Formula bar has three parts:

>> **Name box:** The left-most drop-down button that displays the address of the current cell address or its range name (if you've assigned one as described in Chapter 6).

>> **Formula bar buttons:** The three buttons to the immediate right of the vertical ellipsis (used to narrow or widen the Name box). These buttons are Cancel (with an *X*), Enter (with a check mark), and Insert Function (with *fx*). When you start making or editing a cell entry, the Cancel (an *X*) and Enter (a check mark) buttons become active.

>> **Cell contents:** The third area to the immediate right of the Insert Function button takes up the rest of the bar and expands as necessary to display really long cell entries that won't fit in the normal area.

REMEMBER

The cell contents portion of the Formula bar is important because it *always* shows you the contents of the cell even when the worksheet does not. (When you're dealing with a formula, Excel displays only the calculated result in the cell in the worksheet and not the formula by which that result is derived.) Additionally, you can edit the contents of the cell in this area at any time. Similarly, when the cell contents area is blank, you know that the cell is empty as well.

TECHNICAL STUFF

HOW YOU ASSIGN 26 LETTERS TO 16,384 COLUMNS

When it comes to labeling the 16,384 columns of an Excel 2019 worksheet, our alphabet with its measly 26 letters is simply not up to the task. To make up the difference, Excel doubles the letters in the cell's column reference so that column AA follows column Z (after which you find column AB, AC, and so on) and then triples them so that column AAA follows column ZZ (after which you get column AAB, AAC, and the like). At the end of this letter tripling, the 16,384th and last column of the worksheet ends up being XFD so that the last cell in the 1,048,576th row has the cell address XFD1048576!

What to do in the Worksheet area

The Worksheet area is where most of the Excel spreadsheet action takes place because it's the place that displays the cells of the current worksheet, and it's right inside the cells that you do all your spreadsheet data entry and formatting, not to mention a great deal of your editing.

REMEMBER

To enter or edit data in a cell, that cell must be current. Excel indicates that a cell is current in three ways:

>> The cell cursor — the dark green border surrounding the cell's entire perimeter — appears in the cell.

>> The address or range name assigned to the cell appears in the Name box of the Formula bar.

>> The cell's column letter(s) and row number are shaded in the column headings and row headings that appear at the top and left of the Worksheet area, respectively.

Moving around the worksheet

An Excel worksheet contains far too many columns and rows for all a worksheet's cells to be displayed at one time, regardless of how large your computer's monitor screen is or how high the screen resolution. (After all, we're talking 17,179,869,184 cells total!) Therefore, Excel offers many methods for moving the cell cursor around the worksheet to the cell where you want to enter new data or edit existing data:

>> Click the desired cell — assuming that the cell is displayed within the section of the sheet visible in the Worksheet area — either by clicking it with your mouse or tapping it on your touchscreen.

>> Click the Name box, type the address of the desired cell, and press the Enter key.

>> Press F5 to open the Go To dialog box, type the address of the desired cell into its Reference text box, and then click OK.

>> Use the cursor keys, as shown in Table 1-1 to move the cell cursor to the desired cell.

>> Use the horizontal and vertical buttons located at the ends of the scroll bars found at the bottom and right edge of the Worksheet area to move to the part of the worksheet that contains the desired cell and then click or tap the cell to put the cell cursor in it.

TABLE 1-1   **Keystrokes for Moving the Cell Cursor**

Keystroke	Where the Cell Cursor Moves
→ or Tab	Cell to the immediate right.
← or Shift+Tab	Cell to the immediate left.
↑	Cell up one row.
↓	Cell down one row.
Home	Cell in Column A of the current row.
Ctrl+Home	First cell (A1) of the worksheet.
Ctrl+End or End, Home	Cell in the worksheet at the intersection of the last column that has data in it and the last row that has data in it (that is, the last cell of the so-called active area of the worksheet).
Page Up	Cell one full screen up in the same column.
Page Down	Cell one full screen down in the same column.
Alt+Page Up	One full screen to the left (assuming that the cell cursor is not in the left-most column of the worksheet)
Alt+Page Down	One full screen to the right (assuming that the cell cursor is not in the right-most column of the worksheet)
Ctrl+→ or End, →	First occupied cell to the right in the same row that is either preceded or followed by a blank cell. If no cell is occupied, the pointer goes to the cell at the very end of the row.
Ctrl+← or End, ←	First occupied cell to the left in the same row that is either preceded or followed by a blank cell. If no cell is occupied, the pointer goes to the cell at the very beginning of the row.
Ctrl+↑ or End, ↑	First occupied cell above in the same column that is either preceded or followed by a blank cell. If no cell is occupied, the pointer goes to the cell at the very top of the column.
Ctrl+↓ or End, ↓	First occupied cell below in the same column that is either preceded or followed by a blank cell. If no cell is occupied, the pointer goes to the cell at the very bottom of the column.
Ctrl+Page Down	The cell pointer's location in the next worksheet of that workbook.
Ctrl+Page Up	The cell pointer's location in the previous worksheet of that workbook.

Note: In the case of those keystrokes that use arrow keys, you must either use the arrows on the cursor keypad or else have the Num Lock disengaged on the numeric keypad of your keyboard.

KEYSTROKE SHORTCUTS FOR MOVING THE CELL CURSOR

Excel offers a wide variety of keystrokes for moving the cell cursor to a new cell. When you use one of these keystrokes, the program automatically scrolls a new part of the worksheet into view, if this is required to move the cell pointer. In Table 1-1, I summarize these keystrokes, including how far each one moves the cell pointer from its starting position.

The keystrokes that combine the Ctrl or End key with an arrow key listed in Table 1-1 are among the most helpful for moving quickly from one edge to the other in large tables of cell entries or for moving from table to table in a section of a worksheet with many blocks of cells.

When you use Ctrl and an arrow key to move from edge to edge in a table or between tables in a worksheet, you hold down Ctrl while you press one of the four arrow keys (indicated by the + symbol in keystrokes, such as Ctrl+→).

When you use End and an arrow-key alternative, you must press and then release the End key *before* you press the arrow key (indicated by the comma in keystrokes, such as End, →). Pressing and releasing the End key causes the End Mode indicator to appear on the Status bar. This is your sign that Excel is ready for you to press one of the four arrow keys.

Because you can keep the Ctrl key depressed while you press the different arrow keys that you need to use, the Ctrl-plus-arrow-key method provides a more fluid method for navigating blocks of cells than the End-then-arrow-key method.

REMEMBER

You can use the Scroll Lock key to "freeze" the position of the cell pointer in the worksheet so that you can scroll new areas of the worksheet in view with keystrokes, such as PgUp (Page Up) and PgDn (Page Down), without changing the cell pointer's original position (in essence, making these keystrokes work in the same manner as the scroll bars).

After engaging Scroll Lock, when you scroll the worksheet with the keyboard, Excel does not select a new cell while it brings a new section of the worksheet into view. To "unfreeze" the cell pointer when scrolling the worksheet via the keyboard, you just press the Scroll Lock key again.

TIPS ON USING THE TOUCH KEYBOARD

TIP

If you're running Excel 2019 on a device that lacks any kind of physical keyboard, you need to open the Touch keyboard and use it to input your spreadsheet data.

To open the standard Touch keyboard, simply tap the Touch Keyboard button that appears on the right side of the Windows 10 taskbar. Doing this displays the Touch keyboard, docked at the bottom of the Excel program window, as shown in Figure 1-7.

FIGURE 1-7:
Windows 10 touchscreen shown after displaying the standard Touch keyboard docked beneath the Excel 2019 program window.

Excel supports undocking the standard Touch keyboard so that it floats within the Excel 2019 program window as well as the selection of a different type of keyboard or supported language. To make any of these changes, tap the Touch Keyboard Settings button (the one with the cog on top of the keyboard icon) followed by one of the following options on its pop-up menu:

» **Standard Keyboard** to switch back to the standard docked Touch Keyboard after changing to one of the other styles

» **Split Keyboard** to change to split-keyboard arrangement that separates the letter keys into two banks of three rows starting with QWERT in the top row on the left and YUIOP in the top row on the right

» **Mobile Keyboard** to change to a much smaller floating version of the standard Touch keyboard that you can drag to reposition anywhere in the Excel program window

- >> **Inking Keyboard** to switch to a keyboard that enables you to write out your Excel entries and edits with your pen (or finger) and then enter them by tapping its Enter key

- >> **Expanded Keyboard** to switch to an expanded version of the standard Windows Touch keyboard that supports the Windows, Alt, and function keys as well as adds an Escape, Delete, Tab, and Caps key

- >> **Dock Keyboard** to switch a floating Standard, Split, Inking, or Expanded Touch Keyboard to docked to fix it at the bottom of the screen beneath the Excel program window (note that the Mobile style keyboard can't be docked)

- >> **Float Keyboard** to switch a docked Standard, Split, Inking, or Expanded Touch Keyboard to floating so that you can drag it around the Excel program window

- >> **Language Preferences** to open Region & Language screen in Windows Settings where you can switch to or add another language to use its keyboard in Excel

- >> **Typing Settings** to open the Type screen in the Windows Settings where you modify the spelling and typing options including the one that automatically displays the selected Touch Keyboard whenever your laptop is in Tablet mode or your tablet has no keyboard attached to it

- >> **Keyboard Tips** to open the Tips app where you can get Windows 10 as well as Office 2019 tips

When docked, the default standard Windows 10 Touch keyboard remains completely separate from the Excel program window so that you still have access to all the cells in the current worksheet when doing your data entry. The standard Windows Touch keyboard is limited mostly to letter keys above a spacebar with a few punctuation symbols (apostrophe, comma, period, and question mark). This keyboard also sports the following special keys:

- >> **Backspace** key (marked with the x in the shape pointing left) to delete characters to the immediate left when entering or editing a cell entry

- >> **Enter** key to complete an entry in the current cell and move the cursor down one row in the same column

- >> **Shift** keys (with an arrow pointing upward) to enter capital letters in a cell entry

- >> **Numeric** key (with the &123) to switch to the Touch keyboard so that it displays a numeric keyboard with a Tab key and extensive punctuation used in entering numeric data in a cell (tap the &123 key a second time to return to the standard QWERTY letter arrangement)

- » **Ctrl** key to run macros to which you've assigned letter keys (see Chapter 12 for details) or to combine with the Left arrow or Right arrow key to jump the cursor to the cell in the last and first column of the current row, respectively

- » **Emoticon** key (with that awful smiley face icon) to switch to a bunch of emoticons that you can enter into a cell entry (tap the Emoticon key a second time to return to standard QWERTY letter arrangement)

- » **Left** arrow (with the < symbol) to move the cell cursor one cell to the immediate left and complete any cell entry in progress

- » **Right** arrow (with the > symbol) to move the cell cursor one cell to the immediate right and complete any cell entry in progress

TIP

If you've enabled Windows speech services on your device, you can dictate your Excel entry or edit by tapping the Microphone button (to the immediate right of the Keyboard Settings button).

When you finish entering your worksheet data with the Windows 10 Touch keyboard, you can close it and return to the normal full screen view of the Excel program window by tapping the Close button.

TIPS ON USING THE SCROLL BARS

You can use the horizontal scroll bar at the bottom of the Worksheet area to scroll back and forth through the columns of a worksheet and the vertical scroll bar to scroll up and down through its rows. To scroll a column or a row at a time in a particular direction, select the appropriate scroll arrow at the ends of the scroll bar. To jump immediately back to the originally displayed area of the worksheet after scrolling through single columns or rows in this fashion, simply click (tap on a touchscreen) the area in the scroll bar that now appears in front of or after the scroll box.

You can resize the horizontal scroll bar making it wider or narrower by dragging the button that appears to the immediate left of its left scroll arrow. Just keep in mind when working in a workbook that contains a whole bunch of worksheets that widening the horizontal scroll bar can hide the display of the workbook's later sheet tabs.

TIP

To scroll very quickly through columns or rows of the worksheet when you have a physical keyboard available, hold down the Shift key and then drag the scroll box in the appropriate direction within the scroll bar until the columns or rows that you want to see appear on the screen in the Worksheet area. When you hold down the Shift key while you scroll, the scroll button within the scroll bar becomes skinny, and a ScreenTip appears next to the scroll bar, keeping you informed of the letter(s) of the columns or the numbers of the rows that you're whizzing through.

If you have a mouse and it's equipped with a wheel, you can use it to scroll directly through the columns and rows of the worksheet without using the horizontal or vertical scroll bars. Simply position the white cross mouse pointer in the center of the Worksheet area and then hold down the wheel button of the mouse. When the mouse pointer changes to a four-pointed arrow with a black dot in its center, drag the mouse pointer in the appropriate direction (left and right to scroll through columns or up and down to scroll through rows) until the desired column or row comes into view in the Worksheet area.

TIP

On a touchscreen device, you can also scroll new parts of a worksheet into view simply by swiping with your finger or stylus to scroll (by dragging it on the screen). To scroll new worksheet columns on the right into view, you swipe right to left. To scroll new worksheet rows from below into view, swipe up, bottom to top. The force with which you slide determines how many columns or rows you scroll through. To return previously displayed columns or rows into view, simply slide in the opposite direction: left to right to scroll columns left and downward to scroll rows up.

REMEMBER

The only disadvantage to using the scroll bars to move around is that the scroll bars bring only new sections of the worksheet into view — they don't actually change the position of the cell cursor. If you want to start making entries in the cells in a new area of the worksheet, you still have to remember to select the cell (by clicking it) or the group of cells (by dragging through them) where you want the data to appear before you begin entering the data.

Surfing the sheets in a workbook

Each new workbook you open in Excel 2019 contains a single blank worksheet with 16,384 columns and 1,048,576 rows (giving you a truly staggering 17,179,869,184 blank cells!). But, that's not all. If ever you need more worksheets in your workbook, you can add them simply by clicking the New Sheet button (indicated by the plus sign in a circle) that appears to the immediate right of the last visible tab (see callout in Figure 1-8) or by selecting Shift+F11.

FIGURE 1-8:
The Sheet Tab scroll buttons, sheet tabs, Next sheet, Previous sheet, and New Sheet buttons enable you to activate your worksheets and add to them.

Tab scroll buttons

Previous sheet   Sheet tabs

New sheet

Next sheet

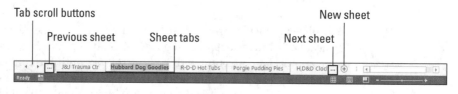

ONE REASON FOR ADDING EXTRA SHEETS TO A WORKBOOK

You may wonder why anyone would ever need more than a single worksheet given just how many cells it already contains. The truth is that it's all about how you choose to structure a particular spreadsheet rather than running out of places to put the data. For example, suppose that you need to create a workbook that contains budgets for all the various departments in your corporation. You may decide to devote an individual work-sheet to each department (with the actual budget spreadsheet tables laid out in the same manner on each sheet) rather than placing all the tables in different sections of the same sheet. Using this kind of one-sheet-per-budget layout makes it much easier for you to enter reoccurring data in multiple sheets at one time as well as to find each budget, print each one as a separate page of a report, and, if ever necessary, to consoli-date the data in a separate summary worksheet.

On the left side of the bottom of the Worksheet area, the Sheet Tab scroll buttons appear followed by the actual tabs for the worksheets in your workbook and the New Sheet button. To activate a worksheet for editing, you select it by clicking its sheet tab. Excel lets you know what sheet is active by displaying the sheet name in boldface type and underlining it to make its tab appear connected to the current sheet.

TIP

Don't forget the Ctrl+Page Down and Ctrl+Page Up shortcut keys for selecting the next and previous sheet, respectively, in your workbook.

If your workbook contains too many sheets for all the tabs to be displayed at the bottom of the Worksheet area, use the Sheet Tab scroll buttons to bring new tabs into view (so that you can then click them to activate them). You click the Next Sheet button (the ellipsis or three periods to the left of the first visible sheet) to scroll the next hidden sheet tab into view or the Last Sheet button (the ellipsis or three periods to the left of the last visible sheet) to scroll the last group of com-pletely or partially hidden tabs into view.

To scroll the very first worksheet in the workbook into view, you can hold down Ctrl as you click the left-pointing Sheet Tab scroll button. To scroll the last sheet into view, you Ctrl+click the right-pointing scroll button.

To display the Activate dialog box that lists all the sheets in the workbook from first to last, right-click either one of the Sheet Tab scroll buttons. You can then scroll into view and click any of the sheets in the workbook simply by clicking its name in the Activate dialog followed by clicking OK.

TIP

On a touchscreen device, remember that the touch equivalent of a right-click with a mouse is to tap and press the graphic element on the screen — the Sheet Tab scroll button in this case — until a circle appears around your finger or stylus. When you then remove your finger or stylus from the screen, the shortcut menu or, in this case, the dialog box associated with the graphic element appears.

Showing off the Status bar

The Status bar is the last component at the very bottom of the Excel program window (see Figure 1-9). The Status bar contains the following:

» **Mode indicator** on the left that shows the current state of the Excel program (Ready, Edit, and so on) as well as any special keys that are engaged (Caps Lock, Num Lock, and Scroll Lock).

» **Record Macro button** to the immediate right of the Mode indicator to begin recording a new macro (this button appears once you record your first macro; see Chapter 12 for details)

» **AutoCalculate indicator** on the right side of the screen that displays the average and sum of all the numerical entries in the current cell selection along with the count of every cell in the selection.

» **Layout selector** that enables you to select between three layouts for the Worksheet area: Normal, the default view that shows only the worksheet cells with the column and row headings; Page Layout View that adds rulers, page margins, and shows page breaks for the worksheet; and Page Break Preview that enables you to adjust the paging of a report. (See Chapter 5 for details.)

» **Zoom slider** that enables you to zoom in and out on the cells in the Worksheet area by dragging the slider to the right or left, respectively.

FIGURE 1-9:
The Status bar displays the program's current standing and enables you to select new worksheet views.

Mode indicator
Record Macro button   AutoCalculate indicator   Layout selector   Zoom slider

TIP

On a touchscreen device, you can work the Zoom slider by using the Pinch and Stretch gesture to increase and decrease the size of the cells displayed in your worksheet. As you stretch your thumb and forefinger apart, you zoom in on the worksheet and the Zoom slider moves to the right and the percentage increases.

As you pinch your fingers together, you zoom out on the worksheet and the Zoom slider moves to the left and the percentage decreases.

TIP

The Num Lock indicator on a physical keyboard equipped with a numeric keypad tells you that you can use the keypad to enter values in the worksheet. This keypad will most often be separate from the regular keyboard (on the right side if you're using a separate keyboard) and embedded in keys on the right side of the keyboard on almost all laptop computers where the keyboard is built in to the computer.

Launching and Quitting Excel

Excel 2019 runs only under the Windows 10 operating system. This means that if your PC is running Windows 7 or (heaven forbid) Windows 8, you must upgrade before you can successfully install and run Excel 2019.

Starting Excel from the Windows 10 Start menu

Windows 10 brings back the good old Start menu that many of you remember from much earlier Windows versions. The Windows 10 Start menu combines the straight menu from earlier days with the tile icons so prominent in Windows 8 Metro view (which reappears only in Windows 10 on tablets or on touchscreen devices when they are in Tablet mode).

To open the Start menu to launch Excel 2019, click the Windows icon on the taskbar or press the Windows key on your keyboard. Then, scroll down to the E section in the list of apps on your device and click Excel.

TIP

To make it easier to launch Excel from the Windows 10 Start menu, you can add its icon to the Start menu as a tile (that you click to launch Excel 2019). Simply right-click the Excel icon in the apps list and select the Pin to Start option on its popup menu. You can also pin an Excel icon to the Windows 10 taskbar. This enables you to launch Excel simply by selecting this button without even opening the Windows Start menu. To pin Excel to the taskbar, launch the program from the Start menu and then right-click the Excel icon on the Windows taskbar and then select the Pin to Taskbar option in the displayed context menu.

Starting Excel from the Windows 10 Search text box

Instead of opening the Windows 10 Start menu and locating the Excel app there, you can launch the program by selecting this item from the Windows Search text box. Simply type **excel** into the text box that appears to the immediate right of the Windows button on the taskbar and click Excel Desktop App at the top of its result list.

TIP

If you want Cortana, the voice-activated online Windows assistant, to launch Excel 2019 for you, click the microphone icon in this text box (that now displays Type Here to Search). When she displays the listening prompt, say, "Cortana, start Microsoft Excel 2019." Or you can simply just say, "Hey Cortana, start Excel." By the way, you can also do this by telling her, "open Excel" or even, launch Excel."

Starting Excel from the Windows 10 Metro view in Tablet mode

TIP

When running Excel 2019 in tablet mode under Windows 10, your Start screen uses tiles in the Metro view introduced in Windows 8. To start Excel from this Start screen, you simply select the Excel program tile either by clicking it if you have a mouse available or tapping it with your finger or stylus.

If you can't locate the Excel program tile among the pinned tiles in the Metro view, you can use the Search feature to find the application and pin it to this Start screen:

1. **From the Start screen, click the Search button on the Windows taskbar (the one with the circle icon between the Back and Task View buttons) and then begin typing** exc **on your physical or virtual keyboard.**

   Windows displays Excel Desktop app in the list under Best Match in the search list.

   If you don't have access to a physical or virtual keyboard, you can locate the Excel app by switching the Start screen from the default of displaying just the pinned tiles to all the applications installed on your device. To do this, tap the All Apps button immediately beneath the Pinned Tiles button, the icon third from top in the upper-left of the Start screen. When you do this, you should see the Excel app button in the E alphabetical listing of all installed applications.

2. **Right-click the Excel app button in the search list to open its pop-up menu.**

   On a touchscreen device, the equivalent to the right-click of the mouse is to tap and hold the Excel menu item with your finger or stylus until the pop-up menu appears. (With the Microsoft Pen, you hold down the button on the pen's side as you tap the Excel app button with the pen tip.)

3. **Select the Pin to Start option in the pop-up menu.**

After pinning an Excel program tile to the Start screen, you can resize it and then move it by dragging and dropping it in your desired block. If you switched to all apps to find the Excel app, you first need to switch the Metro view back to pinned apps by tapping the Pinned Tiles button before you can do this.

Exiting Excel

When you're ready to call it a day and quit Excel, you have a couple of choices for shutting down the program:

>> Press Alt+F4 on your keyboard.

>> Right-click or tap and hold (on a touchscreen device) the Excel program icon on the Windows 10 taskbar and then click or tap the Close Window or Close All Windows item on the pop-up menu.

If you try to exit Excel after working on a workbook and you haven't saved your latest changes, the program displays an alert box querying whether you want to save your changes. To save your changes before exiting, select the Save command button. (For detailed information on saving documents, see Chapter 2.) If you've just been playing around in the worksheet and don't want to save your changes, you can abandon the workbook by selecting the Don't Save button instead.

REMEMBER

QUITTING EXCEL 2019 ON A TOUCHSCREEN DEVICE

If you're running Excel 2019 on a touchscreen device without a physical keyboard (even one with a relatively large screen like my 15-inch Microsoft Surface Book 2), for heaven's sake, don't forget to engage the Touch mode on the Quick Access toolbar (see "Customizing the Quick Access toolbar" earlier in this chapter for details). Turning on Touch mode sufficiently separates the Close button in the very upper-right corner of the Excel screen from the Restore Down button to its immediate left so that when you tap the Close button, you end up actually exiting Excel rather than just shrinking the Excel program window on the Windows desktop!

Help Is on the Way

In Excel 2019, help has its very own tab on the Ribbon. When you select the Help tab, the following command buttons appear on the ribbon:

» **Help** to open a Help task pane with options for selecting or searching for particular help topics as well learning about Excel's features through free online videos (see Figure 1-10). Note that you can also open this Help default task pane by pressing F1.

» **Contact Support** to open a Help task pane containing a text box where you can enter a description of your problem with Excel before clicking its Get Help button to display articles that might help you resolve your issue as well as a Talk to Agent button that enables you to get an agent's help with a Live Chat.

» **Feedback** to open the Feedback screen in the File menu's Backstage view where you can send feedback to Microsoft using the I Like Something, I Don't Like Something, and the I Have a Suggestion option.

» **Show Training** to open the Help task pane with video tutorials that you can run to learn about features such as designing workbooks, using tables and charts, and using formulas and functions.

» **What's New** to open the Help task pane with a list of new features in the version of Excel 2019 you're running.

» **Community** to open the Microsoft Excel Community page in your default web browser with discussions on all sorts of Excel topics where you can post your questions and concerns to the entire Excel online community.

» **Blog Site** to open the Excel blog page in your default web browser, containing articles about all sorts of Excel 2019 applications.

» **Suggest a Feature** to open the Excel's Suggestion Box web page with your default web browser where you can give Microsoft your feedback on Excel 2019 as well as suggest new features for future versions.

TIP

When you get familiar enough with Excel 2019 features that you rarely, if ever, consult help, you can remove the Help tab from the Ribbon. Simply open the Excel Options dialog box (File ⇨ Options), click Customize Ribbon on the left, and then click the Help check box under Main Tabs on the right to remove its check mark before you click OK. Note that after removing the display of the Help tab on the Ribbon, you still open the Help task pane and get all the Excel help you need by pressing F1.

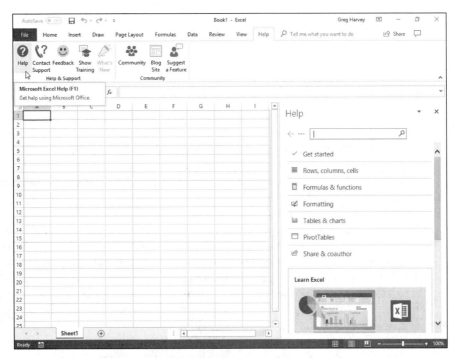

FIGURE 1-10:
The default Help task pane opened by clicking the Help option on the Help tab of the ribbon or by pressing F1.

Using the Tell Me help feature

One of Excel 2019's niftiest help features is the Tell Me help feature available from the Search text box located to the immediate right of the last tab in the Excel Ribbon. (You can press Alt+Q to insert the cursor in the Search text box without having to click it.) As you enter a help topic into this Search text box, Excel displays a list of related Excel commands in a drop-down list.

When you then select one of the items displayed on this list, Excel either selects the associated Ribbon command (no matter which Ribbon tab is currently selected) and waits for you to make a selection from the command's submenu or, in some cases, just goes ahead and completes the associated command sequence for you.

For example, if you type **print** into the Search text box, Excel displays a drop-down list with the following items:

» Preview and Print

» Print

» Print Gridlines

» Print Preview and Print

>> Print Area

>> Get Help on "print"

>> Smart Lookup on "print"

If you select the Preview and Print at the top of the list, a submenu with Print Preview and Print, Quick Print, and Print Preview Full Screen appears. If you select the Quick Print option, the program sends the worksheet directly to the printer. But if you select the Print Preview and Print or the Print Preview Full Screen item, Excel replaces the Worksheet view with a backstage full screen print preview page from which you can print the worksheet.

If you select the Print or Print Gridlines option second on the list, Excel sends the current cell selection directly to your default printer. If you select the Print Area option, a submenu that enables you to set or clear the current print area appears. If you select Print Preview and Print, Excel opens the Print screen in the Backstage with a preview of your printout that you can then send to your printer. (See Chapter 5 for complete details on previewing and printing your worksheets.)

If, however, you select the Get Help on "print" option on the list, Excel opens a submenu with Print a Worksheet or Workbook, Print a Chart, Print Comments, and More Results For options. When you select one of the three print options, Excel opens the Help task pane containing pertinent information on the type of printing selected. If you select More Results For, Excel does an online web search on printing and displays its results in the Help task pane.

In another example, if you type **underline** in the Search text box, Excel displays three items

>> Underline

>> Get Help on "Underline"

>> Smart Lookup on "underline"

If you then select the Underline item, Excel goes ahead and assigns the underlining font attribute to whatever is in the cell that's current in the worksheet.

REMEMBER

If you would rather learn how to complete a task in Excel rather than have the program do it for you, select the Get Help on "xyz" item near the end of the search list. This opens an Excel Help task pane with loads of information about using the commands to accomplish that. To look up the item in question on the web using online resources such as Wikipedia, select the Smart Lookup on "xyz" option instead.

Chapter **2**

Creating a Spreadsheet from Scratch

After you know how to launch Excel 2019, it's time to find out how not to get yourself into trouble when actually using it! In this chapter, you find out how to put all kinds of information into all those little, blank worksheet cells I describe in Chapter 1. Here you find out about the Excel AutoCorrect and AutoComplete features and how they can help cut down on errors and speed up your work. You also get some basic pointers on other smart ways to minimize the drudgery of data entry, such as filling out a series of entries with the AutoFill and Flash Fill features as well as entering the same thing in a bunch of cells all at the same time.

After discovering how to fill a worksheet with all this raw data, you find out what has to be the most important lesson of all — how to save all that information in a secure place, such as your computer's hard drive or in the cloud on your OneDrive, so that you don't ever have to enter the stuff again!

So What Ya Gonna Put in That New Workbook of Yours?

When you launch Excel 2019, the Excel Start screen with the Home tab selected similar to the one shown in Figure 2-1 appears, separated into two panes. In the left navigation pane, Excel lists the names of all the other tabs available when you first start Excel before you open a new or existing workbook file: New, Open, Account, Feedback, and Options.

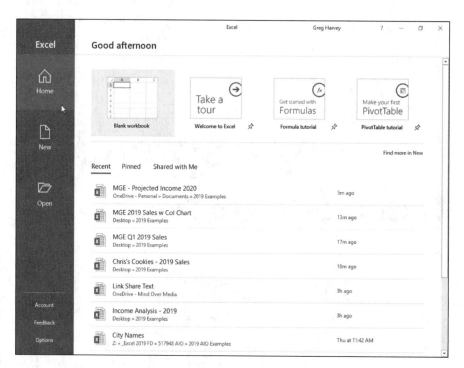

FIGURE 2-1:
The Excel 2019 Start screen with the Home tab selected that appears when you first launch the program.

In the Welcome pane on the right side of the Start screen (which says "Good afternoon" in Figure 2-1), Excel displays a row of thumbnail images of several templates that you can use when starting a new workbook. Templates create new workbooks that follow a particular form, such as an event budget or daily work schedule. These new workbooks generated from a template contain ready-made tables and lists often with sample data and headings that you can then edit and change as needed. Then, when you finish, you can save the new customized workbook with a new filename.

The template thumbnails in the top row of the Start screen begin with a Blank Workbook template immediately followed by a Welcome to Excel template and Formula Tutorial template. To explore even more templates that you can use as the basis for your new workbook, click the Find More in New link under the row of the thumbnails or click the New tab in the navigation pane to open the New screen with several rows different style templates.

If none of the example workbooks offered by the list of templates displayed on the New screen suits your needs, you can use the Search for Online Templates text box to find many more templates that match the search terms you enter. Right below, you can also click any of the links (Business, Personal, Lists, Financial Management, and so on) in the Suggested Searches to bring up and display a whole hoard of templates of a particular type.

TIP

I highly recommend opening the Welcome to Excel template at some point early in your exploration of Excel 2019. When you click its template thumbnail, Excel immediately opens a new Welcome to Excel1 workbook replete with no less than 12 worksheets: Start, Add, Fill, Split, Transpose, Sort& Filter, Tables, Drop-Downs, Analyze, Charts, PivotTables, and Learn More. The Add feature lets you experiment with the all-powerful Sum function and the Fill worksheet lets you try out the Flash Fill feature both discussed later in this chapter. The Analyze worksheet lets you experiment with the new Quick Analysis feature covered in Chapter 3. The Chart worksheet lets you test the Recommended Charts feature discussed in Chapter 10. After playing with any or all of these new features, you can close the Welcome to Excel1 workbook without saving your changes.

When you select any one of the template thumbnails other than Blank Workbook, Welcome to Excel and the other tutorial templates, Excel opens a dialog box that contains a larger version of the template thumbnail along with the name, a brief description, download size, and rating. To then download the template and create a new workbook from it in Excel, you click the Create button. If, on perusing the information in this dialog box, you decide that this isn't the template you want to use after all, click the Close button or simply press Esc.

To start a new workbook devoid of any labels and data, you click the Blank Workbook template in the Excel 2019 Start screen. When you do, Excel opens a new workbook automatically named Book1 or the next unused name, such as Book2. This workbook contains a single blank worksheet, automatically named Sheet1. To begin to work on a new spreadsheet, you simply start entering information in the Sheet1 worksheet of the Book1 Workbook window.

The ins and outs of data entry

Here are a few simple guidelines (a kind of data-entry etiquette, if you will) to keep in mind when you create a spreadsheet in Sheet1 of your new blank workbook:

>> Whenever you can, organize your information in tables of data that use adjacent (neighboring) columns and rows. Start the tables in the upper-left corner of the worksheet and work your way down the sheet, rather than across the sheet, whenever possible. When it's practical, separate each table by no more than a single column or row.

>> When you set up these tables, don't skip columns and rows just to "space out" the information. In Chapter 3, you see how to place as much white space as you want between information in adjacent columns and rows by widening columns, heightening rows, and changing the alignment.

>> Reserve a single column at the left edge of the table for the table's row headings.

>> Reserve a single row at the top of the table for the table's column headings.

>> If your table requires a title, put the title in the row above the column headings. Put the title in the same column as the row headings. You can get information on how to center this title across the columns of the entire table in Chapter 3.

In Chapter 1, I make a big deal about how big each of the worksheets in a workbook is. You may wonder why I'm now on your case about not using that space to spread out the data that you enter into it. After all, given all the real estate that comes with each Excel worksheet, you'd think conserving space would be one of the last things you'd have to worry about.

You'd be 100 percent correct . . . except for one little, itty-bitty thing: Space conservation in the worksheet equals memory conservation. You see, while a table of data grows and expands into columns and rows in new areas of the worksheet, Excel decides that it had better reserve a certain amount of computer memory and hold it open just in case you go crazy and fill that area with cell entries. Therefore, if you skip columns and rows that you really don't need to skip (just to cut down on all that cluttered data), you end up wasting computer memory that could store more information in the worksheet.

You must remember this . . .

Now you know: The amount of computer memory available to Excel determines the ultimate size of the spreadsheet you can build, not the total number of cells in the worksheets of your workbook. Should you run out of memory, you effectively run out of space — no matter how many columns and rows are still available. To maximize the information you can get into a single worksheet, always adopt the "covered wagon" approach to worksheet design by keeping your data close together.

Doing the Data-Entry Thing

Begin by reciting (in unison) the basic rule of worksheet data entry. All together now:

> To enter data in a worksheet, position the cell pointer in the cell where you want the data and then begin typing the entry.

Before you can position the cell pointer in the cell where you want the entry, Excel must be in Ready mode (look for Ready as the Program indicator at the beginning of the Status bar). When you start typing the entry, however, Excel goes through a mode change from Ready to Enter (and *Enter* replaces *Ready* as the Program indicator). If you're not in Ready mode, try pressing Esc on your keyboard.

And if you're doing data entry on a worksheet on a device that doesn't have a physical keyboard, for heaven's sake, open the Touch keyboard and keep it open (preferably floating) in the Excel window during the whole time you're doing data entry. (See "Tips on using the Touch keyboard" in Chapter 1 for details on displaying and using the virtual keyboard on a touchscreen device.)

As soon as you begin typing in Enter mode, the characters that you type in a cell in the Worksheet area simultaneously appear on the Formula bar near the top of the screen. Typing something in the current cell also triggers a change to the Formula bar because two new buttons, Cancel and Enter, between the Name box drop-down button and the Insert Function button become active (indicated by changing from light gray to black).

As you continue to type, Excel displays your progress on the Formula bar and in the active cell in the worksheet (see Figure 2-2). However, the insertion point (the flashing vertical bar that acts as your cursor) appears only at the end of the characters displayed in the cell.

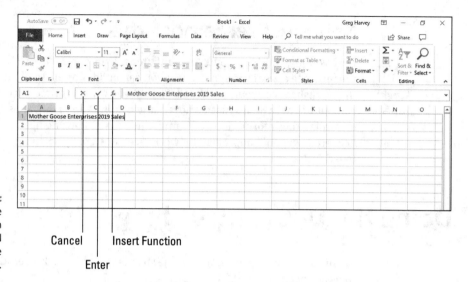

FIGURE 2-2:
What you type appears both in the current cell and on the Formula bar.

Cancel

Insert Function

Enter

After you finish typing your cell entry, you still have to get it into the cell so that it stays put. When you do this, you also change the program from Enter mode back to Ready mode so that you can move the cell pointer to another cell and, perhaps, enter or edit the data there.

To complete your cell entry and, at the same time, get Excel out of Enter mode and back into Ready mode, you can select the Enter button on the Formula bar or press the Enter key or one of the arrow keys (↓, ↑, →, or ←) on your physical or virtual keyboard. You can also press the Tab key or Shift+Tab keys to complete a cell entry.

TIP

When you complete a cell entry with any of the keyboard keys — Enter, Tab, Shift+Tab, or any of the arrow keys — you not only complete the entry in the current cell but get the added advantage of moving the cell pointer to a neighboring cell in the worksheet that requires editing or data entry.

Now, even though each of these alternatives gets your text into the cell, each does something a little different afterward, so please take note:

» If you select the Enter button (the one with the check mark) on the Formula bar, the text goes into the cell, and the cell pointer just stays in the cell containing the brand-new entry.

» If you press the Enter key on a physical or virtual keyboard, the text goes into the cell, and the cell pointer moves down to the cell below in the next row.

» If you press one of the arrow keys, the text goes into the cell, and the cell pointer moves to the next cell in the direction of the arrow. Press ↓, and the cell pointer moves below in the next row just as it does when you finish off a cell entry with the Enter key. Press → to move the cell pointer right to the cell in the next column; press ← to move the cell pointer left to the cell in the previous column; and press ↑ to move the cell pointer up to the cell in the next row above.

>> If you press Tab, the text goes into the cell, and the cell pointer moves to the adjacent cell in the column on the immediate right (the same as pressing the → key). If you press Shift+Tab, the cell pointer moves to the adjacent cell in the column on the immediate left (the same as pressing the ← key) after putting in the text.

No matter which of the methods you choose when putting an entry in its place, as soon as you complete your entry in the current cell, Excel deactivates the Formula bar along with the Cancel and Enter buttons. Thereafter, the data you entered continues to appear in the cell in the worksheet (with certain exceptions that I discuss later in this chapter), and every time you put the cell pointer into that cell, the data will reappear on the Formula bar as well.

If, while still typing an entry or after finishing typing but prior to completing the entry, you realize that you're just about to stick it in the wrong cell, you can clear and deactivate the Formula bar by selecting the Cancel button (the one with the X in it) or by pressing Esc on your keyboard. If, however, you don't realize that you had the wrong cell until after you enter your data there, you can use Undo (Ctrl+Z) to remove it. However, if don't realize the error right away and continue making other data entries, you have to go back and either move the entry to the correct cell (something you find out how to do in Chapter 4) or delete the entry (see Chapter 4) and then re-enter the data in the correct cell.

TECHNICAL STUFF

GETTING THE ENTER KEY TO PUT THE CELL POINTER WHERE YOU WANT IT

Excel automatically advances the cell pointer to the next cell down in the column every time you press Enter to complete the cell entry. If you want to customize Excel so that pressing Enter doesn't move the cell pointer when the program enters your data, or to have it move the cell pointer to the next cell up, left, or right, open the Advanced tab of the Excel Options dialog box (Alt+FTA).

To prevent the cell pointer from moving at all, select the After Pressing Enter, Move Selection check box to remove its check mark. To have the cell pointer move in another direction, select the Direction pop-up list box right below followed by the new direction option you want to use (Right, Up, or Left). When you finish changing the settings, click OK or press Enter.

It Takes All Types

Unbeknownst to you while you go about happily entering data in your spreadsheet, Excel constantly analyzes the stuff you type and classifies it into one of three possible data types: a piece of *text*, a *value*, or a *formula*.

If Excel finds that the entry is a formula, the program automatically calculates the formula and displays the computed result in the worksheet cell (you continue to see the formula itself, however, on the Formula bar). If Excel is satisfied that the entry does not qualify as a formula (I give you the qualifications for an honest-to-goodness formula a little later in this chapter), the program then determines whether the entry should be classified as text or as a value.

Excel makes this distinction between text and values so that it knows how to align the entry in the worksheet. It aligns text entries with the left edge of the cell and values with the right edge. Because most formulas work properly only when they are fed values, by differentiating text from values, the program knows which will and will not work in the formulas that you build. Suffice to say that you can really foul up your formulas if they refer to any cells containing text where Excel expects values to be.

The telltale signs of text

A text entry is simply an entry that Excel can't pigeonhole as either a formula or value. This makes text the catchall category of Excel data types. As a practical rule, most text entries (also known as *labels*) are a combination of letters and punctuation or letters and numbers. Text is used mostly for titles, headings, and notes in the worksheet.

You can tell right away whether Excel has accepted a cell entry as text because text entries automatically align at the left edge of their cells. If the text entry is wider than the cell can display, the data spills into the neighboring cell or cells on the right, *as long as those cells remain blank.*

If, sometime later, you enter information in a cell that contains spillover text from a cell to its left, Excel cuts off the spillover of the long text entry (see Figure 2-3). Not to worry: Excel doesn't actually lop these characters off the cell entry — it simply shaves the display to make room for the new entry. To redisplay the seemingly missing portion of the long text entry, you have to widen the column that contains the cell where the text is entered. (To find out how to do this, skip ahead to Chapter 3.)

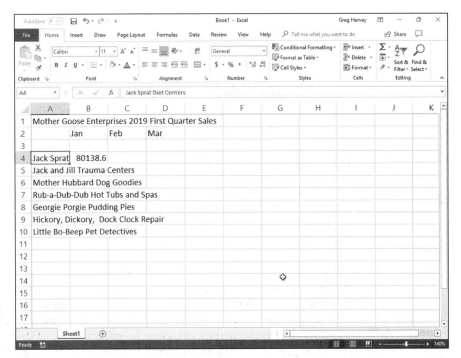

FIGURE 2-3:
Entries in cells to the right cut off the spillover text in cells on the left.

How Excel evaluates its values

Values are the building blocks of most of the formulas that you create in Excel. As such, values come in two flavors: numbers that represent quantities (14 stores or $140,000 dollars) and numbers that represent dates (*July 30, 2005*) or times (2 p.m.).

TECHNICAL STUFF

TO EXCEL, TEXT IS NOTHING BUT A BIG ZERO

Use the AutoCalculate indicator to prove to yourself that Excel gives all text entries the value of 0 (zero). As an example, enter the number **10** in one cell and then some stupid piece of text, such as **Excel is like a box of chocolates**, in the cell directly below. Then drag up so that both cells (the one with 10 and the one with the text) are highlighted. Take a gander at the AutoCalculate indicator on the Status bar, and you see that it reads AVERAGE: 10, COUNT: 2, and SUM: 10, proving that the text adds nothing to the total value of these two cells.

You can tell whether Excel has accepted your entry as a value because values automatically align at the right edge of their cells. If the value that you enter is wider than the column containing the cell can display, Excel automatically converts the value to (of all things) *scientific notation*, as in 1.2E+10 when you enter 12 billion in a standard width cell (that's 12 plus nine zeros). To restore a value that's been converted into that weird scientific notation stuff to a regular number, simply widen the column for that cell. (Read how in Chapter 3.)

Verifying Excel's got your number

When building a new worksheet, you'll probably spend a lot of your time entering numbers, representing all types of quantities from money that you made (or lost) to the percentage of the office budget that went to coffee and donuts. (You mean you don't get donuts?)

To enter a numeric value that represents a positive quantity, like the amount of money you made last year, just select a cell, type the numbers — for example, **459600** — and complete the entry in the cell by clicking the Enter button, pressing the Enter key, and so on. To enter a numeric value that represents a negative quantity, such as the amount of money spent on office snacks last year, begin the entry with the minus sign or hyphen (–) before typing the numbers and then complete the entry. For example, **–175** (that's not too much to spend on coffee and donuts when you just made $459,600).

If you're trained in accounting, you can enclose the negative number (that's *expense* to you) in parentheses. You'd enter it like this: **(175)**. If you go to all the trouble to use parentheses for your negatives (expenses), Excel goes ahead and automatically converts the number so that it begins with a minus sign; if you enter **(175)** in the Office Snacks expense cell, Excel spits back –175. (Relax, you can find out how to get your beloved parentheses back for the expenses in your spreadsheet in Chapter 3.)

With numeric values that represent dollar amounts, like the amount of money you made last year, you can include dollar signs ($) and commas (,) just as they appear in the printed or handwritten numbers you're working from. Just be aware that when you enter a number with commas, Excel assigns a number format to the value that matches your use of commas. (For more information on number formats and how they are used, see Chapter 3.) Likewise, when you preface a financial figure with a dollar sign, Excel assigns an appropriate dollar-number format to the value (one that automatically inserts commas between the thousands).

When entering numeric values with decimal places, use the period as the decimal point. When you enter decimal values, the program automatically adds a zero before the decimal point (Excel inserts 0.34 in a cell when you enter .34) and drops trailing zeros entered after the decimal point (Excel inserts 12.5 in a cell when you enter **12.50**).

If you don't know the decimal equivalent for a value that contains a fraction, you can just go ahead and enter the value with its fraction. For example, if you don't know that 2.1875 is the decimal equivalent for $2\frac{3}{16}$, just type **2$\frac{3}{16}$** (making sure to add a space between the 2 and 3) in the cell. After completing the entry, when you put the cell pointer in that cell, you see $2\frac{3}{16}$ in the cell of the worksheet, but 2.1875 appears on the Formula bar. As you see in Chapter 3, it's then a simple trick to format the display of $2\frac{3}{16}$ in the cell so that it matches the 2.1875 on the Formula bar.

REMEMBER

If you need to enter simple fractions, such as ¾ or ⅝, you must enter them as a mixed number preceded by zero; for example, enter **0 ¾** or **0 ¾** (be sure to include a space between the zero and the fraction). Otherwise, Excel thinks that you're entering the dates March 4 (3/4) or May 8 (5/8).

When entering in a cell a numeric value that represents a percentage (so much out of a hundred), you have this choice:

>> You can divide the number by 100 and enter the decimal equivalent (by moving the decimal point two places to the left like your teacher taught you; for example, enter **.12** for 12 percent).

>> You can enter the number with the percent sign (for example, enter **12%**).

Either way, Excel stores the decimal value in the cell (0.12 in this example). If you use the percent sign, Excel assigns a percentage-number format to the value in the worksheet so that it appears as 12%.

How to fix your decimal places (when you don't even know they're broken)

If you find that you need to enter a whole slew of numbers that use the same number of decimal places, you can turn on Excel's Fixed Decimal setting and have the program enter the decimals for you. This feature really comes in handy when you have to enter hundreds of financial figures that all use two decimal places (for example, for the number of cents).

To *fix* the number of decimal places in a numeric entry, follow these steps:

1. **Click File ⇨ Options ⇨ Advanced or press Alt+FTA.**

   The Advanced tab of the Excel Options dialog box opens.

2. **Select the Automatically Insert a Decimal Point check box in the Editing Options section to fill it with a check mark.**

   By default, Excel fixes the decimal place two places to the left of the last number you type. To change the default Places setting, go to Step 3; otherwise move to Step 4.

3. **(Optional) Select or enter a new number in the Places text box or use the spinner buttons to change the value.**

   For example, you could change the Places setting to 3 to enter numbers with the following decimal placement: 00.000.

4. **Click OK or press Enter.**

   Excel displays the Fixed Decimal status indicator on the Status bar to let you know that the Fixed Decimal feature is now active.

After fixing the decimal place in numeric values, Excel automatically adds a decimal point to any numeric value that you enter using the number of places you selected; all you do is type the digits and complete the entry in the cell. For example, to enter the numeric value 100.99 in a cell after fixing the decimal point to two places, type the digits **10099** without adding any period for a decimal point. When you complete the cell entry, Excel automatically inserts a decimal point two places from the right in the number you typed, leaving 100.99 in the cell.

When you're ready to return to normal data entry for numerical values (where you enter any decimal points yourself), open the Advanced tab of the Excel Options dialog box (Alt+FTA), select the Automatically Insert a Decimal Point check box again, this time to clear it, and then click OK or press Enter. Excel removes the Fixed Decimal indicator from the Status bar.

TECHNICAL STUFF

DON'T GET IN A FIX OVER YOUR DECIMAL PLACES!

When the Fixed Decimal setting is on, Excel adds a decimal point to all the numeric values that you enter. However, if you want to enter a number without a decimal point, or one with a decimal point in a position different from the one called for by this feature, you have to remember to type the decimal point (period) yourself. For example, to enter the number 1099 instead of 10.99 when the decimal point is fixed at two places, type **1099** followed immediately by a period (.) in the cell.

And, for heaven's sake, please don't forget to turn off the Fixed Decimal feature before you work on another worksheet or exit Excel. Otherwise, when you intend to enter values, such as 20, you'll end up with 0.2 instead, and you won't have a clue what's going on!

Tapping on the old ten-key

You can make the Fixed Decimal feature work even better when entering numeric data on a physical keyboard that has a separate ten-key numeric keypad. All you do is select the block of cells where you want to enter numbers (see "Entries all around the block," later in this chapter) and then press Num Lock so that you can enter all the data for this cell selection from the numeric keypad (à la ten-key adding machine).

Using this approach, all you have to do to enter the range of values in each cell is type the number's digits and press Enter on the numeric keypad. Excel inserts the decimal point in the proper place while it moves the cell pointer down to the next cell. Even better, when you finish entering the last value in a column, pressing Enter automatically moves the cell pointer to the cell at the top of the next column in the selection.

Look at Figures 2-4 and 2-5 to see how you can make the ten-key method work for you. In Figure 2-4, the Fixed Decimal feature is turned on (using the default of two decimal places), and the block of cells from B3 through D9 is selected. You also see that six entries have already been made in cells B3 through B8 and a seventh, 30834.63, is about to be completed in cell B9. To make this entry when the Fixed Decimal feature is on, you simply type **3083463** from the numeric keypad.

FIGURE 2-4:
To enter the value 30834.63 in cell B9, type **3083463** and press Enter.

In Figure 2-5, check out what happens when you press Enter (on either the regular keyboard or the numeric keypad). Not only does Excel automatically add the decimal point to the value in cell B9, but it also moves the cell pointer up and over to cell C3 where you can continue entering the values for this column.

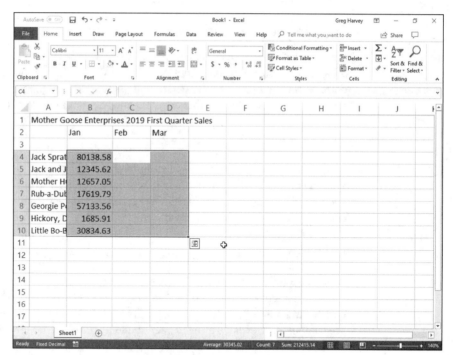

FIGURE 2-5:
Press Enter to
complete the
30834.63 entry in
cell B9. Excel
automatically
moves the cell
pointer up and
over to cell C3.

Entering dates with no debate

At first look, it may strike you a bit odd to enter dates and times as values in the cells of a worksheet rather than text. The reason for this is simple, really: Dates and times entered as values can be used in formula calculations, whereas dates and times entered as text cannot. For example, if you enter two dates as values, you can then set up a formula that subtracts the more recent date from the older date and returns the number of days between them. This kind of thing just couldn't happen if you were to enter the two dates as text entries.

Excel determines whether the date or time that you type is a value or text by the format that you follow. If you follow one of Excel's built-in date-and-time formats, the program recognizes the date or time as a value. If you don't follow one of the built-in formats, the program enters the date or time as a text entry — it's as simple as that.

Excel recognizes the following time formats:

3 AM or **3 PM**

3 A or **3 P** (upper- or lowercase a or p — Excel inserts 3:00 AM or 3:00 PM)

3:21 AM or **3:21 PM** (upper- or lowercase am or pm)

3:21:04 AM or **3:21:04 PM** (upper- or lowercase am or pm)

15:21

15:21:04

REMEMBER

Excel isn't fussy, so you can enter the AM or PM designation in the date in any manner — uppercase letters, lowercase letters, or even a mix of the two.

Excel knows the following date formats. (Month abbreviations always use the first three letters of the name of the month: Jan, Feb, Mar, and so forth.)

November 6, 2012 or **November 6, 12** (appear in cell as 6-Nov-12)

11/6/12 or **11-6-12** (appear in cell as 11/6/2012)

6-Nov-12 or **6/Nov/12** or even **6Nov12** (all appear in cell as 6-Nov-12)

11/6 or **6-Nov** or **6/Nov** or **6Nov** (all appear in cell as 6-Nov)

Nov-06 or **Nov/06** or **Nov06** (all appear in cell as 6-Nov)

Make it a date in the 21st century

Contrary to what you might think, when entering dates in the 21st century, you need to enter only the last two digits of the year. For example, to enter the date January 6, 2019, in a worksheet, I enter **1/6/19** in the target cell. Likewise, to put the date February 15, 2020, in a worksheet, I enter **2/15/20** in the target cell.

REMEMBER

Entering only the last two digits of dates in the 21st century works only for dates in the first three decades of the new century (2000 through 2029). To enter dates for the years 2030 on, you need to input all four digits of the year.

TECHNICAL STUFF

THE DATING GAME

Dates are stored as serial numbers that indicate how many days have elapsed from a particular starting date; times are stored as decimal fractions indicating the elapsed part of the 24-hour period. Excel supports two date systems: the 1900 date system used by Excel in Windows, where January 1, 1900, is the starting date (serial number 1) and the 1904 system used by Excel for the Macintosh, where January 2, 1904, is the starting date.

If you ever get ahold of a workbook created with Excel for the Macintosh that contains dates that seem all screwed up when you open the file, you can rectify this problem by opening the Advanced tab of the Excel Options dialog box (File ➪ Options ➪ Advanced or Alt+FTA) and then selecting the Use 1904 Date System check box in the When Calculating This Workbook section before you click OK.

This also means, however, that to put in dates in the first three decades of the 20th century (1900 through 1929), you must enter all four digits of the year. For example, to put in the date July 21, 1925, you have to enter **7/21/1925** in the target cell. Otherwise, if you enter just the last two digits (**25**) for the year part of the date, Excel enters a date for the year 2025 and not 1925!

Excel 2019 always displays all four digits of the year in the cell and on the Formula bar even when you only enter the last two. For example, if you enter **11/06/18** in a cell, Excel automatically displays 11/6/2018 in the worksheet cell (and on the Formula bar when that cell is current).

Therefore, by looking at the Formula bar, you can always tell when you've entered a 20th rather than a 21st century date in a cell even if you can't keep straight the rules for when to enter just the last two digits rather than all four. (Read Chapter 3 for information on how to format your date entries so that only the last digits display in the worksheet.)

TIP

For information on how to perform simple arithmetic operations between the dates and time you enter in a worksheet and have the results make sense, see the information about dates in Chapter 3.

Fabricating those fabulous formulas!

As entries go in Excel, formulas are the real workhorses of the worksheet. If you set up a formula properly, it computes the correct answer when you enter the formula into a cell. From then on, the formula stays up to date, recalculating the results whenever you change any of the values that the formula uses.

You let Excel know that you're about to enter a formula (rather than some text or a value) in the current cell by starting the formula with the equal sign (=). Most simple formulas follow the equal sign with a built-in function, such as SUM or AVERAGE. (See the section "Inserting a function into a formula with the Insert Function button," later in this chapter, for more information on using functions in formulas.) Other simple formulas use a series of values or cell references that contain values separated by one or more of the following mathematical operators:

+ (plus sign) for addition

– (minus sign or hyphen) for subtraction

* (asterisk) for multiplication

/ (slash) for division

^ (caret) for raising a number to an exponential power

For example, to create a formula in cell C2 that multiplies a value entered in cell A2 by a value in cell B2, enter the following formula in cell C2: **=A2*B2**.

To enter this formula in cell C2, follow these steps:

1. **Select cell C2.**

2. **Type the entire formula =A2*B2 in the cell.**

3. **Press Enter.**

Or

1. **Select cell C2.**

2. **Type = (equal sign).**

3. **Select cell A2 in the worksheet by using the mouse or the keyboard.**

This action places the cell reference A2 in the formula in the cell (as shown in Figure 2-6).

4. **Type * (Shift+8 on the top row of the keyboard).**

The asterisk is used for multiplication rather than the × symbol you used in school.

5. **Select cell B2 in the worksheet with the mouse, keyboard, or by tapping it on the screen (when using a touchscreen device).**

This action places the cell reference B2 in the formula (as shown in Figure 2-7).

6. **Click the Enter button on the Formula bar to complete the formula entry while keeping the cell pointer in cell C2.**

Excel displays the calculated answer in cell C2 and the formula =A2∗B2 in the Formula bar (as shown in Figure 2-8).

FIGURE 2-6:
To start the formula, type = and then select cell A2.

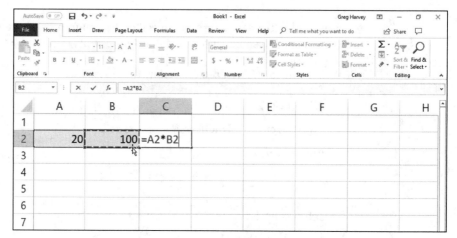

FIGURE 2-7:
To complete the
second part of
the formula,
type * and select
cell B2.

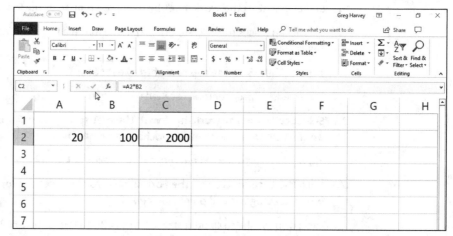

FIGURE 2-8:
Click the Enter
button, and Excel
displays the
answer in cell C2
while the formula
appears in the
Formula bar
above.

When you finish entering the formula =A2*B2 in cell C2 of the worksheet, Excel displays the calculated result, depending on the values currently entered in cells A2 and B2. The major strength of the electronic spreadsheet is the capability of formulas to change their calculated results automatically to match changes in the cells referenced by the formulas.

Now comes the fun part: After creating a formula like the preceding one that refers to the values in certain cells (rather than containing those values itself), you can change the values in those cells, and Excel automatically recalculates the formula, using these new values and displaying the updated answer in the worksheet! Using the example shown in Figure 2-8, suppose that you change the value in cell B2 from 100 to 50. The moment that you complete this change in cell B2, Excel recalculates the formula and displays the new answer, 1000, in cell C2.

If you want it, just point it out

The method of selecting the cells you use in a formula, rather than typing their cell references, is *pointing.* On most devices on which you're running Excel 2019, pointing is quicker than typing and certainly reduces the risk that you might mistype a cell reference. When you type a cell reference, you can easily type the wrong column letter or row number and not realize your mistake by looking at the calculated result returned in the cell. But when you directly select the cell that you want to use in a formula (by clicking or tapping it or even using the arrow keys to move the cell cursor to it), you have less chance of entering the wrong cell reference.

TIP

On a small touchscreen device with a tiny viewing area such as a small tablet or even smartphone, sliding to scroll to the proper column and row and then tapping the cell to select and add its reference to a new formula may be even more challenging than typing the formula's cell references on the device's virtual keyboard. This is when I recommend typing instead of pointing for creating new formulas. Just be aware that when you type the first letter of your cell's column reference into a formula, Excel automatically displays a list of all the built-in functions whose names start with that letter. This list immediately disappears as soon as you type the second letter of the column (if the cell has one) or the first digit of its row number. Also, be sure to double-check that the cell references you type into the formula refer to the cells you really want to use.

Altering the natural order of operations

Many formulas that you create perform more than one mathematical operation. Excel performs each operation, moving from left to right, according to a strict pecking order (the natural order of arithmetic operations). In this order, multiplication and division pull more weight than addition and subtraction and, therefore, perform first, even if these operations don't come first in the formula (when reading from left to right).

Consider the series of operations in the following formula:

    =A2+B2*C2

If cell A2 contains the number 5, B2 contains the number 10, and C2 contains the number 2, Excel evaluates the following formula:

    =5+10*2

In this formula, Excel multiplies 10 times 2 to equal 20 and then adds this result to 5 to produce the result 25.

If you want Excel to perform the addition between the values in cells A2 and B2 before the program multiplies the result by the value in cell C2, enclose the addition operation in parentheses as follows:

```
=(A2+B2)*C2
```

The parentheses around the addition tell Excel that you want this operation performed before the multiplication. If cell A2 contains the number 5, B2 contains the number 10, and C2 contains the number 2, Excel adds 5 and 10 to equal 15 and then multiplies this result by 2 to produce the result 30.

In fancier formulas, you may need to add more than one set of parentheses, one within another (like the wooden Russian dolls that nest within each other) to indicate the order in which you want the calculations to take place. When nesting parentheses, Excel first performs the calculation contained in the most inside pair of parentheses and then uses that result in further calculations as the program works its way outward. For example, consider the following formula:

```
=(A4+(B4-C4))*D4
```

Excel first subtracts the value in cell C4 from the value in cell B4, adds the difference to the value in cell A4, and then finally multiplies that sum by the value in D4.

Without the additions of the two sets of nested parentheses, left to its own devices, Excel would first multiply the value in cell C4 by that in D4, add the value in A4 to that in B4, and then perform the subtraction.

TIP

Don't worry too much when nesting parentheses in a formula if you don't pair them properly so that you have a right parenthesis for every left parenthesis in the formula. If you do not include a right parenthesis for every left one, Excel displays an alert dialog box that suggests the correction needed to balance the pairs. If you agree with the program's suggested correction, you simply click the Yes button. However, be sure that you only use parentheses: ( ). Excel balks at the use of brackets — [ ] — or braces — { } — in a formula by giving you an Error alert box.

Formula flub-ups

Under certain circumstances, even the best formulas can appear to have freaked out after you get them in your worksheet. You can tell right away that a formula's gone haywire because instead of the nice calculated value you expected to see in the cell, you get a strange, incomprehensible message in all uppercase letters beginning with the number sign (#) and ending with an exclamation point (!) or, in one case, a question mark (?). This weirdness, in the parlance of spreadsheets, is as an *error value.* Its purpose is to let you know that some element — either in the formula itself or in a cell referred to by the formula — is preventing Excel from returning the anticipated calculated value.

TIP

When one of your formulas returns one of these error values, an alert indicator (in the form of an exclamation point in a diamond) appears to the left of the cell when it contains the cell pointer, and the upper-left corner of the cell contains a tiny green triangle. When you position the mouse pointer on this alert indicator, Excel displays a brief description of the formula error and adds a drop-down button to the immediate right of its box. When you click this button, a pop-up menu appears with a number of related options. To access online help on this formula error, including suggestions on how to get rid of the error, click the Help on This Error item on this pop-up menu.

The worst thing about error values is that they can contaminate other formulas in the worksheet. If a formula returns an error value to a cell and a second formula in another cell refers to the value calculated by the first formula, the second formula returns the same error value, and so on down the line.

After an error value shows up in a cell, you have to discover what caused the error and edit the formula in the worksheet. In Table 2-1, I list some error values that you might run into in a worksheet and then explain the most common causes.

TABLE 2-1   **Error Values That You May Encounter from Faulty Formulas**

What Shows Up in the Cell	What's Going On Here?
#DIV/0!	Appears when the formula calls for division by a cell that either contains the value 0 or, as is more often the case, is empty. Division by zero is a no-no in mathematics.
#NAME?	Appears when the formula refers to a *range name* (see Chapter 6 for info on naming ranges) that doesn't exist in the worksheet. This error value appears when you type the wrong range name or fail to enclose in quotation marks some text used in the formula, causing Excel to think that the text refers to a range name.
#NULL!	Appears most often when you insert a space (where you should have used a comma) to separate cell references used as arguments for functions.
#NUM!	Appears when Excel encounters a problem with a number in the formula, such as the wrong type of argument in an Excel function or a calculation that produces a number too large or too small to be represented in the worksheet.
#REF!	Appears when Excel encounters an invalid cell reference, such as when you delete a cell referred to in a formula or paste cells over the cells referred to in a formula.
#VALUE!	Appears when you use the wrong type of argument or operator in a function, or when you call for a mathematical operation that refers to cells that contain text entries.

Fixing Those Data Entry Flub-Ups

We all wish we were perfect, but alas, because so few of us are, we are best off preparing for those inevitable times when we mess up. When entering vast quantities of data, it's easy for those nasty little typos to creep into your work. In your pursuit of the perfect spreadsheet, here are things you can do. First, get Excel to correct certain data entry typos automatically when they happen with its AutoCorrect feature. Second, manually correct any disgusting little errors that get through, either while you're still in the process of making the entry in the cell or after the entry has gone in.

You really AutoCorrect that for me

The AutoCorrect feature is a godsend for those of us who tend to make the same stupid typos over and over. With AutoCorrect, you can alert Excel 2019 (along with the other Office 2019 apps you use, such as Word and PowerPoint) to your own particular typing gaffes and tell the program how it should automatically fix them for you.

When you first install Excel, the AutoCorrect feature already knows to automatically correct two initial capital letters in an entry (by lowercasing the second capital letter), to capitalize the name of the days of the week, and to replace a set of predefined text entries and typos with particular substitute text.

You can add to the list of text replacements at any time when using Excel. These text replacements can be of two types: typos that you routinely make along with the correct spelling, and abbreviations or acronyms that you type all the time along with their full forms.

To add to the replacements, follow these steps:

1. **Click File ⇨ Options ⇨ Proofing or press Alt+FTP and then click the AutoCorrect Options button or press Alt+A.**

   Excel opens the AutoCorrect dialog box shown in Figure 2-9.

2. **On the AutoCorrect tab in this dialog box, enter the typo or abbreviation in the Replace text box.**

3. **Enter the correction or full form in the With text box.**

4. **Click the Add button or press Enter to add the new typo or abbreviation to the AutoCorrect list.**

5. **Click the OK button to close the AutoCorrect dialog box.**

FIGURE 2-9:
Use the Replace and With options in the AutoCorrect dialog box to add all typos and abbreviations you want Excel to automatically correct or fill out.

Cell editing etiquette

Despite the help of AutoCorrect, some mistakes are bound to get you. How you correct them really depends upon whether you notice before or after completing the cell entry.

» If you catch the mistake before you complete an entry, you can delete it by pressing your Backspace key until you remove all the incorrect characters from the cell. Then you can retype the rest of the entry or the formula before you complete the entry in the cell.

» If you don't discover the mistake until after you've completed the cell entry, you have a choice of replacing the whole thing or editing just the mistakes.

» When dealing with short entries, you'll probably want to take the replacement route. To replace a cell entry, position the cell pointer in that cell, type your replacement entry, and then click the Enter button or press Enter.

» When the error in an entry is relatively easy to fix and the entry is on the long side, you'll probably want to edit the cell entry rather than replace it. To edit the entry in the cell, simply double-click or double-tap the cell or select the cell and then press F2.

» Doing either one reactivates the Formula bar and the Enter and Cancel buttons once again and placing the insertion point in the cell entry in the worksheet. (If you double-click or double-tap, the insertion point positions itself wherever you click; press F2, and the insertion point positions itself after the last character in the entry.)

>> Notice also that the mode indicator changes to Edit. While in this mode, you can use the mouse or the arrow keys to position the insertion point at the place in the cell entry that needs fixing.

In Table 2-2, I list the keystrokes that you can use to reposition the insertion point in the cell entry and delete unwanted characters. If you want to insert new characters at the insertion point, simply start typing. If you want to delete existing characters at the insertion point while you type new ones, press the Insert key on your keyboard to switch from the normal insert mode to overtype mode. To return to normal insert mode, press Insert a second time. When you finish making corrections to the cell entry, you must complete the edits by pressing Enter before Excel updates the contents of the cell.

TABLE 2-2   ## Keystrokes for Fixing Those Cell Entry Flub-Ups

Keystroke	What the Keystroke Does
Delete	Deletes the character to the right of the insertion point
Backspace	Deletes the character to the left of the insertion point
→	Moves the insertion point one character to the right
←	Moves the insertion point one character to the left
↑	Moves the insertion point, when it is at the end of the cell entry, to its preceding position to the left
End or ↓	Moves the insertion point after the last character in the cell entry
Home	Moves the insertion point in front of the first character of the cell entry
Ctrl+→	Moves the insertion point in front of the next word in the cell entry
Ctrl+←	Moves the insertion point in front of the current word (when it's within a word) or preceding word (when it's between words) in the cell entry
Insert	Switches between insert and overtype mode

REMEMBER While Excel is in Edit mode, you must re-enter the edited cell contents by either clicking the Enter button on the Formula bar or pressing the Enter key or pressing Tab or the Shift+Tab combination. You can use the arrow keys as a way to complete an entry only when the program is in Enter mode. When the program is in Edit mode, the arrow keys move the insertion point only through the entry that you're editing, not to a new cell.

A TALE OF TWO EDITS: CELL VERSUS FORMULA BAR EDITING

Excel gives you a choice between editing a cell's contents either in the cell or on the Formula bar. Whereas most of the time, editing right in the cell is just fine, when dealing with really long entries (like humongous formulas that go on forever or text entries that take up paragraphs), you may prefer to do your editing on the Formula bar. This is because Excel 2019 automatically adds up and down scroll arrow buttons to the end of the Formula bar when a cell entry is too long to display completely on a single row. These scroll arrow buttons enable you to display each line of the cell's long entry without expanding the Formula bar (as in earlier versions of Excel) and thereby obscuring the top part of the Worksheet area.

To edit the contents in the Formula bar rather than in the cell itself, use the appropriate scroll arrow button to display the line with the contents that needs editing and then position the I-beam mouse pointer at the place in the text or number(s) that requires modification to set the insertion cursor.

Taking the Drudgery Out of Data Entry

Before leaving the topic of data entry, I feel duty-bound to cover some of the shortcuts that really help to cut down on the drudgery of this task. These data-entry tips include the AutoComplete, AutoFill, and Flash Fill features as well as doing data entry in a preselected block of cells and making the same entry in a bunch of cells all at the same time.

I'm just not complete without you

AutoComplete in Excel 2019 is a sometimes helpful feature that you need to be aware as you enter new data in a worksheet. In an attempt to cut down on your typing load, our friendly software engineers at Microsoft came up with the Auto-Complete feature.

AutoComplete tries to act like a mind reader, anticipating what you might want to enter next based on existing entries made in the same worksheet column. This feature comes into play only when you're entering a column of text entries. (It does not come into play when entering values or formulas or when entering a row of text entries.)

When entering a column of text entries, AutoComplete looks at the kinds of text entries that you make in that column and automatically enables you to make duplicates of them in subsequent rows as soon as you type sufficient letters uniquely matching an earlier entry. Excel does this by completing the letters in new cell entry (which are selected shown by gray shading) to make it match an earlier entry. You can then accept this suggestion and complete the duplicate entry (by pressing Enter or an arrow key or clicking the Enter button) or override it by continuing to type the missing letters of a different entry that starts with the same letter(s).

For example, suppose that I enter **Capital Investments** (one of the many investment firms that our company uses) in cell A2 and then move the cell pointer down to cell A3 in the row below and press **C** (lowercase or uppercase, it doesn't matter). AutoComplete immediately fills in the remainder of the familiar entry — *apital Investments* — in this cell after the C. To enter the suggested duplicate in this cell, all I have to do is press Enter or the down or right arrow key or click the Enter button on the Formula bar.

Now this is great if I happen to need Capital Investments as the row heading in both cells A2 and A3. Anticipating that I might be typing a different entry that just happens to start with the same letter as the one above, AutoComplete automatically selects everything after the first letter in the suggested duplicated entry it filled in (from *apital* on, in this example) indicated by gray-shading these letters. This enables me to replace the suggested duplicate text supplied by AutoComplete just by continuing to type nonmatching letters.

If you override a duplicate supplied by AutoComplete in a column by typing one of your own (as in the example of the Capital Investments entry automatically corrected to Cook Investments in cell A3), you effectively shut down its capability to supply any more suggested duplicates for that particular letter (in this case, C). For instance, in my example, after changing Capital Investments to Cook Investments in cell A3, AutoComplete doesn't do anything if I then just type **C** in cell A4. AutoComplete doesn't kick in again until I type a new entry that begins with either **Ca** or **Co** in rows below in column A.

TIP

If you find that the AutoComplete feature is really making it hard for you to enter a series of cell entries that all start with the same or similar letters but are otherwise not alike, you can turn off the AutoComplete feature. Select File ➪ Options ➪ Advanced or press Alt+FTA to open the Advanced tab of the Excel Options dialog box. Then, select the Enable AutoComplete for Cell Values check box in the Editing Options section to remove its check mark before clicking OK.

Fill 'er up with AutoFill

Many of the worksheets that you create with Excel require the entry of a series of sequential dates or numbers. For example, a worksheet may require you to title the columns with the 12 months, from January through December, or to number the rows from 1 to 100.

Excel's AutoFill feature makes short work of this kind of repetitive task. All you have to enter is the initial value in that series. In most cases, AutoFill is smart enough to figure out how to fill out the series for you when you drag the fill handle to the right (to take the series across columns to the right) or down (to extend the series to the rows below).

The AutoFill (or fill) handle looks like this — + — and appears only when you position the mouse on the lower-right corner of the active cell (or the last cell, when you've selected a block of cells). If you drag a cell selection with the white-cross mouse pointer rather than the AutoFill handle, Excel simply extends the cell selection to those cells you drag through (see Chapter 3). If you drag a cell selection with the arrowhead pointer, Excel moves the cell selection (see Chapter 4).

On a touchscreen device, you make the Excel fill handle appear by tapping the active cell's lower selection handle (indicated by a circle) and then tapping the AutoFill item on the mini-toolbar that then appears. You can then fill a series by dragging this fill handle with your finger or a stylus.

When creating a series with the fill handle, you can drag in only one direction at a time. For example, you can fill the series or copy the entry to the range to the left or right of the cell that contains the initial values, or you can fill the series or copy to the range above or below the cell containing the initial values. You can't, however, fill or copy the series to two directions at the same time (such as down and to the right by dragging the fill handle diagonally).

As you drag the fill handle, the program keeps you informed of whatever entry will be entered into the last cell selected in the range by displaying that entry next to the mouse pointer (a kind of AutoFill tips, if you will). After extending the range with the fill handle, Excel either creates a series in all of the cells that you select or copies the entire range with the initial value. To the right of the last entry in the filled or copied series, Excel also displays a drop-down button that contains a shortcut menu of options. You can use this shortcut menu to override Excel's default filling or copying. For example, when you use the fill handle, Excel copies an initial value (such as 10) into every cell in the range. But, if you wanted a sequential series (such as 10, 11, 12, and so on), you do this by selecting the Fill Series command on the AutoFill Options shortcut menu.

In Figures 2-10 and 2-11, I illustrate how to use AutoFill to enter a row of months, starting with January in cell B2 and ending with June in cell G2. To do this, you simply enter **Jan** in cell B2 and then position the mouse pointer (or your finger or stylus) on the fill handle in the lower-right corner of this cell before you drag through to cell G2 on the right (as shown in Figure 2-10). When you release the mouse button or remove your finger or stylus from the touchscreen, Excel fills in the names of the rest of the months (Feb through Jun) in the selected cells (as shown in Figure 2-11). Excel keeps the cells with the series of months selected, giving you another chance to modify the series. (If you went too far, you can drag the fill handle to the left to cut back on the list of months; if you didn't go far enough, you can drag it to the right to extend the list of months farther.)

FIGURE 2-10:
To enter a series of months, enter the first month and then drag the fill handle in a direction to add sequential months.

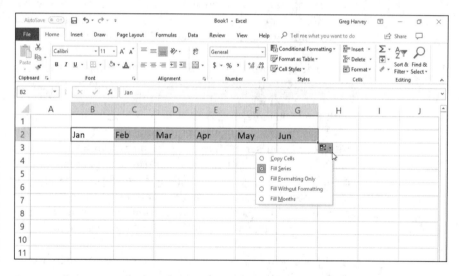

FIGURE 2-11:
Release the mouse button, and Excel fills the cell selection with the missing months.

Also, you can use the options on the AutoFill Options drop-down menu shown in Figure 2-11. To display this menu, you click the drop-down button that appears on the fill handle (to the right of Jun) to override the series created by default. To have Excel copy Jan into each of the selected cells, select Copy Cells on this menu. To have the program fill the selected cells with the formatting used in cell B2 (in this case, the cell has had bold applied to it — see Chapter 3 for details on formatting cells), you select Fill Formatting Only on this menu. To have Excel fill in the series of months in the selected cells without copying the formatting used in cell B2, you select the Fill Without Formatting command from this shortcut menu.

See Table 2-3 to see some of the different initial values that AutoFill can use and the types of series that Excel can create from them.

TABLE 2-3 ## Samples of Series You Can Create with AutoFill

Value Entered in First Cell	Extended Series Created by AutoFill in the Next Three Cells
June	July, August, September
Jun	Jul, Aug, Sep
Tuesday	Wednesday, Thursday, Friday
Tue	Wed, Thu, Fri
4/1/99	4/2/99, 4/3/99, 4/4/99
Jan-00	Feb-00, Mar-00, Apr-00
15-Feb	16-Feb, 17-Feb, 18-Feb
10:00 PM	11:00 PM, 12:00 AM, 1:00 AM
8:01	9:01, 10:01, 11:01
Quarter 1	Quarter 2, Quarter 3, Quarter 4
Qtr2	Qtr3, Qtr4, Qtr1
Q3	Q4, Q1, Q2
Product 1	Product 2, Product 3, Product 4

Working with a spaced series

AutoFill uses the initial value that you select (date, time, day, year, and so on) to design the series. All the sample series I show in Table 2-3 change by a factor of one (one day, one month, or one number). You can tell AutoFill to create a series that changes by some other value: Enter two sample values in neighboring cells that describe the amount of change you want between each value in the series. Make these two values the initial selection that you extend with the fill handle.

For example, to start a series with Saturday and enter every other day across a row, enter **Saturday** in the first cell and **Monday** in the cell next door. After selecting both cells, drag the fill handle across the cells to the right as far as you need to fill out a series based on these two initial values. When you release the mouse button or remove your finger or stylus from the screen, Excel follows the example set in the first two cells by entering every other day (Wednesday to the right of Monday, Friday to the right of Wednesday, and so on).

Copying with AutoFill

You can use AutoFill to copy a text entry throughout a cell range (rather than fill in a series of related entries). To copy a text entry to a cell range, engage the Ctrl key while you click and drag the fill handle. When you do, a plus sign appears to the right of the fill handle — your sign that AutoFill will *copy* the entry in the active cell instead of creating a series using it. You can also tell because the entry that appears as the AutoFill tip next to the fill handle while you drag contains the same text as the original cell. If you decide after copying an initial label or value to a range that you should have used it to fill in a series, click the drop-down button that appears on the fill handle at the cell with the last copied entry and then select the Fill Series command on the AutoFill Options shortcut menu that appears.

REMEMBER

Although holding down Ctrl while you drag the fill handle copies a text entry, just the opposite is true when it comes to values! Suppose that you enter the number **17** in a cell and then drag the fill handle across the row — Excel just copies the number 17 in all the cells that you select. If, however, you hold down Ctrl while you drag the fill handle, Excel then fills out the series (17, 18, 19, and so on). If you forget and create a series of numbers when you only need the value copied, rectify this situation by selecting the Copy Cells command on the AutoFill Options short-cut menu.

Creating custom lists for AutoFill

In addition to varying the increment in a series created with AutoFill, you can also create your own custom series. For example, say your company has offices in the following locations and you get tired of typing the sequence in each new spread-sheet that requires them:

>> New York

>> Chicago

>> Atlanta

>> New Orleans

>> San Francisco

>> Los Angeles

After creating a custom list with these locations, you can enter the entire sequence of cities simply by entering New York in the first cell and then dragging the Fill handle to the blank cells where the rest of the cities should appear.

To create this kind of custom series, follow these steps:

1. **Click File ⇨ Options ⇨ Advanced or press Alt+FTA and then scroll down and click the Edit Custom Lists button in the General section to open the Custom Lists dialog box (as shown in Figure 2-12).**

   If you've already gone to the time and trouble of typing the custom list in a range of cells, go to Step 2. If you haven't yet typed the series in an open worksheet, go to Step 4.

2. **Click in the Import List from Cells text box and then select the range of cells in the worksheet containing the custom list (see Chapter 3 for details).**

   As soon as you start selecting the cells in the worksheet by dragging your mouse or Touch pointer, Excel automatically collapses the Options dialog box to the minimum to get out of the way. The moment you release the mouse button or remove your finger or stylus from the screen, Excel automatically restores the Options dialog box to its normal size.

3. **Click the Import button to copy this list into the List Entries list box.**

   Skip to Step 6.

4. **Select the List Entries list box and then type each entry (in the desired order), being sure to press Enter after typing each one.**

   When all the entries in the custom list appear in the List Entries list box in the order you want them, proceed to Step 5.

5. **Click the Add button to add the list of entries to the Custom Lists list box.**

   Finish creating all the custom lists you need, using the preceding steps. When you're done, move to Step 6.

6. **Click OK twice, the first time to close the Custom Lists dialog box and the second to close the Excel Options dialog box and return to the current worksheet in the active workbook.**

After adding a custom list to Excel, from then on you need only enter the first entry in a cell and then use the fill handle to extend it to the cells below or to the right.

TIP

If you don't even want to bother with typing the first entry, use the AutoCorrect feature — refer to the section "You really AutoCorrect that for me," earlier in this chapter — to create an entry that fills in as soon as you type your favorite acronym for it (such as *ny* for New York).

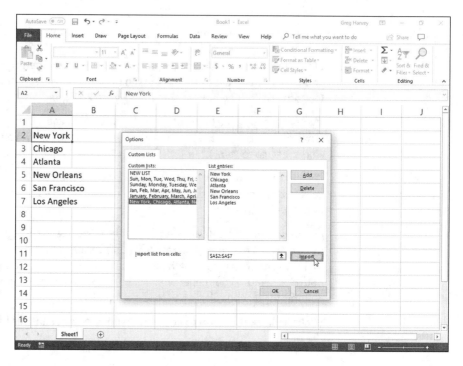

FIGURE 2-12:
Creating a custom company location list from a range of existing cell entries.

Doing AutoFill on a touchscreen

TIP

To fill out a data series using your finger or stylus when using Excel on a touch-screen tablet without access to a mouse or touchpad, you use the AutoFill button that appears on the mini-toolbar as the fill handle as follows:

1. **Tap the cell containing the initial value in the series you want AutoFill to extend.**

Excel selects the cell and displays selection handles (with circles) in the upper-left and lower-right corners.

2. **Tap and hold the cell until the mini-toolbar appears.**

When summoned by touch, the mini-toolbar appears as a single row of command buttons, from Paste to AutoFill, terminated by a Show Context Menu button (with a black triangle pointing downward).

3. **Tap the AutoFill button on the mini-toolbar.**

Excel closes the mini-toolbar and adds an AutoFill button to the currently selected cell (the blue downward-pointing arrow in the square that appears in the lower-right corner of the cell).

4. **Drag the AutoFill button through the blank cells in the same column or row into which the data series sequence is to be filled.**

As you drag your finger or stylus through blank cells, the Name box on the Formula bar keeps informed of the next entry in the data series. When you release your finger or stylus from the touchscreen after selecting the last blank cell to be filled, Excel fills out the data series in the selected range.

Doing AutoFill with the Fill button on the Home tab

TIP

If you're using Excel 2019 on a touchscreen tablet without the benefit of a mouse or touchpad, you can do AutoFill from the Ribbon (you may also want to use this method if you find that using the fill handle to create a series of data entries with AutoFill is too taxing even with a physical mouse).

You simply use the Fill button on the Home tab of the Ribbon to accomplish your AutoFill operations as follows:

1. Enter the first entry (or entries) upon which the series is to be based in the first cell(s) to hold the new data series in your worksheet.

2. Select the cell range where the series is to be created, across a row or down a column, being sure to include the cell with the initial entry or entries in this range.

3. Click the Fill button on the Home tab followed by Series on its drop-down menu or press Alt+HFIS.

The Fill button is located in the Editing group right below the AutoSum button (the one with the Greek sigma). When you select the Series option, Excel opens the Series dialog box.

4. Click the AutoFill option button in the Type column followed by the OK button in the Series dialog box.

Excel enters a series of data based on the initial value(s) in your selected cell range just as though you'd selected the range with the fill handle.

Note that the Series dialog box contains a bunch of options that you can use to further refine and control the data series that Excel creates. In a linear data series, if you want the series to increment more than one step value at a time, you can increase it in the Step Value text box. Likewise, if you want your linear or AutoFill series to stop when it reaches a particular value, you enter that into the Stop Value text box.

REMEMBER

When you're entering a series of dates with AutoFill that increment on anything other than the day, remember the Date Unit options in the Series dialog box enable you to specify other parts of the initial date to increment in the series. Your choices include Weekday, Month, or Year.

Fill it in a flash

Excel 2019's Flash Fill feature gives you the ability to take a part of the data entered into one column of a worksheet table and enter just that data in a new table column using only a few keystrokes. The series of entries appears in the new column, literally in a flash (thus its name, Flash Fill). The second Excel 2019 detects a pattern in your initial data entries, the rest of the entries in that series immediately appears in blank cells in rows below that you can then enter with a single keystroke. And the beauty is that all this happens without the need for you to construct or copy any kind of formula.

The best way to understand Flash Fill is to see it in action. In Figure 2-13, you see a new data table consisting of four columns. The cells in the first column of this table contain the full names of clients (first, middle, and last), all together in one entry. The second, third, and fourth columns need to have just the first, middle, and surnames, respectively, entered into them (so that particular parts of the clients' names can be used in the greetings of form e-mails and letters as in, "Hello Keith," or "Dear Mr. Harper,").

FIGURE 2-13:
Data Table containing full names that need to be split up in separate columns using Flash Fill.

Rather than manually enter the first, middle, or last names in the respective columns (or attempt to copy the entire client name from column A and then edit out the parts not needed in First Name, Middle Name, and Last Name columns), you can use Flash Fill to quickly and effectively do the job. And here's how you do it:

1. **Type** Keith **in cell B2 and complete the entry with the ↓ or Enter key.**

   When you complete this entry with the down-arrow key or Enter key on your keyboard, Excel moves the cell pointer to cell B3 where you only have to type the first letter of the next name for Flash Fill to get the picture.

2. **In Cell B3, only type** J, **the first letter of the second client's first name.**

   Flash Fill immediately does an AutoFill-type maneuver by suggesting the rest of the second client's first name, Jonas, as the text to enter in this cell. At the same time, Flash Fill suggests entering all the remaining first names from the full names in column A in column B (see Figure 2-13).

3. **Complete the entry of Jonas in cell B3 by pressing the Enter key or an arrow key.**

   The moment you complete the data entry in cell B3, the First Name column's done: Excel enters all the other first names in column B at the same time (take that, Barry Allen)!

To complete this example name table by entering the middle and last names in columns C and D, respectively, you simply repeat these steps in those columns. You enter the first middle name, **Austen**, from cell A2 in cell C2 and then type **W** in cell C3. Complete the entry in cell C3 and the middle name entries in that column are done. Likewise, you enter the first last name, **Harper**, from cell A2 in cell D2 and then type **S** in cell D3. Complete the entry in cell D3, and the last name entries for column D are done, completing the entire data table.

By my count, completing the data entry in this Client Name table required me to make a total of 26 keystrokes, 20 of which were for typing in the first, middle, and last name of the first client along with the initial letters of the first, middle, and last name of the second client and the other six to complete these entries. If Column A of this Client Name table contains the full names of hundreds or even thousands of clients, these 26 keystrokes are insignificant compared to the number that would be required to manually enter their first, middle, and last names in its separate First Name, Middle Name, and Last Name columns or even to edit down copies of the full names in each of them.

REMEMBER

Keep in mind that Flash Fill works perfectly at extracting parts of longer data entries in a column provided that all the entries follow the same pattern and use the same type of separators (spaces, commas, dashes, and the like). For example, in Figure 2-13, there's an anomaly in the full name entries in cell A9 where only the middle initial with a period is entered instead of the full middle name. In this case, Flash Fill simply enters M in cell C9 and you have to manually edit its entry to add the necessary period. Also, remember that Flash Fill's usefulness isn't restricted to all-text entries as in my example Client Name table. It can also parse entries that mix text and numbers such as part numbers (AJ-1234, RW-8007, and so forth).

Inserting special symbols

Excel makes it easy to enter special symbols, such as foreign currency indicators, and special characters, such as the trademark and copyright symbols, into your cell entries. To add a special symbol or character to a cell entry you're making or editing, select Insert ⇨ Symbol on the Ribbon or press Alt+NU to open the Symbol dialog box.

The Symbol dialog box contains two tabs: Symbols and Special Characters. To insert a mathematical or foreign currency symbol on the Symbols tab, select its symbol in the list box and then click the Insert button. (You can also do this by double-clicking or double-tapping the symbol.) To insert characters, such as foreign language or accented characters from other character sets, click the Subset drop-down button followed by the name of the set in the drop-down list and the desired characters in the list box. You can often insert commonly used currency and mathematical symbols, such as the pound or plus-or-minus symbol, by selecting them directly from the Recently Used Symbols section at the bottom of this tab, provided that other symbols that you've inserted of late haven't replaced them.

To insert special characters, such as the registered trademark, paragraph symbol, and so forth, you click the Special Characters tab of the Symbol dialog box followed by the symbol in the scrolling list and the Insert button. (You can insert one of these special characters by double-clicking or double-tapping it also.)

When you finish inserting special symbols and characters, close the Symbol dialog box by pressing Esc or clicking the Close button with an X in its upper-right corner.

Entries all around the block

When you want to enter a table of information in a new worksheet, you can simplify the job of entering the data if you select all the empty cells in which you want to make entries before you begin entering any information. Just position the cell pointer in the first cell of what is to become the data table and then select all the cells in the subsequent columns and rows. (For information on the ways to select a range of cells, see Chapter 3.) After you select the block of cells, you can begin entering the first entry.

When you select a block of cells (also known as a *range*) before you enter information, Excel restricts data entry to that range as follows:

>> The program automatically advances the cell pointer to the next cell in the range when you click the Enter button on the Formula bar or press the Enter key to complete each cell entry.

>> In a cell range that contains several different rows and columns, Excel advances the cell pointer down each row of the column while you make your entries. When the cell pointer reaches the cell in the last row of the column, the cell pointer advances to the first selected row in the next column to the right. If the cell range uses only one row, Excel advances the cell pointer from left to right across the row.

>> When you finish entering information in the last cell in the selected range, Excel positions the cell pointer in the first cell of the now-completed data table. To deselect the cell range, select a single cell in the worksheet (inside or outside the selected range — it doesn't matter) or press one of the arrow keys.

WARNING

Be sure that you don't press one of the arrow keys to complete a cell entry within a preselected cell range instead of clicking the Enter button or pressing Enter. Pressing an arrow key deselects the range of cells when Excel moves the cell pointer. To move the cell pointer around a cell range without deselecting the range, try these methods:

>> Press Enter to advance to the next cell down each row and then across each column in the range. Press Shift+Enter to move up to the previous cell.

>> Press Tab to advance to the next cell in the column on the right and then down each row of the range. Press Shift+Tab to move left to the previous cell.

>> Press Ctrl+. (period) to move from one corner of the range to another.

Data entry express

You can save a lot of time and energy when you want the same entry (text, value, or formula) to appear in many cells of the worksheet; you can enter the information in all the cells in one operation. You first select the cell ranges to hold the information. (Excel lets you select more than one cell range for this kind of thing — see Chapter 3 for details.) Then you construct the entry on the Formula bar and press Ctrl+Enter to put the entry into all the selected ranges.

REMEMBER

The key to making this operation a success on a physical keyboard is to hold the Ctrl key down while you press Enter so that Excel inserts the entry on the Formula bar into all the selected cells. If you forget to hold Ctrl and you just press Enter, Excel places the entry in the first cell only of the selected cell range. On the Windows virtual keyboard, you just tap Ctrl followed by Enter in succession.

You can also speed up data entry in a list that includes formulas by making sure that the Extend Data Range Formats and Formulas check box is selected in the Editing Options section of the Advanced tab in the Excel Options dialog box (click File ⇨ Options ⇨ Advanced or press Alt+FTA). When this check box is selected,

Excel automatically formats new data that you type in the last row of a list to match that of like data in earlier rows and copies down formulas that appear in the preceding rows. Note, however, that for this feature to kick in, you must manually enter the formulas and format the data entries in at least three rows preceding the new row.

How to Make Your Formulas Function Even Better

Earlier in this chapter, I show you how to create formulas that perform a series of simple mathematical operations, such as addition, subtraction, multiplication, and division. (See the section "Fabricating those fabulous formulas!") Instead of creating complex formulas from scratch out of an intricate combination of these operations, you can find an Excel function to get the job done.

A *function* is a predefined formula that performs a particular type of computation. All you have to do to use a function is supply the values that the function uses when performing its calculations. (In the parlance of the Spreadsheet Guru, such values are the *arguments of the function.*) As with simple formulas, you can enter the arguments for most functions either as a numerical value (for example, **22** or **−4.56**) or, as is more common, as a cell reference (**B10**) or as a cell range (**C3:F3**).

Just as with a formula you build yourself, each function you use must start with an equal sign (=) so that Excel knows to enter the function as a formula rather than as text. Following the equal sign, you enter the name of the function (in uppercase or lowercase — it doesn't matter, as long as you spell the name correctly). Following the name of the function, you enter the arguments required to perform the calculations. All function arguments are enclosed in a pair of parentheses.

REMEMBER

If you type the function directly in a cell, remember not to insert spaces between the equal sign, function name, and the arguments enclosed in parentheses. Some functions use more than one value when performing their designated calculations. When this is the case, you separate each argument of the function with a comma (not a space).

After you type the equal sign and begin typing the first few letters of the name of the function you want to use, a drop-down list showing all the functions that begin with the letters you've typed appears immediately beneath the cell. When you see the name of the function you want to use on this list, double-click it or select its name and then press Tab and Excel finishes entering the function name in the cell and on the Formula bar as well as adding the left parenthesis that marks the beginning of the arguments for the function.

Excel then displays all the arguments that the function takes beneath the cell, and you can indicate any cell or cell range that you want to use as the first argument by either pointing to it or typing its cell or range references. When the function uses more than one argument, you can point to the cells or cell ranges or enter the addresses for the second argument right after you enter a comma (,) to complete the first argument.

After you finish entering the last argument, you need to close off the function by typing a right parenthesis to mark the end of the argument list. The display of the function name along with its arguments that appeared beneath the cell when you first selected the function from the drop-down list then disappears. Click the Enter button or press Enter (or the appropriate arrow key) to then insert the function into the cell and have Excel calculate the answer.

Inserting a function into a formula with the Insert Function button

Although you can enter a function by typing it directly in a cell, Excel provides an Insert Function command button on the Formula bar you can use to select any of Excel's functions. When you select this button, Excel opens the Insert Function dialog box (shown in Figure 2-14) where you can select the function you want to use. After you select your function, Excel opens the Function Arguments dialog box. In this dialog box, you can specify the function arguments. The real boon comes when you're starting to use an unfamiliar function or one that's kind of complex (some of these puppies can be hairy). You can get loads of help in completing the argument text boxes in the Function Arguments dialog box by clicking the Help on This Function link in the lower-left corner.

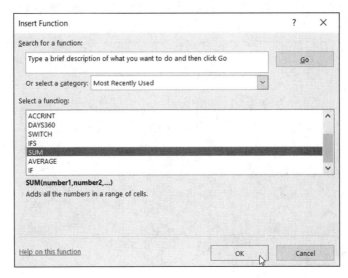

FIGURE 2-14: Select the function you want to use in the Insert Function dialog box.

The Insert Function dialog box contains three boxes: a Search for a Function text box, an Or Select a Category drop-down list box, and a Select a Function list box. When you open the Insert Function dialog box, Excel automatically selects Most Recently Used as the category in the Select a Category drop-down list box and displays the functions you usually use in the Select a Function list box.

If your function isn't among the most recently used, you must then select the appropriate category of your function in the Select a Category drop-down list box. If you don't know the category, you must search for the function by typing a description of its purpose in the Search for a Function text box and then press Enter or click the Go button. For example, to locate all the Excel functions that total values, you enter **total** in the Search for a Function list box and click the Go button. Excel then displays its list of recommended functions for calculating totals in the Select a Function list box. You can peruse the recommended functions by selecting each one. While you select each function in this list, the Insert Function dialog box shows you the required arguments followed by a description, at the bottom of the dialog box, of what the function does.

After you locate and select the function that you want to use, click the OK button to insert the function into the current cell and open the Function Arguments dialog box. This dialog box displays the required arguments for the function along with any that are optional. For example, suppose that you select the SUM function (the crown jewel of the Most Recently Used function category) in the Select a Function list box and then select OK. As soon as you do, the program inserts

```
SUM( )
```

in the current cell and on the Formula bar (following the equal sign), and the Function Arguments dialog box showing the SUM arguments appears on the screen (as shown in Figure 2-15). This is where you add the arguments for the SUM function.

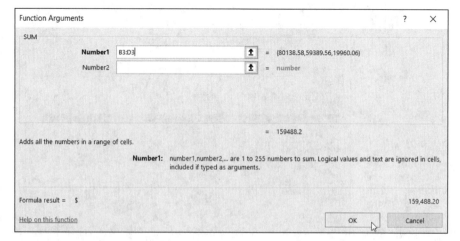

FIGURE 2-15:
Specify the arguments to use in the selected function in the Function Arguments dialog box.

As shown in Figure 2-15, you can sum up to 255 numbers in the Function Arguments dialog box. What's not obvious, however (there's always some trick, huh?), is that these numbers don't have to be in single cells. In fact, most of the time you'll be selecting a whole slew of numbers in nearby cells (in a multiple cell selection — that range thing) that you want to total.

To select your first number argument in the dialog box, you select the cell (or block of cells) in the worksheet while the insertion point is in the Number1 text box. Excel then displays the cell address (or range address) in the Number1 text box while, at the same time, showing the value in the cell (or values, if you select a bunch of cells) in the box to the right. Excel displays the total near the bottom of the Function Arguments dialog box after the words *Formula result=.*

When selecting cells, you can minimize this arguments dialog box to just the contents of the Number1 text box by dragging the cell pointer through the cells to sum in the worksheet. After you minimize the arguments dialog box while selecting the cells for the first argument, you can then expand it again by releasing the mouse button.

You can also reduce the dialog box to the Number1 argument text box by clicking the Minimize Dialog Box button on the right of the text box, selecting the cells, and then clicking the Maximize Dialog Box button (the only button displayed on the far right) or by pressing the Esc key. Instead of minimizing the dialog box, you can also temporarily move it out of the way by clicking on any part and then dragging the dialog box to its new destination on the screen.

If you're adding more than one cell (or a bunch of cells) in a worksheet, press the Tab key or click the Number2 text box to move the insertion point to that text box. (Excel responds by extending the argument list with a Number3 text box.) Here is where you specify the second cell (or cell range) to add to the one now showing in the Number1 text box. After you select the cell or second cell range, the program displays the cell address(es), the numbers in the cell(s) to the right, and the running total near the bottom of the Function Arguments dialog box after *Formula result=* (as shown in Figure 2-15). You can minimize the entire Function Arguments dialog box down to just the contents of the argument text box you're dealing with (Number2, Number3, and so on) by clicking its particular Minimize Dialog Box button if the dialog box obscures the cells that you need to select.

When you finish pointing out the cells or bunch of cells to sum, click the OK button to close the Function Arguments dialog box and put the SUM function in the current cell.

Editing a function with the Insert Function button

You can also use the Insert Function button to edit formulas that contain functions right from the Formula bar. Select the cell with the formula and function to edit before you select the Insert Function button (the one sporting the *fx* that appears immediately in front of the current cell entry on the Formula bar).

As soon as you select the Insert Function button, Excel opens the Function Arguments dialog box where you can edit its arguments. To edit just the arguments of a function, select the cell references in the appropriate argument's text box (marked Number1, Number2, Number3, and so on) and then make whatever changes are required to the cell addresses or select a new range of cells.

Excel automatically adds any cell or cell range that you highlight in the worksheet to the current argument. If you want to replace the current argument, you need to highlight it and remove its cell addresses by pressing the Delete key before you highlight the new cell or cell range to use as the argument. (Remember that you can always minimize this dialog box or move it to a new location if it obscures the cells you need to select.)

When you finish editing the function, press Enter or click the OK button in the Function Arguments dialog box to put it away and update the formula in the worksheet.

I'd be totally lost without AutoSum

Before leaving this fascinating discussion on entering functions, I want you to get to the AutoSum tool in the Editing group on the Home tab of the Ribbon. Look for the Greek sigma (Σ) symbol. This little tool is worth its weight in gold. In addition to entering the SUM, AVERAGE, COUNT, MAX, or MIN functions, it also selects the most likely range of cells in the current column or row that you want to use as the function's argument and then automatically enters them as the function's argument. Nine times out of ten, Excel selects (with the *marquee* or moving dotted line) the correct cell range to total, average, count, and so forth. For that tenth case, you can manually correct the range by simply dragging the cell pointer through the block of cells to sum.

Simply select the AutoSum button followed by Sum on the drop-down menu on the Home tab when you want to insert the SUM function into the current cell. The quicker method to select this function is to press Alt+= (the Alt key plus the equal to symbol on the top row).

If you want to use the AutoSum button to insert another function, such as AVERAGE, COUNT, MAX, or MIN, you need to click its drop-down button and select the name of the desired function on its pop-up menu (click Count Numbers on the menu to insert the COUNT function). If you select the More Functions command on this menu, Excel opens the Insert Function dialog box as though you had clicked the *fx* button on the Formula bar.

In Figure 2-16, check out how to use AutoSum to total the sales of Jack Sprat Diet Centers in row 3. Position the cell pointer in cell E3 where the first-quarter total is to appear and then select Sum on the AutoSum drop-down menu (or press Alt+=). Excel inserts SUM (equal sign and all) onto the Formula bar; places a marquee around cells B3, C3, and D3; and uses the cell range B3:D3 as the argument of the SUM function.

AutoSum button

FIGURE 2-16:
To total Jack Sprat Diet Centers first quarter sales for row 3, click the AutoSum button after you select cell E3 and then click Enter.

Now look at the worksheet after you insert the function in cell E3 (see Figure 2-17). The calculated total appears in cell E3 while the following SUM function formula appears in the Formula bar:

```
=SUM(B3:D3)
```

After entering the function to total the sales of Jack Sprat Diet Centers, you can copy this formula to total sales for the rest of the companies by dragging the fill handle down column E until the cell range E3:E11 is highlighted (as shown in Figure 2-17).

FIGURE 2-17:
The worksheet with the first-quarter totals calculated with AutoSum.

Look at Figure 2-18 to see how you can use AutoSum to total the January sales for all the Mother Goose Enterprises in column B. Position the cell pointer in cell B12 where you want the total to appear. Select Sum on the AutoSum's drop-down menu, and Excel places the marquee around cells B3 through B11 and correctly enters the cell range `B3:B11` as the argument of the SUM function.

FIGURE 2-18:
Select AutoSum in cell B12 and click Enter to total the January sales for all companies in column B.

In Figure 2-19, you see the worksheet after inserting the function in cell B12 and using the AutoFill feature to copy the formula to cells C12 and E12 to the right. (To use AutoFill, drag the fill handle through the cells to the right until you reach cell E12. Release the mouse button or remove your finger or stylus from the touchscreen.)

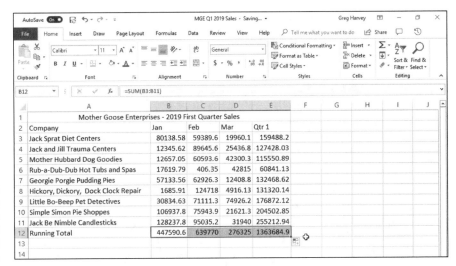

FIGURE 2-19:
The worksheet after copying the SUM function formulas using the fill handle.

Sums via Quick Analysis Totals

For those of you who don't have the time or patience for adding totals to your worksheet tables with AutoSum and AutoFill, Excel 2019's Totals feature on the Quick Analysis tool is just the thing. The Quick Analysis tool offers a bevy of features for doing anything from adding conditional formatting (see Chapter 3), charts (see Chapter 10), pivot tables (see Chapter 9), and sparklines (see Chapter 10) to your worksheet tables. And it turns out Quick Analysis is also a whiz at adding running totals and sums to the rows and columns of your new worksheet tables.

To use the Quick Analysis tool, all you have to do is select the worksheet table's cells (see Chapter 3 for details) and then click the Quick Analysis tool that automatically appears in the lower-right corner of the last selected cell. When you do, a palette of options (from Formatting to Sparklines) appears right beneath the tool.

To add totals to your selected table data, simply click the Totals button. You can then use your mouse or Touch pointer to have Live Preview show you totals in a new row at the bottom by highlighting Running Total or in a new column on the right by highlighting Sum (shown in Figure 2-20). To actually add the SUM formulas with the totals to a new row or column, you simply click the Running Total or Sum button.

To add the running totals to the sample worksheet table shown in Figure 2-20, you simply select the table of data, A2 through D11, and click the Quick Analysis tool followed by the Totals and Running Total buttons. Add a column of quarterly running totals down the rows in the cell range E3:E11 by selecting the Quick Analysis tool again and then selecting Totals followed by the Sum option (displaying the Sigma on a shaded column) that is to the immediate right of the Running option. Finally, enter a **Qtr1 Total** heading at the top of the column in cell E2, and you're done!

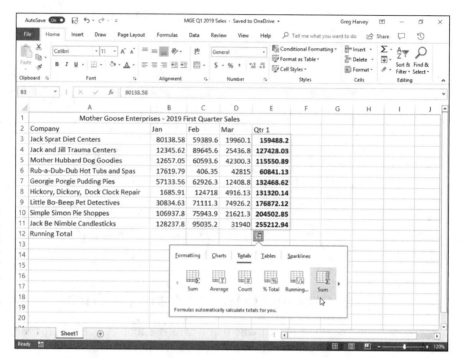

FIGURE 2-20:
Using Totals on the Quick Analysis tool to add a row of running monthly totals or a column of quarterly totals to a selected worksheet table.

TIP

If you have trouble selecting the Quick Analysis tool to open its palette for any reason, simply select the cells to be calculated and then press Ctrl+Q or right-click the cell selection and click the Quick Analysis item on its context menu.

Making Sure That the Data Is Safe and Sound

All the work you do in creating worksheets in any previously unsaved workbook (with the generic name Book1, Book2, and the like) is at risk until you save the workbook as a disk file, normally on your computer's hard drive. Should you lose power or should your computer crash for any reason before you save the workbook, you're out of luck. You have to re-create each keystroke — a painful task made all the worse because it's so unnecessary. To avoid this unpleasantness altogether, adopt this motto: Save your work any time that you enter more information than you could possibly bear to lose.

TIP

To encourage frequent saving on your part after you first save your workbook file on a local drive such as your computer's hard disk, Excel even provides you with a Save button on the Quick Access toolbar (the one with the picture of a floppy disk, the very first on the toolbar). You don't even have to take the time and trouble to select the Save command from the File pull-down menu (opened by selecting File) or even press Ctrl+S; you can simply click this tool whenever you want to save new work on disk. If you're saving your workbook file in an online location, such as a folder on your OneDrive or SharePoint site, Excel 2019 goes one further by activating its AutoSave feature that automatically saves any further editing changes you make to the workbook without you having to bother with the Save button!

When you click the Save button, press Ctrl+S, or select File ⇨ Save for the first time, Excel 2019 displays the Save As screen similar to the one shown in Figure 2-21. This screen is divided into two columns: a left column where you select the general location for saving the new workbook file and a right column that shows a list of folders and sometimes files saved in the selected location.

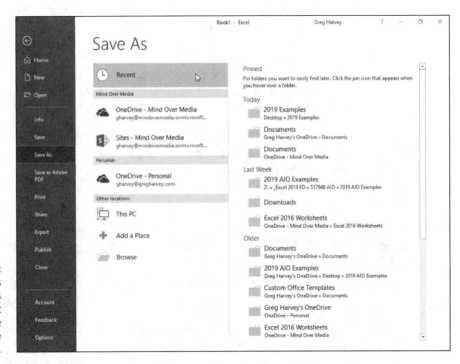

FIGURE 2-21:
The Save As screen appears after you select the Save command to save a new workbook.

As you continue to work with Excel saving files in various locations, when you open the Save As screen, Excel automatically selects Recent as the default location and displays a list of folders (both local and in the cloud) in which you've recently saved workbooks. To save the new workbook in one of the recently used folders, simply click its folder icon to select it. Excel 2019 will then display a list of any subfolders and workbook files that already saved in that folder beneath a File Name text box (displaying "Enter File Name Here") and a Save as Type drop-down list box (with Excel Workbook *xlsx as the default). To save your file, simply click the File Name text box (which removes the *Enter File Name Here* text), type the name for your new workbook, and click the Save button to the right of the Save As Type drop-down list box.

TIP

Excel replaces the folders in the Recent list as you continue to save more and more workbook files in various local and online locations. If you have a favorite location for saving your Excel workbooks and want its folder to always appear on this list, you can pin its folder by right-clicking the folder and then choosing Pin to List on the pop-up menu that appears.

If the folder in which you want to save the new workbook file (either locally or online) is not displayed in the Recent list, you first need to select its location before entering its new filename. To save the new workbook on your OneDrive or SharePoint site, select OneDrive or the name of the SharePoint site in the left column of the Save As screen. Excel will then select the default folder for the online site. To save the workbook in that default folder, all you have to do is name the workbook in the File Name text box before you click the Save button. To save the file in another OneDrive or SharePoint folder listed beneath the File Name and Save As Type boxes, click it before entering your filename and clicking Save.

To save the file locally — on your computer's hard drive or a virtual drive on your local area network — select This PC under the Other Locations heading in the left column of the Save As screen. Then, select the folder from its list in the right column and name the workbook in its File Name text box before you click Save.

TECHNICAL STUFF

ONEDRIVE TO SAVE THEM ALL

You've undoubtedly heard of the cloud, but your understanding of it may yet be as nebulous as its name. OneDrive (formerly known as SkyDrive) is the descriptive name that Microsoft has given the space in the cloud that it lends to its users who sign up for a Windows account. The great thing about saving a workbook file in a folder on your OneDrive is that you then can open it for further editing and printing from any device running a version of Excel that has Internet access. For example, if you save a workbook file that you create in Excel on your office desktop computer, you can then open it for more editing on your laptop at home or even your Windows tablet or smartphone at the local coffee shop. For more information on OneDrive and how to set it up on your computer, select the Learn More link under Get OneDrive for Windows and Take Your Files with You Anywhere on the Excel Save As screen.

If you're not sure where the folder in which you want to save the new workbook is located, click the Browse button in the Other Locations section. Excel then opens the Save As dialog box with the default location for saving workbook files showing a list of the subfolders it contains. (This default location just happens to be the Documents folders on your OneDrive until you change it, as described in the following section.)

In the Save As dialog box, you can use the navigation pane on the left to select the drive and folder where the new workbook should be stored. After you select the folder in which you want to save your new workbook in the Save As dialog box, you then need to replace the temporary document name (Book1, Book2, and so forth) with a more descriptive filename in the File Name text box, select a new file format in the Save As Type drop-down list box right below, and select a new drive and folder before you save the workbook as a disk file.

When you finish making changes in the Save As dialog box, click the Save button or press Enter to have Excel 2019 save your work. When Excel saves your workbook file, the program saves all the information in every worksheet in your workbook (including the last position of the cell cursor) in the designated folder and drive.

REMEMBER

You don't have to fool with the Save As dialog box again unless you want to rename the workbook or save a copy of it in a different folder. If you want to do these things, you must select File ⇨ Save As or press Alt+FA to choose the Save As command rather than clicking the Save button on the Quick Access toolbar or pressing Ctrl+S.

Changing the default file location

Whenever you open the Save As dialog box to save a new workbook file, Excel 2019 automatically selects the folder listed in the Default Local File Location text box on the Save tab of the Excel Options dialog box (File ⇨ Options ⇨ Save or Alt+FTS).

When you first start using Excel, the default folder is the Documents on your One-Drive. For example, the directory path of the default folder where Excel 2019 automatically saves new workbook files on my computer is

```
C:\Users\gharv\OneDrive\Documents
```

The very generic Documents folder may not be the place on your OneDrive where you want all the new workbooks you create automatically saved. To change the default file location to another folder on your computer, follow these steps:

1. **Click File ⇨ Options ⇨ Save or press Alt+FTS to open the Save tab of the Excel Options dialog box.**

   The Default Local File Location text box displays the directory path to the current default folder.

2. **Click in the Default Local File Location text box.**

   To edit part of the path (such as the Documents folder name after your username or remove OneDrive to designate a local drive), insert the mouse pointer at that place in the path to set the insertion point.

3. **Edit the existing path or replace it with the path to another folder in which you want all future workbooks to save to automatically.**

4. **Click OK to close the Excel Options dialog box.**

The difference between the XLSX and XLS file formats

Excel 2019 supports the use of the XML-based file format first introduced in Excel 2007 (which Microsoft officially calls the Microsoft Office Open XML format). This default file format is touted as being more efficient in saving data, resulting in smaller file size and offering superior integration with external data sources (especially when these resources are web-based ones supporting XML files). This XML-based file format carries the filename extension .xlsx and is the file format in which Excel automatically saves any new workbook you create.

WARNING

The only problem with this newfangled XML-based file format is that it can't be opened by earlier Excel versions (before Excel 2007). Therefore, if someone who needs to work with the workbook you've just created isn't using Excel 2007 or hasn't yet upgraded to Excel 2019, you need to save the new workbook in the earlier file format used in Excel versions 97 through 2003 with the old .xls filename extension. To do this, click the Save As Type drop-down button in the Save As dialog box and then click Excel 97-2003 Workbook (*.xls) in the drop-down menu.

REMEMBER

Filename extensions, such as .xlsx and .xls, do not appear as part of the filename (even though they are appended) in the File Name text box in the Excel Save As dialog box unless you've specifically changed Windows' folder options to show them. To make this change in Windows 10, open the File Explorer and then deselect the File Name Extensions check box on the View tab in the dialog box.

TIP

Excel 2019 also supports a special binary file format called Excel Binary Workbook that carries the .xlsb filename extension. Select this binary format for huge spreadsheets that you create that have to be compatible with earlier versions of Excel.

Saving the Workbook as a PDF File

The PDF (Portable Document File) file format developed by Adobe Systems Incorporated enables people to open and print documents without access to the original programs with which the documents were created.

Excel 2019 enables you to save your workbook files directly in this special PDF file format. You can readily share your Excel 2019 workbooks with users who don't have Excel installed on their computers by saving them as PDF files. All they need to open and print the PDF copy of the workbook file is the free Adobe Reader software (which they can download from the Adobe website at www.adobe.com).

To save your workbook as a PDF file, you simply select the PDF option on the Save as Type drop-down list in the Save As dialog box. Excel then adds PDF-specific options to the bottom of the Save As dialog box, with the Standard (Publishing Online and Printing) button under the Optimize For heading and the Open File after Publishing check box selected.

If you want to make the resulting PDF file as small as possible (because your worksheet is so large), click the Minimum Size (Publishing Online) button under the Optimize For heading. If you want to change which parts of the workbook are saved in the resulting PDF (Excel automatically saves all ranges in the active worksheet of the workbook), click the Options button directly beneath the Minimum Size (Publishing Online) option and make the appropriate changes in the Options dialog box before you click OK.

If you don't need to edit the filename (Excel automatically appends .pdf to the current filename) or the folder location in the Save As dialog box, simply click the Save button. Excel then saves a copy of the workbook in a PDF file format and, provided you don't deselect the Open File after Publishing check box, automatically opens the workbook for your inspection in Adobe Reader. After viewing the PDF version in Adobe Reader, you can then return to your worksheet in Excel by clicking the Reader's Close button (or pressing Alt+F4).

REMEMBER

If you create an Excel 2019 workbook that incorporates new features not supported in earlier versions of Excel, instead of saving the workbook as an .xls file, thereby losing all of its 2010 enhancements, consider saving it as a PDF file. That way, coworkers still using pre-2010 Excel versions can still access the data in all its glory via Adobe Reader.

TIP

When you need coworkers or clients who don't have access to Excel on their devices to review and comment on a worksheet you've created, use the File ➪ Save as Adobe PDF command to convert the worksheet with the new PDFMaker add-in. This app enables you to convert all or part of the current workbook to PDF file format as well as preview the result in the Adobe PDF Reader or Acrobat software installed on your computer. You can send the converted PDF file to your coworker or client as an e-mail attachment from your Adobe software, and they can open the file in their copy of the Adobe PDF software to add comments, which they can then send back to you either in the PDF file format or as a converted Excel worksheet file.

Document Recovery to the Rescue

Excel 2019 offers a document recovery feature that can help you in the event of a computer crash because of a power failure or some sort of operating system freeze or shutdown. The AutoRecover feature saves your workbooks at regular intervals. In the event of a computer crash, Excel displays a Document Recovery task pane the next time you start Excel after rebooting the computer.

TIP

When you first start using Excel 2019, the AutoRecover feature is set to automatically save changes to your workbook (provided that the file has already been saved) every ten minutes. You can shorten or lengthen this interval as you see fit. Select File ➪ Options ➪ Save or press Alt+FTS to open the Excel Options dialog box with the Save tab selected. Use the spinner buttons or enter a new automatic save interval into the text box marked Save AutoRecover Information Every 10 Minutes before clicking OK.

After re-launching Excel 2019 after a computer crash that prevents you from saving your workbook file, the program opens with the Document Recovery task pane on the left side of the screen. This Document Recovery task pane shows the available versions of the workbook files that were open at the time of the computer crash. The original version of the workbook file is identified, including when it was saved, as is the recovered version of the file (displaying an .xlsb file extension) and when it was saved.

To open the recovered version of a workbook (to see how much of the work it contains that was unsaved at the time of the crash), position the mouse pointer over the AutoRecover version, and click its drop-down menu button followed by Open. After you open the recovered version, you can then (if you choose) save its changes by selecting the Save button on the Quick Access toolbar or by selecting File ➪ Save.

To save the recovered version of a workbook without bothering to first open it, click the recovered version's drop-down button in the Document Recovery task pane, and then select Save As. To abandon the recovered version permanently (leaving you with *only* the data in the original version), click the Close button at the bottom of the Document Recovery task pane. When you do this, an alert dialog box appears, giving you the chance to retain the recovered versions of the file for later viewing. To retain the files for later viewing, select the Yes (I Want to View These Files Later) radio button before clicking OK. To retain only the original versions of the files shown in the task pane, select the No (Remove These Files. I Have Saved the Files I Need) radio button instead.

WARNING

The AutoRecover feature only works on Excel workbooks that you've saved at least one time (as explained in the earlier section "Making Sure That the Data Is Safe and Sound"). In other words, if you build a new workbook and don't bother to save and rename it prior to experiencing a computer crash, the AutoRecover feature will not bring back any part of it. For this reason, it is very important that you get into the habit of saving new workbooks with the Save button on the Quick Access toolbar very shortly after beginning to work on worksheets. Or use the trusty keyboard shortcut Ctrl+S.

2

Editing Without Tears

IN THIS PART . . .

Select and format worksheet data.

Adjust worksheet columns and rows.

Rearrange data in worksheet tables.

Delete worksheet data.

Use Cut, Copy, and Paste.

Preview pages before printing.

Print a whole worksheet or just selected cell ranges.

Visit www.dummies.com/extras/excel2019 for great Dummies content online.

IN THIS CHAPTER

» Selecting the cells to format

» Formatting data tables with the Format as Table command button

» Using various number formats on cells containing values

» Adjusting column width and row height in a worksheet

» Hiding columns and rows in a worksheet

» Formatting cell ranges from the Home tab of the Ribbon

» Formatting cell ranges using Styles and the Format Painter

» Formatting cells under certain conditions

Chapter **3**

Making It All Look Pretty

I n spreadsheet programs like Excel, you normally don't worry about how the stuff looks until after you enter all the data in the worksheets of your workbook and save it all safe and sound (see Chapters 1 and 2). Only then do you pretty up the information so that it's clearer and easy to read.

After you decide on the types of formatting that you want to apply to a portion of the worksheet, you can select all the cells to beautify and then click the appropriate tool or choose the menu command to apply those formats to the cells.

However, before you discover all the fabulous formatting features you can use to dress up cells, you need to know how to pick the group of cells that you want to apply the formatting to — that is, *selecting the cells* or, alternatively, *making a cell selection.*

Be aware, also, that entering data into a cell and formatting that data are two completely different things in Excel. Because they're separate, you can change the entry in a formatted cell, and new entries assume the cell's formatting. This enables you to format blank cells in a worksheet, knowing that when you get around to making entries in those cells, those entries automatically assume the formatting you assign to those cells.

Choosing a Select Group of Cells

Given the monotonously rectangular nature of the worksheet and its components, it shouldn't come as a surprise to find that all the cell selections you make in the worksheet have the same kind of cubist feel to them. After all, worksheets are just blocks of cells of varying numbers of columns and rows.

A *cell selection* (or *cell range*) is whatever collection of neighboring cells you choose to format or edit. The smallest possible cell selection in a worksheet is just one cell: the so-called *active cell.* The cell with the cell cursor is really just a single cell selection. The largest possible cell selection in a worksheet is all the cells in that worksheet (the whole enchilada, so to speak). Most of the cell selections you need for formatting a worksheet will probably fall somewhere in between, consisting of cells in several adjacent columns and rows.

Excel shows a cell selection in the worksheet by highlighting in color the entire block of cells within the extended cell cursor, except for the active cell that keeps its original color. (Figure 3-1 shows several cell selections of different sizes and shapes.)

In Excel, you can select more than one cell range at a time (a phenomenon somewhat ingloriously called a *noncontiguous* or *nonadjacent selection*). In fact, although Figure 3-1 appears to contain several cell selections, it's really just one big, nonadjacent cell selection with cell D12 (the active one) as the cell that was selected last.

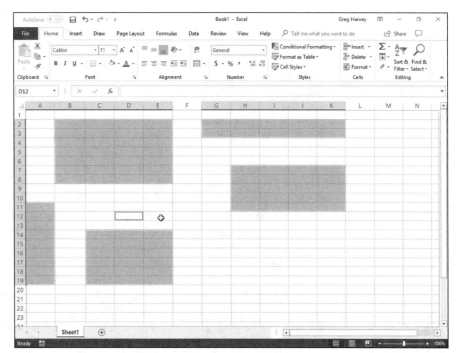

FIGURE 3-1:
Several cell
selections of
various shapes
and sizes.

Point-and-click cell selections

A mouse (provided that the device you're running Excel 2019 on has a mouse) is a natural for selecting a range of cells. Just position the mouse pointer (in its thick, white cross form) on the first cell and then click and drag in the direction that you want to extend the selection.

>> To extend the cell selection to columns to the right, drag your mouse to the right, highlighting neighboring cells as you go.

>> To extend the selection to rows to the bottom, drag your mouse down.

>> To extend the selection down and to the right at the same time, drag your mouse diagonally toward the cell in the lower-right corner of the block you're highlighting.

Shifty cell selections

To speed up the old cell-selection procedure, you can use the Shift+click method, which goes as follows:

1. **Click the first cell in the selection.**

   This selects that cell.

2. **Position the mouse pointer in the last cell in the selection.**

   This is kitty-corner from the first cell in your selected rectangular block.

3. **Press the Shift key and hold it down while you click the mouse button again.**

   When you click the mouse button the second time, Excel selects all the cells in the columns and rows between the first cell and last cell.

The Shift key works with the mouse like an *extend* key to extend a selection from the first object you select through to, and including, the second object you select. See the section "Extend that cell selection," later in this chapter. Using the Shift key enables you to select the first and last cells, as well as all the intervening cells in a worksheet or all the document names in a list.

If, when making a cell selection with the mouse, you notice that you include the wrong cells before you release the mouse button, you can deselect the cells and resize the selection by moving the pointer in the opposite direction. If you already released the mouse button, click the first cell in the highlighted range to select just that cell (and deselect all the others) and then start the whole selection process again.

Adding to and subtracting from cell selections

To select a nonadjacent cell selection made up of more than one nontouching block of cells, drag through the first cell range and release the mouse button. Then hold down the Ctrl key while you click the first cell of the second range and drag the pointer through the cells in this range. As long as you hold down Ctrl while you select the subsequent ranges, Excel doesn't deselect any of the previously selected cell ranges.

The Ctrl key can work with the mouse like an *add* or *subtract* key in Excel 2019. As an add key, you use it to include non-neighboring objects in the current worksheet. See the section "Nonadjacent cell selections with the keyboard," later in this chapter. By using the Ctrl key, you can add to the selection of cells in a worksheet or to the document names in a list without having to deselect those already selected.

TIP

To use the Ctrl key to deselect a range of cells within the current cell selection, hold down the Ctrl key and drag through the range that you want to deselect (subtract from the selected range) before releasing the mouse button and Ctrl key.

Touchy-feely cell selections

TIP

If you're running Excel 2019 on a touchscreen device such as a Windows tablet (like the Microsoft Surface Pro) or a computer (such as the Surface Laptop), you simply use your finger or stylus to make your cell selections. Simply tap the first cell in the selection (the equivalent of clicking with a mouse) and then drag the selection handle (one of the two circles that appears in the upper-left and lower-right corner of the cell) through the rest of the adjacent cells to extend the cell selection and select the entire range.

REMEMBER

Keep in mind that you can select only one range at a time on a touchscreen when you're dragging through the cells directly on the screen with your finger or a stylus. The Shift and Ctrl key range selection and extender techniques (discussed in the previous two sections) only work when dragging through cells indirectly with a mouse or on a computer touchpad using the Shift and Ctrl keys on a physical keyboard.

Going for the "big" cell selections

You can select the cells in entire columns or rows or even all the cells in the worksheet by applying the following clicking-and-dragging techniques to the worksheet frame:

>> To select every single cell in a particular column, click its column letter on the frame at the top of the worksheet document window.

>> To select every cell in a particular row, click its row number on the frame at the left edge of the document window.

>> To select a range of entire columns or rows, drag through the column letters or row numbers on the frame surrounding the workbook.

>> To select more than entire columns or rows that are not right next to each other (that old noncontiguous stuff, again), press and hold down the Ctrl key while you click the column letters or row numbers of the columns or rows that you want to add to the selection.

TIP

>> To select every cell in the worksheet, press Ctrl+A or click the Select All button, which is the button with the triangle pointing downward on the diagonal (which reminds me of the corner of a dog-eared book page). It's in the upper-left corner of the workbook frame, formed by the intersection of the row with the column letters and the column with the row numbers.

Selecting the cells in a table of data, courtesy of AutoSelect

Excel provides a quick way (called AutoSelect) to select all the cells in a table of data entered as a solid block with your mouse. To use AutoSelect, simply follow these steps:

1. Click the first cell of the table to select it.

This is the cell in the table's upper-left corner.

2. Hold down the Shift key while you double-click the right or bottom edge of the selected cell with the arrowhead mouse pointer (see Figure 3-2).

Double-clicking the bottom edge of the cell causes the cell selection to expand to the cell in the last row of the first column (as shown in Figure 3-3). If you double-click the right edge of the cell, the cell selection expands to the cell in the last column of the first row.

3a. Double-click somewhere on the right edge of the cell selection (refer to Figure 3-3) if the cell selection now consists of the first column of the table.

This selects all the remaining rows of the table of data (as shown in Figure 3-4).

3b. Double-click somewhere on the bottom edge of the current cell selection if the cell selection now consists of the first row of the table.

This selects all the remaining rows in the table.

FIGURE 3-2: Position the mouse pointer on the first cell's bottom edge to select all cells of the table's first column.

FIGURE 3-3:
Hold down Shift while you double-click the bottom edge of the first cell to extend the selection down the column.

FIGURE 3-4:
Hold down Shift as you double-click the right edge of the current selection to extend it across the rows of the table.

TIP

Although the preceding steps may lead you to believe that you have to select the first cell of the table when you use AutoSelect, you can actually select any of the cells in the four corners of the table. Then, when expanding the cell selection in the table with the Shift key depressed, you can choose whatever direction you like to either select the first or last row of the table or the first or last column. (Choose left, by clicking the left edge; right, by clicking the right edge; up, by clicking the top edge; or down, by clicking the bottom edge.) After expanding the cell selection to include either the first or last row or first or last column, you need to click whichever edge of that current cell selection that will expand it to include all the remaining table rows or columns.

Keyboard cell selections

If you're not keen on using the mouse, you can use the keyboard to select the cells you want. Sticking with the Shift+click method of selecting cells, the easiest way to select cells with the keyboard is to combine the Shift key with other keystrokes that move the cell cursor. (I list these keystrokes in Chapter 1.)

Start by positioning the cell cursor in the first cell of the selection and then holding the Shift key while you press the appropriate cell pointer movement keys. When you hold the Shift key while you press direction keys — such as the arrow keys ($\uparrow$, $\rightarrow$, $\downarrow$, $\leftarrow$), PgUp, or PgDn — Excel anchors the selection on the current cell, moves the cell cursor, and highlights cells as it goes.

TIP

When making a cell selection this way, you can continue to alter the size and shape of the cell range with the cell pointer movement keys as long as you don't release the Shift key. After you release the Shift key, pressing any of the cell pointer movement keys immediately collapses the selection, reducing it to just the cell with the cell cursor.

Extend that cell selection

If holding the Shift key while you move the cell cursor is too tiring, you can place Excel in Extend mode by pressing (and promptly releasing) F8 before you press any cell pointer movement key. Excel displays the Extend Selection indicator on the left side of the Status bar — when you see this indicator, the program will select all the cells that you move the cell cursor through (just as though you were holding down the Shift key).

After you highlight all the cells you want in the cell range, press F8 again (or Esc) to turn off Extend mode. The Extend Selection indicator disappears from the Status bar, and then you can once again move the cell cursor with the keyboard without highlighting everything in your path. In fact, when you first move the pointer, all previously selected cells are deselected.

AutoSelect keyboard style

For the keyboard equivalent of AutoSelect with the mouse (see the "Selecting the cells in a table of data, courtesy of AutoSelect" section), you combine the use of the F8 key (Extend key) or the Shift key with the Ctrl+arrow keys or End+arrow keys to zip the cell cursor from one end of a block to the other and merrily select all the cells in that path.

To select an entire table of data with a keyboard version of AutoSelect, follow these steps:

1. **Position the cell cursor in the first cell.**

   That's the cell in the upper-left corner of the table.

2. **Press F8 (or hold the Shift key) and then press Ctrl+ → to extend the cell selection to the cells in the columns on the right.**

3. **Then press Ctrl+↓ to extend the selection to the cells in the rows below.**

REMEMBER

The directions in the preceding steps are somewhat arbitrary — you can just as well press Ctrl+↓ before you press Ctrl+→. Just be sure (if you're using the Shift key instead of F8) that you don't let up on the Shift key until after you finish performing these two directional maneuvers. Also, if you press F8 to get the program into Extend mode, don't forget to press this key again to get out of Extend mode after the table cells are all selected, or you'll end up selecting cells that you don't want included when you next move the cell cursor.

Nonadjacent cell selections with the keyboard

Selecting more than one cell range is a little more complicated with the keyboard than it is with the mouse. When using the keyboard, you alternate between *anchoring* the cell cursor and moving it to select the cell range and *unanchoring* the cell cursor and repositioning it at the beginning of the next range. To unanchor the cell cursor so that you can move it into position for selecting another range, press Shift+F8. This puts you in Add to Selection mode, in which you can move to the first cell of the next range without selecting any more cells. Excel lets you know that the cell cursor is unanchored by displaying the Add to Selection indicator on the left side of the Status bar.

To select more than one cell range by using the keyboard, follow these general steps:

1. **Move the cell cursor to the first cell of the first cell range that you want to select.**

2. **Press F8 to get into Extend Selection mode.**

   Move the cell cursor to select all the cells in the first cell range. Alternatively, hold the Shift key while you move the cell cursor.

3. **Press Shift+F8 to switch from Extend Selection mode to Add to Selection mode.**

   The Add to Selection indicator appears in the Status bar.

4. Move the cell cursor to the first cell of the next nonadjacent range that you want to select.

5. Press F8 again to get back into Extend Selection mode and then move the cell cursor to select all the cells in this new range.

6. If you still have other nonadjacent ranges to select, repeat Steps 3, 4, and 5 until you select and add all the cell ranges that you want to use.

Cell selections à la Go To

If you want to select a large cell range that would take a long time to select by pressing various cell pointer movement keys, use the Go To feature to extend the range to a far distant cell. All you gotta do is follow this pair of steps:

1. Position the cell cursor in the first cell of the range and then press F8 to anchor the cell cursor and get Excel into Extend Selection mode.

2. Press F5 or Ctrl+G to open the Go To dialog box, type the address of the last cell in the range (the cell kitty-corner from the first cell), and then click OK or press Enter.

REMEMBER

Because Excel is in Extend Selection mode at the time you use the Go To feature to jump to another cell, the program not only moves the cell cursor to the designated cell address but selects all the intervening cells as well. After selecting the range of cells with the Go To feature, don't forget to press F8 (the Extend Selection key) again to prevent the program from messing up your selection by adding more cells the next time you move the cell cursor.

Using the Format as Table Gallery

Here's a formatting technique that doesn't require you to do any prior cell selecting. (Kinda figures, doesn't it?) The Format as Table feature is so automatic that the cell cursor just has to be within the table of data prior to you clicking the Format as Table command button in the Styles group on the Home tab. Clicking the Format as Table command button opens its rather extensive Table Styles gallery with the formatting thumbnails divided into three sections — Light, Medium, and Dark — each of which describes the intensity of the colors used by its various formats.

As soon as you click one of the table formatting thumbnails in this Table Styles gallery, Excel makes its best guess as to the cell range of the data table to apply it to (indicated by the marquee around its perimeter), and the Format As Table dialog box, similar to the one shown in Figure 3-5, appears.

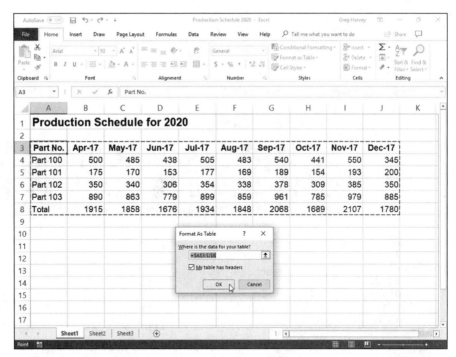

FIGURE 3-5:
Selecting a
format from the
Table Styles
gallery and
indicating its
range in the
Format As Table
dialog box.

This dialog box contains a Where Is the Data for Your Table text box that shows the address of the cell range currently selected by the marquee and a My Table Has Headers check box.

If Excel does not correctly guess the range of the data table you want to format, drag through the cell range to adjust the marquee and the range address in the Where Is the Data for Your Table text box. If your data table doesn't use column headers or, if the table has them, but you still don't want Excel to add Filter dropdown buttons to each column heading, deselect the My Table Has Headers check box before you click the OK button.

WARNING

The table formats in the Table Styles gallery are not available if you select multiple nonadjacent cells before you click the Format as Table command button on the Home tab.

After you click the OK button in the Format As Table dialog box, Excel applies the formatting of the thumbnail you clicked in the gallery to the data table. Additionally, the Design tab appears under the Table Tools contextual tab at the end of the Ribbon, and the table is selected with the Quick Analysis tool appearing in the lower-right corner, as shown in Figure 3-6.

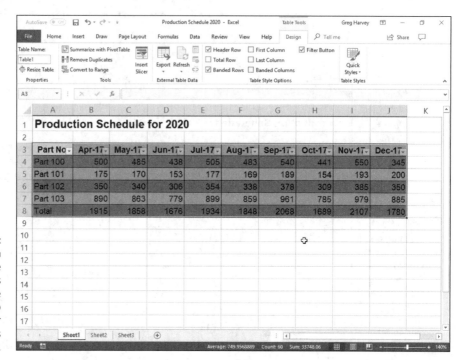

FIGURE 3-6:
After you select a format from the Table Styles gallery, the Design tab appears under the Table Tools contextual tab.

TIP

The Design tab enables you to use Live Preview to see how your table would appear. Simply click the Table Styles continuation button on the Design tab of the Ribbon (or Quick Styles button, if it's displayed) and then position the mouse pointer over any of the format thumbnails in the Table Styles drop-down palette to see the data in your table appear in that table format. Click the button with the triangle pointing downward to scroll up new rows of table formats in the Table Styles group; click the button with the triangle pointing upward to scroll down rows without opening the Table Styles gallery and possibly obscuring the actual data table in the Worksheet area. Click the More button (the one with the horizontal bar above the downward-pointing triangle) to redisplay the Table gallery and then mouse over the thumbnails in the Light, Medium, and Dark sections to have Live Preview apply them to the table.

Whenever you assign a format in the Table Styles gallery to one of the data tables in your workbook, Excel automatically assigns that table a generic range name (Table1, Table2, and so on). You can use the Table Name text box in the Properties group on the Design tab to rename the data table to give it a more descriptive range name. (See Chapter 6 for all you need to know about naming cell ranges.)

REMEMBER

You can also use the Tables option on the Quick Analysis tool to format your worksheet data as a table. Simply select the table data (including headings) as a cell range in the worksheet and then click the Tables option on the Quick Analysis tool, followed by the Table option below at the very beginning of the Tables options. Excel then assigns the Table Style Medium 9 style to your table while at same time selecting the Design tab on the Ribbon. Then if you're not too keen on this table style, you can use Live Preview in the Tables Styles gallery on this tab to find the table formatting that you do want to use.

Customizing table formats

In addition to enabling you to select a new format from the Table Styles gallery, the Design tab contains a Table Style Options group containing a bunch of check boxes that enable you to customize the look of the selected table format even further:

» **Header Row** to display the top row with the labels that identify the type of data in each column as well as the Filter buttons for sorting and filtering data in the first row of the table. (This check box is selected by default.)

» **Total Row** to have Excel add a Total Row to the bottom of the table that displays the sums of each column that contains values. To apply another Statistical function to the values in a particular column, click the cell in that column's Total Row to display a drop-down list button and then select the function — Average, Count, Count Numbers, Max, Min, Sum, StdDev (Standard Deviation), or Var (Variance).

» **Banded Rows** to have Excel apply shading to every other row in the table.

» **First Column** to have Excel display the row headings in the first column of the table in bold.

» **Last Column** to have Excel display the row headings in the last column of the table in bold.

» **Banded Columns** to have Excel apply shading to every other column in the table.

» **Filter Button** to have Excel display drop-down buttons to the right of the entries when the table's Header Row is displayed that you can use to sort and filter the data in that column. (This check box is selected by default.)

When you finish selecting and/or customizing the formatting of your data table, click a cell outside of the table to remove the Table Tools contextual tab (with its Design tab) from the Ribbon. If later, you decide that you want to further experiment with the table's formatting, click any of the table's cells to redisplay the Table Tools' Design tab at the end of the Ribbon.

Creating a new custom Table Style

Excel 2019 lets you create your own custom styles to add to the Tables Styles gallery and use in formatting your worksheet tables. Once created, a custom Table Style not only applies just the kind of formatting you want for your worksheet tables but can also be reused on tables of data in any worksheet you create or edit in the future. You can even designate one of the custom styles you create as the new Table Style default for your workbook so that it's automatically applied when you later format a data table in its worksheets with the Tables option on the Quick Analysis toolbar.

To create a custom Table Style, you follow these steps:

1. **Format the data in your worksheet as a table using one of the existing styles (as described in the previous section).**

2. **On the Design contextual tab of the Tables Tool tab, click the Table Styles More drop-down button and then select the New Table Style option near the bottom of the gallery.**

    The New Table Style dialog box, shown in Figure 3-7, appears.

3. **Replace the generic, table style name, Table Style 1, with a more descriptive name in the Name text box.**

4. **Modify each of the individual table components in the Table Elements list box (from Whole Table through Last Total Cell) with the custom formatting you want included in your new custom table style.**

    To customize the formatting for a table element, select its name in the Table Element list box. After you select the element, click the Format button to open the Format Cells dialog box where you can change that element's font style and/or color on its Font tab, the border style and/or color on its Border tab, or the fill effect and/or color on its Fill tab. (See the "Futzing with the Fonts," "Bring on the borders!," and "Applying fill colors, patterns, and gradient effects to cells" sections later in this chapter for details on adjusting these different formats.)

    Note that when customizing a First or Second Column or Row Stripe element (that controls the shading or banding of table's column or row), in addition to changing the fill for the banding on the Fill tab of the Format Cells dialog box, you can also increase how many columns or rows are banded by increasing the number in the Stripe Size drop-down list that appears when you select one of the Stripe elements.

    As you assign new formatting to a particular table element, Excel displays a description of the formatting change below the Element Formatting heading of New Table Style dialog box, as long as that table element remains selected in the Table Element list box. When you add a new fill color to a particular element, this color appears in the Preview area of this dialog box regardless of which component is selected in the Table Element list box.

5. **(Optional) If you want your new custom table style to become the default table style for all the data tables you format in your workbook, select the Set as Default Table Style for This Document check box.**

6. **Click the OK button to save the settings for your new custom table style and close the New Table Style dialog box.**

FIGURE 3-7:
Use the options in the New Table Style dialog box to create a new custom table style to add to the Table Styles gallery.

As soon as you close the New Table Style dialog box, a thumbnail of the new custom table style you just created appears at the very beginning of the truncated Table Styles gallery that appears on the Design tab of the Table Tools font. You can then apply the newly created style to the currently selected table of data (the sample table you formatting in order to create the new style) by clicking this thumbnail. When you next open the entire Table Styles gallery to format other tables of data that you add to your worksheets, the thumbnail of the custom style you created will appear in its own Custom section at the very top of the gallery.

TIP

If you made changes to the fill formatting for the First or Second Column Stripe element in the custom table style, don't forget to select the Banded Rows check box in Table Styles Options section on the Table Tools Design tab to make it appear in the formatted data table. So, too, if you made changes to the First or Second Row Stripe, you need to select the Banded Rows check box to make these formats appear.

To further modify, copy (in order to use its settings as the basis for a new custom style), delete, or add a custom style to the Quick Analysis toolbar, right-click its thumbnail image in the Table Styles gallery and then choose the Modify, Duplicate, Delete, or Add Gallery to Quick Access Toolbar option on its context menu.

Cell Formatting from the Home Tab

Some spreadsheet tables or ranges within them require a lighter touch than the Format as Table command button offers. For example, you may have a data table where the only emphasis you want to add is to make the column headings bold at the top of the table and to underline the row of totals at the bottom (done by drawing a borderline along the bottom of the cells).

The formatting buttons that appear in the Font, Alignment, and Number groups on the Home tab enable you to accomplish just this kind of targeted cell formatting. See Table 3-1 for a complete rundown on how to use each of these formatting buttons.

TABLE 3-1 **Formatting Command Buttons in the Font, Alignment, and Number Groups on the Home Tab**

Group	Button Name	Function
Font		
	Font	Displays a Font drop-down menu from which you can select a new font for your cell selection
	Font Size	Displays a Font Size drop-down menu from which you can select a new font size for your cell selection — click the Font Size text box and enter the desired point size if it doesn't appear on the drop-down menu
	Increase Font Size	Increases the current font size of the cell selection (as it appears in the Font Size drop-down list box) by one point
	Decrease Font Size	Decreases the current font size of the cell selection (as it appears in the Font Size drop-down list box) by one point
	Bold	Applies boldface to the entries in the cell selection
	Italic	Italicizes the entries in the cell selection
	Underline	Underlines the entries in the cell selection
	Borders	Displays a Borders drop-down menu from which you can select a border style for the cell selection
	Fill Color	Displays a Color drop-down palette from which you can select a new background color for the cell selection
	Font Color	Displays a Color drop-down palette from which you can select a new font color for the cell selection

Group	Button Name	Function
Alignment		
	Align Left	Aligns all the entries in the cell selection with the left edge of their cells
	Center	Centers all the entries in the cell selection within their cells
	Align Right	Aligns all the entries in the cell selection with the right edge of their cells
	Decrease Indent	Decreases the margin between entries in the cell selection and their left cell borders by about one character width
	Increase Indent	Increases the margin between the entries in the cell selection and their left cell borders by about one character width
	Top Align	Aligns the entries in the cell selection with the top border of their cells
	Middle Align	Vertically centers the entries in the cell selection between the top and bottom borders of their cells
	Bottom Align	Aligns the entries in the cell selection with the bottom border of their cells
	Orientation	Displays a drop-down menu with options for changing the angle and direction of the entries in the cell selection
	Wrap Text	Wraps the entries in the cell selection that spill over their right borders onto multiple lines within the current column width
	Merge & Center	Merges the cell selection into a single cell and centers the entry in the first cell between its new left and right border — click the Merge and Center drop-down button to display a menu of options that enable you to merge the cell selection into a single cell without centering the entries, as well as to split up a merged cell back into its original individual cells
Number		
	Number Format	Displays the number format applied to the active cell in the cell selection — click its drop-down button to display a menu showing the active cell in cell selection formatted with all of Excel's major number formats
	Accounting Number Format	Formats the cell selection using the Accounting number format that adds a dollar sign, uses commas to separate thousands, displays two decimal places, and encloses negative values in a closed pair of parentheses — click the Accounting Number Format's drop-down button to display a menu of other major Currency number formats from which you can choose
	Percent Style	Formats the cell selection using the Percentage number format that multiplies the values by 100 and adds a percent sign with no decimal places
	Comma Style	Formats the cell selection with the Comma Style number format that uses commas to separate thousands, displays two decimal places, and encloses negative values in a closed pair of parentheses
	Increase Decimal	Adds a decimal place to the values in the cell selection
	Decrease Decimal	Removes a decimal place from the values in the cell selection

Don't forget about the tooltips that appear when you highlight one of these formatting command buttons with your mouse or Touch pointer. These tooltips not only give you a short description of the button's function, but also display any shortcut keys for quickly adding or removing attributes from the entries in the cell selection.

Formatting Cells Close to the Source with the Mini-bar

Excel 2019 makes it easy to apply common formatting changes to a cell selection right within the Worksheet area thanks to the mini-toolbar feature, nicknamed the mini-bar (makes me thirsty just thinking about it!).

To display the mini-bar, select the cells that need formatting and then right-click somewhere in the cell selection. The cell range's context menu along with the mini-bar then appears near the cell selection. When you select a tool in the mini-bar, such as Font or Font Size pop-up button, the context menu disappears (see Figure 3-8).

FIGURE 3-8:
Use the buttons on the mini-bar to apply common formatting changes to the cell selection within the Worksheet area.

As you can see in this figure, the mini-bar contains most of the buttons from the Font group of the Home tab (with the exception of the Underline button). It also contains the Center and Merge & Center buttons from the Alignment group (see the "Altering the Alignment" section, later in this chapter) and the Accounting Number Format, Percent Style, Comma Style, Increase Decimal, and Decrease Decimal buttons from the Number group (see the "Understanding the number formats" section, later in this chapter). Simply click these buttons to apply their formatting to the current cell selection.

Additionally, the mini-bar contains the Format Painter button from the Clipboard group of the Home tab that you can use to copy the formatting in the active cell to a cell selection you make (see the "Fooling Around with the Format Painter" section, later in this chapter for details).

Using the Format Cells Dialog Box

Although the command buttons in the Font, Alignment, and Number groups on the Home tab give you immediate access to the most commonly used formatting commands, they do not represent all of Excel's formatting commands by any stretch of the imagination.

To have access to all the formatting commands, you need to open the Format Cells dialog box shown in Figure 3-9 by doing any of the following:

» Click the More Number Formats option at the very bottom of the drop-down menu attached to the Number Format button.

» Click the Number Format Dialog Box launcher in the lower right of the Number group.

» Press Ctrl+1.

As you can see in Figure 3-9, the Format Cells dialog contains six tabs: Number, Alignment, Font, Border, Fill, and Protection. In this chapter, I show you how to use them all except the Protection tab. For information on that tab, see Chapter 6.

TIP

The keystroke shortcut that opens the Format Cells dialog box — Ctrl+1 — is one worth knowing. Just press the Ctrl key plus the *number* 1 key, and not the *function key* F1.

FIGURE 3-9:
The Format Cells
dialog box gives
you access to a
wide range of
format settings to
apply to the
selected cell
range.

Understanding the number formats

As I explain in Chapter 2, how you enter values into a worksheet determines the type of number format that they get. Here are some examples:

» If you enter a financial value complete with the dollar sign and two decimal places, Excel assigns a Currency number format to the cell along with the entry.

» If you enter a value representing a percentage as a whole number followed by the percent sign without any decimal places, Excel assigns the cell the Percentage number format that follows this pattern along with the entry.

» If you enter a date (dates are values, too) that follows one of the built-in Excel number formats, such as 11/06/13 or 06-Nov-13, the program assigns a Date number format that follows the pattern of the date along with a special value representing the date.

Although you can format values in this manner as you go along (which is necessary in the case of dates), you don't have to do it this way. You can always assign a number format to a group of values before or after you enter them. Formatting numbers after you enter them is often the most efficient way to go because it's just a two-step procedure:

1. **Select all the cells containing the values that need dressing up.**

2. **Select the number format that you want to use from the formatting command buttons on the Home tab or the options available on the Number tab in the Format Cells dialog box.**

TIP

Even if you're a really, really good typist and prefer to enter each value exactly as you want it to appear in the worksheet, you still have to resort to using number formats to make the values that are calculated by formulas match the others you enter. This is because Excel applies a General number format (which the Format Cells dialog box defines: "General format cells have no specific number format.") to all the values it calculates, as well as any you enter that don't exactly follow one of the other Excel number formats. The biggest problem with the General format is that it has the nasty habit of dropping all leading and trailing zeros from the entries. This makes it very hard to line up numbers in a column on their decimal points.

You can view this sad state of affairs in Figure 3-10, which is a sample worksheet with the first-quarter 2019 sales figures for Mother Goose Enterprises before any of the values have been formatted. Notice how the decimal in the numbers in the monthly sales figures columns zig and zag because they aren't aligned on the decimal place. This is the fault of Excel's General number format; the only cure is to format the values with a uniform number format.

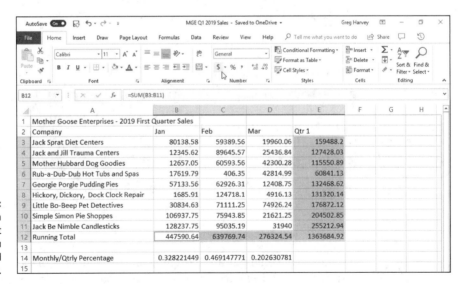

FIGURE 3-10:
Numbers with decimals don't align when you choose General formatting.

	A	B	C	D	E
1	Mother Goose Enterprises - 2019 First Quarter Sales				
2	Company	Jan	Feb	Mar	Qtr 1
3	Jack Sprat Diet Centers	80138.58	59389.56	19960.06	159488.2
4	Jack and Jill Trauma Centers	12345.62	89645.57	25436.84	127428.03
5	Mother Hubbard Dog Goodies	12657.05	60593.56	42300.28	115550.89
6	Rub-a-Dub-Dub Hot Tubs and Spas	17619.79	406.35	42814.99	60841.13
7	Georgie Porgie Pudding Pies	57133.56	62926.31	12408.75	132468.62
8	Hickory, Dickory, Dock Clock Repair	1685.91	124718.1	4916.13	131320.14
9	Little Bo-Beep Pet Detectives	30834.63	71111.25	74926.24	176872.12
10	Simple Simon Pie Shoppes	106937.75	75943.85	21621.25	204502.85
11	Jack Be Nimble Candlesticks	128237.75	95035.19	31940	255212.94
12	Running Total	447590.64	639769.74	276324.54	1363684.92
13					
14	Monthly/Qtrly Percentage	0.328221449	0.469147771	0.202630781	
15					

Accounting for the dollars and cents in your cells

Given the financial nature of most worksheets, you probably use the Accounting number format more than any other. Applying this format is easy because you can assign it to the cell selection simply by clicking the Accounting Number Format button on the Home tab.

REMEMBER

The Accounting number format adds a dollar sign, commas between thousands of dollars, and two decimal places to any values in a selected range. If any of the values in the cell selection are negative, this number format displays them in parentheses (the way accountants like them). If you want a minus sign in front of your negative financial values rather than enclosing them in parentheses, select the Currency format on the Number Format drop-down menu or on the Number tab of the Format Cells dialog box.

You can see in Figure 3-11 that only the cells containing totals are selected (cell ranges E3:E10 and B10:D10). This cell selection was then formatted with the Accounting number format by simply clicking its command button (the one with the $ icon, naturally) in the Number group on the Ribbon's Home tab.

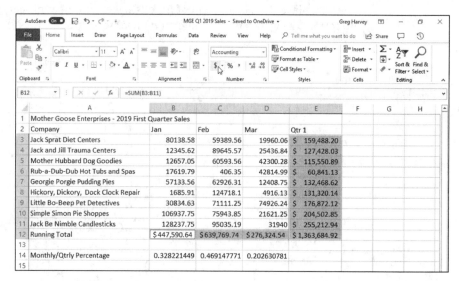

FIGURE 3-11:
The totals in the Mother Goose sales table after clicking the Accounting Number Format button on the Home tab.

	A	B	C	D	E	F	G	H
1	Mother Goose Enterprises - 2019 First Quarter Sales							
2	Company	Jan	Feb	Mar	Qtr 1			
3	Jack Sprat Diet Centers	80138.58	59389.56	19960.06	$ 159,488.20			
4	Jack and Jill Trauma Centers	12345.62	89645.57	25436.84	$ 127,428.03			
5	Mother Hubbard Dog Goodies	12657.05	60593.56	42300.28	$ 115,550.89			
6	Rub-a-Dub-Dub Hot Tubs and Spas	17619.79	406.35	42814.99	$ 60,841.13			
7	Georgie Porgie Pudding Pies	57133.56	62926.31	12408.75	$ 132,468.62			
8	Hickory, Dickory, Dock Clock Repair	1685.91	124718.1	4916.13	$ 131,320.14			
9	Little Bo-Beep Pet Detectives	30834.63	71111.25	74926.24	$ 176,872.12			
10	Simple Simon Pie Shoppes	106937.75	75943.85	21621.25	$ 204,502.85			
11	Jack Be Nimble Candlesticks	128237.75	95035.19	31940	$ 255,212.94			
12	Running Total	$447,590.64	$639,769.74	$276,324.54	$ 1,363,684.92			
13								
14	Monthly/Qtrly Percentage	0.328221449	0.469147771	0.202630781				
15								

TIP

Although you could put all the figures in the table into the Accounting number format to line up the decimal points, this would result in a superabundance of dollar signs in a fairly small table. In this example, I only formatted the monthly and quarterly totals with the Accounting number format.

"Look, Ma, no more format overflow!"

When I apply the Accounting number format to the selection in the cell ranges of E3:E10 and B10:D10 in the sales table shown in Figure 3-11, Excel adds dollar signs, commas between the thousands, a decimal point, and two decimal places to the highlighted values. At the same time, Excel automatically widens columns B, C, D, and E just enough to display all this new formatting. In versions of Excel earlier than Excel 2003, you had to widen these columns yourself, and instead of the perfectly aligned numbers, you were confronted with columns of #######s in cell ranges E3:E10 and B10:D10. Such pound signs (where nicely formatted dollar totals should be) serve as overflow indicators, declaring that whatever formatting you added to the value in that cell has added so much to the value's display that Excel can no longer display it within the current column width.

Fortunately, Excel eliminates the format overflow indicators when you're formatting the values in your cells by automatically widening the columns. The only time you'll ever run across these dreaded #######s in your cells is when you take it upon yourself to narrow a worksheet column manually (see the section "Calibrating Columns," later in this chapter) to the extent that Excel can no longer display all the characters in its cells with formatted values.

Currying your cells with the Comma Style

The Comma Style format offers a good alternative to the Currency format. Like Currency, the Comma Style format inserts commas in larger numbers to separate thousands, hundred thousands, millions, and . . . well, you get the idea.

This format also displays two decimal places and puts negative values in parentheses. What it doesn't display is dollar signs. This makes it perfect for formatting tables where it's obvious that you're dealing with dollars and cents or for larger values that have nothing to do with money.

The Comma Style format also works well for the bulk of the values in the sample first-quarter sales worksheet. Check out Figure 3-12 to see this table after I format the cells containing the monthly sales for all the Mother Goose Enterprises with the Comma Style format. To do this, select the cell range B3:D9 and click the Comma Style button — the one with the comma icon (,) — in the Number group on the Home tab.

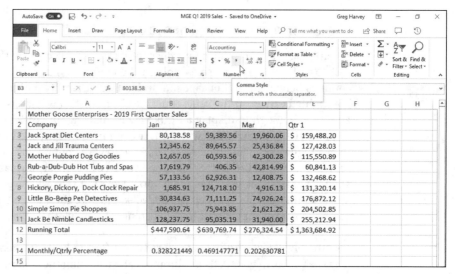

FIGURE 3-12:
Monthly sales figures after formatting cells with the Comma Style number format.

Note how, in Figure 3-12, the Comma Style format takes care of the earlier decimal alignment problem in the quarterly sales figures. Moreover, Comma Style–formatted monthly sales figures align perfectly with the Currency format–styled monthly totals in row 10. If you look closely (you may need a magnifying glass for this one), you see that these formatted values no longer abut the right edges of their cells; they've moved slightly to the left. The gap on the right between the last digit and the cell border accommodates the right parenthesis in negative values, ensuring that they, too, align precisely on the decimal point.

Playing around with Percent Style

Many worksheets use percentages in the form of interest rates, growth rates, inflation rates, and so on. To insert a percentage in a cell, type the percent sign (%) after the number. To indicate an interest rate of 12 percent, for example, you enter **12%** in the cell. When you do this, Excel assigns a Percentage number format and, at the same time, divides the value by 100 (that's what makes it a percentage) and places the result in the cell (0.12 in this example).

Not all percentages in a worksheet are entered by hand in this manner. Some may be calculated by a formula and returned to their cells as raw decimal values. In such cases, you should add a Percent format to convert the calculated decimal values to percentages (done by multiplying the decimal value by 100 and adding a percent sign).

The sample first-quarter-sales worksheet just happens to have some percentages calculated by formulas in row 12 that need formatting (these formulas indicate what percentage each monthly total is of the first-quarter total in cell E10). In

Figure 3-13, these values reflect Percent Style formatting. To accomplish this feat, you simply select the cells and click the Percent Style button in the Number group on the Home tab. (Need I point out that it's the button with the % symbol?)

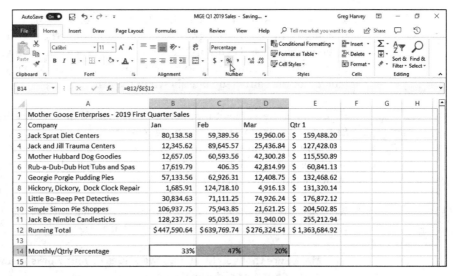

FIGURE 3-13:
Monthly-to-quarterly sales percentages with Percentage number formatting.

Deciding how many decimal places

You can increase or decrease the number of decimal places used in a number entered by using the Accounting Number Format, Comma Style, or Percent Style button in the Number group of the Home tab simply by clicking the Increase Decimal button or the Decrease Decimal button in this group. Each time you click the Increase Decimal button (the one with the arrow pointing left), Excel adds another decimal place to the number format you apply.

The values behind the formatting

Make no mistake about it — all that these fancy number formats do is spiff up the presentation of the values in the worksheet. Like a good illusionist, a particular number format sometimes appears to transform some entries, but in reality, the entries are the same old numbers you started with. For example, suppose that a formula returns the following value:

```
25.6456
```

Now suppose that you format the cell containing this value with the Accounting Number Format button on the Home tab. The value now appears as follows:

$25.65

This change may lead you to believe that Excel rounded the value up to two decimal places. In fact, the program has rounded up only the *display* of the calculated value — the cell still contains the same old value of 25.6456. If you use this cell in another worksheet formula, Excel uses the behind-the-scenes value in its calculation, not the spiffed-up one shown in the cell.

WARNING

If you want the values to match their formatted appearance in the worksheet, Excel can do that in a single step. Be forewarned, however, that this is a one-way trip. You can convert all underlying values to the way they are displayed by selecting a single check box, but you can't return them to their previous state by deselecting this check box.

Well, because you insist on knowing this little trick anyway, here goes (just don't write and try to tell me that you weren't warned):

1. **Make sure that you format all the values in your worksheet with the correct number of decimal places.**

You must do this step before you convert the precision of all values in the worksheet to their displayed form.

2. **Click File ⇨ Options ⇨ Advanced or press Alt+FTA to open the Advanced tab of the Excel Options dialog box.**

3. **In the When Calculating This Workbook section, select the Set Precision as Displayed check box (to fill it with a check mark).**

Excel displays the Data Will Permanently Lose Accuracy alert dialog box.

4. **Go ahead (live dangerously) and click the OK button or press Enter to convert all values to match their display. Click OK again to close the Excel Options dialog box.**

TIP

Save the workbook with the calculated values. After converting all the values in a worksheet by selecting the Set Precision as Displayed check box, open the Save As dialog box (select File ⇨ Save As or press Alt+FA). Edit the filename in the File Name text box (maybe by appending **as Displayed** to the current filename) before you click the Save button or press Enter. That way, you'll have two copies: the original workbook file with the values as entered and calculated by Excel and the new *as Displayed* version.

Make it a date!

In Chapter 2, I mention that you can easily create formulas that calculate the differences between the dates and times that you enter in your worksheets. The only problem is that when Excel subtracts one date from another date or one time from another time, the program automatically formats the calculated result in a corresponding date or time number format as well. For example, if you enter 8-15-19 in cell B4 and 4/15/19 in cell C4 and in cell D4 enter the following formula for finding the number of elapsed days between the two dates:

```
=B4–C4
```

Excel correctly returns the result of 122 (days) using the General number format. However, when dealing with formulas that calculate the difference between two times in a worksheet, you have to reformat the result that appears in a corresponding time format into the General format. For example, suppose that you enter 8:00 AM in cell B5 and 4:00 PM in cell C5 and then create in cell D5 the following formula for calculating the difference in hours between the two times:

```
=C5–B5
```

You then have to convert the result in cell D5 — that automatically appears as 8:00 AM — to the General format. When you do this, the fraction 0.333333 — representing its fraction of the total 24-hour period — replaces 8:00 AM in cell D5. You can then convert this fraction of a total day into the corresponding number of hours by multiplying this cell by 24 and formatting the cell with the General format.

Ogling some of the other number formats

Excel supports more number formats than just the Accounting, Comma Style, and Percentage number formats. To use them, select the cell range (or ranges) you want to format and select Format Cells on the cell shortcut menu (right-click somewhere in the cell selection to activate this menu) or just press Ctrl+1 to open the Format Cells dialog box.

After the Format Cells dialog box opens with the Number tab displayed, you select the desired format from the Category list box. Some number formats — such as Date, Time, Fraction, and Special — give you further formatting choices in a Type list box. Other number formats, such as Number and Currency, have their own particular boxes that give you options for refining their formats. When you click the different formats in these list boxes, Excel shows what effect this would have on the first of the values in the current cell selection in the Sample area above. When the sample has the format that you want to apply to the current cell selection, you just click OK or press Enter to apply the new number format.

Excel contains a nifty category of number formats called Special. The Special category contains the following four number formats that may interest you:

>> **Zip Code:** Retains any leading zeros in the value (important for zip codes and of absolutely no importance in arithmetic computations). Example: 00123.

>> **Zip Code + 4:** Automatically separates the last four digits from the first five digits and retains any leading zeros. Example: 00123-5555.

>> **Phone Number:** Automatically encloses the first three digits of the number in parentheses and separates the last four digits from the previous three with a dash. Example: (999) 555-1111.

>> **Social Security Number:** Automatically puts dashes in the value to separate its digits into groups of three, two, and four. Example: 666-00-9999.

These Special number formats really come in handy when creating data lists in Excel that often deal with stuff like zip codes, telephone numbers, and sometimes even Social Security numbers (see Chapter 11 for more on creating and using data lists).

Calibrating Columns

For those times when Excel 2019 doesn't automatically adjust the width of your columns to your complete satisfaction, the program makes changing the column widths a breeze. The easiest way to adjust a column is to do a *best-fit,* using the AutoFit feature. With this method, Excel automatically determines how much to widen or narrow the column to fit the longest entry currently in the column.

Here's how to use AutoFit to get the best fit for a column:

1. **Position the mouse on the right border of the worksheet frame with the column letter at the top of the worksheet.**

   The pointer changes to a double-headed arrow pointing left and right.

2. **Double-click the mouse button.**

   Excel widens or narrows the column width to suit the longest entry.

You can apply a best-fit to more than one column at a time. Simply select all the columns that need adjusting (if the columns neighbor one another, drag through their column letters on the frame; if they don't, Ctrl+click the individual column letters). After you select the columns, double-click any of the right borders on the frame.

Best-fit à la AutoFit doesn't always produce the expected results. A long title that spills into several columns to the right produces a very wide column when you use best-fit.

TIP

When AutoFit's best-fit won't do, drag the right border of the column (on the frame) until it's the size you need instead of double-clicking it. This manual technique for calibrating the column width also works when more than one column is selected. Just be aware that all selected columns assume whatever size you make the one that you're actually dragging.

You can also set the widths of columns from the Format button's drop-down list in the Cells group on the Home tab. When you click this drop-down button, the Cell Size section of this drop-down menu contains the following width options:

» **Column Width** to open the Column Width dialog box where you enter the number of characters that you want for the column width before you click OK

» **AutoFit Column Width** to have Excel apply best-fit to the columns based on the widest entries in the current cell selection

» **Default Width** to open the Standard Width dialog box containing the standard column width of 8.47 characters that you can apply to the columns in the cell selection

Rambling rows

The story with adjusting the heights of rows is pretty much the same as that with adjusting columns except that you do a lot less row adjusting than you do column adjusting. That's because Excel automatically changes the height of the rows to accommodate changes to their entries, such as selecting a larger font size or wrapping text in a cell. I discuss both of these techniques in the upcoming section "Altering the Alignment." Most row-height adjustments come about when you want to increase the amount of space between a table title and the table or between a row of column headings and the table of information without actually adding a blank row. (See the section "From top to bottom," later in this chapter, for details.)

To increase the height of a row, drag the bottom border of the row frame down until the row is high enough and then release the mouse button. To shorten a row, reverse this process and drag the bottom row-frame border up. To use AutoFit to best-fit the entries in a row, you double-click the bottom row-frame border.

As with columns, you can also adjust the height of selected rows using row options in the Cell Size section on the Format button's drop-down menu on the Home tab:

>> **Row Height** to open the Row Height dialog box where you enter the number of points in the Row Height text box and then click OK

>> **AutoFit Row Height** to return the height of selected rows to the best fit

Now you see it, now you don't

A funny thing about narrowing columns and rows: You can get carried away and make a column so narrow or a row so short that it actually disappears from the worksheet! This can come in handy for those times when you don't want part of the worksheet visible. For example, suppose you have a worksheet that contains a column listing employee salaries — you need these figures to calculate the departmental budget figures, but you would prefer to leave sensitive info off most printed reports. Rather than waste time moving the column of salary figures outside the area to be printed, you can just hide the column until after you print the report.

Hiding worksheet columns

Although you can hide worksheet columns and rows by just adjusting them out of existence, Excel does offer an easier method of hiding them, via the Hide & Unhide option on the Format button's drop-down menu (located in the Cells group of the Home tab). Suppose that you need to hide column B in the worksheet because it contains some irrelevant or sensitive information that you don't want printed. To hide this column, you could follow these steps:

1. **Select any cell in column B to designate it as the column to hide.**

2. **Click the drop-down button attached to the Format button in the Cells group on the Home tab.**

   Excel opens the Format button's drop-down menu.

3. **Click Hide & Unhide ⇨ Hide Columns on the drop-down menu.**

That's all there is to it — column B goes *poof!* All the information in the column disappears from the worksheet. When you hide column B, notice that the row of column letters in the frame now reads A, C, D, E, F, and so forth.

TIP

You could just as well have hidden column B by right-clicking its column letter on the frame and then selecting the Hide command on the column's shortcut menu.

Now, suppose that you've printed the worksheet and need to make a change to one of the entries in column B. To unhide the column, follow these steps:

1. **Position the mouse pointer on column letter A in the frame and drag the pointer right to select both columns A and C.**

   You must drag from A to C to include hidden column B as part of the column selection — don't click while holding down the Ctrl key or you won't get B.

2. **Click the drop-down button attached to the Format button in the Cells group on the Home tab.**

3. **Click Hide & Unhide ⇨ Unhide Columns on the drop-down menu.**

Excel brings back the hidden B column, and all three columns (A, B, and C) are selected. You can then click the mouse pointer on any cell in the worksheet to deselect the columns.

You could also unhide column B by selecting columns A through C, right-clicking either one of them, and then selecting the Unhide command on the column shortcut menu.

Hiding worksheet rows

The procedure for hiding and unhiding rows of the worksheet is essentially the same as for hiding and unhiding columns. The only difference is that after selecting the rows to hide, you click Hide & Unhide ⇨ Hide Rows on the Format button's drop-down menu and Hide & Unhide ⇨ Unhide Rows to bring them back.

Don't forget that you can use the Hide and Unhide options on the rows' shortcut menu to make selected rows disappear and then reappear in the worksheet.

Futzing with the Fonts

When you start a new worksheet, Excel 2019 assigns a uniform font and type size to all the cell entries you make. The default font is Microsoft's Calibri font (the so-called Body Font) in 11-point size. Although this font may be fine for normal entries, you may want to use something with a little more zing for titles and headings in the worksheet.

If you don't especially care for Calibri as the standard font, modify it from the General tab of the Excel Options dialog box (File ⇨ Options or Alt+FT). Look for the Use This as the Default Font drop-down list box (containing Body Font as the default choice) in the When Creating New Workbooks section and then select the name of the new font you want to make standard from this drop-down list. If you want a different type size, choose the Font Size drop-down list box and a new point size on its drop-down menu or enter the new point size for the standard font directly into the Font Size text box.

Using the buttons in the Font group on the Home tab, you can make most font changes (including selecting a new font style or new font size) without having to resort to changing the settings on the Font tab in the Format Cells dialog box (Ctrl+1):

>> To select a new font for a cell selection, click the drop-down button next to the Font combo box and then select the name of the font you want to use from the list box. Excel displays the name of each font that appears in this list box in the actual font named (so that the font name becomes an example of what the font looks like — onscreen anyway).

>> To change the font size, click the drop-down button next to the Font Size combo box, select the new font size or click the Font Size text box, type the new size, and then press Enter.

You can also add the attributes of **bold**, *italic*, <u>underlining</u>, or `strikethrough` to the font you use. The Font group of the Home tab contains the Bold, Italic, and Underline buttons, which not only add these attributes to a cell selection but remove them as well. After you click any of these attribute tools, notice that the tool becomes shaded whenever you position the cell cursor in the cell or cells that contain that attribute. When you click a selected format button to remove an attribute, Excel no longer shades the attribute button when you select the cell.

Although you'll probably make most font changes with the Home tab on the Ribbon, on rare occasions you may find it more convenient to make these changes from the Font tab in the Format Cells dialog box (Ctrl+1).

The Font tab in the Format Cells dialog box brings together under one roof fonts, font styles (bold and italics), effects (strikethrough, superscript, and subscript), and color changes. When you want to make many font-related changes to a cell selection, working in the Font tab may be your best bet. One of the nice things about using this tab is that it contains a Preview box that shows you how your font changes appear (onscreen at least).

To change the color of the entries in a cell selection, click the Font Color button's drop-down menu in the Font group on the Home tab and then select the color you want the text to appear in the drop-down palette. You can use Live Preview to see what the entries in the cell selection look like in a particular font color by moving the mouse pointer over the color swatches in the palette before you select one by clicking it (assuming, of course, that the palette doesn't cover the cells).

REMEMBER

If you change font colors and then print the worksheet with a black-and-white printer, Excel renders the colors as shades of gray. The Automatic option at the top of the Font Color button's drop-down menu picks up the color assigned in Windows as the window text color. This color is black unless you change it in your display properties. (For help on this subject, please refer to *Microsoft Windows 10 For Dummies,* by Andy Rathbone — and be sure to tell Andy that Greg sent ya!)

Altering the Alignment

The horizontal alignment assigned to cell entries when you first make them is simply a function of the type of entry it is: All text entries are left-aligned, and all values are right-aligned with the borders of their cells. However, you can alter this standard arrangement anytime it suits you.

The Alignment group of the Home tab contains three normal horizontal alignment tools: the Align Left, Center, and Align Right buttons. These buttons align the current cell selection exactly as you expect them to. On the right side of the Alignment group, you usually find the special alignment button called Merge & Center.

Despite its rather strange name, you'll want to get to know this button. You can use it to center a worksheet title across the entire width of a table in seconds (or faster, depending upon your machine). Figure 3-12 shows you how this works. To center the title, Mother Goose Enterprises – 2019 First Quarter Sales, entered in cell A1 over the entire table (which extends from column A through E), select the cell range A1:E1 (the width of the table) and then click the Merge & Center button in the Alignment group on the Ribbon's Home tab.

In Figure 3-14, you see the result: The cells in row 1 of columns A through E are merged into one cell, and now the title is properly centered in this "super" cell and consequently over the entire table.

TIP

If you ever need to split up a supercell that you've merged with Merge & Center back into its original, individual cells, select the cell and then simply click the Merge & Center button in the Alignment group on the Home tab again. You can also do this by clicking the drop-down button attached to the Merge & Center button on the Home tab and then clicking Unmerge Cells on this drop-down menu (a few more steps, I'd say!).

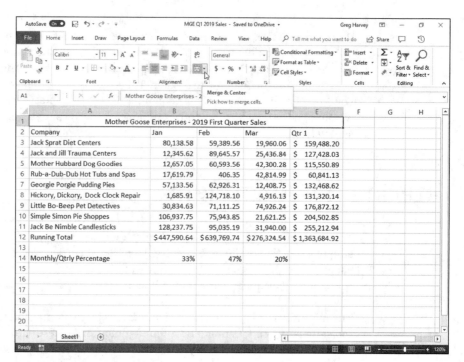

FIGURE 3-14:
A worksheet title
after merging and
centering it
across columns
A through E.

Intent on indents

In Excel 2019, you can indent the entries in a cell selection by clicking the Increase Indent button. The Increase Indent button in the Alignment group of the Home tab sports a picture of an arrow pushing the lines of text to the right. Each time you click this button, Excel indents the entries in the current cell selection to the right by a little over a character width of the standard font. (See the section "Futzing with the Fonts," earlier in this chapter, if you don't know what a standard font is or how to change it.)

You can remove an indent by clicking the Decrease Indent button (to the immediate left of the Increase Indent button) on the Home tab with the picture of the arrow pushing the lines of text to the left. Additionally, you can change how many characters an entry indents with the Increase Indent button (or outdents with the Decrease Indent button). Open the Format Cells dialog box (Ctrl+1). Select the Alignment tab, and then alter the value in the Indent text box (by typing a new value in this text box or by dialing up a new value with its spinner buttons).

From top to bottom

Left, right, and *center* alignment all refer to the horizontal positioning of a text entry in relation to the left and right cell borders (that is, horizontally). You can also align entries in relation to the top and bottom borders of their cells (that is, vertically). Normally, all entries align vertically with the bottom of the cells (as though they were resting on the very bottom of the cell). You can also vertically center an entry in its cell or align it with the top of its cell.

To change the vertical alignment of a cell range that you've selected, click the appropriate button (Top Align, Middle Align, or Bottom Align) in the Alignment group on the Home tab.

Tampering with how the text wraps

Traditionally, column headings in worksheet tables have been a problem — you had to keep them really short or abbreviate them if you wanted to avoid widening all the columns more than the data warranted. You can avoid this problem in Excel by using the Wrap Text button in the Alignment group on the Home tab (the one to the immediate right of the Orientation button). In Figure 3-15, I show a new worksheet in which cells B2:H2 contain the names of various companies within the vast Mother Goose Enterprises conglomerate. Every company name that spills over to a column on the right that contains another name is truncated except for the Little Bo Peep Pet Detectives name in the last column in cell H2.

FIGURE 3-15:
A new worksheet with truncated column headings in row 2.

Rather than widen columns B through H sufficiently to display the company names, I use the Wrap Text feature to avoid widening the columns as much as these long company names would otherwise require, as shown in Figure 3-16. To create the effect shown here, I select the cells with the column headings, B2:H2, and then click the Wrap Text button in the Alignment group on the Home tab.

Selecting Wrap Text breaks up the long text entries (that either spill over or cut off) in the selection into separate lines. To accommodate more than one line in a cell, the program automatically expands the row height so that the entire wrapped-text entry is visible.

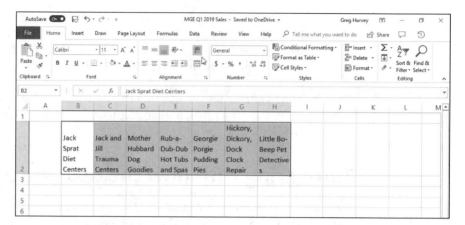

FIGURE 3-16:
Worksheet after using Wrap Text to display all the headings without widening their columns.

When you select Wrap Text, Excel continues to use the horizontal and vertical alignment you specify for the cell. You can use any of the Horizontal alignment options found on the Alignment tab of the Format Cells dialog box (Ctrl+1), including Left (Indent), Center, Right (Indent), Justify, or Center Across Selection. However, you can't use the Fill option or Distributed (Indent) option. Select the Fill option on the Horizontal drop-down list box only when you want Excel to repeat the entry across the entire width of the cell.

If you want to wrap a text entry in its cell and have Excel justify the text with both the left and right borders of the cell, select the Justify option from the Horizontal drop-down list box in the Alignment tab in the Format Cells dialog box.

TIP

You can break a long text entry into separate lines by positioning the insertion point in the cell entry (or on the Formula bar) at the place where you want the new line to start and pressing Alt+Enter. Excel expands the row containing the cell (and the Formula bar above) when it starts a new line. When you press Enter to complete the entry or edit, Excel automatically wraps the text in the cell, according to the cell's column width and the position of the line break.

Reorienting cell entries

Instead of wrapping text entries in cells, you may find it more beneficial to change the orientation of the text by rotating the text up (in a counterclockwise direction) or down (in a clockwise direction). Peruse Figure 3-17 for a situation where changing the orientation of the wrapped column headings works much better than just wrapping them in their normal orientation in the cells.

FIGURE 3-17:
Column headings
rotated 90°
counterclockwise.

This example shows the same column headings for the sample order form I introduced in Figure 3-15 after rotating them 90 degrees counterclockwise. To make
this switch with the cell range B2:H2 selected, click the Orientation button in the
Alignment group on the Home tab and then click the Rotate Text Up option on the
drop-down menu.

Figure 3-18 shows the same headings rotated up at a 45-degree angle. To create
what you see in this figure, you click the Angle Counterclockwise option on the
Orientation button's drop-down menu after making the same cell selection,
B2:H2.

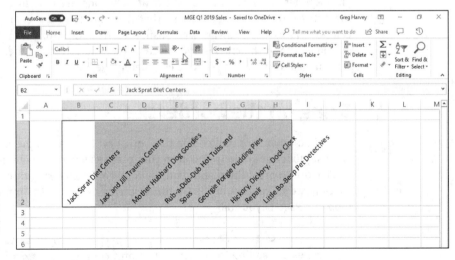

FIGURE 3-18:
Column headings
rotated 45°
counterclockwise.

If you need to set the rotation of the entries in a spreadsheet at angles other than 45 and 90 degrees (up or down), you need to click the Format Cell Alignment option on the Orientation button's drop-down menu. Doing so opens the Alignment tab of the Format Cells dialog box (or press Ctrl+1 and click the Alignment tab) where you can then use the controls in the Orientation section to set the angle and number of degrees.

To set a new angle, enter the number of degrees in the Degrees text box, click the appropriate place on the semicircular diagram, or drag the line extending from the word *Text* in the diagram to the desired angle.

REMEMBER

To angle text up using the Degrees text box, enter a positive number between 1 and 45 in the text box. To angle the text down, enter a negative number between −1 and −45.

TIP

To set the text vertically so that each letter is above the other in a single column, select the Vertical Text option on the Orientation button's drop-down menu on the Home tab.

Shrink to fit

For those times when you need to prevent Excel from widening the column to fit its cell entries (as might be the case when you need to display an entire table of data on a single screen or printed page), use the Shrink to Fit text control.

Select the Alignment tab of the Format Cells dialog box (Ctrl+1) and then select the Shrink to Fit check box in the Text Control section. Excel reduces the font size of the entries to the selected cells so that they don't require changing the current column width. Just be aware when using this Text Control option that, depending on the length of the entries and width of the column, you can end up with some text entries so small that they're completely illegible!

Bring on the borders!

The gridlines you normally see in the worksheet to separate the columns and rows are just guidelines to help you keep your place as you build your spreadsheet. You can choose to print them with your data or not by checking or clearing the Print check box that appears in the Gridlines section of the Sheet Options group on the Ribbon's Page Layout tab.

To emphasize sections of the worksheet or parts of a particular table, you can add borderlines or shading to certain cells. Don't confuse the *borderlines* that you add to accent a particular cell selection with the *gridlines* used to define cell borders in the worksheet — borders that you add print regardless of whether you print the worksheet gridlines.

TIP

To see the borders that you add to the cells in a worksheet, remove the gridlines normally displayed in the worksheet by clearing the View check box in the Gridlines section of the Sheet Options group on the Ribbon's Page Layout tab.

To add borders to a cell selection, click the drop-down button attached to the Borders button in the Font group on the Home tab. This displays a drop-down menu with all the border options you can apply to the cell selection (see Figure 3-19) where you click the type of line you want to apply to all its cells.

FIGURE 3-19:
Select borders for a cell selection on the Borders drop-down menu opened with the Borders button on the Home tab.

When selecting options on this drop-down menu to determine where you want the borderlines drawn, keep these things in mind:

>> To have Excel draw borders only around the outside edges of the entire cell selection (in other words, following the path of the expanded cell cursor), click the Outside Borders or the Thick Box Border options on this menu. To draw the outside borders yourself around an unselected cell range in the active worksheet, click the Draw Border option, drag the mouse (using the Pencil mouse pointer) through the range of cells, and then click the Borders button on the Home tab's Font group.

>> If you want borderlines to appear around all four edges of each cell in the cell selection (like a paned window), select the All Borders option on this drop-down menu. If you want to draw the inside and outside borders yourself around an unselected cell range in the active worksheet, click the Draw Border Grid option, drag the mouse (using the Pencil mouse pointer) through the range of cells, and then click the Borders button on the Home tab.

To change the type of line, line thickness, or color of the borders you apply to a cell selection, you must open the Format Cells dialog box and use the options on its Border tab (click More Borders at the bottom of the Borders button's drop-down menu or press Ctrl+1 and then click the Border tab).

To select a new line thickness or line style for a border you're applying, click its example in the Style section. To change the color of the border you want to apply, click the color sample on the Color drop-down palette. After you select a new line style and/or color, apply the border to the cell selection by clicking the appropriate line in either the Presets or Border section of the Border tab before you click OK.

To get rid of existing borders in a worksheet, you must select the cell or cells that presently contain them and then click the No Border option at the top of the second section on the Borders button's drop-down menu.

Applying fill colors, patterns, and gradient effects to cells

You can also add emphasis to particular sections of the worksheet or one of its tables by changing the fill color of the cell selection and/or applying a pattern or gradient to it.

If you're using a black-and-white printer, you want to restrict your color choices to light gray in the color palette. Additionally, you want to restrict your use of pattern styles to the very open ones with few dots when enhancing a cell selection that contains any kind of entries (otherwise, the entries will be almost impossible to read when printed).

To choose a new fill color for the background of a cell selection, you can click the Fill Color button's drop-down menu in the Font group on the Home tab and then select the color you want to use in the drop-down palette. Remember that you can use Live Preview to see what the cell selection looks like in a particular fill color by moving the mouse pointer over the color swatches. Click one to select it.

To choose a new pattern for a cell selection, you must open the Format Cells dialog box (Ctrl+1), and then click the Fill tab. To change the pattern of the cell selection, click a pattern swatch from the Pattern Style button's pattern palette. To add a fill color to the pattern you select, click its color swatch in the Background Color section of the Fill tab.

If you want to add a gradient effect to the cell selection that goes from one color to another in a certain direction, click the Fill Effects button on the Fill tab to open the Fill Effects dialog box. This dialog box contains a Gradient tab with controls that enable you to determine the two colors to use as well as shading style and variant.

After you select the colors and styles of the gradient, check the Sample swatch in the Fill Effects dialog box. When you have it the way you want it, click OK to close the Fill Effects dialog box and return to the Format Cells dialog box. The selected gradient effect then appears in its Sample area on the Fill tab in the Format Cells dialog box. Unfortunately, this is one area where Live Preview doesn't work, so you're just going to have to click its OK button to apply the gradient to the cell selection to see how it actually looks in the worksheet.

REMEMBER

Although you can't select new patterns or gradients (only colors) with the Fill Color button on the Home tab, you can remove fill colors, patterns, and gradients assigned to a cell selection by clicking the No Fill option on the Fill Color button's drop-down menu.

Doing It in Styles

In Excel 2019, vibrant cell styles are a snap to assign to your worksheet data using the Cell Styles gallery opened by selecting the Cell Styles button in the Styles group on the Ribbon's Home tab. The Cell Styles gallery contains loads of ready-made styles you can immediately apply to the current cell selection. Simply click the desired style sample in the gallery after using the Live Preview feature to determine which style looks best on your data.

Creating a new style for the gallery

To create a new style for the gallery by example, manually format a single cell with all the attributes you want (font, font size, font color, bold, italic, underlining, fill color, pattern, borders, orientation, and so on) and then click the Cell Styles button on the Home tab followed by the New Cell Style option at the bottom of the gallery. Excel then opens a Style dialog box where you replace the generic style name (Style 1, Style 2, and so on) with your own descriptive name before you click OK.

Excel then adds a sample of your new style — the style name formatted, with the new style's attributes — to a Custom section at the top of the Cell Styles gallery. To apply this custom style to a cell selection, you then only have to click its sample in the Custom section of the Cell Styles gallery.

REMEMBER

The custom cell styles you create don't become part of the current workbook until the next time you save the workbook. Therefore, you need to remember to click the Save button on the Quick Access toolbar or press Ctrl+S to save your changes after creating a new cell style if you want that style to remain part of the workbook's Cell Styles gallery the next time you open the workbook in Excel.

Copying custom styles from one workbook into another

Excel makes it easy to copy custom cell styles that you've saved as part of one workbook into the workbook you're currently working on. To copy custom styles from one workbook to another, follow these steps:

1. **Open the workbook that needs the custom styles added to it from another existing workbook.**

   This can be a brand-new workbook or one that you've opened for editing (see Chapter 4).

2. **Open the workbook that has the custom styles you want to copy saved as part of it.**

   See the previous section, "Creating a new style for the gallery," for tips on how to create and save cell styles.

3. **Switch back to the workbook into which you want to copy the saved custom styles.**

   You can do this by clicking the workbook's button on the Windows taskbar or using the Flip feature by pressing Alt+Tab until you select the workbook's thumbnail in the center of the display.

4. **Click the Cell Styles button on the Home tab followed by Merge Styles in the Cell Styles gallery or press Alt+HJM.**

   Excel opens the Merge Styles dialog box.

5. **Click the name of the open workbook file that contains the custom styles to copy in the Merge Styles From list box and then click OK.**

After you close the Merge Styles dialog box, Excel adds all the custom styles from the designated workbook into the current workbook, adding them to the Custom section of its Cell Styles gallery. To retain the custom styles you just imported, save the current workbook (click the Save button on the Quick Access toolbar or press Ctrl+S). Then, you can switch back to the workbook containing the original custom styles you just copied and close its file (press Alt+FC).

Fooling Around with the Format Painter

Using cell styles to format ranges of worksheet cells is certainly the way to go when you have to apply the same formatting repeatedly in the workbooks you create. However, there may be times when you simply want to reuse a particular cell format and apply it to particular groups of cells in a single workbook without ever bothering to open the Cell Styles gallery.

For those occasions when you feel the urge to format on the fly (so to speak), use the Format Painter button (the paintbrush icon) in the Clipboard group on the Home tab. This wonderful little tool enables you to take the formatting from a particular cell that you fancy up and apply its formatting to other cells in the worksheet simply by selecting those cells.

To use the Format Painter to copy a cell's formatting to other worksheet cells, just follow these easy steps:

1. **Format an example cell or cell range in your workbook, selecting whatever fonts, alignment, borders, patterns, and color you want it to have.**

2. **Select one of the cells you just fancied up and click the Format Painter button in the Clipboard group on the Home tab.**

   The mouse pointer changes from the standard thick, white cross to a thick, white cross with an animated paintbrush by its side, and you see a marquee around the selected cell with the formatting to be used by the Format Painter.

3. **Drag the white-cross-plus-animated-paintbrush pointer (the Format Painter pointer) through all the cells you want to format.**

   As soon as you release the mouse button, Excel applies all the formatting used in the example cell to all the cells you just selected!

To keep the Format Painter selected so that you can format a bunch of different cell ranges with the Format Painter pointer, double-click the Format Painter button on the Home tab after you select the sample cell with the desired formatting. To stop formatting cells with the Format Painter pointer, you simply click the Format Painter button on the Home tab again (it remains selected when you double-click it) to restore the button to its unselected state and return the mouse pointer to its normal thick, white cross shape.

You can use the Format Painter to restore a cell range that you gussied all up back to its boring default (General) cell format. To do this, click an empty, previously unformatted cell in the worksheet before you click the Format Painter button and then use the Format Painter pointer to drag through the cells you want returned to the default General format.

Using the Format Painter on a touchscreen has a very limited application: You can only copy the formatting from the one cell to another by first tapping the format-ted cell and then tapping the cell to be formatting. Unfortunately, you can't for-mat an entire cell range by dragging your finger or stylus as you can with the mouse.

Conditional Formatting

Before leaving behind the scintillating subject of cell formatting, there's one more formatting button in the Styles group of the Home tab of which you need to be aware. The Conditional Formatting button enables you to apply provisional for-matting to a cell range based solely on the categories into which its current values fall. The cool thing about this kind of conditional formatting is that should you edit the numbers in the cell range so that their values fall into other categories, the program automatically changes their cell formatting to suit.

When you click the Conditional Formatting button in the Styles group of the Home tab, a drop-down menu appears with the following options:

>> **Highlight Cells Rules** opens a continuation menu with various options for defining formatting rules that highlight the cells in the cell selection that contain certain values, text, or dates; that have values greater or less than a particular value; or that fall within a certain ranges of values.

>> **Top/Bottom Rules** opens a continuation menu with various options for defining formatting rules that highlight the top and bottom values, percent-ages, and above and below average values in the cell selection.

>> **Data Bars** opens a palette with different color data bars that you can apply to the cell selection to indicate their values relative to each other by clicking the data bar thumbnail.

>> **Color Scales** opens a palette with different two- and three-colored scales that you can apply to the cell selection to indicate their values relative to each other by clicking the color scale thumbnail.

» **Icon Sets** opens a palette with different sets of icons that you can apply to the cell selection to indicate their values relative to each other by clicking the icon set.

» **New Rule** opens the New Formatting Rule dialog box where you define a custom conditional formatting rule to apply to the cell selection.

» **Clear Rules** opens a continuation menu where you can remove conditional formatting rules for the cell selection by clicking the Clear Rules from Selected Cells option, for the entire worksheet by clicking the Clear Rules from Entire Sheet option, or for just the current data table by clicking the Clear Rules from This Table option. If you're working with a Pivot Table (as described in Chapter 9), you can clear the conditional formatting from it by clicking the Clear Rules from This PivotTable option at the very bottom of this menu.

» **Manage Rules** opens the Conditional Formatting Rules Manager dialog box where you edit and delete particular rules as well as adjust their rule precedence by moving them up or down in the Rules list box.

Formatting with scales and markers

The easiest conditional formatting that you can apply to a worksheet cell range is using the pop-up palettes of graphical scales and markers attached to the Data Bars, Color Scales, and Icon Sets options on the Conditional Formatting button's drop-down menu:

» **Data Bars** represent the relative values in the cell selection by the length of the color bar in each cell and are great for helping you quickly spot the lower and higher values within a large range of data.

» **Color Scales** classify the relative values in a cell selection with a color gradation using a one-, two-, or three-color scale and are great for identifying the distribution of values across a large range of data.

» **Icon Sets** classify the values in the cell selection into particular graphic sets arranged in four categories, and each icon within a set represents a range of values that go from high to low. Icon sets are great for quickly identifying the different ranges of values in a range of data.

Figure 3-20 shows you an example of cell ranges (containing identical values) using each of the three formatting types. The values in the first range (B2:B12) are conditionally formatted using blue Gradient Fill Data Bars. The values in the second range (D2:D12) are conditionally formatted using the Green, Yellow, Red Color Scale. The values in the third range (F2:F12) are conditionally formatted using the 3 Arrows (Colored) Icon Set.

FIGURE 3-20:
Sample worksheet with three identical cell ranges formatted with Excel's Data Bars, Color Scales, and Icon Sets options.

In Figure 3-20, the particular conditional formatting types Excel assigned to each cell range can be interpreted as follows:

>> **Data bars** added to the cells in the first cell range, B2:B12, represent the relative size of its values graphically, much like a standard bar chart.

>> **Color scales** applied to the second range, D2:D12, represent the relative size of the values in the range by color and hue (red hues applied to the lower values, yellow to the middle values, and green to the higher values).

>> **Directional icons** applied to the third cell range, F2:F12, represent the relative size of the values in the range with arrow icons pointing in different directions (arrows pointing straight down for the lower values, straight up for the higher values, and sideways for middling values).

Highlighting cells ranges

The Highlight Cells Rules and Top/Bottom Rules options on Excel's Conditional Formatting drop-down menu enable you to quickly identify cell entries of particular interest in various cell ranges in your worksheet.

The options on the Highlight Cells Rules continuation menu enable you to set formats that identify values that are greater than, less than, equal to, or even between particular values that you set. This menu also contains an option for setting special formats for identifying cells that contain particular text (such as Yes, No, or even Maybe answers in a data list) or certain dates (such as project milestones and deadlines).

TIP

Perhaps one of the most useful options on the Highlight Cells Rules continuation menu is the Duplicate Values option that enables you to flag duplicate entries in a cell range by assigning them a special formatting. Doing this not only makes it easy to visually identify duplicate entries in a data list or table but also to find them electronically by searching for their particular formatting characteristics. (See Chapter 6 for details on searching your worksheets.)

The options on the Top/Bottom Rules continuation menu enable you to specially format and, therefore, easily identify values in data tables and lists that are either above or below the norm. These options not only include those for automatically formatting all values in a range that are among the top 10 highest or lowest (either in value or percentage) but also above or below the average (as calculated by dividing the total by the number of values).

REMEMBER

In addition to using the ready-made rules for conditional formatting located on the Highlight Cells Rules and Top/Bottom Rules continuation menus, you can also create your own custom rules. When you create a custom rule, you not only specify the rule type that identifies which values or text entries to format, but also you format the colors and other aspects included in the formatting. (For details on creating custom conditional formats, consult my *Excel 2019 All-in-One For Dummies*.)

Formatting via the Quick Analysis tool

One of the quickest and easiest ways to apply Data Bars, Color Scales, Icon Set, Greater Than, or Top 10% conditional formatting to a data table is with the Excel 2019's Quick Analysis tool. The coolest thing about applying conditional formatting in this manner is that Live Preview lets you visualize how your data looks with a particular type of conditional formatting before you actually apply it.

To assign conditional formatting with the Quick Analysis tool, select the data in your table that you wanted formatted and then select the Quick Analysis tool. By default, the Formatting option is selected when Excel displays the tool's palette so that all you have to do is highlight each of the formatting options with your mouse or Touch pointer to see how they will look on your data.

Figure 3-21 shows you the Live Preview of the financial data in the Mother Goose 2016 Sales table with the Data Bars conditional formatting (as the Data Bars button is highlighted in the Formatting options). To assign this conditional format to the financial data in the selected table, you simply click the Data Bars button on the Quick Analysis palette. To preview how the data would look formatted with another conditional format, you simply highlight its button with the mouse or Touch pointer.

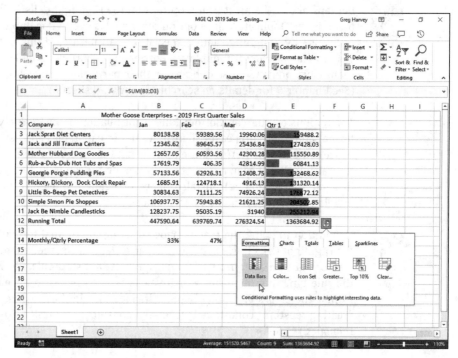

FIGURE 3-21:
Previewing conditional formatting in a data table using the Quick Analysis tool.

Note that if you click the Greater Than button on the Quick Analysis palette, Excel displays a Greater Than dialog box where you specify the threshold value in the Format Cells That Are Greater Than text box, as well as select the color of the formatting for all the cells above that threshold in the drop-down list to its right.

With all the other kinds of conditional formats (Data Bars, Color Scales, Icon Set, and Top 10%), Excel just goes ahead and applies the first (default) option for that kind of formatting that you find on the Conditional Formatting button's drop-down menus on the Ribbon.

Chapter **4**

Going Through Changes

Picture this: You just finished creating, formatting, and printing a major project with Excel — a workbook with your department's budget for the next fiscal year. Because you finally understand a little bit about how the Excel thing works, you finish the job in crack time. You're actually ahead of schedule.

You turn the workbook over to your boss so that she can check the numbers. With plenty of time for making those inevitable last-minute corrections, you're feeling on top of this situation.

Then comes the reality check — your boss brings the document back, and she's plainly agitated. "We forgot to include the estimates for the temps and our over-time hours. They go right here. While you're adding them, can you move these rows of figures up and those columns over?"

As she continues to suggest improvements, your heart begins to sink. These modifications are in a different league than, "Let's change these column headings from bold to italic and add shading to that row of totals." Clearly, you're looking at a lot more work on this baby than you had contemplated. Even worse, you're looking at making structural changes that threaten to unravel the very fabric of your beautiful worksheet.

As the preceding fable points out, editing a worksheet in a workbook can occur on different levels:

>> You can make changes that affect the contents of the cells, such as copying a row of column headings or moving a table to a new area in a particular worksheet.

>> You can make changes that affect the structure of a worksheet itself, such as inserting new columns or rows (so that you can enter new data originally left out) or deleting unnecessary columns or rows from an existing table so that you don't leave any gaps.

>> You can even make changes to the number of worksheets in a workbook (by either adding or deleting sheets).

In this chapter, you discover how to make these types of changes safely to a workbook. As you see, the mechanics of copying and moving data or inserting and deleting rows are simple to master. It's the impact that such actions have on the worksheet that takes a little more effort to understand. Not to worry! You always have the Undo feature to fall back on for those (hopefully rare) times when you make a little tiny change that throws an entire worksheet into complete and utter chaos.

In the final section of this chapter ("Eliminating Errors with Text to Speech"), you find out how to use the Text to Speech feature to check out and confirm the accuracy of the data entries you make in your worksheets. With Text to Speech, you can listen to your computer read back a series of cell entries while you visually corroborate their accuracy from the original source document. Text to Speech can make this sort of routine and otherwise labor-intensive editing much easier and greatly increase the accuracy of your spreadsheets.

Opening Your Workbooks for Editing

Before you can do any damage — I mean, make any changes — in a workbook, you have to open it up in Excel. To open a workbook from within Excel, you can select File ⇨ Open, press Alt+FO, or use the old standby keyboard shortcuts Ctrl+O or Ctrl+F12.

REMEMBER

When you use the Ctrl+F12 shortcut, as opposed to any of the other methods for opening a workbook, Excel 2019 bypasses the Open screen in the Backstage and takes you directly to the Open dialog box. This is fine provided that the workbook file you need to work with is in the currently open folder (by default, this is the Documents folder on your OneDrive, unless you've opened files from another folder and drive during your work session).

If you've just launched Excel 2019 and don't yet have any workbooks open, you can open the workbook for editing by selecting it on the list of files under the Recent heading displayed in the left pane of the Start screen. If the file you want to edit is not in this list, click the Open Other Workbooks link at the bottom of this left pane to have Excel take you to the Open screen.

Opening files in the Open screen

When the Open screen is first displayed in the Excel 2019 Backstage (shown in Figure 4-1) the Recent option in the Places pane on the left is selected. If the file you want to open isn't shown in this list in the right-hand pane, you need to select one of the other Places options:

>> **OneDrive** to open a workbook file that's saved in the cloud in one of your folders on your Windows OneDrive (for more information on OneDrive or to open an account, visit `https://onedrive.live.com/about`). When you select the OneDrive option, the right-hand pane lists folders on your OneDrive that you accessed recently as well as the Browse button that enables you to locate other folders in the Open dialog box.

>> **This PC** to open a workbook file saved locally on your computer's hard drive or a network drive to which you have access. When you select this option, the right-hand pane lists folders on your local and network drives that you accessed recently as well as a Documents button that displays the Open dialog box giving you access to the files saved in all your local and network drives and folders.

>> **Add a Place** to add access to a folder on your SharePoint site or OneDrive. When you select this option, the right-hand pane contains an Office 365 SharePoint and OneDrive button. Click the Office 365 SharePoint button to log into a SharePoint site for which you have a user ID and password to add its folders to the Open screen under the Computer option. Select the OneDrive option to log into your Windows Live account (for which you have a user ID and password) to add your space in the cloud to the Open screen under the OneDrive option.

>> **Browse** to display the Open dialog box (shown in Figure 4-1) where you can select a workbook for editing from any folders saved on the local, network, or online drives available to you.

FIGURE 4-1:
Use the OneDrive
option in the
Open screen
to open an
online workbook
file for editing.

Operating the Open dialog box

After you select a folder and drive in the Excel 2019 Open screen or its Browse button or press the Ctrl+F12 shortcut from within Excel, the program displays an Open dialog box similar to the one shown in Figure 4-2. The Open dialog box is divided into panes: Navigation pane on the left, where you can select a new folder to open, and main pane on the right showing the icons for all the subfolders in the current folder, as well as the documents that Excel can open.

The folder with contents displayed in the Open dialog box is either the one designated as the Default File Location on the Save tab of the Excel Options dialog box, the folder you last opened during your current Excel work session, or the folder you selected in the Open screen of the Backstage view.

To open a workbook in another folder, select the Quick Access option in the Navigation pane (to see a list of frequently used folders in the main pane) or one of the location icons displayed in this pane to access that folder. You can display a list of folders on a particular location by clicking the Expand Folders button (the one with the triangle pointing to the right) to the left of its name.

FIGURE 4-2:
Selecting the
workbook file to
open for editing
in Excel in the
Open dialog box.

If you open a new folder and it appears empty of all files (and you know that it's not an empty folder), this just means the folder doesn't contain any of the types of files that Excel can open directly (such as workbooks, template files, and macro sheets). To display all the files, whether or not Excel can open them directly (meaning without some sort of conversion), click the drop-down button that appears next to the drop-down list box that currently displays All Excel Files and then click All Files on its drop-down menu.

When the icon for the workbook file you want to work with appears in the Open dialog box, you can then open it either by clicking its file icon and then clicking the Open button or, if you're handy with the mouse, by just double-clicking the file icon.

REMEMBER

You can use the slider attached to the Change Your View drop-down list button located in upper-right corner of the Open dialog box to change the way folder and file icons appear in the dialog box. When you select Large Icons or Extra Large Icons on this slider (or anywhere in between), the Excel workbook icons actually show a preview of the data in the upper-left corner of the first worksheet when the file is saved with the preview picture option turned on:

>> To enable the preview feature when saving workbooks in Excel 2019, select the Save Thumbnail check box in the Save As dialog box before saving the file for the first time.

>> To enable the preview feature when saving workbooks in Excel 97 through 2003, click the Save Preview Picture check box on the Summary tab of the workbook's Properties dialog box (File ⇨ Properties) before saving the file for the first time.

This preview of part of the first sheet can help you quickly identify the workbook you want to open for editing or printing. To have the workbook file's preview displayed in the Open dialog box without changing the current icon view, click the Show the Preview Pane button to the immediate right of the Change Your View drop-down button.

Changing the Recent files settings

Excel 2019 automatically keeps a running list of the last 50 files you opened in the Recent Workbooks list on the Open screen in the Backstage when the default Recent Workbooks option is selected rather than Shared With Me (which displays a list of all the Excel workbook files that coworkers or clients have shared on a OneDrive or SharePoint web site). If you want, you can have Excel fewer files in this list.

To change the number of recently opened files that appear, follow these simple steps:

1. **Select File ⇨ Options ⇨ Advanced or press Alt+FTA to open the Advanced tab of the Excel Options dialog box.**

2. **Type a new entry (between 1 and 50) in the Show This Number of Recent Documents text box located in the Display section or use the spinner buttons to increase or decrease this number.**

3. **Click OK or press Enter to close the Excel Options dialog box.**

REMEMBER

If you don't want any files displayed in the Recent Workbooks list, either on the Excel or Open screen in the Backstage view, enter **0** in the Show This Number of Recent Documents text box or select it with the spinner buttons.

TIP

Select the Quickly Access This Number of Recent Workbooks check box on the Advanced tab of the Excel Options dialog box (right below the Show This Number of Recent Workbooks option) to have Excel display the four most recently opened workbooks as menu items at the bottom of the File menu in the Backstage view. That way, you can open any of them by clicking its button even when the Open screen is not displayed in the Backstage view. If four workbook files is too many or not sufficient, you can decrease or increase the number of files shown at the bottom of the File menu by replacing 4 in the text box that appears to the right of the Quickly Access This Number of Recent Workbooks check box option.

Opening multiple workbooks

If you know that you're going to edit more than one of the workbook files shown in the list box of the Open dialog box, you can select multiple files in the list box, and Excel will then open all of them (in the order they're listed) when you click the Open button or press Enter.

REMEMBER

Remember that in order to select multiple files that appear sequentially in the Open dialog box, you click the first filename and then hold down the Shift key while you click the last filename. To select files that aren't listed sequentially, you need to hold down the Ctrl key while you click the various filenames.

After the workbook files are open in Excel, you can then switch documents by clicking the Task View button on the Windows 10 taskbar and then clicking the thumbnail of the workbook you want to edit or by using the Flip feature (Alt+Tab) to select the workbook's thumbnail. You can also switch files within Excel 2019 by using the View➪Switch Windows command and selecting its filename on its drop-down menu (See Chapter 7 for detailed information on working on more than one worksheet at a time.)

Find workbook files

The only problem you can encounter in opening a document from the Open dialog box is locating the filename. Everything's hunky-dory as long as you can see the workbook filename listed in the Open dialog box or know which folder to open in order to display it. But what about those times when a file seems to migrate mysteriously and can't be found on your computer?

For those times, you need to use the Search Documents text box in the upper-right corner of the Open dialog box. To find a missing workbook, click this text box and then begin typing characters used in the workbook's filename or contained in the workbook itself.

As soon as Windows 10 finds any matches for the characters you type, the names of the workbook files (and other Excel files, such as templates and macro sheets) appear in the Open dialog box. When the workbook you want to open is listed, you can open it by clicking its icon and filename followed by the Open button, or by double-clicking it.

Using the Open file options

The drop-down button attached to the Open command button at the bottom of the Open dialog box enables you to open the selected workbook file(s) in a special way, including:

>> **Open Read-Only:** This command opens the files you select in the Open dialog box's list box in a read-only state, which means that you can look but you can't touch. (Actually, you can touch; you just can't save your changes in the original workbook.) To save changes in a read-only file, you must use the Save As command (File ⇨ Save As or Alt+FA) and give the workbook file a new location and/or filename. (Refer to Chapter 2.)

>> **Open as Copy:** This command opens a copy of the files you select in the Open dialog box. Use this method of opening files as a safety net: If you mess up the copies, you always have the originals to fall back on.

>> **Open in Browser:** This command opens workbook files you save as web pages (which I describe in Chapter 12) in your favorite web browser. This command isn't available unless the program identifies that the selected file or files were saved as web pages rather than plain old Excel workbook files.

>> **Open in Protected View:** This command opens the workbook file in Protected View mode that keeps you from making any changes to the contents of its worksheets until you click the Enable Editing button that appears in the orange Protected View panel at the top of the screen.

>> **Open and Repair:** This command attempts to repair corrupted workbook files before opening them in Excel. When you select this command, a dialog box appears, giving you a choice between attempting to repair the corrupted file or opening the recovered version, extracting data from the corrupted file, and placing it in a new workbook (which you can save with the Save command). Click the Repair button to attempt to recover and open the file. Click the Extract Data button if you tried unsuccessfully to have Excel repair the file.

Much Ado about Undo

Before you start tearing into the workbook that you just opened, get to know the Undo feature, including how it can put right many of the things that you could inadvertently mess up. The Undo command button on the Quick Access toolbar is a regular chameleon button. When you delete the cell selection by pressing the Delete key, the Undo button's ScreenTip reads Undo Clear (Ctrl+Z). If you move some entries to a new part of the worksheet by dragging it, the Undo command button ScreenTip changes to Undo Drag and Drop (Ctrl+Z).

In addition to clicking the Undo command button (in whatever guise it appears), you can also choose this command by pressing Ctrl+Z (perhaps for *unZap*).

The Undo command button on the Quick Access toolbar changes in response to whatever action you just took; that is, it changes after each action. If you forget to strike when the iron is hot, so to speak, and don't use the Undo feature to restore the worksheet to its previous state *before* you choose another command, you then need to consult the drop-down menu on the Undo button. Click its drop-down button that appears to the right of the Undo icon (the curved arrow pointing to the left). After the Undo drop-down menu appears, click the action on this menu that you want undone. Excel will then undo this action and all actions that precede it in the list (which are selected automatically).

Undo is Redo the second time around

After using the Undo command button on the Quick Access toolbar, Excel 2019 activates the Redo command button to its immediate right. If you delete an entry from a cell by pressing the Delete key and then click the Undo command button or press Ctrl+Z, the ScreenTip that appears when you position the mouse pointer over the Redo command button reads Redo Clear (Ctrl+Y).

When you click the Redo command button or press Ctrl+Y, Excel redoes the thing you just undid. Actually, this sounds more complicated than it is. It simply means that you use Undo/Redo to switch between the result of an action and the state of the worksheet just before that action until you decide how you want the worksheet (or until the cleaning crew turns off the lights and locks up the building).

What to do when you can't Undo?

Just when you think it is safe to begin gutting the company's most important workbook, I really feel that I have to tell you that (yikes!) Undo doesn't work all the time! Although you can undo your latest erroneous cell deletion, bad move, or unwise copy, you can't undo your latest rash save. (You know, like when you meant to choose Save As from the File menu in the Backstage view to save the edited worksheet under a different document name but chose Save and ended up saving the changes as part of the current document.)

Unfortunately, Excel doesn't let you know when you are about to take a step from which there is no return — until it's too late. After you've gone and done the unundoable and you click the Undo button where you expect its ScreenTip to say Undo *blah, blah*, it now reads Can't Undo.

One exception to this rule is when the program gives you advance warning (which you should heed). When you choose a command that is normally possible but because you're low on memory or the change will affect so much of the worksheet, or both, Excel knows that it can't undo the change if it goes through with it, the program displays an alert box telling you that there isn't enough memory to undo this action and asking whether you want to go ahead anyway. If you click the Yes button and complete the edit, just realize that you do so without any possibility of pardon. If you find out, too late, that you deleted a row of essential formulas (that you forgot about because you couldn't see them), you can't bring them back with Undo. In such a case, you would have to close the file (File⇨Close) and *NOT save your changes.*

Doing the Old Drag-and-Drop Thing

The first editing technique you need to learn is *drag and drop.* As the name implies, you can use this technique to pick up a cell selection and drop it into a new place on the worksheet. Although drag and drop is primarily a technique for moving cell entries around a worksheet, you can adapt it to copy a cell selection, as well.

To use drag and drop to move a range of cell entries (one cell range at a time), follow these steps:

1. **Select a cell range.**

2. **Position the mouse pointer on one edge of the extended cell cursor that now surrounds the entire cell range.**

   Your signal that you can start dragging the cell range to its new position in the worksheet is when the pointer changes to the outlined arrowhead pointing to a smaller, black four-way arrow.

3. **Drag your selection to its destination.**

   Drag your selection by depressing and holding down the primary mouse button — usually the left one — while moving the mouse.

   While you drag your selection, you actually move only the outline of the cell range, and Excel keeps you informed of what the new cell range address would be (as a kind of drag-and-drop ScreenTip) if you were to release the mouse button at that location.

   Drag the outline until it's positioned where you want the entries to appear (as evidenced by the cell range in the drag-and-drop ScreenTip).

4. **Release the mouse button.**

   The cell entries within that range reappear in the new location as soon as you release the mouse button.

In Figures 4-3 and 4-4, I show how you can drag and drop a cell range. In Figure 4-3, I select the cell range A10:E10 (containing the quarterly totals) to move it to row 12 to make room for sales figures for two new companies (Simple Simon Pie Shoppes and Jack Be Nimble Candlesticks, which hadn't been acquired when this workbook was first created). In Figure 4-4, you see the Mother Goose Enterprises – 2016 Sales worksheet right after completing this move.

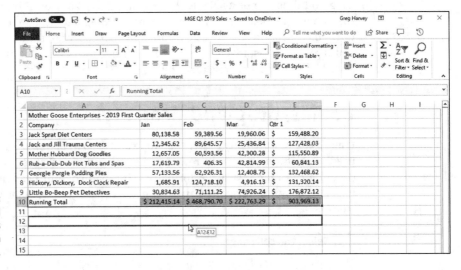

FIGURE 4-3:
Dragging the cell selection to its new position in a worksheet.

FIGURE 4-4:
A worksheet after dropping the cell selection into its new place.

The arguments for the SUM functions in cell range B13:E13 do not keep pace with the change — it continues to sum only the values in rows 3 through 9 after the move. However, as soon as you enter the sales figures for these new enterprises in columns B through D in rows 10 and 11, Excel shows off its smarts and updates the formulas in row 12 and column E to include the new entries. For example, the SUM(B3:B9) formula in B12 magically becomes SUM(B3:B11).

Drag and drop is not available when using Excel 2019 on a touchscreen device that's not equipped with a mouse. Instead of drag and drop, you have to use the Cut and Paste or Copy and Paste commands that appear in the pop-up menu when you tap and hold somewhere in your cell selection. (See "Cut and Paste, Digital Style" later in this chapter, for details.)

Copies, drag-and-drop style

What if you want to copy rather than drag and drop a cell range? Suppose that you need to start a new table in rows farther down the worksheet, and you want to copy the cell range with the formatted title and column headings for the new table. To copy the formatted title range in the sample worksheet, follow these steps:

1. **Select the cell range.**

   In the case of Figures 4-3 and 4-4, that's cell range A1:E2.

2. **Hold the Ctrl key down while you position the mouse pointer on an edge of the selection (that is, the expanded cell cursor).**

   The pointer changes from a thick, shaded cross to an outlined arrowhead with a + (plus sign) to the right of it with the drag-and-drop ScreenTip beside it. The plus sign next to the pointer is your signal that drag and drop will *copy* the selection rather than *move* it.

3. **Drag the cell-selection outline to the place where you want the copy to appear and release the mouse button.**

If, when using drag and drop to move or copy cells, you position the outline of the selection so that it overlaps any part of cells that already contain entries, Excel displays an alert box that asks whether you want to replace the contents of the destination cells. To avoid replacing existing entries and to abort the entire drag-and-drop mission, click the Cancel button in this alert box. To go ahead and exterminate the little darlings, click OK or press Enter.

Insertions courtesy of drag and drop

Like the Klingons of *Star Trek* fame, spreadsheets, such as Excel, never take prisoners. When you place or move a new entry into an occupied cell, the new entry completely replaces the old as though the old entry never existed in that cell.

To insert the cell range you're moving or copying within a populated region of the worksheet without wiping out existing entries, hold down the Shift key while you drag the selection. (If you're copying, you have to get ambitious and hold down both the Shift and Ctrl keys at the same time!)

With the Shift key depressed while you drag, instead of a rectangular outline of the cell range, you get an I-beam shape that shows where the selection will be inserted if you release the mouse button along with the address of the cell range (as a kind of Insertion ScreenTip). When you move the I-beam shape, notice that it wants to attach itself to the column and row borders while you move it. After you position the I-beam at the column or row border where you want to insert the cell range, release the mouse button. Excel inserts the cell range, moving the existing entries to neighboring blank cells (out of harm's way).

TIP

When inserting cells with drag and drop, it may be helpful to think of the I-beam shape as a pry bar that pulls apart the columns or rows along the axis of the I. Also, sometimes after moving a range to a new place in the worksheet, instead of the data appearing, you see only #######s in the cells. (Excel 2019 doesn't automatically widen the new columns for the incoming data as it does when formatting the data.) Remember that the way to get rid of the #######s in the cells is by widening those troublesome columns enough to display all the data-plus-formatting; and the easiest way to do this kind of widening is by double-clicking the right border of the column.

I HELD DOWN THE SHIFT KEY JUST AS YOU SAID . . .

Drag and drop in Insert mode is one of Excel's most finicky keyboard features. Sometimes you can do everything just right and still get the alert box warning you that Excel is about to replace existing entries instead of pushing them aside. When you see this alert box, always click the Cancel button! Fortunately, you can insert things with the Insert commands without worrying about which way the I-beam selection goes (see the "Staying in Step with Insert" section, later in this chapter).

Copying Formulas with AutoFill

Copying with drag and drop (by holding down the Ctrl key) is useful when you need to copy a bunch of neighboring cells to a new part of the worksheet. Frequently, however, you just need to copy a single formula that you just created to a bunch of neighboring cells that need to perform the same type of calculation (such as totaling columns of figures). This type of formula copy, although quite common, can't be done with drag and drop. Instead, use the AutoFill feature (read about this in Chapter 2) or the Copy and Paste commands. (See the section "Cut and Paste, Digital Style," later in this chapter.)

TIP

Don't forget the Totals option on the Quick Analysis tool. You can use it to create a row or a column of totals at the bottom or right edge of a data table in a flash. Simply select the table as a cell range and click the Quick Analysis button followed by Totals in its palette. Then click the Sum button at the beginning of the palette to create formulas that total the columns in a new row at the bottom of the table and/or the Sum button at the end of the palette to create formulas that total the rows in a new column at the right end.

Here's how you can use AutoFill to copy one formula to a range of cells. In Figure 4-5, you can see the Mother Goose Enterprises – 2019 Sales worksheet with all the companies, but this time with only one monthly total in row 12, which is in the process of being copied through cell E12.

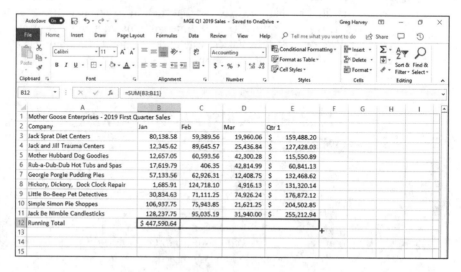

FIGURE 4-5:
Copying a formula to a cell range with AutoFill.

Figure 4-6 shows the worksheet after dragging the fill handle in cell B12 to select the cell range C12:E12 (where this formula should be copied).

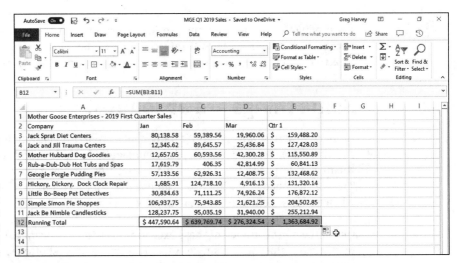

FIGURE 4-6:
The worksheet after copying the formula totaling the monthly (and quarterly) sales.

Relatively speaking

Figure 4-6 shows the worksheet after the formula in a cell is copied to the cell range C12:E12 and cell B12 is active. Notice how Excel handles the copying of formulas. The original formula in cell B12 is as follows:

```
=SUM(B3:B11)
```

When the original formula is copied to cell C12, Excel changes the formula slightly so that it looks like this:

```
=SUM(C3:C11)
```

Excel adjusts the column reference, changing it from B to C, because I copied from left to right across the rows.

When you copy a formula to a cell range that extends down the rows, Excel adjusts the row numbers in the copied formulas rather than the column letters to suit the position of each copy. For example, cell E3 in the Mother Goose Enterprises – 2019 Sales worksheet contains the following formula:

```
=SUM(B3:D3)
```

When you copy this formula to cell E4, Excel changes the copy of the formula to the following:

```
=SUM(B4:D4)
```

Excel adjusts the row reference to keep current with the new row 4 position. Because Excel adjusts the cell references in copies of a formula relative to the direction of the copying, the cell references are known as *relative cell references*.

Some things are absolutes!

All new formulas you create naturally contain relative cell references unless you say otherwise. Because most copies you make of formulas require adjustments of their cell references, you rarely have to give this arrangement a second thought. Then, every once in a while, you come across an exception that calls for limiting when and how cell references are adjusted in copies.

One of the most common of these exceptions is when you want to compare a range of different values with a single value. This happens most often when you want to compute what percentage each part is to the total. For example, in the Mother Goose Enterprises – 2019 Sales worksheet, you encounter this situation in creating and copying a formula that calculates what percentage each monthly total (in the cell range B14:D14) is of the quarterly total in cell E12.

Suppose that you want to enter these formulas in row 14 of the Mother Goose Enterprises – 2019 Sales worksheet, starting in cell B14. The formula in cell B14 for calculating the percentage of the January-sales-to-first-quarter-total is very straightforward:

```
=B12/E12
```

This formula divides the January sales total in cell B12 by the quarterly total in E12 (what could be easier?). Look, however, at what would happen if you dragged the fill handle one cell to the right to copy this formula to cell C14:

```
=C12/F12
```

The adjustment of the first cell reference from B12 to C12 is just what the doctor ordered. However, the adjustment of the second cell reference from E12 to F12 is a disaster. Not only do you not calculate what percentage the February sales in cell C12 are of the first quarter sales in E12, but you also end up with one of those horrible #DIV/0! error things in cell C14.

To stop Excel from adjusting a cell reference in a formula in any copies you make, convert the cell reference from relative to absolute. You do this by pressing the function key F4, after you put Excel in Edit mode (F2). Excel indicates that you make the cell reference absolute by placing dollar signs in front of the column letter and row number. For example, in Figure 4-7, cell B14 contains the correct formula to copy to the cell range C14:D14:

```
=B12/$E$12
```

FIGURE 4-7:
Copying the formula for computing the ratio of monthly to quarterly sales with an absolute cell reference.

Look at the worksheet after this formula is copied to the range C14:D14 with the fill handle and cell C14 is selected (see Figure 4-8). Notice that the Formula bar shows that this cell contains the following formula:

```
=C12/$E$12
```

FIGURE 4-8:
The worksheet after copying the formula with the absolute cell reference.

Because E12 was changed to $E$12 in the original formula, all the copies have this same absolute (non-changing) reference.

TIP

If you goof up and copy a formula where one or more of the cell references should have been absolute but you left them all relative, edit the original formula as follows:

1. **Double-click the cell with the formula or press F2 to edit it.**

2. **Position the insertion point somewhere on the reference you want to convert to absolute.**

3. **Press F4.**

4. **When you finish editing, click the Enter button on the Formula bar and then copy the formula to the messed-up cell range with the fill handle.**

WARNING

Be sure to press F4 only once to change a cell reference to completely absolute as I describe earlier. If you press the F4 function key a second time, you end up with a so-called *mixed reference*, where only the row part is absolute and the column part is relative (as in E$12). If you then press F4 again, Excel comes up with another type of mixed reference, where the column part is absolute and the row part is relative (as in $E12). If you go on and press F4 yet again, Excel changes the cell reference back to completely relative (as in E12). After you're back where you started, you can continue to use F4 to cycle through this same set of cell reference changes all over again.

TIP

If you're using Excel 2019 on a device without access to a physical keyboard with function keys (such as a touchscreen tablet), the only way to convert cell addresses in your formulas from relative to absolute or some form of mixed address is to open the Touch keyboard and use it add the dollar signs before the column letter and/or row number in the appropriate cell address on the Formula bar.

Cut and Paste, Digital Style

Instead of using drag and drop or AutoFill, you can use the old standby Cut, Copy, and Paste commands to move or copy information in a worksheet. These commands use the Office Clipboard as a kind of electronic halfway house where the information you cut or copy remains until you decide to paste it somewhere. Because of this Clipboard arrangement, you can use these commands to move or copy information to any other workbook open in Excel or even to other programs running in Windows (such as a OneNote or Word 2019 document).

To move a cell selection with Cut and Paste, follow these steps:

1. **Select the cells you want to move.**

2. **Click the Cut command button in the Clipboard group on the Home tab (the button with the scissors icon).**

If you prefer, you can choose Cut by pressing Ctrl+X.

Whenever you choose the Cut command in Excel, the program surrounds the cell selection with a *marquee* (a dotted line that travels around the cells' outline) and displays the following message on the Status bar:

```
Select destination and press ENTER or choose Paste
```

3. **Move the cell cursor to the new range to which you want the information moved, or click the cell in the upper-left corner of the new range.**

4. **Press Enter to complete the move operation.**

If you're feeling ambitious, click the Paste command button in the Clipboard group on the Home tab or press Ctrl+V.

Notice that when you indicate the destination range, you don't have to select a range of blank cells that matches the shape and size of the cell selection you're moving. Excel needs to know only the location of the cell in the upper-left corner of the destination range to figure out where to put the rest of the cells.

Copying a cell selection with the Copy and Paste commands follows an identical procedure to the one you use with the Cut and Paste commands. After selecting the range to copy, you can get the information into the Clipboard by clicking the Copy button on the Ribbon's Home tab, selecting Copy from the cell's shortcut menu, or pressing Ctrl+C.

Paste it again, Sam . . .

An advantage to copying a selection with the Copy and Paste commands and the Clipboard is that you can paste the information multiple times. Just make sure that, instead of pressing Enter to complete the first copy operation, you click the Paste button on the Home tab of the Ribbon or press Ctrl+V.

When you use the Paste command to complete a copy operation, Excel copies the selection to the range you designate without removing the marquee from the original selection. This is your signal that you can select another destination range (in either the same or a different document).

After you select the first cell of the next range where you want the selection copied, choose the Paste command again. You can continue in this manner, pasting the same selection to your heart's content. When you make the last copy, press Enter instead of clicking the Paste command button or pressing Ctrl+V. If you forget and select Paste, get rid of the marquee around the original cell range by pressing the Esc key.

Keeping pace with Paste Options

Right after you click the Paste button on the Home tab of the Ribbon or press Ctrl+V to paste cell entries that you copy (not cut) to the Clipboard, Excel displays a Paste Options button with the label, (Ctrl), to its immediate right at the end of the pasted range. When you click this drop-down button or press the Ctrl key, a palette similar to the one shown in Figure 4-9 appears with three groups of buttons (Paste, Paste Values, and Other Paste Options).

You can use these paste options to control or restrict the type of content and formatting that's included in the pasted cell range. The paste options (complete with the hot key sequences you can type to select them) on the Paste Options palette include:

- **Paste (P):** Excel pastes all the stuff in the cell selection (formulas, formatting, you name it).

- **Formulas (F):** Excel pastes all the text, numbers, and formulas in the current cell selection without their formatting.

- **Formulas & Number Formatting (O):** Excel pastes the number formats assigned to the copied values along with their formulas.

- **Keep Source Formatting (K):** Excel copies the formatting from the original cells and pastes this into the destination cells (along with the copied entries).

- **No Borders (B):** Excel pastes all the stuff in the cell selection without copying any borders applied to its cell range.

- **Keep Source Column Widths (W):** Excel makes the width of the columns in the destination range the same as those in the source range when it copies their cell entries.

- **Transpose (T):** Excel changes the orientation of the pasted entries. For example, if the original cells' entries run down the rows of a single column of the worksheet, the transposed pasted entries will run across the columns of a single row.

- **Values (V):** Excel pastes only the calculated results of any formulas in the source cell range.

- **Values & Number Formatting (A):** Excel pastes the calculated results of any formulas along with all the formatting assigned to the labels, values, and formulas in the source cell range into the destination range. This means that all the labels and values in the destination range appear formatted just like the source range, even though all the original formulas are lost and only the calculated values are retained.

- **Values & Source Formatting (E):** Excel pastes the calculated results of any formulas along with all formatting assigned to the source cell range.

- **Formatting (R):** Excel pastes only the formatting (and not the entries) copied from the source cell range to the destination range.

- **Paste Link (N):** Excel creates linking formulas in the destination range so that any changes that you make to the entries in cells in the source range are immediately brought forward and reflected in the corresponding cells of the destination range.

- **Picture (U):** Excel pastes only the pictures in the copied cell selection.

- **Linked Picture (I):** Excel pastes a link to the pictures in the copied cell selection.

REMEMBER

The options that appear on the Paste Options palette are context sensitive. This means that the particular paste options available on the palette depend directly upon the type of cell entries previously copied to the Office Clipboard. Additionally, you can access this same palette of paste options by clicking the drop-down button that appears directly beneath the Paste button on the Ribbon instead of clicking the Paste Options button that appears at the end of the pasted range in the worksheet or pressing the Ctrl key on your keyboard.

Paste it from the Clipboard task pane

The Office Clipboard can store multiple cuts and copies from any program running under Windows (not just Excel). In Excel, this means that you can continue to paste stuff from the Clipboard into a workbook even after finishing a move or copy operation (even when you do so by pressing the Enter key rather than using the Paste command).

To open the Office Clipboard in its own task pane to the immediate left of the Worksheet area (see Figure 4-10), click the Dialog Box launcher in the lower-right corner of the Clipboard group on the Ribbon's Home tab.

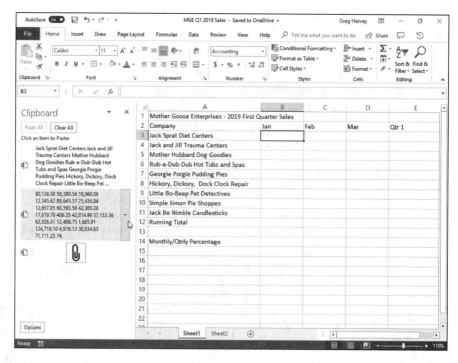

FIGURE 4-10:
The Clipboard task pane appears on the left side of the Excel Worksheet area.

To paste an item from the Clipboard into a worksheet, click the cell in the worksheet where you want the item to be copied before you click item in the Clipboard task pane. If the Clipboard item is composed of a series of text or values, Excel will paste the into the cells of the worksheet starting at the current cell. If the item is a graphic, Excel will pasted in the vicinity of the current cell (see Chapter10 for details on working with graphics in your worksheets).

You can paste all the items stored in the Office Clipboard into the current worksheet by clicking the Paste All button at the top of the Clipboard task pane. To clear the Office Clipboard of all the current items, click the Clear All button. To delete only a particular item from the Office Clipboard, position the mouse pointer over the item in the Clipboard task pane until its drop-down button appears. Click this drop-down button, and then select Delete from the pop-up menu (refer to Figure 4-10).

TIP

To have the Clipboard task pane appear automatically after making two cuts or copies to the Clipboard in an Excel workbook, click the Show Office Clipboard Automatically option on the task pane's Options button menu. To open the Clipboard task pane in the Excel program window by pressing Ctrl+CC, click Show Office Clipboard When Ctrl+C Pressed Twice on the task pane's Options button. Pressing Ctrl+CC only opens the task pane. You still have to click the Close button on the Office Clipboard to close the task pane.

So what's so special about Paste Special?

Normally, unless you fool around with the Paste Options (see the section "Keeping pace with Paste Options," earlier in this chapter), Excel copies all the information in the range of cells you selected: formatting, as well the formulas, text, and other values you enter. You can use the Paste Special command to specify which entries and formatting to use in the current paste operation. Many of the Paste Special options are also available on the Paste Options palette.

To paste particular parts of a cell selection while discarding others, click the drop-down button that appears at the bottom of the Paste command button on the Ribbon's Home tab. Then, click Paste Special on its drop-down menu to open the Paste Special dialog box, shown in Figure 4-11.

The options in the Paste Special dialog box include:

>> **All** to paste all the stuff in the cell selection (formulas, formatting, you name it).

>> **Formulas** to paste all the text, numbers, and formulas in the current cell selection without their formatting.

>> **Values** to convert formulas in the current cell selection to their calculated values.

>> **Formats** to paste only the formatting from the current cell selection, leaving the cell entries in the dust.

>> **Comments** to paste only the notes that you attach to their cells (kind of like electronic self-stick notes — see Chapter 6 for details).

>> **Validation** to paste only the data validation rules into the cell range that you set up with the Data Validation command (which enables you to set what value or range of values is allowed in a particular cell or cell range).

>> **All Using Source Theme** to paste all the information plus the cell styles applied to the cells.

>> **All Except Borders** to paste all the stuff in the cell selection without copying any borders you use there.

>> **Column Widths** to apply the column widths of the cells copied to the Clipboard to the columns where the cells are pasted.

>> **Formulas and Number Formats** to include the number formats assigned to the pasted values and formulas.

>> **Values and Number Formats** to convert formulas to their calculated values and include the number formats you assign to all the pasted values.

>> **All Merging Conditional Formats** to paste Conditional Formatting into the cell range.

- >> **None** to prevent Excel from performing any mathematical operation between the data entries you cut or copy to the Clipboard and the data entries in the cell range where you paste.

- >> **Add** to add the data you cut or copy to the Clipboard and the data entries in the cell range where you paste.

- >> **Subtract** to subtract the data you cut or copy to the Clipboard from the data entries in the cell range where you paste.

- >> **Multiply** to multiply the data you cut or copy to the Clipboard by the data entries in the cell range where you paste.

- >> **Divide** to divide the data you cut or copy to the Clipboard by the data entries in the cell range where you paste.

- >> **Skip Blanks** check box when you want Excel to paste everywhere except for any empty cells in the incoming range. In other words, a blank cell cannot overwrite your current cell entries.

- >> **Transpose** check box when you want Excel to change the orientation of the pasted entries. For example, if the original cells' entries run down the rows of a single column of the worksheet, the transposed pasted entries will run across the columns of a single row.

- >> **Paste Link** button when you're copying cell entries and you want to establish a link between copies you're pasting and the original entries. That way, changes to the original cells automatically update in the pasted copies.

Let's Be Clear About Deleting Stuff

No discussion about editing in Excel would be complete without a section on getting rid of the stuff you put into cells. You can perform two kinds of deletions in a worksheet:

- >> **Clearing a cell:** Clearing just deletes or empties the cell's contents without removing the cell from the worksheet, which would alter the layout of the surrounding cells.

- >> **Deleting a cell:** Deleting gets rid of the whole kit and caboodle — cell structure along with all its contents and formatting. When you delete a cell, Excel has to shuffle the position of entries in the surrounding cells to plug up any gaps made by the action.

Sounding the all clear!

To get rid of just the contents of a cell selection rather than delete the cells and their contents, select the range of cells to clear and then simply press the Delete key.

If you want to get rid of more than just the contents of a cell selection, click the Clear button (the one with the eraser) in the Editing group on the Ribbon's Home tab and then click one of the following options on its drop-down menu:

>> **Clear All:** Gets rid of all formatting and notes, as well as entries in the cell selection (Alt+HEA)

>> **Clear Formats:** Deletes only the formatting from the cell selection without touching anything else (Alt+HEF)

>> **Clear Contents:** Deletes only the entries in the cell selection just like pressing the Delete key (Alt+HEC)

>> **Clear Comments:** Removes the notes in the cell selection but leaves everything else behind (Alt+HEM)

>> **Clear Hyperlinks:** Removes the active hyperlinks (see Chapter 12) in the cell selection but leaves its descriptive text (Alt+HEL)

>> **Remove Hyperlinks:** Removes the active hyperlinks in the cell selection along with all the formatting (Alt+HER)

Get these cells outta here!

To delete the cell selection rather than just clear out its contents, select the cell range, click the drop-down button attached to the Delete command button in the Cells group of the Home tab, and then click Delete Cells on the drop-down menu (or press Alt+HDD). The Delete dialog box opens, showing options for filling in the gaps created when the cells currently selected are blotted out of existence:

>> **Shift Cells Left:** This default option moves entries from neighboring columns on the right to the left to fill in gaps created when you delete the cell selection by clicking OK or pressing Enter.

>> **Shift Cells Up:** Select this to move entries up from neighboring rows below.

>> **Entire Row:** Select this to remove all the rows in the current cell selection.

>> **Entire Columns:** Select this to delete all the columns in the current cell selection.

TIP

If you know that you want to shift the remaining cells to the left after deleting the cells in the current selection, you can simply click the Delete command button on the Home tab of the Ribbon. This is the same thing as opening the Delete dialog box and then clicking OK when the default Shift Cells Left button is selected.

To delete an entire column or row from the worksheet, you can select the column or row on the Workbook window frame, right-click the selection, and then click Delete from the column's or row's shortcut menu.

REMEMBER

You can also delete entire columns and rows selected in the worksheet by clicking the drop-down button attached to the Delete command button on the Ribbon's Home tab and then clicking the Delete Sheet Columns (Alt+HDC) option or the Delete Sheet Rows option (Alt+HDR) on the drop-down menu.

WARNING

Deleting entire columns and rows from a worksheet is risky business unless you are sure that the columns and rows in question contain nothing of value. Remember, when you delete an entire row from the worksheet, you delete *all information from column A through XFD* in that row (and you can see only a very few columns in this row). Likewise, when you delete an entire column from the worksheet, you delete *all information from row 1 through 1,048,576* in that column.

Staying in Step with Insert

For those inevitable times when you need to squeeze new entries into an already populated region of the worksheet, you can insert new cells in the area rather than go through all the trouble of moving and rearranging several individual cell ranges. To insert a new cell range, select the cells (many of which are already occupied) where you want the new cells to appear and then click the drop-down button on the right end of the Insert command button (rather than the button itself) in the Cells group of the Home tab and then click Insert Cells on the drop-down menu (or press Alt+HII). The Insert dialog box opens with the following option buttons:

>> **Shift Cells Right:** Select this to shift existing cells to the right to make room for the ones you want to add before clicking OK or pressing Enter.

>> **Shift Cells Down:** Use this default to instruct the program to shift existing entries down before clicking OK or pressing Enter.

>> **Entire Row** or **Entire Column:** When you insert cells with the Insert dialog box, you can insert complete rows or columns in the cell range by selecting either of these radio buttons. You can also select the row number or column letter on the frame before you select the Insert command.

TIP

If you know that you want to shift the existing cells to the right to make room for the newly inserted cells, you can simply click the Insert command button on the Ribbon's Home tab (this is the same thing as opening the Insert dialog box and then clicking OK when the Shift Cells Right button is selected).

REMEMBER

Remember that you can also insert entire columns and rows in a worksheet by right-clicking the selection and then clicking Insert on the column's or row's shortcut menu.

WARNING

As when you delete whole columns and rows, inserting entire columns and rows affects the entire worksheet, not just the part you see. If you don't know what's out in the hinterlands of the worksheet, you can't be sure how the insertion will affect — perhaps even sabotage — stuff (especially formulas) in the other unseen areas. I suggest that you scroll all the way out in both directions to make sure that nothing's out there.

Stamping Out Your Spelling Errors

If you've become as poor a speller as I have, you'll be relieved to know that Excel 2019 has a built-in spell checker that can catch and remove all those embarrassing little spelling errors. With this in mind, you no longer have any excuse for putting out worksheets with typos in the titles or headings.

To check the spelling in a worksheet, you have the following options:

>> Click the Spelling command button on the Ribbon's Review tab

>> Press Alt+RS

>> Press F7

Any way you do it, Excel begins checking the spelling of all text entries in the worksheet. When the program comes across an unknown word, it displays the Spelling dialog box, similar to the one shown in Figure 4-12.

Excel suggests replacements for the unknown word shown in the Not in Dictionary text box with a likely replacement in the Suggestions list box of the Spelling dialog box. If that replacement is incorrect, you can scroll through the Suggestions list and click the correct replacement. Use the Spelling dialog box options as follows:

FIGURE 4-12:
Check your spelling from the Spelling dialog box.

>> **Ignore Once** and **Ignore All:** When Excel's spell check comes across a word its dictionary finds suspicious but you know is viable, click the Ignore Once button. If you don't want the spell checker to bother querying you about this word again, click the Ignore All button.

>> **Add to Dictionary:** Click this button to add the unknown (to Excel) word — such as your name — to a custom dictionary so that Excel won't flag it again when you check the spelling in the worksheet later on.

>> **Change:** Click this button to replace the word listed in the Not in Dictionary text box with the word Excel offers in the Suggestions list box.

>> **Change All:** Click this button to change all occurrences of this misspelled word in the worksheet to the word Excel displays in the Suggestions list box.

>> **AutoCorrect:** Click this button to have Excel automatically correct this spelling error with the suggestion displayed in the Suggestions list box (by adding the misspelling and suggestion to the AutoCorrect dialog box; for more, read Chapter 2).

>> **Dictionary Language:** To switch to another dictionary (such as a United Kingdom English dictionary, or a French dictionary when checking French terms in a multilingual worksheet), click this drop-down button and then select the name of the desired language in the list.

>> **Options button:** To open the Proofing tab in the Excel Options dialog box where you can modify the current Excel spell-check settings such as Ignore Words in Uppercase, Ignore Words with Numbers, and the like.

Notice that the Excel spell checker not only flags words not found in its built-in or custom dictionary but also flags occurrences of double words in a cell entry (such as *total total*) and words with unusual capitalization (such as *NEw York* instead of *New York*). By default, the spell checker ignores all words with numbers and all Internet addresses. If you want it to ignore all words in uppercase letters as well, click the Options button at the bottom of the Spelling dialog box, and then select the Ignore Words in UPPERCASE check box before clicking OK.

TIP

You can check the spelling of just a particular group of entries by selecting the cells before you click the Spelling command button on the Review tab of the Ribbon or press F7.

REMEMBER

Excel also has a Thesaurus pane that enables you to find synonyms for the label entered into the cell that's current when you open the pane (or that you type into its text box). To open the Thesaurus pane, select Review⇨Thesaurus in the Proofing group at the beginning of the Review tab on the Ribbon or press Shift+F7. Excel then opens a pane showing a list of all the synonyms for the label in the current cell or the term manually entered in its text box. To view more synonyms for a particular term in the list, select it. To replace the label entered in the current cell with a term in the Thesaurus list, select Insert on the term's drop-down menu.

Eliminating Errors with Text to Speech

The good news is that Excel 2019 still supports the Text to Speech feature first introduced way back in Excel 2003. This feature enables your computer to read aloud any series of cell entries in the worksheet. By using Text to Speech, you can check your printed source while the computer reads aloud the values and labels that you've actually entered — a real nifty way to catch and correct errors that may otherwise escape unnoticed.

REMEMBER

The Text to Speech translation feature requires no prior training or special microphones: All that's required is a pair of speakers or headphones connected to your computer.

Now for the bad news: Text to Speech is not available from any of the tabs on the Ribbon. The only way to access Text to Speech is by adding its Speak Cells command buttons as custom buttons on the Quick Access toolbar or to a custom tab on the Ribbon.

Here are the steps for adding the Text to Speech command buttons to the Quick Access toolbar (shown in Figure 4-13):

1. **Click the Customize Quick Access Toolbar button at the end of the toolbar followed by the More Commands on the Customize Quick Access toolbar drop-down menu.**

    The Excel Options dialog box opens with the Customize Access Toolbar tab selected.

2. **Click Commands Not in the Ribbon on the Choose Commands From drop-down menu and scroll down the list until you see the Speak Cells command.**

   The Text to Speech command buttons include Speak Cells, Speak Cells – Stop Speaking Cells, Speak Cells by Columns, Speak Cells by Rows, and Speak Cells on Enter.

3. **Click the Speak Cells button in the Choose Commands From list box on the left and then click the Add button to add it to the Quick Access toolbar following the Redo button.**

4. **Click the Add button repeatedly until you've added the remaining Text to Speech buttons to the custom group: Speak Cells – Stop Speaking Cells, Speak Cells by Columns, Speak Cells by Rows, and Speak Cells on Enter.**

   To reposition the speech command buttons on the Quick Access toolbar, select the button and then move it up or down in the list (which corresponds to left and right, respectively, on the toolbar) with the Move Up and Move Down.

5. **Click the OK button to close the Excel Options dialog box.**

Figure 4-13 shows the Quick Access toolbar above my Ribbon in my Excel 2019 program window after I added the speech buttons to it.

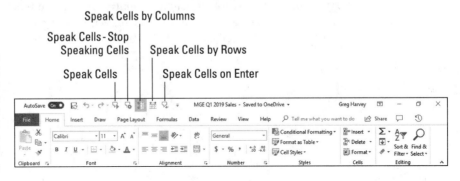

Speak Cells by Columns

Speak Cells - Stop
Speaking Cells   Speak Cells by Rows

Speak Cells   Speak Cells on Enter

FIGURE 4-13: After adding the Speak Cells buttons to the Quick Access toolbar, you can use them to check cell entries audibly.

After adding the Text to Speech commands as custom Speak Cells buttons to your Quick Access toolbar, you can use them to corroborate spreadsheet entries and catch those hard-to-spot errors as follows:

1. **Select the cells in the worksheet whose contents you want read aloud by Text to Speech.**

2. **Click the Speak Cells button on the Quick Access toolbar to have the computer read the entries in the selected cells.**

By default, the Text to Speech feature reads the contents of each cell in the cell selection by reading down each column and then across the rows. If you want Text to Speech to read across the rows and then down the columns, click the Speak Cells by Rows button on the Quick Access toolbar (the button with the two opposing horizontal arrows).

3. **To have the Text to Speech feature read each cell entry while you press the Enter key (at which point the cell cursor moves down to the next cell in the selection), click the Speak Cells on Enter custom button (the button with the curved arrow Enter symbol) on your Quick Access toolbar.**

   As soon as you click the Speak Cells on Enter button, the computer tells you, "Cells will now be spoken on Enter." After selecting this option, you need to press Enter each time that you want to hear an entry read to you.

4. **To pause the Text to Speech feature when you're not using the Speak Cells on Enter option (Step 3) and you locate a discrepancy between what you're reading and what you're hearing, click the Stop Speaking button (the Speak Cells group button with the x).**

REMEMBER

After you click the Speak Cells on Enter button on the Quick Access toolbar, the Text to Speech feature speaks aloud each new cell entry you make after you complete it by pressing any of the keys — Enter, Tab, Shift+Tab, one of the arrow keys, and so forth — that move the cell pointer upon making the cell entry. Text to Speech does not, however, speak a cell entry that you complete by clicking the Enter button on the Formula bar because this action does not move the cell pointer upon completing the cell entry.

Chapter **5**

Printing the Masterpiece

For most people, getting data down on paper is what spreadsheets are all about (all the talk about a so-called paperless office to the contrary). Everything — all the data entry, all the formatting, all the formula checking, all the things you do to get a spreadsheet ready — is really just preparation for printing its information.

In this chapter, you find out just how easy it is to print reports with Excel 2019. Thanks to the program's Print screen in Backstage view (Alt+FP), its Page Layout worksheet view, and its handy Page Layout tab on the Ribbon, you discover how to produce top-notch reports the first time you send the document to the printer (instead of the second or even the third time around).

The only trick to printing a worksheet is getting used to the paging scheme and learning how to control it. Many of the worksheets you create with Excel are not only longer than one printed page, but also wider. Word processors, such as Word 2019, page the document only vertically; they won't let you create a document wider than the page size you're using. Spreadsheet programs like Excel 2019, however, often have to break up pages both vertically and horizontally to print a worksheet document (a kind of tiling of the print job, if you will).

When breaking a worksheet into pages, Excel first pages the document vertically down the rows in the first columns of the print area (just like a word processor). After paging the first columns, the program pages down the rows of the second set of columns in the print area. Excel pages down and then over until the entire document included in the current print area (which can include the entire worksheet or just sections) is paged.

When paging the worksheet, Excel doesn't break up the information within a row or column. If not all the information in a row will fit at the bottom of the page, the program moves the entire row to the following page. If not all the information in a column will fit at the right edge of the page, the program moves the entire column to a new page. (Because Excel pages down and then over, the column may not appear on the next page of the report.)

You can deal with such paging problems in several ways, and in this chapter, you see all of them! After you have these page problems under control, printing is a proverbial piece of cake.

Previewing Pages in Page Layout View

Excel 2019's Page Layout view gives you instant access to the paging of the current worksheet. Activate this feature by clicking the Page Layout View button (the center one) to the immediate left of the Zoom slider on the Status bar or by clicking the Page Layout command button on the Ribbon's View tab (Alt+WP). As you can see in Figure 5-1, when you switch to Page Layout view, Excel adds horizontal and vertical rulers to the column letter and row number headings. In the

Worksheet area, this view shows the margins for each printed page, any headers and footers defined for the report, and the breaks between each page. (Often, you have to use the Zoom slider to reduce the screen magnification to display the page breaks onscreen.)

FIGURE 5-1:
Viewing a
spreadsheet in
Page Layout view.

TIP

To see all the pages in the active worksheet, drag the slider button in the Zoom slider on the Status bar to the left until you decrease the screen magnification sufficiently to display all the pages of data.

REMEMBER

Excel displays rulers using the default units for your computer (inches on a U.S. computer and centimeters on a European machine). To change the units, open the Advanced tab of the Excel Options dialog box (File⇨Options⇨Advanced or Alt+FTA) and then select the appropriate unit (Inches, Centimeters, or Millimeters) on the Ruler Units drop-down menu in the Display section.

The Ruler check box on the View tab acts as a toggle switch so that the first time you click this box, Excel removes the rulers from the Page Layout view, and the second time you click it, the program adds them again.

Using the Backstage Print Screen

To save paper and your sanity, print your worksheet directly from the Print screen in Excel's Backstage view by selecting File⇨Print (or simply pressing Ctrl+P or Ctrl+F2) so that you can check everything before sending it to the printer (unlike when using the Quick Print command that immediately begins the printing). As you see in Figure 5-2, the Print screen shows you at-a-glance your current print settings along with a preview of the first page of the printout.

FIGURE 5-2:
The Print screen in Backstage view shows your current print settings plus a preview of the printout.

TIP

You can also add a Print Preview and Print command button to the Quick Access toolbar that opens this Print screen in the Backstage view. Simply click the Customize Quick Access Toolbar button followed by the Print Preview and Print option on its drop-down menu to add this button at the end of the toolbar. Then click this button anytime you want to preview a report before sending it to your printer.

You can use the Print Preview feature in the Print screen before you print any worksheet, section of worksheet, or entire workbook. Because of the peculiarities in paging worksheet data, you often need to check the page breaks for any report that requires more than one page. The print preview area in the Print panel shows you exactly how the worksheet data will page when printed. If necessary, you can return to the worksheet where you can make changes to the page settings from the Page Layout tab on the Ribbon before sending the report to the printer when everything looks okay.

When Excel displays a full page in the print preview area, you can barely read its contents. To increase the view to actual size to verify some of the data, click the Zoom to Page button in the lower-right corner of the Print panel. Check out the difference in Figure 5-3 — you can see what the first page of the four-page report looks like after I zoom in by clicking this Zoom to Page button.

FIGURE 5-3:
Page 1 of a four-page report after clicking the Zoom to Page button.

After you enlarge a page to actual size, use the scroll bars to bring new parts of the page into view in the print preview area. To return to the full-page view, click the Zoom to Page button a second time to deselect it.

Excel indicates the number of pages in a report at the bottom of the print preview area. If your report has more than one page, you can view pages that follow by clicking the Next Page button to the right of the final page number. To review a page you've already seen, back up a page by clicking the Previous Page button to the left of the first page number. (The Previous Page button is gray if you're on the first page.)

TIP

To display markers indicating the current left, right, top, and bottom margins along with the column widths, click the Show Margins button to the immediate left of the Zoom to Page button. You can then modify the column widths as well as the page margins by dragging the appropriate marker (see "Massaging the margins" later in this chapter for details).

When you finish previewing the report, the Print screen offers you the following options for changing certain print settings before you send it to the printer:

>> **Print** button with the **Number of Copies** combo box: Use this button to print the spreadsheet report using the current print settings listed on the panel. Use the combo box to indicate the number of copies you want when you need multiple copies printed.

>> **Printer** drop-down button: Use this button to select a new printer or fax to send the spreadsheet report to when more than one device is installed. (Excel automatically displays the name of the printer that's installed as the default printer in Windows.)

>> **Settings** drop-down buttons: These include a **Print What** drop-down button with attendant **Pages** combo boxes: Use the Print What drop-down button to choose between printing only the active (selected) worksheets in the workbook (the default), the entire workbook, the current cell selection in the current worksheet, and the currently selected table in the current worksheet. Use the Pages combo boxes to restrict what's printed to just the range of pages you enter in these boxes or select with their spinner buttons.

Beneath the combo boxes, you find drop-down list buttons to collate the pages of the report, and switch the page orientation from Portrait (aligned with the short side) to Landscape (aligned with the long side). Additionally, you can select a paper size based on your printer's capabilities other than the default 8.5" x 11" letter, and customize the size of the report's margins (top, bottom, left, and right, as well as the margins for any header and footer on the page).

Printing the Current Worksheet

As long as you want to use Excel's default print settings to print all the cells in the current worksheet, printing in Excel 2019 is a breeze. Simply add the Quick Print button to the Quick Access toolbar (by clicking the Customize Quick Access Toolbar button followed by Quick Print on its drop-down menu).

After adding the Quick Print button to the Quick Access toolbar, you can use this button to print a single copy of all the information in the current worksheet, including any charts and graphics — but not including comments you add to cells. (See Chapter 6 for details about adding comments to your worksheet and Chapter 10 for details about charts and graphics.)

When you click the Quick Print button, Excel routes the print job to the Windows print queue, which acts like a middleman and sends the job to the printer. While Excel sends the print job to the print queue, Excel displays a Printing dialog box to inform you of its progress (displaying such updates as *Printing Page 2 of 3*). After this dialog box disappears, you are free to go back to work in Excel. To stop the printing while the job is still being sent to the print queue, click the Cancel button in the Printing dialog box.

If you don't realize that you want to cancel the print job until after Excel finishes shipping it to the print queue (that is, while the Printing dialog box appears onscreen), you must do the following:

1. **Click the printer icon in the Notification area at the far right of the Windows 10 taskbar (to the immediate left of the current time) with the secondary mouse button to open its shortcut menu.**

   This printer icon displays the ScreenTip *1 document(s) pending for so-and-so*. For example, when I'm printing, this message reads *1 document(s) pending for Greg* when I position the mouse pointer over the printer icon.

2. **Right-click the printer icon and then select the Open All Active Printers command from its shortcut menu.**

   This opens the dialog box for the printer with the Excel print job in its queue (as described under the Document Name heading in the list box).

3. **Select the Excel print job that you want to cancel in the list box of your printer's dialog box.**

4. **Select Document ⇨ Cancel from the menu and then click Yes to confirm you want to cancel the print job.**

5. **Wait for the print job to disappear from the queue in the printer's dialog box and then click the Close button to return to Excel.**

UNDERSTANDING AND USING THE PRINT AREA

Excel includes a special printing feature called Print Area. Click Print Area ⇨ Set Print Area on the Ribbon's Page Layout tab or press Alt+PRS to define any cell selection on the current worksheet as the print area. Note that you can define a separate print area for each worksheet in your workbook. After you define the print area, Excel then prints this cell selection anytime you print the worksheet with the Quick Print button added to the Quick Access toolbar.

After you define the print area, its cell range is the only one you can print for the active worksheet (regardless of what other Print What option you select in the Settings section of the Backstage Print screen). That is, unless you click the Ignore Print Area option at the very bottom of the Print What drop-down list or clear the print area. To clear the print area (and return to the printing defaults that Excel establishes in the Print dialog box), click Print Area ⇨ Clear Print Area on the Page Layout tab or simply press Alt+PRC.

You can also define and clear the print area from the Sheet tab of the Page Setup dialog box by clicking the Dialog Box launcher in the Page Setup group on the Ribbon's Page Layout tab. To define the print area from this dialog box, click the Print Area text box on the Sheet tab to insert the cursor and then select the cell range or ranges in the worksheet (remembering that you can reduce the Page Setup dialog box to just this text box by clicking the Print Area Collapse/Expand button). To clear the print area from this dialog box, select the cell addresses in the Print Area text box and press the Delete key.

My Page Was Set Up!

About the only thing the slightest bit complex in printing a worksheet is figuring out how to get the pages right. Fortunately, the command buttons in the Page Setup group on the Ribbon's Page Layout tab give you a great deal of control over what goes on which page.

Three groups of buttons on the Page Layout tab help you get your page settings exactly as you want them. The Page Setup group, the Scale to Fit group, and the Sheet Options group are described in the following sections.

TIP

To see the effect of changes you make in the Worksheet area, put the worksheet into Page Layout view by clicking the Page Layout button on the Status bar while you work with the command buttons in the Page Setup, Scale to Fit, and Sheet Options groups on the Page Layout tab of the Ribbon.

Using the buttons in the Page Setup group

The Page Setup group of the Page Layout tab contains the following important command buttons:

» **Margins** button to select one of three preset margins for the report or to set custom margins on the Margins tab of the Page Setup dialog box. (See "Massaging the margins" that follows in this chapter.)

» **Orientation** button to switch between Portrait and Landscape mode for printing. (See the "Getting the lay of the landscape" section, later in this chapter.)

» **Size** button to select one of the preset paper sizes, set a custom size, or change the printing resolution or page number on the Page tab of the Page Setup dialog box.

» **Print Area** button to set and clear the print area. (See the nearby "Understanding and using the print area" sidebar.)

» **Breaks** button to insert or remove page breaks. (See "Solving Page Break Problems" later in this chapter.)

» **Background** button to open the Sheet Background dialog box where you can select a new graphic image or photo to use as a background for the current worksheet. (This button changes to Delete Background as soon as you select a background image.)

» **Print Titles** button to open the Sheet tab of the Page Setup dialog box where you can define rows of the worksheet to repeat at the top and columns of the worksheet to repeat at the left as print titles for the report. (See "Putting out the print titles" later in this chapter.)

Massaging the margins

The Normal margin settings that Excel applies to a new report use standard top, bottom, left, and right margins of ¾ inch with just over ¼ inch separating the header and footer from the top and bottom margin, respectively.

In addition to the Normal margin settings, the program enables you to select two other standard margins from the Margins button's drop-down menu:

» **Wide** margins with 1-inch top, bottom, left, and right margins and ½ inch separating the header and footer from the top and bottom margin, respectively

» **Narrow** margins with a top and bottom margin of ¾ inch and a left and right margin of ¼ inch with 0.3 inch separating the header and footer from the top and bottom margin, respectively

Frequently, you find yourself with a report that takes up a full printed page and then just enough to spill over onto a second, mostly empty, page. To squeeze the last column or the last few rows of the worksheet data onto Page 1, try selecting Narrow on the Margins button's drop-down menu.

If that doesn't do it, you can try manually adjusting the margins for the report from the Margins tab of the Page Setup dialog box or by dragging the margin markers in the preview area of the Print screen in the Backstage view (Press Ctrl+P and click the Show Margins button). To get more columns on a page, try reducing the left and right margins. To get more rows on a page, try reducing the top and bottom margins.

To open the Margins tab of the Page Setup dialog box (shown in Figure 5-4), select Custom Margins on the Margins button's drop-down menu. There, enter the new settings in the Top, Bottom, Left, and Right text boxes — or select the new margin settings with their respective spinner buttons.

FIGURE 5-4:
Adjust your report margins from the Margins tab in the Page Setup dialog box.

TIP

Select one or both Center on Page options in the Margins tab of the Page Setup dialog box (refer to Figure 5-4) to center a selection of data (that takes up less than a full page) between the current margin settings. In the Center on Page section, select the Horizontally check box to center the data between the left and right margins. Select the Vertically check box to center the data between the top and bottom margins.

When you click the Show Margins button in the Print screen in the Excel Backstage view (Ctrl+P) to modify the margin settings directly, you can also massage the column widths as well as the margins. (See Figure 5-5.) To change one of the margins, position the mouse pointer on the desired margin marker (the pointer shape changes to a double-headed arrow) and drag the marker with your mouse in the appropriate direction. When you release the mouse button, Excel redraws the page, using the new margin setting. You may gain or lose columns or rows, depending on what kind of adjustment you make. Changing the column widths is the same story: Drag the column marker to the left or right to decrease or increase the width of a particular column.

FIGURE 5-5:
Drag a marker to adjust its margin in the page preview area of the Print screen when the Show Margins button is selected.

Show Margins

Getting the lay of the landscape

The drop-down menu attached to the Orientation button in the Page Setup group of the Ribbon's Page Layout tab contains two options:

» **Portrait** (the default), where the printing runs parallel to the short edge of the paper

» **Landscape,** where the printing runs parallel to the long edge of the paper

Because many worksheets are far wider than they are tall (such as budgets or sales tables that track expenditures over 12 months), you may find that wider worksheets page better if you switch the orientation from Portrait mode (which accommodates fewer columns on a page because the printing runs parallel to the short edge of the page) to Landscape mode.

In Figure 5-6, you can see the Print Preview window with the first page of a report in Landscape mode in the Page Layout view. For this report, Excel can fit three more columns of information on this page in Landscape mode than it can in Portrait mode. However, because this page orientation accommodates fewer rows, the total page count for this report increases from two pages in Portrait mode to four pages in Landscape mode.

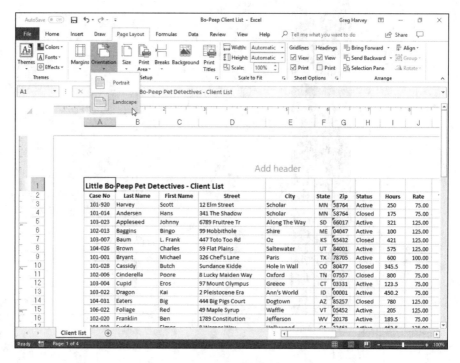

FIGURE 5-6:
A Landscape mode report in Page Layout view.

Putting out the print titles

Excel's Print Titles feature enables you to print particular row and column headings on each page of the report. Print titles are important in multipage reports where the columns and rows of related data spill over to other pages that no longer show the row and column headings on the first page.

REMEMBER

Don't confuse print titles with the header of a report (see "From Header to Footer" later in this chapter). Even though both are printed on each page, header information prints in the top margin of the report; print titles always appear in the body of the report — at the top, in the case of rows used as print titles, and on the left, in the case of columns.

To designate rows and/or columns as the print titles for a report, follow these steps:

1. **Click the Print Titles button on the Page Layout tab on the Ribbon or press Alt+PI.**

The Page Setup dialog box appears with the Sheet tab selected (see Figure 5-7).

To designate worksheet rows as print titles, go to Step 2a. To designate worksheet columns as print titles, go to Step 2b.

2a. **Click in the Rows to Repeat at Top text box and then drag through the rows with information you want to appear at the top of each page in the worksheet below. If necessary, reduce the Page Setup dialog box to just the Rows to Repeat at Top text box by clicking the text box's Collapse/Expand button.**

For the example shown in Figure 5-7, I clicked the Collapse/Expand button associated with the Rows to Repeat at Top text box and then dragged through rows 1 and 2 in column A of the Little Bo-Peep Pet Detectives – Client List worksheet. Excel entered the row range $1:$2 in the Rows to Repeat at Top text box.

Excel indicates the print-title rows in the worksheet by placing a dotted line (that moves like a marquee) on the border between the titles and the information in the body of the report.

2b. **Click in the Columns to Repeat at Left text box and then drag through the range of columns with the information you want to appear at the left edge of each page of the printed report in the worksheet below. If necessary, reduce the Page Setup dialog box to just the Columns to Repeat at Left text box by clicking the text box's Collapse/Expand button.**

Excel indicates the print-title columns in the worksheet by placing a dotted line (that moves like a marquee) on the border between the titles and the information in the body of the report.

3. **Click OK or press Enter to close the Page Setup dialog box.**

The dotted line showing the border of the row and/or column titles disappears from the worksheet.

FIGURE 5-7:
Specify the rows and columns to use as print titles on the Sheet tab of the Page Setup dialog box.

In Figure 5-7, rows 1 and 2 containing the worksheet title and column headings for the Little Bo-Peep Pet Detectives client database are designated as the print titles for the report in the Page Setup dialog box. In Figure 5-8, you can see the Print Preview window with the second page of the report. Note how these print titles appear on all pages of the report.

REMEMBER

To clear print titles from a report if you no longer need them, open the Sheet tab of the Page Setup dialog box and then delete the row and column ranges from the Rows to Repeat at Top and the Columns to Repeat at Left text boxes. Click OK or press Enter.

Using the buttons in the Scale to Fit group

If your printer supports scaling options, you're in luck. You can always get a worksheet to fit on a single page simply by selecting the 1 Page option on the Width and Height drop-down menus attached to their command buttons in the Scale to Fit group on the Ribbon's Page Layout tab. When you select these options, Excel figures out how much to reduce the size of the information you're printing to fit it all on one page.

FIGURE 5-8:
Page 2 of a sample report in Print Preview with defined print titles.

After clicking the Page Break Preview button on the Status bar, you might preview this page in the Print screen in the Backstage view (Ctrl+P) and find that the printing is just too small to read comfortably. Go back to the Normal worksheet view (Esc), select the Page Layout tab on the Ribbon, and try changing the number of pages in the Width and Height drop-down menus in the Scale to Fit group.

TIP

Instead of trying to stuff everything on one page, check out how your worksheet looks if you fit it on two pages across. Try this: Select 2 Pages on the Width button's drop-down menu on the Page Layout tab and leave 1 Page selected in the Height drop-down list button. Alternatively, see how the worksheet looks on two pages down: Select 1 Page on the Width button's drop-down menu and 2 Pages on the Height button's drop-down menu.

TIP

After using the Width and Height Scale to Fit options, you may find that you don't want to scale the printing. Cancel scaling by selecting Automatic on both the Width and Height drop-down menus and then entering **100** in the Scale text box (or select 100% with its spinner buttons).

Using the Print buttons in the Sheet Options group

The Sheet Options group on the Page Layout tab of the Ribbon contains two very useful Print check boxes (neither of which is selected automatically). The first is in the Gridlines column and the second is in the Headings column:

>> Select the Print check box in the Gridlines column to print the column and row gridlines on each page of the report.

>> Select the Print check box in the Headings column to print the row headings with the row numbers and the column headings with the column letters on each page of the report.

Select both check boxes (by clicking them to put check marks in them) when you want the printed version of your spreadsheet data to closely match its onscreen appearance. This is useful when you need to use the cell references on the printout to help you later locate the cells in the actual worksheet that need editing.

TIP

From Header to Footer

Headers and footers are simply standard text that appears on every page of the report. A header prints in the top margin of the page, and a footer prints — you guessed it — in the bottom margin. Both are centered vertically in the margins. Unless you specify otherwise, Excel does not automatically add either a header or footer to a new workbook.

Use headers and footers in a report to identify the document used to produce the report and display the page numbers and the date and time of printing.

TIP

The place to add a header or footer to a report is in Page Layout view. You can switch to this view by clicking the Page Layout View button on the Status bar or by clicking the Page Layout View button on the Ribbon's View tab, or by just pressing Alt+WP.

When the worksheet is in Page Layout view, position the mouse pointer over the section in the top margin of the first page marked Add Header or in the bottom margin of the first page marked Add Footer.

To create a centered header or footer, click the center section of this header/footer area to set the insertion point in the middle of the section. To add a left-aligned header or footer, click the left section to set the insertion point flush with the left edge. To add a right-aligned header or footer, click the right section to set the insertion point flush with the right edge.

REMEMBER

Immediately after setting the insertion point in the left, center, or right section of the header/footer area, Excel adds a Header & Footer Tools contextual tab with its own Design tab (see Figure 5-9). The Design tab is divided into Header & Footer, Header & Footer Elements, Navigation, and Options groups.

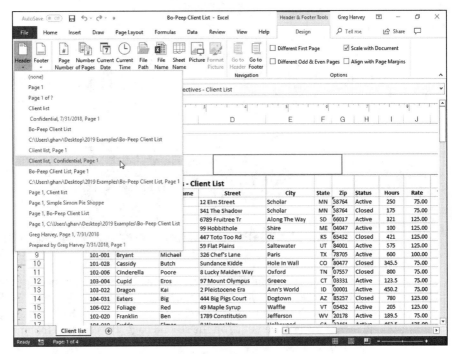

FIGURE 5-9: Defining a new header using the buttons on the Design tab of the Header & Footer Tools contextual tab.

Adding an Auto Header and Footer

The Header and Footer command buttons on the Design tab of the Header & Footer Tools contextual tab enable you to add stock headers and footers in an instant. Simply click the appropriate command button and then click the header or footer example you want to use on the Header or Footer drop-down menu that appears.

To create the centered header and footer for the report shown in Figure 5-10, I selected Client List, Confidential, Page 1 on the Header command button's drop-down menu. Client List is the name of the worksheet; Confidential is stock text; and Page 1 is, of course, the current page number.

To set up the footer, I chose Page 1 of ? in the Footer command button's drop-down menu (which puts the current page number with the total number of pages in the report). You can select this paging option on either the Header or Footer button's drop-down menu.

FIGURE 5-10:
The first page of a report in Page Layout view shows you how the header and footer will print.

Check out the results in Figure 5-10, which is the first page of the report in Page Layout view. Here you can see the header and footer as they will print. You can also see how choosing Page 1 of ? works in the footer: On the first page, you see the centered footer Page 1 of 4; on the second page, the centered footer reads Page 2 of 4.

TIP

If, after selecting some stock header or footer info, you decide that you no longer need either the header or footer printed in your report, you can remove it. Simply click the (None) option at the top of the Header button's or Footer button's drop-down menu. (Remember that the Design tab with the Header and Footer command buttons under the Header & Footer Tools contextual tab is selected on the Ribbon the moment you click the header or footer in Page Layout view.)

Creating a custom header or footer

Most of the time, the stock headers and footers available on the Header button's and Footer button's drop-down menus are sufficient for your report-printing needs. Occasionally, however, you may want to insert information not available in these list boxes or in an arrangement that Excel doesn't offer in the ready-made headers and footers.

For those times, you need to use the command buttons that appear in the Header & Footer Elements group of the Design tab on the Header & Footer Tools contextual tab. These command buttons enable you to blend your own information with that generated by Excel into different sections of the custom header or footer you're creating.

The command buttons in the Header & Footer Elements group include

- **Page Number:** Click this button to insert the &[Page] code that puts in the current page number.

- **Number of Pages:** Click this button to insert the &[Pages] code that puts in the total number of pages.

- **Current Date:** Click this button to insert the &[Date] code that puts in the current date.

- **Current Time:** Click this button to insert the &[Time] code that puts in the current time.

- **File Path:** Click this button to insert the &[Path]&[File] codes that put in the directory path along with the name of the workbook file.

- **File Name:** Click this button to insert the &[File] code that puts in the name of the workbook file.

- **Sheet Name:** Click this button to insert the &[Tab] code that puts in the name of the worksheet as shown on the sheet tab.

- **Picture:** Click this button to insert the &[Picture] code that inserts the image that you select from the Insert Picture dialog box that enables you to select a local image (using the From File option) or download one from an online source (using the Bing Image Search, OneDrive, or Facebook and Flickr options). See Chapter 10 for more details on inserting graphics.

- **Format Picture:** Click this button to apply the formatting that you choose from the Format Picture dialog box to the &[Picture] code that you enter with the Insert Picture button without adding any code of its own.

To use these command buttons in the Header & Footer Elements group to create a custom header or footer, follow these steps:

1. **Put your worksheet into Page Layout view by clicking the Page Layout View button on the Status bar or by clicking View ⇨ Page Layout View on the Ribbon or pressing Alt+WP.**

   In Page Layout view, the text Click to Add Header appears centered in the top margin of the first page and the text Click to Add Footer appears centered in the bottom margin.

2. **Position the mouse pointer in the top margin to create a custom header or the bottom margin to create a custom footer and then click the pointer in the left, center, or right section of the header or footer to set the insertion point and left-align, center, or right-align the text.**

When Excel sets the insertion point, the text Click to Add Header and Click to Add Footer disappears and the Design tab on the Header & Footer Tools contextual tab becomes active on the Ribbon.

3. **To add program-generated information to your custom header or footer (such as the filename, worksheet name, current date, and so forth), click the information's corresponding command button in the Header & Footer Elements group.**

Excel inserts the appropriate header/footer code preceded by an ampersand (&) into the header or footer. These codes are replaced by the actual information (filename, worksheet name, graphic image, and the like) as soon as you click another section of the header or footer or finish the header or footer by clicking the mouse pointer outside of it.

4. **(Optional) To add your own text to the custom header or footer, type it at the insertion point.**

When joining program-generated information indicated by a header/footer code with your own text, be sure to insert the appropriate spaces and punctuation. For example, to have Excel display Page 1 of 4 in a custom header or footer, you do the following:

(a) *Type the word* **Page** *and press the spacebar.*

(b) *Click the Page Number command button and press the spacebar again.*

(c) *Type the word* **of** *and press the spacebar a third time.*

(d) *Click the Number of Pages command button.*

This inserts *Page &[Page] of &[Pages]* in the custom header (or footer).

5. **(Optional) To modify the font, font size, or some other font attribute of your custom header or footer, drag through its codes and text, click the Home tab, and then click the appropriate command button in the Font group.**

In addition to selecting a new font and font size for the custom header or footer, you can add bold, italic, underlining, and a new font color to its text with the Bold, Italic, Underline, and Font Color command buttons on the Home tab.

6. **After you finish defining and formatting the codes and text for your custom header or footer, click a cell in the Worksheet area to deselect the header or footer area.**

Excel replaces the header/footer codes in the custom header or footer with the actual information, while at the same time removing the Header & Footer Tools contextual tab from the Ribbon.

Figure 5-11 shows you a custom footer I added to a spreadsheet in Page Layout view. This custom footer blends my own text, Preliminary Client List, with a program-generated sheet name, date, and time information, and uses all three sections: left-aligned page information, centered Preliminary Client List text, and right-aligned current date and time.

FIGURE 5-11:
Spreadsheet in Page Layout view showing the custom footer.

Creating first-page headers and footers

Excel 2019 enables you to define a header or footer for the first page that's different from all the rest of the pages. Simply click the Different First Page check box to put a check mark in it. (This check box is part of the Options group of the Design tab on the Header & Footer Tools contextual tab that appears when you're defining or editing a header or footer in Page Layout view.)

After selecting the Different First Page check box, go ahead and define the unique header and/or footer for just the first page (now marked First Page Header or First Page Footer). Then, on the second page of the report, define the header and/or footer (marked simply Header or Footer) for the remaining pages of the report (see "Adding an Auto Header and Footer" and "Creating a custom header or footer" earlier in the chapter for details).

TIP

Use this feature when your spreadsheet report has a cover page that needs no header or footer. For example, suppose that you have a report that needs the current page number and total pages centered at the bottom of all pages except the cover page. To do this, select the Different First Page check box on the Design tab of the Header & Footer Tools contextual tab on the Ribbon. Then define a centered Auto Footer that displays the current page number and total pages (Page 1 of ?) on the second page of the report, leaving the Click to Add Footer text intact on the first page.

Excel will correctly number both the total number of pages in the report and the current page number without printing this information on the first page. For example, if your report has six pages (including the cover page), the second page footer will read Page 2 of 6; the third page, Page 3 of 6; and so on, even if the first printed page has no footer.

Creating even and odd page headers and footers

If you plan to do two-sided printing or copying of your spreadsheet report, you may want to define one header or footer for the even pages and another for the odd pages of the report. That way, the header or footer information (such as the report name or current page) alternates between being right-aligned on the odd pages (printed on the front side of the page) and being left-aligned on the even pages (printed on the back of the page).

To create an alternating header or footer for a report, you click the Different Odd & Even Pages check box to put a check mark in it. (This check box is in the Options group of the Design tab on the Header & Footer Tools contextual tab that appears when you're defining or editing a header or footer in Page Layout view.)

After that, create a header or footer on the first page of the report (now marked Odd Page Header or Odd Page Footer) in the third, right-aligned section of the header or footer area and then re-create this header or footer on the second page (now marked Even Page Header or Even Page Footer), this time in the first, left-aligned section.

Solving Page Break Problems

The Page Break preview feature in Excel 2019 enables you to spot and fix page break problems in an instant, such as when the program wants to split information across different pages that you know should always be on the same page.

Figure 5-12 shows a worksheet in Page Break Preview with an example of a bad vertical page break that you can remedy by adjusting the location of the page break on Page 1 and Page 3. Given the page size, orientation, and margin settings for this report, Excel breaks the page between columns K and L. This break separates the Paid column (L) from all the others in the client list, effectively putting this information on its own Page 3 and Page 4 (not shown in Figure 5-12).

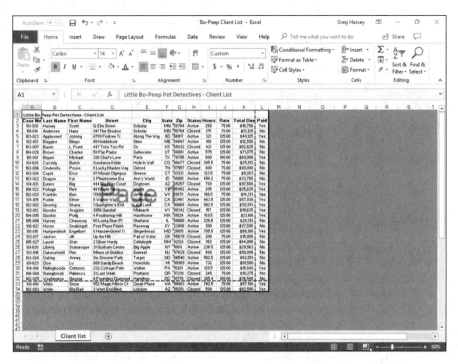

FIGURE 5-12:
Preview page breaks in a report with Page Break Preview.

To prevent the data in the Paid column from printing on its own pages, you need to move the page break to a column on the left. In this case, I moved the page break between columns G (with the zip-code data) and H (containing the account status information) so that the name and address information stays together on Page 1 and Page 2 and the other client data is printed together on Page 3 and

Page 4. Figure 5-13 shows vertical page breaks in the Page Break Preview worksheet view, which you can accomplish by following these steps:

1. **Click the Page Break Preview button (the third one in the cluster to the left of the Zoom slider) on the Status bar, or click View ⇨ Page Break Preview on the Ribbon or press Alt+WI.**

   This takes you into a Page Break Preview worksheet view that shows your worksheet data at a reduced magnification (60 percent of normal in Figure 5-13) with the page numbers displayed in large light type and the page breaks shown by heavy lines between the columns and rows of the worksheet.

   The first time you choose this command, Excel displays a Welcome to Page Break Preview dialog box. To prevent this dialog box from reappearing each time you use Page Break Preview, click the Do Not Show This Dialog Again check box before you close the Welcome to Page Break Preview dialog box.

2. **Click OK or press Enter to get rid of the Welcome to Page Break Preview dialog box.**

3. **Position the mouse pointer somewhere on the page break indicator (one of the heavy lines surrounding the representation of the page) that you need to adjust; when the pointer changes to a double-headed arrow, drag the page indicator to the desired column or row and release the mouse button.**

   For the example shown in Figure 5-13, I dragged the page break indicator between Page 1 and Page 3 to the left so that it's between columns G and H. Excel placed the page break at this point, which puts all the name and address information together on Page 1 and Page 2. This new page break then causes all the other columns of client data to print together on Page 3 and Page 4.

4. **After you finish adjusting the page breaks in Page Break Preview (and, presumably, printing the report), click the Normal button (the first one in the cluster to the left of the Zoom slider) on the Status bar, or click View ⇨ Normal on the Ribbon or press Alt+WL to return the worksheet to its regular view of the data.**

TIP

You can also insert your own manual page breaks at the cell cursor's position by clicking Insert Page Break on the Breaks button's drop-down menu on the Page Layout tab (Alt+PBI) and remove them by clicking Remove Page Break on this menu (Alt+PBR). When the cell cursor is in the top row of the print area and you insert a page break, Excel inserts a single vertical break along the left edge of the current column in the report. When the cell cursor is in one of the rows below, Excel inserts both a vertical and horizontal page break along the left edge of the current column and the top edge of the current row.

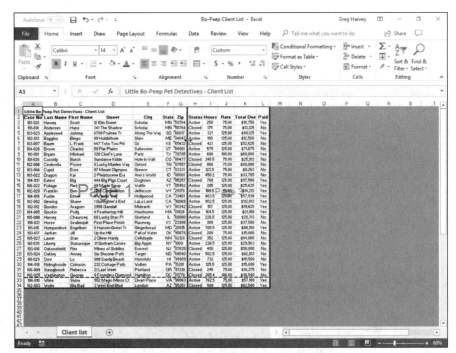

FIGURE 5-13:
Page 1 of the report after adjusting the page breaks in the Page Break Preview worksheet view.

To remove all manual page breaks that you've inserted into a report, click Reset All Page Breaks on the Breaks button's drop-down menu (Alt+PBA).

Letting Your Formulas All Hang Out

A basic printing technique that you may need occasionally is printing the formulas in a worksheet instead of printing the calculated results of the formulas. You can check over a printout of the formulas in your worksheet to make sure that you haven't done anything stupid (like replace a formula with a number or use the wrong cell references in a formula) before you distribute the worksheet company-wide.

Before you can print a worksheet's formulas, you have to display the formulas, rather than their results, in the cells by clicking the Show Formulas button (the one with the icon that looks like a page of a calendar with a tiny 15 that's above the Error Checking button) in the Formula Auditing group on the Ribbon's Formulas tab (Alt+MH).

Excel then displays the contents of each cell in the worksheet the way it appears in the Formula bar or when you're editing it in the cell. Notice that value entries lose their number formatting, formulas appear in their cells (Excel widens the columns with best-fit so that the formulas appear in their entirety), and long text entries no longer spill into neighboring blank cells.

TIP

Excel allows you to toggle between the normal cell display and the formula cell display by pressing Ctrl+`. (That is, press Ctrl and the key with the tilde on top.) This key — usually found in the upper-left corner of your keyboard — does double-duty as a tilde and a weird backward accent mark. (Don't confuse that backward accent mark with the apostrophe that appears on a key below the quotation mark!)

After Excel displays the formulas in the worksheet, you are ready to print it as you would any other report. You can include the worksheet column letters and row numbers as headings in the printout so that if you do spot an error, you can pinpoint the cell reference right away.

REMEMBER

To include the row and column headings in the printout, put a check mark in the Print check box in the Headings column on the Sheet Options group of the Page Layout tab of the Ribbon before you send the report to the printer.

After you print the worksheet with the formulas, return the worksheet to normal by clicking the Show Formulas button on the Formulas tab of the Ribbon or by pressing Ctrl+`.

3

Getting Organized and Staying That Way

Explore ways to navigate larger worksheets.

Add comments to cells in a worksheet.

Find and replace data in a worksheet.

Add (and delete) worksheets to a workbook.

Open multiple windows on a worksheet to compare data in separate areas not visible on the same screen.

Juggle the information from one worksheet to another and even from one workbook to another.

Visit `www.dummies.com/extras/excel2019` for great Dummies content online.

Chapter **6**

Maintaining the Worksheet

E ach worksheet in an Excel 2019 workbook offers an immense place in which to store information. But because even a regular size computer monitor (which is quite large when compared to a regular Windows tablet or smartphone screen) lets you see only a tiny bit of any of the worksheets in a workbook at a time, the issue of keeping on top of information is not a small one (pun intended).

Although the Excel worksheet employs a coherent cell-coordinate system that you can use to get anywhere in the great big worksheet, you have to admit that this A1, B2 stuff — although highly logical — remains fairly alien to human thinking.

(I mean, saying, "Go to cell IV88," just doesn't have anywhere near the same impact as saying, "Go to the corner of Hollywood and Vine.") Consider for a moment the difficulty of coming up with a meaningful association between a 2015 depreciation table and its location in the cell range AC50:AN75 so that you can remember where to find it in your income tax worksheet.

In this chapter, I show you some of the more effective techniques for maintaining and keeping on top of information. You find out how to change the perspective on a worksheet by zooming in and out on the information, how to split the document window into separate panes so that you can display different sections of the worksheet at the same time, and how to keep particular rows and columns on the screen at all times.

And, as if that weren't enough, you also see how to add comments to cells, assign descriptive, English-type names to cell ranges (like Hollywood_and_Vine!), and use the Find and Replace commands to locate and, if necessary, replace entries anywhere in the worksheet. Finally, you see how to control when Excel recalculates the worksheet and how to limit where changes can be made.

Zooming In and Out

So what to do when trying to edit the company's huge spreadsheet on your fancy new Microsoft Surface tablet with its not-so-generous 10.6-inch screen or even on your 15-inch screen laptop? Does this mean that you're doomed to straining your eyes to read all the information in those tiny cells, or you're scrolling like mad trying to locate a table you can't seem to find? Never fear, the Zoom feature is here in the form of the Zoom slider on the Status bar. You can use the Zoom slider to quickly increase the magnification of part of the worksheet or shrink it down to the tiniest size.

You can use the Zoom slider on the Status bar of the Excel window in several ways, depending upon the device you're using:

>> Drag the Zoom slider button to the left or the right on the slider to decrease or increase the magnification percentage (with 10% magnification being the lowest percentage when you drag all the way to the left on the slider and 400% magnification being the highest percentage when you drag all the way to the right).

>> Click the Zoom Out (with the minus sign) or the Zoom In button (with the plus sign) at either end of the slider to decrease or increase the magnification percentage by 10%.

TIP

» On a touchscreen, use the stretch-and-pinch gesture with your thumb and forefinger on your touchscreen device to quickly zoom in and out on the cells of your worksheet and move the Zoom slider at the same time.

In Figure 6-1, you can see a blowup of the worksheet after increasing it to 200% magnification (twice the normal size). To blow up a worksheet like this, drag the Zoom slider button to the right until 200% appears on the Status bar to the left of the slider. (You can also do this by clicking View➪Zoom and then clicking the 200% button in the Zoom dialog box, if you really want to go to all that trouble.) One thing's for sure: You don't have to go after your glasses to read the names in those enlarged cells! The only problem with 200% magnification is that you can see only a few cells at one time.

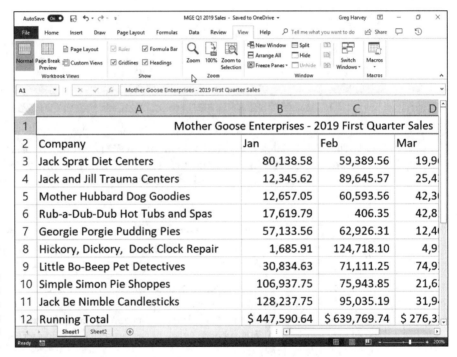

FIGURE 6-1:
Zooming a sample worksheet to 200% magnification.

	A	B	C	D
1	Mother Goose Enterprises - 2019 First Quarter Sales			
2	Company	Jan	Feb	Mar
3	Jack Sprat Diet Centers	80,138.58	59,389.56	19,9
4	Jack and Jill Trauma Centers	12,345.62	89,645.57	25,4
5	Mother Hubbard Dog Goodies	12,657.05	60,593.56	42,3
6	Rub-a-Dub-Dub Hot Tubs and Spas	17,619.79	406.35	42,8
7	Georgie Porgie Pudding Pies	57,133.56	62,926.31	12,4
8	Hickory, Dickory, Dock Clock Repair	1,685.91	124,718.10	4,9
9	Little Bo-Beep Pet Detectives	30,834.63	71,111.25	74,9
10	Simple Simon Pie Shoppes	106,937.75	75,943.85	21,6
11	Jack Be Nimble Candlesticks	128,237.75	95,035.19	31,9
12	Running Total	$ 447,590.64	$ 639,769.74	$ 276,3

In Figure 6-2, check out the same worksheet, this time at 40% magnification. To reduce the display to this magnification, you drag the Zoom slider button to the left until 40% appears on the Status bar in front of the slider.

Whew! At 40% of normal screen size, the only thing you can be sure of is that you can't read a thing! However, notice that with this bird's-eye view, you can see at a glance how far over and down the data in this worksheet extends and how much empty space there is in the worksheet.

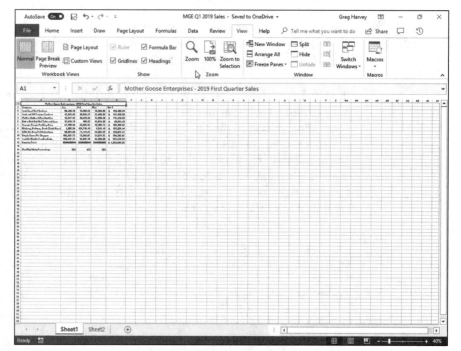

FIGURE 6-2:
Zooming a
sample
worksheet
to 40%
magnification.

The Zoom dialog box (View⇨Zoom or Alt+WQ) offers five precise magnification settings — 200%, 100% (normal screen magnification), 75%, 50%, and 25%. To use other percentages besides those, you have the following options:

>> If you want to use precise percentages other than the five preset percentages (such as 150% or 85%) or settings greater or less than the highest or lowest percentage (such as 400% or 10%), click within the Custom button's text box in the Zoom dialog box, type the new percentage, and press Enter.

>> If you don't know what percentage to enter in order to display a particular cell range on the screen, select the range, click View⇨Zoom to Selection on the Ribbon or press Alt+WG or the Fit Selection option in the Zoom dialog box. Excel figures out the percentage necessary to fill your screen with just the selected cell range.

REMEMBER

To quickly return to 100% (normal) magnification in the worksheet after selecting any another percentage, all you have to do is click the bar in the center of the Zoom slider on the Status bar or click the 100% button on the View tab of the Ribbon.

TIP

You can use the Zoom feature to locate and move to a new cell range in the worksheet. First, select a small magnification, such as 50%. Then locate the cell range you want to move to and select one of its cells. Finally, use the Zoom feature to return the screen magnification to 100%. When Excel returns the display to normal size, the cell you select and its surrounding range appear onscreen.

Splitting the Worksheet into Window Panes

Although zooming in and out on the worksheet can help you get your bearings, it can't bring together two separate sections so that you can compare their data on the screen (at least not at a normal size where you can actually read the information). To manage this kind of trick, split the Worksheet area into separate panes and then scroll the worksheet in each pane so that they display the parts you want to compare.

Splitting the window is easy. Look at Figure 6-3 to see an Income Analysis worksheet after splitting its worksheet window horizontally into two panes and scrolling up rows 36 through 44 in the lower pane. Each pane has its own vertical scroll bar, which enables you to scroll different parts of the worksheet into view.

To split a worksheet into two (upper and lower) horizontal panes, you simply position the cell pointer at the place in the worksheet where you want to split the worksheet and then click the Split button on the Ribbon's View tab (or press Alt+WS).

The key to the panes created with the Split button is the cell in the worksheet where you position the pointer *before* selecting this command button:

>> To split the window into two horizontal panes, position the cell pointer in column A of the row where you want to split the worksheet.

>> To split the window into two vertical panes, position the cell pointer in row 1 of the column where you want to split the worksheet.

>> To split the window into four panes — two horizontal and two vertical — position the cell cursor in the cell at the lower-right junction of the new window panes so that the vertical pane is split along the left edge of the current cell and the horizontal pane along the top edge of the current cell.

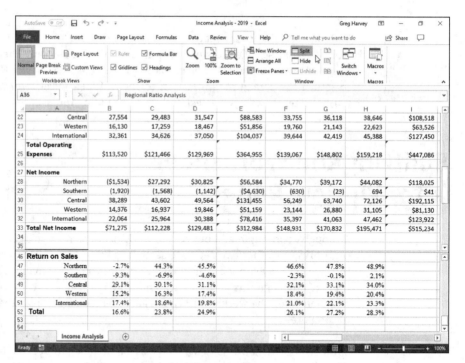

After you split the worksheet window, Excel displays a split bar (a thin, light gray bar) along the row or column where the window split occurs. If you position the mouse or Touch pointer anywhere on the split bar, the pointer changes from a white-cross to a split pointer shape (with black arrowheads pointing in opposite directions from parallel separated lines).

You can increase or decrease the size of the current window panes by dragging the split bar up or down or left or right with the split pointer. You can make the panes in a Workbook window disappear by double-clicking anywhere on the split bar (you can also do this by selecting View ⇨ Split again).

Fixed Headings with Freeze Panes

Panes are great for viewing different parts of the same worksheet that normally can't be seen together. You can also use panes to freeze headings in the top rows and first columns so that the headings stay in view at all times, no matter how you scroll through the worksheet. Frozen headings are especially helpful when you work with a table that contains information that extends beyond the rows and columns shown onscreen.

In Figure 6-4, you can see just such a table. The Income Analysis worksheet contains more rows and columns than you can see at one time (unless you decrease the magnification to about 40% with Zoom, which makes the data too small to read). In fact, this worksheet continues down to row 52 and over to column P.

By dividing the worksheet into four panes between rows 2 and 3 and columns A and B and then freezing them on the screen, you can keep the column headings in row 2 that identify each column of information on the screen while you scroll the worksheet up and down to review information on income and expenses. Additionally, you can keep the row headings in column A on the screen while you scroll the worksheet to the right.

Refer to Figure 6-4 to see the worksheet right after splitting the window into four panes and freezing them. To create and freeze these panes, follow these steps:

1. **Position the cell cursor in cell B3.**

2. **Click View ➪ Freeze Panes on the Ribbon and then click Freeze Panes on the drop-down menu or press Alt+WFF.**

   In this example, Excel freezes the top and left pane above row 3 and left of column B.

When Excel sets up the frozen panes, the borders of frozen panes are represented by a single line rather than the thin gray bar, as is the case when simply splitting the worksheet into panes.

See what happens when you scroll the worksheet up after freezing the panes (shown in Figure 6-5). In this figure, I scrolled the worksheet up so that rows 33 through 52 of the table appear under rows 1 and 2. Because the vertical pane with the worksheet title and column headings is frozen, it remains onscreen. (Normally, rows 1 and 2 would have been the first to disappear when you scroll the worksheet up.)

FIGURE 6-5:
The Income Analysis worksheet after scrolling the rows up to display additional income and expense data.

	A	B	C	D	E	F	G	H	I
1	**Regional Income 2019**								
2		Jan	Feb	Mar	Qtr 1	Apr	May	Jun	Qtr 2
33	**Total Net Income**	$71,275	$112,228	$129,481	$312,984	$148,931	$170,832	$195,471	$515,234
34									
35									
36	**Regional Ratio Analysis**								
37		Jan	Feb	Mar		Apr	May	Jun	
38	**Gross Profit on Sales**								
39	Northern	81.5%	81.7%	81.9%		82.0%	82.2%	82.4%	
40	Southern	68.2%	68.5%	68.8%		69.0%	69.3%	69.6%	
41	Central	50.0%	50.5%	50.9%		51.4%	51.8%	52.2%	
42	Western	32.3%	32.9%	33.5%		34.1%	34.7%	35.3%	
43	International	42.9%	43.5%	44.0%		44.5%	45.0%	45.5%	
44	**Total**	49.0%	49.5%	49.9%		50.4%	50.8%	51.3%	
45									
46	**Return on Sales**								
47	Northern	-2.7%	44.3%	45.5%		46.6%	47.8%	48.9%	
48	Southern	-9.3%	-6.9%	-4.6%		-2.3%	-0.1%	2.1%	
49	Central	29.1%	30.1%	31.1%		32.1%	33.1%	34.0%	
50	Western	15.2%	16.3%	17.4%		18.4%	19.4%	20.4%	
51	International	17.4%	18.6%	19.8%		21.0%	22.1%	23.3%	
52	**Total**	16.6%	23.8%	24.9%		26.1%	27.2%	28.3%	
53									
54									

Look to Figure 6-6 to see what happens when you scroll the worksheet to the right. In this figure, I scroll the worksheet so that the data in columns M through P appear after the data in column A. Because the first column is frozen, it remains onscreen, helping you identify the various categories of income and expenses for each month.

TIP Click Freeze Top Row or Freeze First Column on the Freeze Panes button's drop-down menu to freeze the column headings in the top row of the worksheet or the row headings in the first column of the worksheet, regardless of where the cell cursor is located in the worksheet.

FIGURE 6-6:
The Income
Analysis
worksheet after
scrolling the
columns left to
display the last
group of columns
in this table.

To unfreeze the panes in a worksheet, click View ⇨ Freeze Panes on the Ribbon and then click Unfreeze Panes on the Freeze Panes button's drop-down menu or press Alt+WFF. Choosing this option removes the frozen panes, leaving the split panes displayed in the light, indicating that these panes are no longer frozen. You can then remove the split panes by clicking the Split button on the View tab of the Ribbon.

Electronic Sticky Notes

You can add text comments to particular cells in an Excel worksheet. *Comments* act kind of like electronic pop-up versions of sticky notes. For example, you can add a comment to yourself to verify a particular figure before printing the worksheet or to remind yourself that a particular value is only an estimate (or even to remind yourself that it's your anniversary and to pick up a little something special for your spouse on the way home!).

TIP

In addition to using notes to remind yourself of something you've done or that remains to be done, you can also use a comment to mark your current place in a large worksheet. You can then use the comment's location to quickly find your starting place the next time you work with that worksheet.

Adding a comment to a cell

To add a comment to a cell, follow these steps:

1. **Move the cell pointer to or click the cell to which you want to add the comment.**

2. **Click the New Comment command button on the Ribbon's Review tab (Alt+RC) or the Comment button on the Insert tab (Alt+NC2) or press Shift+F2.**

   A new text box appears (similar to the one shown in Figure 6-7). This text box contains the name of the user as it appears in the User Name text box on the General tab in the Excel Options dialog box (Alt+FT) and the insertion point located at the beginning of a new line right below the user name.

3. **Type the text of your comment in the text box that appears.**

4. **When you finish entering the comment text, click somewhere on the worksheet outside of the text box.**

   Excel marks the location of a comment in a cell by adding a tiny triangle in the upper-right corner of the cell. (This triangular indicator appears in red on a color monitor.)

5. **To display the comment in a cell, position the thick white cross mouse or Touch pointer somewhere in the cell with the note indicator.**

FIGURE 6-7:
Adding a new comment to a cell in the Comment box.

Comments in review

When you have a workbook with sheets that contain a whole bunch of comments, you probably won't want to take the time to position the mouse pointer over each of its cells in order to read each one. For those times, you need to click the Show All Comments command button on the Ribbon's Review tab (or press Alt+RA). When you click Show All Comments on the Review tab, Excel displays all the comments in the workbook (as shown in Figure 6-8).

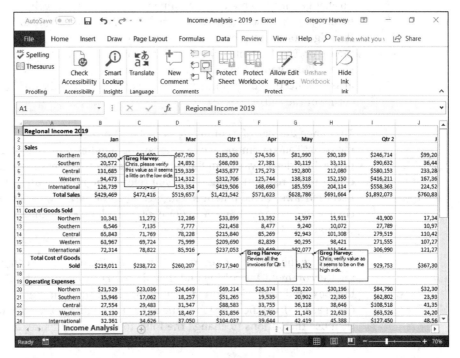

FIGURE 6-8:
Use the Show All Comments button on the Review tab to review the comments added to a worksheet.

With the Review tab selected in the Ribbon, you can then move back and forth from comment to comment by clicking its Next and Previous command buttons in the Comments group (or by pressing Alt+RN and Alt+RV, respectively). After you finish reviewing the comments in your workbook, you can hide their display by clicking the Comments button next to the Share button on the line with the Ribbon tabs or the Show All Comments command button on the Review tab of the Ribbon or pressing Alt+RH a second time.

Editing comments in a worksheet

To edit the contents of a comment (whether or not it's one you created), select it by clicking the Next or Previous command button in the Comments group of the Review tab and then click the Edit Comment button (which replaces New Comment) or right-click the cell with the comment and select Edit Comment from the cell's shortcut menu. You can also do this by selecting the cell with the comment and then pressing Shift+F2.

To change the placement of a comment in relation to its cell, you select the comment by clicking somewhere on it and then position the mouse pointer on one of the edges of its text box. When a four-headed arrow appears at the tip of the mouse or Touch pointer, you can drag the text box to a new place in the worksheet. When you release the mouse button, finger, or stylus, Excel redraws the arrow connecting the comment's text box to the note indicator in the upper-right corner of the cell.

To change the size of a comment's text box, you select the comment, position the mouse or Touch pointer on one of its sizing handles, and then drag in the appropriate direction (away from the center of the box to increase its size or toward the center to decrease its size). When you release the mouse button finger, or stylus, Excel redraws the comment's text box with the new shape and size. When you change the size and shape of a comment's text box, Excel automatically wraps the text to fit in the new shape and size.

To change the font of the comment text, select the text of the comment (by selecting the comment for editing and then dragging through the text), right-click the text box, and then click Format Comment on its shortcut menu (or you can press Ctrl+1 as I do). On the Font tab of the Format Cells dialog box that appears, you can then use the options to change the font, font style, font size, or color of the text displayed in the selected comment.

TIP

To delete a comment, select the cell with the comment in the worksheet or click the Next or Previous command buttons on the Review tab of the Ribbon until the comment is selected and then click the Delete command button in the Comments group (Alt+RD). Excel removes the comment along with the note indicator from the selected cell.

REMEMBER

You can also delete all comments in the selected range by clicking Clear Comments from the Clear button's drop-down menu (the one with the eraser icon in the Editing group) on the Home tab of the Ribbon (Alt+HEM).

Getting your comments in print

When printing a worksheet, you can print comments along with worksheet data by selecting the At End of Sheet or As Displayed on Sheet option on the Comments drop-down list on the Sheet tab of the Page Setup dialog box. Open this dialog box by clicking the Dialog Box launcher in the lower-right corner of the Page Setup group on the Ribbon's Page Layout tab (Alt+PSO).

The Range Name Game

By assigning descriptive names to cells and cell ranges, you can go a long way toward keeping on top of the location of important information in a worksheet. Rather than try to associate random cell coordinates with specific information, you just have to remember a name. You can also use range names to designate the cell selection that you want to print or use in other Office 2019 programs, such as Microsoft Word or Access. Best of all, after you name a cell or cell range, you can use this name with the Go To feature to not only locate the range but select all its cells as well.

TIP

I've always been a fan of using range names in worksheets for all the previous versions of Excel designed for desktop and laptop computers. With this new version of Excel designed for touchscreen devices, such as Windows 10 tablets and smartphones, as well, I'm bordering on becoming a fanatic about their use. Believe me, you can save yourself oodles of time and tons of frustration by locating and selecting the data tables and lists in your worksheets on these touch devices via range names. Contrast simply tapping their range names on Excel's Name box's drop-down list to go to and select them to having first to swipe and swipe to locate and display their cells before dragging through their cells with your finger or stylus.

If I only had a name . . .

When assigning range names to a cell or cell range, you need to follow a few guidelines:

>> **Range names must begin with a letter of the alphabet, not a number.**

For example, instead of 01Profit, use Profit01.

>> **Range names cannot contain spaces.**

Instead of a space, use the underscore (Shift+hyphen) to tie the parts of the name together. For example, instead of Profit 01, use Profit_01.

>> **Range names cannot correspond to cell coordinates in the worksheet.**

For example, you can't name a cell Q1 because this is a valid cell coordinate. Instead, use something like Q1_sales.

>> **Range names must be unique within their scope** — that is, all of the worksheets in the workbook when the scope is set to Workbook (as it is by default) or just a specific sheet in the workbook when the scope is set to a particular worksheet, such as Sheet1 or Income Analysis (when the sheet is named).

To name a cell or cell range in a worksheet, follow these steps:

1. **Select the single cell or range of cells that you want to name.**

2. **Click Formulas ⇨ Defined Names ⇨ Define Name (Alt+MZND) to open the New Name dialog box, as shown in Figure 6-9.**

3. **Type the name for the selected cell or cell range in the Name Box.**

4. **(Optional) To limit the scope of the range name to a particular worksheet rather than the entire workbook (the default), click the drop-down button in the Scope drop-down list box and then click the name of sheet to which the range is to be restricted.**

5. **(Optional) To add a comment describing the function and/or extent of the range name, click the Comment text box and then type your comments.**

6. **Check the cell range that the new range name will encompass in the Refers to text box and make an adjustment, if necessary.**

If this cell range is not correct, click the Collapse button (the up arrow button) to the right of the Refers To text box to condense the New Dialog box to the Refers To text box and then click the appropriate cell or drag through the appropriate range before you click Expand button (the down arrow to the right of the text box) to restore the New Name dialog box to its normal size.

7. **Click the OK button to complete the definition of the range name and to close the New Range name dialog box.**

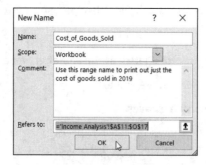

FIGURE 6-9:
Naming a cell range in the worksheet in the New Name dialog box.

To quickly name a cell or cell range in a worksheet from the Name Box on the Formula bar, follow these steps:

1. **Select the single cell or range of cells that you want to name.**

2. **Click the cell address for the current cell that appears in the Name Box on the far left of the Formula bar.**

   Excel selects the cell address in the Name Box.

3. **Type the name for the selected cell or cell range in the Name Box.**

   When typing the range name, you must follow Excel's naming conventions: Refer to the bulleted list of cell-name do's and don'ts earlier in this section for details.

4. **Press Enter.**

To select a named cell or range in a worksheet, click the range name on the Name Box drop-down list. To open this list, click the drop-down arrow button that appears to the right of the cell address on the Formula bar.

You can also accomplish the same thing by selecting Home⇨Find & Select (with the binoculars icon)⇨Go To or by pressing F5 or Ctrl+G to open the Go To dialog box (see Figure 6-10). Double-click the desired range name in the Go To list box (alternatively, select the name followed by OK). Excel moves the cell cursor directly to the named cell. If you select a cell range, all the cells in that range are selected as well.

FIGURE 6-10:
Select the named cell range to go to in a workbook.

Name that formula!

Cell names are not only a great way to identify and find cells and cell ranges in your spreadsheet, but they're also a great way to make out the purpose of your formulas. For example, suppose that you have a simple formula in cell K3 that calculates the total due to you by multiplying the hours you work for a client (in cell I3) by the client's hourly rate (in cell J3). Normally, you would enter this formula in cell K3 as

```
=I3*J3
```

However, if you assign the name Hours to cell I3 and the name Rate to cell J3, in cell K3 you could enter the formula

```
=Hours*Rate
```

I don't think there's anyone who would dispute that the function of the formula =Hours*Rate is much easier to understand than =I3*J3.

To enter a formula using cell names rather than cell references, follow these steps (see Chapter 2 to brush up on how to create formulas):

1. **Assign range names to the individual cells as I describe earlier in this section.**

   For this example, give the name Hours to cell I3 and the name Rate to cell J3.

2. **Place the cell cursor in the cell where the formula is to appear.**

   For this example, put the cell cursor in cell K3.

3. **Type = (equal sign) to start the formula.**

4. **Select the first cell referenced in the formula by selecting its cell (either by clicking the cell or moving the cell cursor into it).**

   For this example, you select the Hours cell by selecting cell I3.

5. **Type the arithmetic operator to use in the formula.**

   For this example, you would type * (asterisk) for multiplication. (Refer to Chapter 2 for a list of the other arithmetic operators.)

6. **Select the second cell referenced in the formula by selecting its cell (either by clicking the cell or moving the cell cursor into it).**

   For this example, you select the Rate cell by selecting cell J3.

7. **Click the Enter button or press Enter to complete the formula.**

   In this example, Excel enters the formula =Hours*Rate in cell K3.

WARNING

You can't use the fill handle to copy a formula that uses cell names, rather than cell addresses, to other cells in a column or row that perform the same function (see Chapter 4). When you copy an original formula that uses names rather than addresses, Excel copies the original formula without adjusting the cell references to the new rows and columns. See the upcoming "Naming constants" section to find a way to use your column and row headings to identify the cell references in the copies, and include the original formula from which the copies are made.

Naming constants

Certain formulas use constant values, such as an 8.25% tax rate or a 10% discount rate. If you don't want to have to enter these constants into a cell of the worksheet in order to use the formulas, you create range names that hold their values and then use their range names in the formulas you create.

For example, to create a constant called *tax_rate* (of 8.25%), follow these steps:

1. **Click the Define Name button on the Ribbon's Formulas tab or press Alt+MMD to open the New Name dialog box.**

2. **In the New Name dialog box, type the range name (tax_rate in this example) into the Name text box.**

   Be sure to adhere to the cell range naming conventions when entering this new name.

3. **(Optional) To limit the scope of range name defined to just a particular worksheet instead of the entire workbook, click the name of the sheet on the Scope drop-down list.**

   Normally, you're safer sticking with the default selection of Workbook as the Scope option so that you can use your constant in a formula on any of its sheets. Only change the scope to a particular worksheet when you want to use the same range name on multiple sheets of the workbook or you're sure that you'll use it only in formulas on that worksheet.

4. **Click in the Refers To text box after the equal to sign (=) and replace (enter) the current cell address with the constant value (8.25% in this example) or a formula that calculates the constant.**

5. **Click OK to close the New Name dialog box.**

After you assign a constant to a range name by using this method, you can apply it to the formulas that you create in the worksheet in one of two ways:

» Type the range name to which you assign the constant at the place in the formula where its value is required.

>> Click the Use in Formula command button on the Formulas tab (or press Alt+MS) and then click the constant's range name on the drop-down menu that appears.

TIP

When you copy a formula that uses a range name containing a constant, its values remain unchanged in all copies of the formula that you create with the fill handle. (In other words, range names in formulas act like absolute cell addresses in copied formulas — see Chapter 4 for more on copying formulas.)

Also, when you update the constant by changing its value in the Edit Name dialog box — opened by clicking the range name in the Name Manager dialog box (Alt+MN) and then clicking its Edit button — all the formulas that use that constant (by referring to the range name) are automatically updated (recalculated) to reflect this change.

Seek and Ye Shall Find . . .

When all else fails, you can use Excel's Find feature to locate specific information in the worksheet. Select Home➪Find & Select (with the binoculars icon)➪Find or press Ctrl+F, Shift+F5, or even Alt+HFDF to open the Find and Replace dialog box (isn't it great to have choices!).

In the Find What drop-down box of this dialog box, enter the text or values you want to locate and then select the Find Next button or press Enter to start the search. Select the Options button in the Find and Replace dialog box to expand the search options (as shown in Figure 6-11).

When you search for a text entry with the Find and Replace feature, be mindful of whether the text or number you enter in the Find What text box is separate in its cell or occurs as part of another word or value. For example, if you enter the characters **in** in the Find What text box and you don't select the Match Entire Cell Contents check box, Excel finds

>> The *In* in Regional Income 2019 in cell A1

>> The *In* in International in A8, A16, A24, and so on

>> The *in* in Total Operating Expenses in cell A25

If you select the Match Entire Cell Contents check box in the Find and Replace dialog box before starting the search, Excel would not consider *anything in the sheet to be a match* because all entries have other text surrounding the text you're searching for. If you had the state abbreviation for Indiana (IN) in a cell by itself and had chosen the Match Entire Cell Contents option, Excel would find that cell.

When you search for text, you can also specify whether you want Excel to match the case you use (uppercase or lowercase) when entering the search text in the Find What text box. By default, Excel ignores case differences between text in cells of your worksheet and the search text you enter in the Find What text box. To conduct a case-sensitive search, you need to select the Match Case check box (available when you click the Options button to expand the Find and Replace dialog box, shown in Figure 6-10).

If the text or values that you want to locate in the worksheet have special formatting, you can specify the formatting to match when conducting the search.

To have Excel match the formatting assigned to a particular cell in the worksheet, follow these steps:

1. **Click the drop-down button on the right of the Format button in the Find and Replace dialog box and choose the Choose Format from Cell option on the pop-up menu.**

    Excel adds an ink dropper icon to the normal white cross mouse and Touch pointer.

2. **Click the ink dropper pointer in the cell in the worksheet that contains the formatting you want to match.**

    The formatting in the selected worksheet appears in the Preview text box in the Find and Replace dialog box, and you can then search for that formatting in other places in the worksheet by clicking the Find Next button or by pressing Enter.

To select the formatting to match in the search from the options on the Find Format dialog box (which are identical to those of the Format Cells dialog box), follow these steps:

1. **Click the Format button or click its drop-down button and select Format from its menu.**

2. **Select the formatting options to match from the various tabs (refer to Chapter 3 for help on selecting these options) and click OK.**

When you use either of these methods to select the kinds of formatting to match in your search, the No Format Set button (located between the Find What text box and the Format button) changes to a Preview button. The word *Preview* in this button appears in whatever font and attributes Excel picks up from the sample cell or through your selections in the Find Format dialog box. To reset the Find and Replace to search across all formats again, select Format⇨Clear Find Format, and No Format Set will appear again between the Find What and Format buttons.

When you search for values in the worksheet, be mindful of the difference between formulas and values. For example, say cell K24 of your worksheet contains the computed value $15,000 (from a formula that multiplies a value in cell I24 by that in cell J24). If you type **15000** in the Find What text box and press Enter to search for this value, instead of finding the value 15000 in cell K24, Excel displays an alert box with the following message:

```
Microsoft Excel cannot find the data you're searching for
```

This is because the value in this cell is calculated by the formula

```
=I24*J24
```

The value 15000 doesn't appear in that formula. To have Excel find any entry matching 15000 in the cells of the worksheet, you need to choose Values in the Look In drop-down menu of the Find and Replace dialog box in place of the normally used Formulas option.

TIP

To restrict the search to just the text or values in the text of the comments in the worksheet, choose the Comments option from the Look In drop-down menu.

If you don't know the exact spelling of the word or name or the precise value or formula you're searching for, you can use wildcards, which are symbols that stand for missing or unknown text. Use the question mark (?) to stand for a single unknown character; use the asterisk (*) to stand for any number of missing characters. Suppose that you enter the following in the Find What text box and choose the Values option in the Look In drop-down menu:

7*4

Excel stops at cells that contain the values 74, 704, and 75,234. Excel even finds the text entry 782 4th Street!

If you actually want to search for an asterisk in the worksheet rather than use the asterisk as a wildcard, precede it with a tilde (~), as follows:

~*4

This arrangement enables you to search the formulas in the worksheet for one that multiplies by the number 4. (Remember that Excel uses the asterisk as the multiplication sign.)

The following entry in the Find What text box finds cells that contain Jan, January, June, Janet, and so on.

J?n*

REMEMBER

Normally, Excel searches only the current worksheet for the search text you enter. If you want the program to search all the worksheets in the workbook, you must select the Workbook option from the Within drop-down menu.

When Excel locates a cell in the worksheet that contains the text or values you're searching for, it selects that cell while leaving the Find and Replace dialog box open. (Remember that you can move the Find and Replace dialog box if it obscures your view of the cell.) To search for the next occurrence of the text or value, click the Find Next button or press Enter.

Excel normally searches down the worksheet by rows. To search across the columns first, choose the By Columns option in the Search drop-down menu. To reverse the search direction and revisit previous occurrences of matching cell entries, press the Shift key while you click the Find Next button in the Find and Replace dialog box.

Replacing Cell Entries

If your purpose for finding a cell with a particular entry is so that you can change it, you can automate this process by using the Replace tab on the Find and Replace dialog box. If you select Home ⇨ Find & Select (with the binoculars icon) ⇨ Replace or press Ctrl+H or Alt+HFDR, Excel opens the Find and Replace dialog box with the Replace tab (rather than the Find tab) selected. On the Replace tab, enter the text or value you want to replace in the Find What text box, and then enter the replacement text or value in the Replace With text box.

When you enter replacement text, enter it exactly how you want it to appear in the cell. In other words, if you want to replace all occurrences of Jan in the worksheet with January, enter the following in the Replace With text box:

January

Make sure that you use a capital J in the Replace With text box, even though you can enter the following in the Find What text box (providing you don't check the Match Case check box that appears only when you choose the Options button to expand the Find and Replace dialog box options):

Jan

After specifying what to replace and what to replace it with (as shown in Figure 6-12), you can have Excel replace occurrences within the active worksheet on a case-by-case basis or globally. To have Excel search for replacements in all sheets of your workbook, change the Within option from Sheet to Workbook before you undertake the search and replace.

FIGURE 6-12:
Use Replace options to change particular cell entries.

WARNING

Be careful with global search-and-replace operations; they can really mess up a worksheet in a hurry if you inadvertently replace values, parts of formulas, or characters in titles and headings that you hadn't intended to change. With this in mind, always follow one rule:

Never undertake a global search-and-replace operation on an unsaved worksheet.

Also, verify whether the Match Entire Cell Contents check box (displayed only when you click the Options button) is selected before you begin. You can end up with many unwanted replacements if you leave this check box unselected when you really only want to replace entire cell entries (rather than matching parts in cell entries).

If you do make a mess, immediately click the Undo button on the Quick Access toolbar or press Ctrl+Z to restore the worksheet.

To see each occurrence before you replace it, click the Find Next button or press Enter. Excel selects the next cell with the text or value you enter in the Find What text box. To have the program replace the selected text, click the Replace button. To skip this occurrence, click the Find Next button to continue the search. When you finish replacing occurrences, click the Close button to close the Find and Replace dialog box.

Doing Your Research with Smart Lookup

Excel 2019's Smart Lookup feature enables you to use online resources such as Wikipedia to get information on a particular search entry or cell entry in a worksheet. When you click the Smart Lookup button on the Review tab of the Ribbon (or press Alt+RR), Excel opens a Smart Lookup task pane (similar to the one shown in Figure 6-13) with information about the entry in the current cell of your worksheet under an Explore tab. If you want to do such a lookup on a topic that's not entered in a worksheet cell, type that entry in the Search text box at the very end of the ribbon and then select the Smart Lookup option with the name of that entry in parentheses.

Actually, the very first time you click the Smart Lookup feature, the Smart Lookup task pane displays a "turn on intelligent services to let Office get web results for your highlighted text" message rather than information about the current cell entry. You must then click the Turn On button to proceed with the online search.

Once the Bing Search engine displays information about the current cell entry on the Explore tab of the Smart Lookup task pane, you can scroll down to peruse the particulars and even follow any interesting online details by clicking the appropriate hyperlinks (which open the relevant web page in a separate window in your default browser).

FIGURE 6-13:
Researching
Human
Resources
in the Smart
Lookup task
pane with
Smart Lookup.

If you want a definition for the current cell entry rather than related information about it, simply click the Define tab at the top of the Smart Lookup task pane. Excel then displays a definition for the current term contained in the current cell. If appropriate, the definition will include the latest statistics about the defined term. If you want to hear how the defined term is pronounced, click the speaker icon near the top of the Smart Lookup task pane.

When you're finished researching the term that's entered in the current worksheet cell or the Search text box, close the Smart Lookup task pane by clicking the pane's Close button in its upper-right corner.

Controlling Recalculation

Although extremely important, locating information in a worksheet is only part of keeping on top of the information in a worksheet. In really large workbooks that contain many completed worksheets, you may want to switch to manual recalculation so that you can control when the formulas in the worksheet are calculated. You need this kind of control when you find that Excel's recalculation of formulas each time you enter or change information in cells has slowed the program's response time to a crawl. By holding off recalculations until you are ready to save or print the workbook, you find that you can work with Excel's worksheets without interminable delays.

To put the workbook into manual recalculation mode, you select the Manual option on the Calculation Options button on the Formulas tab of the Ribbon (Alt+MXM). After switching to manual recalculation, Excel displays CALCULATE on the Status bar whenever you make a change to the worksheet that somehow affects the current values of its formulas. Whenever Excel is in manual recalculation and displaying the Calculate mode on the Status bar, you need to bring the formulas up-to-date in your worksheets before saving the workbook (as you would do before you print its worksheets).

To recalculate the formulas in a workbook when calculation is manual, press F9 or Ctrl+= (equal sign) or select the Calculate Now button (the one with a picture of a calculator in the upper-right corner of the Calculation group) on the Formulas tab (Alt+MB).

Excel then recalculates the formulas in all the worksheets of your workbook. If you made changes to only the current worksheet and you don't want to wait around for Excel to recalculate every other worksheet in the workbook, you can restrict the recalculation to the current worksheet. Press Shift+F9 or click the Calculate Sheet button (the one with a picture of a calculator under the worksheet in the lower-right corner of the Calculation group) on the Formulas tab (Alt+MJ).

TIP

If your worksheet contains data tables that perform different what-if scenarios (see Chapter 8 for details), you can have Excel automatically recalculate all parts of the worksheet except for those data tables by clicking Automatic Except Data Tables on the Calculation Options button's drop-down menu on the Formulas tab (Alt+MXE).

REMEMBER

To return a workbook to fully automatic recalculation mode, click the Automatic option on the Calculation Options button's drop-down menu on the Formulas tab (Alt+MXA).

Putting on the Protection

After you more or less finalize a worksheet by checking out its formulas and proofing its text, you often want to guard against any unplanned changes by protecting the document.

Each cell in the worksheet can be locked or unlocked. By default, Excel locks all the cells in a worksheet so that, when you follow these steps, Excel locks the whole thing up tighter than a drum:

1. **Click the Protect Sheet command button in the Protect group on the Review tab on the Ribbon or press Alt+RPS.**

   Excel opens the Protect Sheet dialog box (see Figure 6-14), in which you select the check box options you want to be available when the protection is turned on in the worksheet. By default, Excel selects the Protect Worksheet and Contents of Locked Cells check box at the top of the Protect Sheet dialog box. Additionally, the program selects both the Select Locked Cells and Select Unlocked Cells check boxes in the Allow All Users of This Worksheet To list box below.

2. **(Optional) Click any of the check box options in the Allow All Users of This Worksheet To list box (such as Format Cells or Insert Columns) that you still want to be functional when the worksheet protection is operational.**

3. **If you want to assign a password that must be supplied before you can remove the protection from the worksheet, type the password in the Password to Unprotect Sheet text box.**

4. **Click OK or press Enter.**

   If you type a password in the Password to Unprotect Sheet text box, Excel opens the Confirm Password dialog box. Reenter the password in the Reenter Password to Proceed text box exactly as you typed it in the Password to Unprotect Sheet text box in the Protect Sheet dialog box and then click OK or press Enter.

FIGURE 6-14:
Protection options in the Protect Sheet dialog box.

If you want to go a step further and protect the layout of the worksheets in the workbook, you protect the entire workbook as follows:

1. **Click the Protect Workbook command button in the Changes group on the Ribbon's Review tab or press Alt+RPW.**

   Excel opens the Protect Structure and Windows dialog box, where the Structure check box is selected and the Windows check box is not. With the Structure check box selected, Excel won't let you mess around with the sheets in the workbook (by deleting them or rearranging them). If you want to protect any windows that you set up (as I describe in Chapter 7), you need to select the Windows check box as well.

2. **To assign a password that must be supplied before you can remove the protection from the worksheet, type the password in the Password (Optional) text box.**

3. **Click OK or press Enter.**

   If you type a password in the Password (Optional) text box, Excel opens the Confirm Password dialog box. Reenter the password in the Reenter Password to Proceed text box exactly as you typed it into the Password (Optional) text box in the Protect Structure and Windows dialog box and then click OK or press Enter.

Selecting the Protect Sheet command makes it impossible to make further changes to the contents of any of the locked cells in that worksheet, except for those options that you specifically exempt in the Allow All Users of This Worksheet To list box. (See Step 2 in the first set of steps in this section.) Selecting the Protect Workbook command makes it impossible to make further changes to the layout of the worksheets in that workbook.

Excel displays an alert dialog box with the following message when you try to edit or replace an entry in a locked cell:

```
The cell or chart you are trying to change is on a
protected sheet. To make a change a change,
unprotect this sheet. You might be requested to enter a password.
```

Usually, your intention in protecting a worksheet or an entire workbook is not to prevent all changes but to prevent changes in certain areas of the worksheet. For example, in a budget worksheet, you may want to protect all the cells that contain headings and formulas but allow changes in all the cells where you enter the budgeted amounts. That way, you can't inadvertently wipe out a title or formula in the worksheet simply by entering a value in the wrong column or row (a common occurrence).

To leave certain cells unlocked so that you can still change them after protecting the worksheet or workbook, select all the cells as the cell selection, open the Format Cells dialog box (Ctrl+1), and then click the Locked check box on the Protection tab to remove its check mark. Then, after unlocking the cells that you still want to be able to change, protect the worksheet as described earlier.

To remove protection from the current worksheet or workbook document so that you can again make changes to its cells (whether locked or unlocked), click the Unprotect Sheet or the Unprotect Workbook command button in the Changes group on the Ribbon's Review tab (or press Alt+RPS and Alt+RPW, respectively). If you assign a password when protecting the worksheet or workbook, you must then reproduce the password exactly as you assigned it (including any case differences) in the Password text box of the Unprotect Sheet or Unprotect Workbook dialog box.

You can also protect a worksheet or your workbook from Excel Info screen in the Backstage by clicking the Protect Workbook button (Alt+FIP). Clicking this button opens a menu of protection options, including among others, the familiar Protect Current Sheet to prevent changes to the current worksheet in the Protect Sheet dialog box and Protect Workbook Structure to changes to worksheets and or windows set up in the current workbook in the Protect Structure and Windows dialog box.

Chapter 7

Maintaining Multiple Worksheets

When you're brand-new to spreadsheets, you have enough trouble keeping track of a single worksheet, and the very thought of working with more than one may be a little more than you can take. However, after you get a little experience under your belt, you'll find that working with more than one worksheet in a workbook is no more taxing than working with just a single worksheet.

REMEMBER

Don't confuse the term *workbook* with *worksheet.* The workbook forms the document (file) that you open and save while you work. Each new workbook (file) normally contains a single blank worksheet, to which you can add as many worksheets as you need by clicking the New Sheet button on the Status bar (the one with plus sign in a circle). Multiple worksheets in a single workbook act like the loose-leaf pages in a notebook binder; you can add or remove sheets as needed. To help you keep track of the worksheets in your workbook and navigate between them, Excel provides sheet tabs (Sheet1, Sheet 2, and Sheet3) that are like the tab dividers in a loose-leaf notebook.

Juggling Multiple Worksheets

You need to understand *how* to work with more than one worksheet in a workbook, but it's also important to understand *why* you'd want to do such a crazy thing in the first place. The most common situation is, of course, when you have a bunch of worksheets that are related to each other and, therefore, naturally belong together in the same workbook. For example, consider the case of Mother Goose Enterprises with its different companies: Jack Sprat Diet Centers; Jack and Jill Trauma Center;, Mother Hubbard Dog Goodies; Rub-a-Dub-Dub Hot Tubs and Spas; Georgie Porgie Pudding Pies; Hickory, Dickory, Dock Clock Repair; Little Bo Peep Pet Detectives; Simple Simon Pie Shoppes; and Jack Be Nimble Candlesticks. To keep track of the annual sales for all these companies, you could create a workbook containing a worksheet for each of the nine different companies.

By keeping the sales figures for each company in a different sheet of the same workbook, you gain all the following benefits:

>> You can enter the stuff that's needed in all the sales worksheets (if you select those sheet tabs) just by typing it once into the first worksheet (see the section "Editing en masse," later in this chapter).

>> In order to help you build the worksheet for the first company's sales, you can attach macros to the current workbook so that they are readily available when you create the worksheets for the other companies. (A *macro* is a sequence of frequently performed, repetitive tasks and calculations that you record for easy playback — see Chapter 12 for details.)

>> You can quickly compare the sales of one company with the sales of another (see the section "Opening Windows on Your Worksheets," later in this chapter).

>> You can print all the sales information for each company as a single report in one printing operation. (Read Chapter 5 for specifics on printing an entire workbook or particular worksheets in a workbook.)

>> You can easily create charts that compare certain sales data from different worksheets (see Chapter 10 for details).

>> You can easily set up a summary worksheet with formulas that total the quarterly and annual sales for all nine companies (see the upcoming "Summing Stuff on Different Worksheets" section).

Sliding between the sheets

Each blank workbook that you open contains a single worksheet given the prosaic name, Sheet1. To add more sheets to your workbook, you simply click the New Sheet button on the Status bar (the one with plus sign in a circle). Each worksheet you add with the New Sheet command button is assigned a generic Sheet name with the next available number appended to it, so if you click this button twice in a new workbook containing only Sheet1, Excel adds Sheet2 and Sheet3. These worksheet names appear on tabs at the bottom of the Workbook window.

To go from one worksheet to another, you simply click the tab that contains the name of the sheet you want to see. Excel then brings that worksheet to the top of the stack, displaying its information in the current Workbook window. You can always tell which worksheet is current because its name is in bold type on the tab and its tab appears as an extension of the current worksheet with a bold line appearing along the bottom edge.

The only problem with moving to a new sheet by clicking its sheet tab occurs when you add so many worksheets to a workbook (as I describe in the upcoming section "Don't Short-Sheet Me!") that not all the sheet tabs are visible at any one time, and the sheet tab you want to click is not visible in the workbook indicated on the Status bar by an ellipsis (three periods in a row) that appears immediately after the last visible sheet tab.

To deal with the problem of not having all the sheet tabs visible, Excel provides two tab scrolling buttons on the Status bar before the first sheet tab that you can use to bring new sheet tabs into view:

>> Click the Next tab scroll button (with the triangle pointing right) to bring the next unseen tab of the sheet on the right into view. Hold down the Shift key while you click this button to scroll several tabs at a time. Hold down the Ctrl key while you click this button to bring the last group of sheets, including the last sheet tab, into view.

>> Click the Previous tab scroll button (with the triangle pointing left) to bring the next unseen tab of the sheet on the left into view. Hold down the Shift key while you click this button to scroll several tabs at a time. Hold down the Ctrl key when you click this button to bring the first group of sheet tabs, including the very first tab, into view.

>> Right-click either tab scroll button to open the Activate dialog box (shown in Figure 7-1) showing a list of all the worksheets. To activate a worksheet in this list, select it, followed by OK.

FIGURE 7-1:
Right-click a tab
scroll button to
display the
Activate dialog
box with a list
of all the
worksheets in
your workbook.

REMEMBER

Just don't forget that scrolling the sheet tab into view is not the same thing as selecting it: You still need to click the tab for the desired sheet to bring it to the front of the stack (or select it in the Activate dialog box shown in Figure 7-1).

TIP

To make it easier to find the sheet tab you want to select without having to do an inordinate amount of tab scrolling, drag the tab split bar (the three vertical dots that immediately follow the New Sheet button) to the right. Doing this reveals more sheet tabs on the Status bar, consequently making the horizontal scroll bar shorter. If you don't care at all about using the horizontal scroll bar, you can maximize the number of sheet tabs in view by actually getting rid of this scroll bar. To do this, drag the tab split bar to the right until it's smack up against the vertical split bar.

When you want to restore the horizontal scroll bar to its normal length, you can either manually drag the tab split bar to the left or simply double-click it.

GOING SHEET TO SHEET VIA THE KEYBOARD

You can forget all about the tab scrolling buttons and sheet tabs and just go back and forth through the sheets in a workbook with your keyboard. To move to the next worksheet in a workbook, press Ctrl+PgDn. To move to the previous worksheet in a workbook, press Ctrl+PgUp. The nice thing about using the keyboard shortcuts Ctrl+PgDn and Ctrl+PgUp is that they work whether or not the next or previous sheet tab is displayed in the Workbook window!

Editing en masse

Each time you click a sheet tab, you select that worksheet and make it active, enabling you to make whatever changes are necessary to its cells. You may encounter times, however, when you want to select bunches of worksheets so that you can make the same editing changes to all of them simultaneously. When you select multiple worksheets, any editing change that you make to the current worksheet — such as entering information in cells or deleting stuff from them — affects the same cells in all the selected sheets in exactly the same way.

Suppose you need to set up a new workbook with three worksheets that contain the names of the months across row 3 beginning in column B. Prior to entering January in cell B3 and using the AutoFill handle (as described in Chapter 2) to fill in the 11 months across row 3, you select all three worksheets (Sheet1, Sheet2, and Sheet3, for argument's sake). When you enter the names of the months in the third row of the first sheet, Excel will insert the names of the months in row 3 of all three selected worksheets. (Pretty slick, huh?)

Likewise, suppose you have another workbook in which you need to get rid of Sheet2 and Sheet3. Instead of clicking Sheet2, clicking Home ⇨ Delete ⇨ Delete Sheet on the Ribbon or pressing Alt+HDS, and then clicking Sheet3 and repeating the Delete Sheet command, select both worksheets and then zap them out of existence in one fell swoop by clicking Home ⇨ Delete ⇨ Delete Sheet on the Ribbon or pressing Alt+HDS.

To select a bunch of worksheets in a workbook, you have the following choices:

>> To select a group of neighboring worksheets, click the first sheet tab and then scroll the sheet tabs until you see the tab of the last worksheet you want to select. Hold the Shift key while you click the last sheet tab to select all the tabs in between — the old Shift-click method applied to worksheet tabs.

>> To select a group of non-neighboring worksheets, click the first sheet tab and then hold down the Ctrl key while you click the tabs of the other sheets you want to select.

>> To select all the sheets in the workbook, right-click the tab of the worksheet that you want active and choose Select All Sheets from the shortcut menu that appears.

Excel shows you worksheets that you select by turning their sheet tabs white (although only the active sheet's tab name appears in bold) and displaying [Group] after the filename of the workbook on the Excel window's title bar.

TIP

To deselect the group of worksheets when you finish your group editing, you simply click a nonselected (that is, grayed out) worksheet tab. You can also deselect all the selected worksheets other than the one you want active by right-clicking the tab of the sheet you want displayed in the Workbook window and then clicking Ungroup Sheets on its shortcut menu.

Don't Short-Sheet Me!

For some of you, the single worksheet automatically put into each new workbook that you start is as much as you would ever, ever need (or want) to use. For others of you, a measly, single blank worksheet might seldom, if ever, be sufficient for the type of spreadsheets you create (for example, suppose that your company operates in 10 locations, or you routinely create budgets for 20 different departments or track expenses for 40 account representatives).

TIP

Excel 2019 makes it a snap to insert additional worksheets in a workbook (up to 255 total) — simply click the Insert Worksheet button that appears to the immediate right of the last sheet tab.

To insert a bunch of new worksheets in a row in the workbook, select a group with the same number of tabs as the number of new worksheets you want to add, starting with the tab where you want to insert the new worksheets. Next, click Home ⇨ Insert ⇨ Insert Sheet on the Ribbon or press Alt+HIS.

To delete a worksheet from the workbook, follow these steps:

1. **Click the tab of the worksheet that you want to delete.**

2. **Click Home ⇨ Delete ⇨ Delete Sheet on the Ribbon, press Alt+HDS, or right-click the tab and choose Delete from its shortcut menu.**

   If the sheet you're deleting contains any data, Excel displays a scary message in an alert box about how you're going to delete the selected sheets permanently.

3. **Go ahead and click the Delete button or press Enter if you're sure that you won't be losing any data you need when Excel zaps the entire sheet.**

This is one of those situations where Undo is powerless to put things right by restoring the deleted sheet to the workbook.

To delete a bunch of worksheets from the workbook, select all the worksheets you want to delete and then select Home ⇨ Delete ⇨ Delete Sheet, press Alt+HDS, or choose Delete from the tab's shortcut menu. Then, when you're sure that none of the worksheets will be missed, click the Delete button or press Enter when the alert dialog box appears.

If you find yourself constantly adding a bunch of new worksheets, you may want to think about changing the default number of worksheets so that the next time you open a new workbook, you have a more realistic number of sheets on hand. To change the default number, select File ⇨ Options or press Alt+FT to open the General tab of the Excel Options dialog box. Enter a new number between 1 and 255 in the Include This Many Sheets text box in the When Creating New Workbooks section or select a new number with the spinner buttons before you click OK.

A worksheet by any other name . . .

The sheet names that Excel comes up with for the tabs in a workbook (Sheet1, Sheet2, Sheet3) are, to put it mildly, not very original — and are certainly not descriptive of their function in life! Luckily, you can easily rename a worksheet tab to whatever helps you remember what you put on the worksheet (provided this descriptive name is no longer than 31 characters).

To rename a worksheet tab, just follow these steps:

1. **Double-click the sheet tab or right-click the sheet tab and then click Rename on its shortcut menu.**

The current name on the sheet tab appears selected.

2. **Replace the current name on the sheet tab by typing the new sheet name.**

3. **Press Enter.**

Excel displays the new sheet name on its tab at the bottom of the Workbook window.

SHORT AND SWEET (SHEET NAMES)

Although Excel allows up to 31 characters (including spaces) for a sheet name, you want to keep your sheet names much briefer for two reasons:

- The longer the name, the longer the sheet tab. The longer the sheet tab, the fewer the tabs that can display and the more tab scrolling you have to do to select the sheets you want to work with.

- Should you start creating formulas that use cells in different worksheets (see the upcoming section "Summing Stuff on Different Worksheets" for an example), Excel uses the sheet name as part of the cell reference in the formula. (How else could Excel keep straight the value in cell C1 on Sheet1 from the value in cell C1 on Sheet2?) Therefore, if your sheet names are long, you end up with unwieldy formulas in the cells and on the Formula bar, even when you're dealing with simple formulas that only refer to cells in a couple of different worksheets.

Generally, the fewer characters in a sheet name, the better. Also, remember that each name must be unique — no duplicates allowed.

A sheet tab by any other color . . .

In Excel 2019, you can assign colors to the different worksheet tabs. This feature enables you to color-code different worksheets. For example, you could assign red to the tabs of those worksheets that need immediate checking and blue to the tabs of those sheets that you've already checked.

To assign a color to a worksheet tab, right-click the tab and highlight Tab Color on its shortcut menu to open a submenu containing the Tab Color pop-up palette. Then, click the new color for the tab by clicking its color square on the color palette. After you select a new color for a sheet tab, the name of the active sheet tab appears underlined in the color you just selected. When you make another sheet tab active, the entire tab takes on the assigned color (and the text of the tab name changes to white if the selected color is sufficiently dark enough that black lettering is impossible to read).

REMEMBER

To remove a color from a tab, right-click the sheet tab and highlight the Tab Color option to open the Tab Color pop-up palette. Then, click No Color at the bottom of the Tab Color palette.

Getting your sheets in order

Sometimes, you may find that you need to change the order in which the sheets appear in the workbook. Excel makes this possible by letting you drag the tab of the sheet you want to arrange in the workbook to the place where you want to insert it. While you drag the tab, the mouse or Touch pointer changes to a sheet icon with an arrowhead on it, and the program marks your progress among the sheet tabs (see Figures 7-2 and 7-3 for examples). When you release the mouse button, Excel reorders the worksheets in the workbook by inserting the sheet at the place where you dropped the tab off.

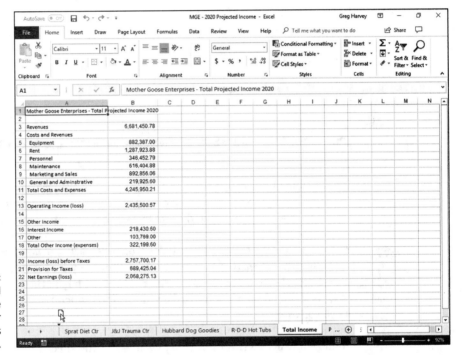

FIGURE 7-2:
Drag the Total Income tab to the front to reorder the sheets in this worksheet.

TIP

If you hold down the Ctrl key while you drag the sheet tab icon, Excel inserts a copy of the worksheet at the place where you release the mouse button. You can tell that Excel is copying the sheet rather than just moving it in the workbook because the pointer shows a plus sign (+) on the sheet tab icon containing the arrowhead. When you release the mouse button or remove your finger or stylus, Excel inserts the copy in the workbook, which is designated by the addition of (2) after the tab name.

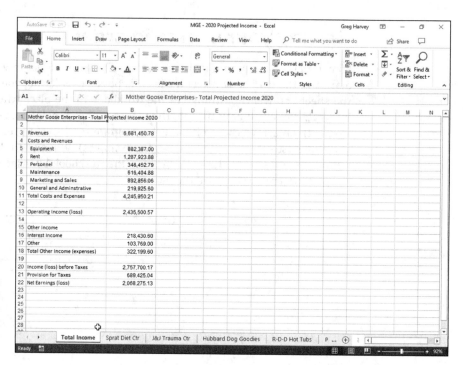

FIGURE 7-3:
The relocated
Total Income
sheet is now at
the front of the
workbook.

For example, if you copy Sheet5 to another place in the workbook, the sheet tab of the copy is named Sheet5 (2). You can then rename the tab to something civilized (see the earlier section "A worksheet by any other name . . ." for details).

You can also move or copy worksheets from one part of a workbook to another by activating the sheet that you want to move or copy and then choosing Move or Copy on its shortcut menu. In the Before Sheet list box in the Move or Copy dialog box, click the name of the worksheet in front of which you want the active sheet moved or copied.

REMEMBER

To move the active sheet immediately ahead of the sheet you select in the Before Sheet list box, simply click OK. To copy the active sheet, be sure to select the Create a Copy check box before you click OK. If you copy a worksheet instead of just moving it, Excel adds a number to the sheet name. For example, if you copy a sheet named Total Income, Excel automatically names the copy of the worksheet Total Income (2), which appears on its sheet tab.

Opening Windows on Your Worksheets

Just as you can split a single worksheet into panes so that you can view and compare different parts of that same sheet on the screen (see Chapter 6), you can split a single workbook into worksheet windows and then arrange the windows so that you can view different parts of each worksheet on the screen.

To open the worksheets that you want to compare in different windows, you simply create new Workbook windows for them (in addition to the one that Excel automatically opens when you open the workbook file itself) and then select the worksheet that you want to display in the new window. You can accomplish this with the following steps:

1. **Click the New Window command button on the View tab or press Alt+WN to create a second worksheet window; then click the tab of the worksheet that you want to display in this second window (indicated by the - 2 that Excel adds to the end of the filename in the title bar).**

2. **Click the New Window command button or press Alt+WN again to create a third worksheet window; then click the tab of the worksheet that you want to display in this third window (indicated by the - 3 that Excel adds to the end of the filename in the title bar).**

3. **Continue clicking the New Window command button or pressing Alt+WN to create a new window and then selecting the tab of the worksheet you want to display in that window for each worksheet you want to compare.**

4. **Click the Arrange All command button on the View tab or press Alt+WA and select one of the Arrange options in the Arrange Windows dialog box (as I describe next); then click OK or press Enter.**

When you open the Arrange Windows dialog box, you're presented with the following options:

» **Tiled:** Select this button to have Excel arrange and size the windows so that they all fit side by side on the screen. (Check out Figure 7-4 to see the screen that appears after you choose the Tiled button to organize four worksheet windows.)

» **Horizontal:** Select this button to have Excel size the windows equally and place them one above the other. (In Figure 7-5, you can see the screen that appears after you choose the Horizontal button to organize these four worksheet windows.)

» **Vertical:** Select this button to have Excel size the windows equally and place them next to each other. (Look at Figure 7-6 to see the screen that appears after you choose the Vertical option to arrange four worksheet windows.)

» **Cascade:** Select this button to have Excel arrange and size the windows so that they overlap one another with only their title bars showing. (See Figure 7-7 for the screen that appears after you select the Cascade option to arrange four worksheet windows.)

>> **Windows of Active Workbook:** Select this check box to have Excel show only the windows that you have open in the current workbook. Otherwise, Excel also displays all the windows in any other workbooks you have open. Yes, it is possible to open more than one workbook — as well as more than one window within each open workbook — provided that the device you're running Excel on has sufficient screen space and memory, and you have enough stamina to keep track of all that information.

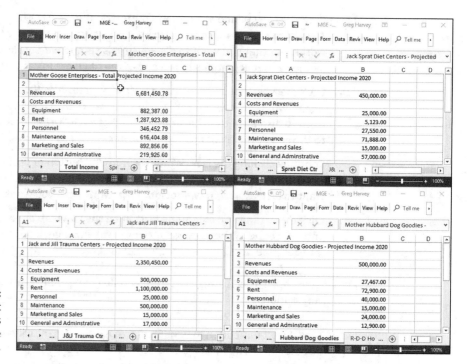

FIGURE 7-4:
Four worksheet windows arranged with the Tiled option.

REMEMBER

After you place windows in one arrangement or another, activate the one you want to use (if it isn't selected already) by clicking it in the Excel program window. Alternatively, position the mouse (or your finger or stylus on a touchscreen) on the Excel program icon on the Windows 10 taskbar to display pop-up thumbnails for each of the worksheet windows you have open. To display the contents of one of the Excel worksheet windows without the others visible, highlight its pop-up thumbnail on the Windows taskbar. To then activate a particular worksheet window from the taskbar, you simply click its thumbnail.

FIGURE 7-5:
Four worksheet windows with the Horizontal option.

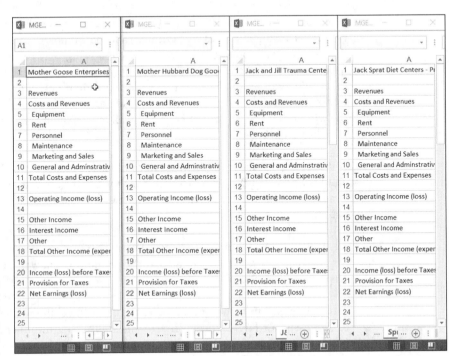

FIGURE 7-6:
Four worksheet windows arranged with the Vertical option.

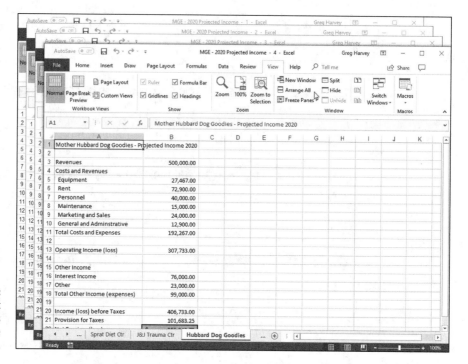

FIGURE 7-7:
Four worksheet
windows
arranged with the
Cascade option.

When you click a worksheet window that has been tiled or placed in the horizontal or vertical arrangement, Excel indicates that the window is selected by displaying the cell pointer around the active cell, highlighting that cell's column and row heading in the worksheet, and displaying its title bar in a regular black font (rather than light gray as in the inactive windows). When you click the title bar of a worksheet window you place in the cascade arrangement, the program displays the window on the top of the stack, as well as displaying the cell pointer in the sheet's active cell.

You can temporarily zoom the window to full size by clicking the Maximize button on the window's title bar. When you finish your work in the full-size worksheet window, return it to its previous arrangement by clicking the window's Restore button.

TIP

To display the next window in a cascade arrangement on the top of the heap with the keyboard, press Ctrl+F6. To display the previous window in a cascade arrangement, press Ctrl+Shift+F6.

If you close one of the windows by clicking Close (the X in the upper-right corner) or by pressing Ctrl+W, Excel doesn't automatically resize the other open windows to fill in the gap. Likewise, if you create another window by clicking the New Window command button on the View tab, Excel doesn't automatically arrange it in with the others. (In fact, the new window just sits on top of the other open windows.)

To fill in the gap created by closing a window or to integrate a newly opened window into the current arrangement, click the Arrange command button to open the Arrange Windows dialog box and click OK or press Enter. (The button you selected last time is still selected; if you want to choose a new arrangement, select a new button before you click OK.)

WARNING

Don't try to close a particular worksheet window by selecting File⇨Close or by pressing Alt+FC because you'll only succeed in closing the entire workbook file, getting rid of all the worksheet windows you created!

When you save your workbook, Excel saves the current window arrangement as part of the file along with all the rest of the changes. If you don't want to save the current window arrangement, close all but one of the windows (by clicking their Close buttons or selecting their windows and then pressing Ctrl+W). Then click that last window's Maximize button and select the tab of the worksheet that you want to display the next time you open the workbook before saving the file.

Comparing Worksheets Side by Side

You can use the View Side by Side command button (the one with the picture of two sheets side by side like tiny tablets of the Ten Commandments) on the Ribbon's View tab to quickly and easily do a side-by-side comparison of any two worksheet windows that you have open. When you click this button (or press Alt+WB after opening two windows), Excel automatically tiles them horizontally (as though you had selected the Horizontal option in the Arrange Windows dialog box), as shown in Figure 7-8.

If you have more than two windows open at the time you click the View Side by Side command button (Alt+WB), Excel opens the Compare Side by Side dialog box where you click the name of the window that you want to compare with the one that's active at the time you choose the command. As soon as you click OK in the Compare Side by Side dialog box, Excel horizontally tiles the active window above the one you just selected.

Immediately below the View Side by Side command button in the Window group of the View tab on the Ribbon, you find the following two command buttons, which are useful when comparing windows side by side:

>> **Synchronous Scrolling:** When this command button is selected (as it is by default), any scrolling that you do in the worksheet in the active window is mirrored and synchronized in the worksheet in the inactive window beneath it. To be able to scroll the worksheet in the active window independently of the inactive window, click the Synchronous Scrolling button to deselect it.

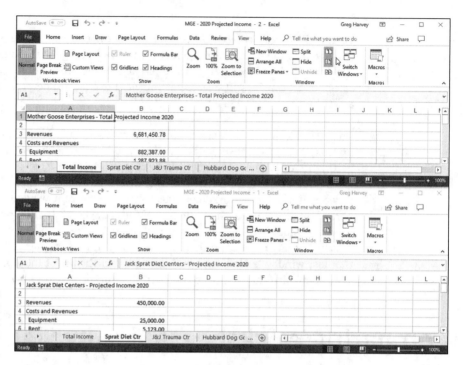

FIGURE 7-8:
Comparing
two worksheet
windows
side by side.

>> **Reset Window Position:** Click this command button after you manually resize the active window (by dragging its size box or an edge of the window) to restore the two windows to their previous side-by-side arrangement.

Shifting Sheets to Other Workbooks

In some situations, you need to move a particular worksheet or copy it from one workbook to another. To move or copy worksheets between workbooks, follow these steps:

1. **Open both the workbook with the worksheet(s) that you want to move or copy and the workbook that is to contain the moved or copied worksheet(s).**

   Select File ➪ Open or press Ctrl+O to open both the workbooks.

2. **Select the workbook that contains the worksheet(s) that you want to move or copy.**

   To select the workbook with the sheet(s) to move or copy, click its pop-up thumbnail on the Windows taskbar.

3. **Select the worksheet(s) that you want to move or copy.**

To select a single worksheet, click its sheet tab. To select a group of neighboring sheets, click the first tab and then hold down Shift while you click the last tab. To select various nonadjacent sheets, click the first tab and then hold down Ctrl while you click each of the other sheet tabs.

4. **Right-click its sheet tab and then click Move or Copy on its shortcut menu.**

Excel opens up the Move or Copy dialog box (similar to the one shown in Figure 7-9) in which you indicate whether you want to move or copy the selected sheet(s) and where to move or copy them.

5. **In the To Book drop-down list box, select the name of the workbook to which you want to copy or move the worksheets.**

If you want to move or copy the selected worksheet(s) to a new workbook rather than to an existing one that you have open, select the (new book) option that appears at the very top of the To Book drop-down list.

6. **In the Before Sheet list box, select the name of the sheet that the worksheet(s) you're about to move or copy should precede. If you want the sheet(s) that you're moving or copying to appear at the end of the workbook, choose the (Move to End) option.**

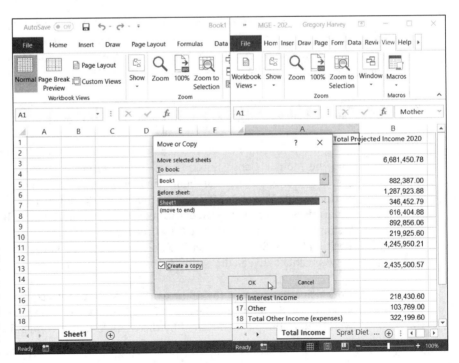

FIGURE 7-9:
Use the Move or Copy dialog box to move or copy from the current workbook into a different workbook.

7. **Select the Create a Copy check box to copy the selected worksheet(s) to the designated workbook (rather than move them).**

8. **Click OK or press Enter to complete the move or copy operation.**

If you prefer a more direct approach, you can move or copy sheets between open workbooks by dragging the sheet tabs from one Workbook window to another. This method works with several sheets or a single sheet; just be sure that you select all the sheet tabs before you begin the drag-and-drop procedure.

TIP

To drag a worksheet from one workbook to another, you must open both workbooks. Click the Arrange All command button on the View tab or press Alt+WA and then select an arrangement (such as Horizontal or Vertical to put the Workbook windows either on top of each other or side by side). Before you close the Arrange Windows dialog box, be sure that the Windows of Active Workbook check box is not selected; that is, does *not* contain a check mark.

After arranging the Workbook windows, drag the worksheet tab from one workbook to another. If you want to copy rather than move the worksheet, hold down the Ctrl key while you drag the sheet icon(s). To locate the worksheet in the new workbook, position the downward-pointing triangle that moves with the sheet icon in front of the worksheet tab where you want to insert it; then release the mouse button or remove your finger or stylus from the touchscreen.

WARNING

This drag-and-drop operation is one of those that you can't reverse by using Excel's Undo feature (see Chapter 4). This means that if you drop the sheet in the wrong workbook, you'll have to go get the wayward sheet yourself and then drag and drop it into the place where it once belonged!

In Figures 7-10 and 7-11, I show how easy it is to move or copy a worksheet from one workbook to another using this drag-and-drop method.

In Figure 7-10, you see two Workbook windows: Book1 new workbook (left pane) and the Mother Goose Enterprises – 2020 Projected Income workbook (right pane). I arranged these Workbook windows with the View Side by Side command button on the View tab. To copy the Sprat Diet Ctr sheet from the Mother Goose Enterprises – 2020 Projected Income workbook to the new Book1 workbook, I simply select the Sprat Diet Ctr sheet tab and drag the sheet icon to its new position before Sheet1 (no need to hold down the Ctrl key as Excel always copies between data between different files).

Now look at Figure 7-11 to see the workbooks after I release the mouse button. As you can see, Excel inserts the copy of the Sprat Diet Ctr worksheet into the Book1 workbook at the place indicated by the triangle that accompanies the sheet icon (before Sheet1 in this example).

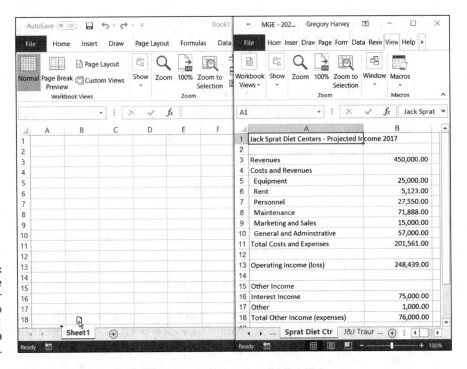

FIGURE 7-10:
Copying the Sprat Diet Ctr worksheet to the Book1 workbook via drag and drop.

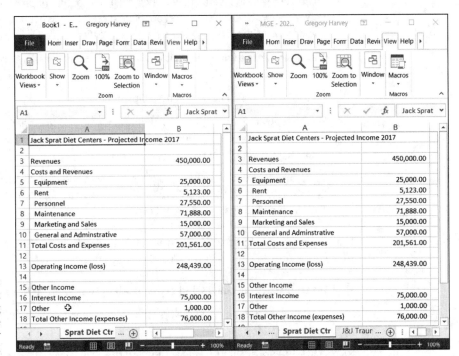

FIGURE 7-11:
Book1 workbook after moving a copy of the Sprat Diet Ctr before Sheet1.

Summing Stuff on Different Worksheets

I'd be remiss if I didn't introduce you to the fascinating subject of creating a *summary worksheet* that recaps or totals the values stored in a bunch of other worksheets in the workbook.

The best way that I can show you how to create a summary worksheet is to walk you through the procedure of making one (entitled Total Projected Income) for the Mother Goose Enterprises – 2020 Projected Income workbook. This summary worksheet totals the projected revenue and expenses for all the companies that Mother Goose Enterprises operates.

Because the Mother Goose Enterprises – 2020 Projected Income workbook already contains nine worksheets with the 2020 projected revenue and expenses for each one of these companies, and because these worksheets are all laid out in the same arrangement, creating this summary worksheet will be a breeze:

1. **I insert a new worksheet in front of the other worksheets in the MGE – 2020 Projected Income workbook and rename its sheet tab from Sheet1 to Total Income.**

   To find out how to insert a new worksheet, refer to this chapter's "Don't Short-Sheet Me!" section. To find out how to rename a sheet tab, read the earlier "A worksheet by any other name . . ." section.

2. **Next, I enter the worksheet title** Mother Goose Enterprises – Total Projected Income 2020 **in cell A1.**

   Do this by selecting cell A1 and then typing the text.

   Finally, I copy the rest of the row headings for column A (containing the revenue and expense descriptions) from the Sprat Diet Ctr worksheet to the Total Income worksheet.

   To do this, select cell A3 in the Total Income sheet and then click the Sprat Diet Ctr tab. Select the cell range A3:A22 in this sheet; then press Ctrl+C, click the Total Income tab again, and press Enter.

I am now ready to create the master SUM formula that totals the revenues of all nine companies in cell B3 of the Total Income sheet:

1. **I start by clicking cell B3 and pressing Alt+= to select the AutoSum feature.**

   Excel then puts =SUM( ) in the cell with the insertion point placed between the two parentheses.

2. **I click the Sprat Diet Ctr sheet tab, and then click its cell B3 to select the projected revenues for the Jack Sprat Diet Centers.**

The Formula bar reads =SUM('Sprat Diet Ctr'!B3) after selecting this cell.

3. **Next, I type a comma (,) — the comma starts a new argument. I click the J&J Trauma Ctr sheet tab and then click its cell B3 to select projected revenues for the Jack and Jill Trauma Centers.**

The Formula bar now reads =SUM('Sprat Diet Ctr'!B3,'J&J Trauma Ctr'!B3) after I select this cell.

4. **I continue in this manner, typing a comma (to start a new argument) and then selecting cell B3 with the projected revenues for all the other companies in the following seven sheets.**

At the end of this procedure, the Formula bar now appears with the whopping SUM formula shown on the Formula bar in Figure 7-12.

5. **To complete the SUM formula in cell B3 of the Total Income worksheet, I then click the Enter button in the Formula bar (I could press Enter on my keyboard, as well).**

In Figure 7-12, note the result in cell B3. As you can see in the Formula bar, the master SUM formula that returns 6,681,450.78 to cell B3 of the Total Income worksheet gets its result by summing the values in B3 in all nine of the supporting worksheets.

FIGURE 7-12:
The Total Income worksheet after I create a SUM formula to total projected revenues for all the Mother Goose companies.

TIP

If you want to select the same cell across multiple worksheets, you can press and hold the Shift key, and then select the last worksheet. All worksheets in between the first and last will be included in the selection, or in this case, the calculation.

All that's left to do now is to use AutoFill to copy the master formula in cell B3 down to row 22, as follows:

1. With cell B3 still selected, I drag the AutoFill handle in the lower-right corner of cell B3 down to cell B22 to copy the formula for summing the values for the nine companies down this column.

2. Then I delete the SUM formulas from cells B4, B12, B14, B15, and B19 (all of which contain zeros because these cells have no income or expenses to total).

In Figure 7-13, you see the first section of the summary Total Income worksheet after I copy the formula created in cell B3 and after I delete the formulas from the cells that should be blank (all those that came up 0 in column B).

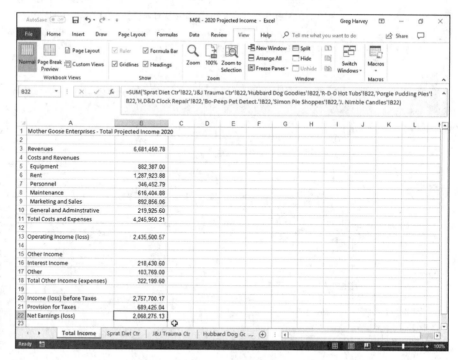

FIGURE 7-13:
The Total Income worksheet after I copy the SUM formula and delete formulas that return zero values.

254   PART 3 **Getting Organized and Staying That Way**

4

Digging Data Analysis

Chapter **8**

Doing What-If Analysis

t would be a big mistake to regard Excel 2019 as merely a fancy calculator that shines at performing static computations, for the program really does excel (if you don't mind the pun) at performing various types of more dynamic *what-if* analysis as well. What-if analysis enables you to explore the possibilities in a worksheet by inputting a variety of promising or probable values into the same equation and letting you see the possible outcomes in black and white (or, at least, in the cells of the spreadsheet).

In Excel 2019, what-if analysis comes in a wide variety of flavors (some of which are more involved than others). In this chapter, I introduce you to these three simple and straightforward methods:

» **Data tables** enable you to see how changing one or two variables affects the bottom line (for example, you may want to know what happens to the net profit if you fall into a 25 percent tax bracket, a 35 percent tax bracket, and so on).

» **Goal seeking** enables you to find out what it takes to reach a predetermined objective, such as how much you have to sell to make a $15 million profit this year.

» **Scenarios** let you set up and test a wide variety of cases, all the way from the best-case scenario (profits grow by 8.5 percent) to the worst-case scenario (you don't make any profit and actually lose money).

Playing What-If with Data Tables

Data tables enable you to enter a series of possible values that Excel then plugs into a single formula. Excel supports two types of data tables: a one-variable data table that substitutes a series of possible values for a single input value in a formula and a two-variable data table that substitutes series of possible values for two input values in a single formula.

Both types of data tables use the very same Data Table dialog box that you open by selecting Data⇨What-If Analysis⇨Data Table on the Ribbon or pressing Alt+AWT. The Data Table dialog box contains two text boxes: Row Input Cell and Column Input Cell.

When creating a one-variable data table, you designate one cell in the worksheet that serves either as the Row Input Cell (if you've entered the series of possible values across columns of a single row) *or* as the Column Input Cell (if you've entered the series of possible values down the rows of a single column).

When creating a two-variable data table, you designate two cells in the worksheet and, therefore, use both text boxes. One cell serves as the Row Input Cell that substitutes the series of possible values you've entered across columns of a single row, and the other cell serves as the Column Input Cell that substitutes the series of possible values you've entered down the rows of a single column.

Creating a one-variable data table

Figure 8-1 shows a 2020 sales projections spreadsheet for which a one-variable data table is to be created. In this worksheet, the projected sales amount in cell B5 is calculated by adding last year's sales total in cell B2 to the amount that I expect it to grow in 2020 (calculated by multiplying last year's total in cell B2 by the growth percentage in cell B3), giving me the formula

```
=B2+(B2*B3)
```

Because I clicked the Create From Selection command button on the Ribbon's Formulas tab after making A2:B5 the selection and accepted the Left Column check box default, the formula uses the row headings in column A and reads:

```
=Sales_2019+(Sales_2019*Growth_2020)
```

FIGURE 8-1:
Sales projection
spreadsheet
with a column of
possible growth
percentages to
plug into a
one-variable
data table.

As you can see in Figure 8-2, I entered a column of possible growth rates ranging from 1% all the way to 5.0% down column B in the range B8:B24. To create the one-variable data table shown in Figure 8-2 that plugs each of these values into the sales growth formula, I follow these simple steps:

1. **Copy the original formula entered in cell B5 into cell C7 by typing = (equal to) and then clicking cell B5 to create the formula** =Projected_Sales_2020.

   The copy of the original formula (to substitute the series of different growth rates in B8:B24 into) is now the column heading for the one-variable data table.

2. **Select the cell range B7:C24.**

   The range of the data table includes the formula along with the various growth rates.

3. **Click Data ⇨ What-If Analysis ⇨ Data Table on the Ribbon.**

   Excel opens the Data Table dialog box.

4. **Click the Column Input Cell text box in the Data Table dialog box and then click cell B3, the Growth_2020 cell with the original percentage, in the worksheet.**

   Excel inserts the absolute cell address, $B$3, into the Column Input Cell text box.

5. Click OK to close the Data Table dialog box.

As soon as you click OK, Excel creates the data table in the range C8:C24 by entering a formula using its TABLE function into this range. Each copy of this formula in the data table uses the growth rate percentage in the same row in column B to determine the possible outcome.

6. Click cell C7 and then click the Format Painter command button in the Clipboard group on the Home tab and drag through the cell range C8:C24.

Excel copies the Accounting number format to the range of possible outcomes calculated by this data table.

FIGURE 8-2:
Sales projection spreadsheet after creating the one-variable data table in the range C8:C24.

REMEMBER

A couple of important things to note about the one-variable data table created in this spreadsheet:

» If you modify any growth-rate percentages in the cell range B8:B24, Excel immediately updates the associated projected sales result in the data table. To prevent Excel from updating the data table until you click the Calculate Now (F9) or Calculate Sheet command button (Shift+F9) on the Formulas tab, click the Calculation Options button on the Formulas tab and then click the Automatic Except for Data Tables option (Alt+MXE).

ARRAY FORMULAS AND THE TABLE FUNCTION IN DATA TABLES

Excel's Data Table feature works by creating a special kind of formula called an array formula in the blank cells of the table. An array formula (enclosed in a pair of curly brackets) is unique in that Excel creates the formulas that it copies into each blank cell of the selection at the time you enter the original formula. (You don't make the formula copies yourself.) As a result, editing changes, such as moving or deleting, are restricted to the entire cell range containing the array formula — it's always all or nothing when editing these babies!

>> If you try to delete any single TABLE formula in the cell range C8:C24, Excel displays a Can't Change Part of a Data Table alert. You must select the entire range of formulas (C8:C24 in this case) before you press Delete or click the Clear or Delete button on the Home tab.

Creating a two-variable data table

To create a two-variable data table, you enter two ranges of possible input values for the same formula in the Data Table dialog box: a range of values for the Row Input Cell across the first row of the table and a range of values for the Column Input Cell down the first column of the table. You then enter the formula (or a copy of it) in the cell located at the intersection of this row and column of input values.

Figure 8-3 illustrates this type of situation. This version of the projected sales spreadsheet uses two variables to calculate the projected sales for year 2020: a growth rate as a percentage of increase over last year's sales (in cell B3 named Growth_2020) and expenses calculated as a percentage of last year's sales (in cell B4 named Expenses_2020). In this example, the original formula created in cell B5 is a bit more complex:

```
=Sales_2019+(Sales_2019*Growth_2020) - (Sales_2019*Expenses_2020)
```

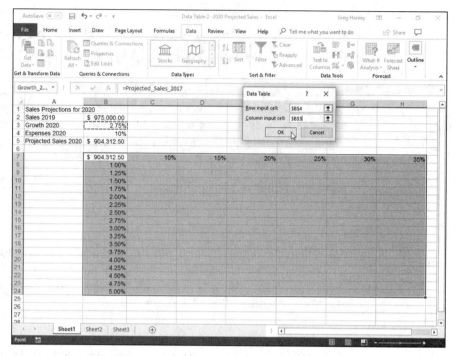

FIGURE 8-3:
Sales projection spreadsheet with a series of possible growth and expense percentages to plug into a two-variable data table.

To set up the two-variable data table, I added a row of possible Expenses_2020 percentages from 10% to 35% in the range C7:H7 to a column of possible Growth_2020 percentages from 1.00% to 5.00% in the range B8:B24. I then copied the original formula named Projected_Sales_2020 from cell B5 to cell B7, the cell at the intersection of this row of Expenses_2020 percentages and column of Growth_2020 percentages with the formula:

```
=Projected_Sales_2020
```

With these few steps, I created the two-variable data table you see in Figure 8-4:

1. **Select the cell range B7:H24.**

   This cell range incorporates the copy of the original formula along with the row of possible expenses and growth-rate percentages.

2. **Click Data ⇨ What-If Analysis ⇨ Data Table on the Ribbon.**

   Excel opens the Data Table dialog box with the insertion point in the Row Input Cell text box.

3. **Click cell B4 to enter the absolute cell address, $B$4, in the Row Input Cell text box.**

4. **Click the Column Input Cell text box and then click cell B3 to enter the absolute cell address, $B$3, in this text box.**

5. **Click OK to close the Data Table dialog box.**

Excel fills the blank cells of the data table with a TABLE formula using B4 as the Row Input Cell and B3 as the Column Input Cell.

6. **Click cell B7, then click the Format Painter command button in the Clipboard group on the Home tab and drag through the cell range C8:H24 to copy the Accounting number format with no decimal places to this range.**

This Accounting number format is too long to display given the current width of columns C through F — indicated by the ###### symbols. With the range C8:H24 still selected from using the Format Painter, Step 7 fixes this problem.

7. **Click the Format command button in the Cells group of the Home tab and then click AutoFit Column Width on its drop-down menu.**

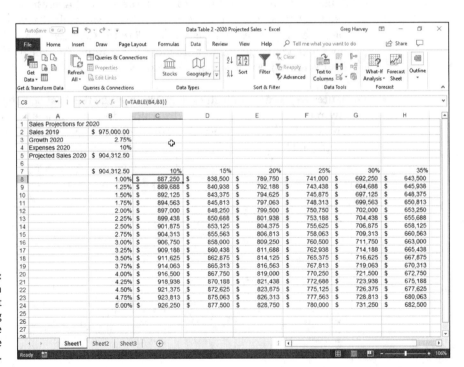

FIGURE 8-4:
Sales projection spreadsheet after creating the two-variable data table in the range C8:H24.

TECHNICAL STUFF

The array formula {=TABLE(B4,B3)} that Excel creates for the two-variable data table in this example specifies both a Row Input Cell argument (B4) and a Column Input Cell argument (B3). (See the nearby "Array formulas and the TABLE function in data tables" sidebar.) Because this single array formula is entered into the entire data table range of C8:H24, any editing (in terms of moving or deleting) is restricted to this range.

Playing What-If with Goal Seeking

Sometimes when doing what-if analysis, you have a particular outcome in mind, such as a target sales amount or growth percentage. When you need to do this type of analysis, you use Excel's Goal Seek feature to find the input values needed to achieve the desired goal.

To use the Goal Seek feature located on the What-If Analysis button's drop-down menu, you need to select the cell containing the formula that will return the result you're seeking (referred to as the *set cell* in the Goal Seek dialog box). Then indicate the target value you want the formula to return as well as the location of the input value that Excel can change to reach this target.

Figures 8-5 and 8-6 illustrate how you can use the Goal Seek feature to find out how much sales must increase to realize first quarter net income of $525,000 (given certain growth, cost of goods sold, and expense assumptions) in a sales forecast table.

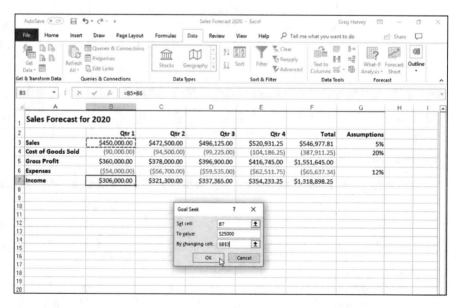

FIGURE 8-5:
Use goal seeking to find out how much sales must increase to reach a target income.

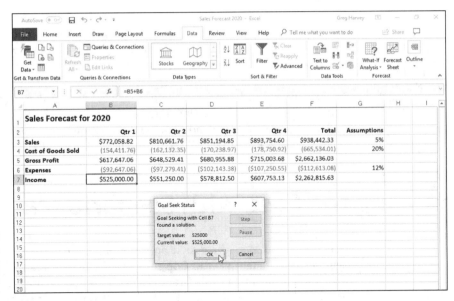

FIGURE 8-6:
Forecast
spreadsheet
showing
goal-seeking
solution.

To find out how much sales must increase to return a net income of $525,000 in the first quarter, select cell B7, which contains the formula that calculates the forecast for the first quarter of 2020 before you select Data⇨What-If Analysis ⇨ Goal Seek on the Ribbon or press Alt+AWG.

This action opens the Goal Seek dialog box, similar to the one shown in Figure 8-5. Because cell B7 is the active cell when you open this dialog box, the Set Cell text box already contains the cell reference B7. You then click in the To Value text box and enter **525000** as the goal. Then, you click the By Changing Cell text box and click cell B3 in the worksheet (the cell that contains the first quarter sales) to enter the absolute cell address, $B$3, in this text box.

Figure 8-6 shows you the Goal Seek Status dialog box that appears when you click OK in the Goal Seek dialog box to have Excel go ahead and adjust the sales figure to reach your desired income figure. As this figure shows, Excel increases the sales in cell B3 from $450,000 to $772,058.82 which, in turn, returns $525,000 as the income in cell B7.

REMEMBER

The Goal Seek Status dialog box informs you that goal seeking has found a solution and that the current value and target value are now the same. When this is not the case, the Step and Pause buttons in the dialog box become active, and you can have Excel perform further iterations to try to narrow and ultimately eliminate the gap between the target and current value.

If you want to keep the values entered in the worksheet as a result of goal seeking, click OK to close the Goal Seek Status dialog box. If you want to return to the original values, click the Cancel button instead.

TIP

To flip between the "after" and "before" values when you've closed the Goal Seek Status dialog box, click the Undo button or press Ctrl+Z to display the original values before goal seeking and click the Redo button or press Ctrl+Y to display the values engendered by the goal-seeking solution.

Making the Case with Scenario Manager

Excel's Scenario Manager option on the What-If Analysis button's drop-down menu on the Data tab of the Ribbon enables you to create and save sets of different input values that produce different calculated results, named *scenarios* (such as Best Case, Worst Case, and Most Likely Case). Because these scenarios are saved as part of the workbook, you can use their values to play what-if simply by opening the Scenario Manager and having Excel show the scenario in the worksheet.

After setting up the various scenarios for a spreadsheet, you can also have Excel create a summary report that shows both the input values used in each scenario as well as the results they produce in your formula.

Setting up the various scenarios

The key to creating the various scenarios for a table is to identify the various cells in the data whose values can vary in each scenario. You then select these cells (known as changing cells) in the worksheet before you open the Scenario Manager dialog box by selecting Data ⇨ What-If Analysis ⇨ Scenario Manager on the Ribbon or by pressing Alt+AWS.

Figure 8-7 shows the Sales Forecast 2020 table after selecting the three changing cells in the worksheet — G3 named Sales_Growth, G4 named COGS (Cost of Goods Sold), and G6 named Expenses — and then opening the Scenario Manager dialog box (Alt+AWS).

I want to create three scenarios using the following sets of values for the three changing cells:

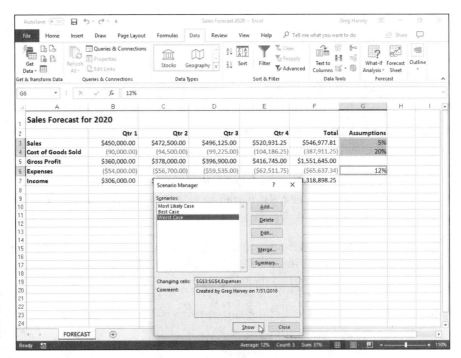

» **Most Likely Case** where the Sales_Growth percentage is 5%, COGS is 20%, and Expenses is 12%

» **Best Case** where the Sales_Growth percentage is 8%, COGS is 18%, and Expenses is 10%

» **Worst Case** where the Sales_Growth percentage is 2%, COGS is 25%, and Expenses is 20%

To create the first scenario, I click the Add button in the Scenario Manager dialog box to open the Add Scenario dialog box, enter **Most Likely Case** in the Scenario Name box, and then click OK. (Remember that the three cells currently selected in the worksheet, G3, G4, and G6, are already listed in the Changing Cells text box of this dialog box.) Note that Excel 2019 automatically selects the Prevent Changes check box under the Protection heading at the bottom of Add Scenario dialog box to prevent users from changing the values in these cells of the worksheet. If you want their values to be hidden as well, be sure to select the Hide option before you click OK.

When you click OK, Excel then displays the Scenario Values dialog box where I accept the following values already entered in each of the three text boxes (from the Sales Forecast for 2017 table), Sales_Growth, COGS, and Expenses, before clicking its Add button:

>> **0.05** in the Sales_Growth text box

>> **0.2** in COGS text box

>> **0.12** in the Expenses text box

TIP

Always assign range names as described in Chapter 6 to your changing cells before you begin creating the various scenarios that use them. That way, Excel always displays the cells' range names rather than their addresses in the Scenario Values dialog box.

After clicking the Add button, Excel redisplays the Add Scenario dialog box where I enter **Best Case** in the Scenario Name box and the following values in the Scenario Values dialog box:

>> **0.08** in the Sales_Growth text box

>> **0.18** in the COGS text box

>> **0.10** in the Expenses text box

After making these changes, I click the Add button again. Doing this opens the Add Scenario dialog box where I enter **Worst Case** as the scenario name and the following scenario values:

>> **0.02** in the Sales_Growth text box

>> **0.25** in the COGS text box

>> **0.20** in the Expenses text box

Because this is the last scenario that I want to add, I then click the OK button instead of Add. Doing this opens the Scenario Manager dialog box again, this time displaying the names of all three scenarios — Most Likely Case, Best Case, and Worst Case — in its Scenarios list box. To have Excel plug the changing values assigned to any of these three scenarios into the Sales Forecast for 2020 table, I click the scenario name in this list box followed by the Show button.

REMEMBER

After adding the various scenarios for a table in your spreadsheet, don't forget to save the workbook after closing the Scenario Manager dialog box if you aren't using AutoSave. That way, you'll have access to the various scenarios each time you open the workbook in Excel simply by opening the Scenario Manager, selecting the scenario name, and clicking the Show button.

Producing a summary report

After adding your scenarios to a table in a spreadsheet, you can have Excel produce a summary report on its own worksheet like the one shown in Figure 8-8. This report displays the changing and resulting values for not only all the scenarios you've defined, but also the current values that are entered into the changing cells in the worksheet table at the time you generate the report.

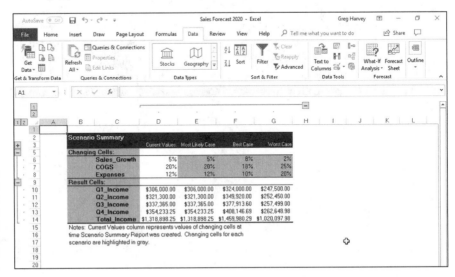

FIGURE 8-8:
Scenario
Summary report
showing the
various scenarios
added to the
Sales Forecast
for 2020 table.

To produce a summary report, open the Scenario Manager dialog box (Data ⇨ What-If Analysis ⇨ Scenario Manager or Alt+AWS) and then click the Summary button to open the Scenario Summary dialog box.

This dialog box gives you a choice between creating a (static) Scenario Summary (the default) and a (dynamic) Scenario PivotTable Report (see Chapter 9). You can also modify the range of cells in the table that is included in the Result Cells section of the summary report by adjusting the cell range in the Result Cells text box before you click OK to generate the report. For this example, I chose the cell range B7:F7 with the named cells, Q1_Income, Q2_Income, Q3_Income, Q4_Income, and Total_Income as the Result Cells for this summary report.

After you click OK, Excel creates the summary report for the changing values in all the scenarios (and the current worksheet) along with the calculated values in the Result Cells on a new worksheet (named Scenario Summary). You can then rename and reposition the Scenario Summary worksheet before you save it as part of the workbook file.

PERFORMING MORE SOPHISTICATED WHAT-IF ANALYSIS

In addition to the straightforward what-if analysis offered by the Scenario Manager, Goal Seek, and Data Table options on the What-If Analysis button's drop-down menu on the Data tab of the Ribbon, Excel 2019 supports a more complex what-if analysis in the form of the Solver add-in program (see Chapter 12 for information on add-ins) and the Forecast Sheet button on the Data tab of the Ribbon. With the Solver, you can create models that not only involve changes to multiple input values but also impose constraints on these inputs or on the results themselves. With Forecast Sheet, you can create a visual forecast (sometimes called an infographic) that uses historical data to generate a chart of the forecasted results. For details on using Solver and Forecast Sheet in Excel 2019, see my *Microsoft Excel 2019 All-in-One For Dummies*.

Chapter **9**

Playing with Pivot Tables

ivot table is Microsoft's name for a special type of summary table that's unique to Excel. Pivot tables are great for summarizing particular values in a data list or database because they do their magic without making you create formulas to perform the calculations. They also enable you to quickly and easily examine and analyze relationships inherent in their data sources; data lists you maintain in Excel; or external database tables you import into Excel from standalone database applications such as Microsoft Office Access, or from a data feed such as Windows Azure Marketplace (as discussed in Chapter 11).

Pivot tables also let you play around with the arrangement of the summarized data — even after you generate the table. This capability of changing the arrangement of the summarized data on the fly simply by rotating row and column headings gives the pivot table its name. And, if you're the type who relates better to data represented in pictorial form, Excel enables you to summarize your data list graphically as a pivot chart using any of the many, many chart types now supported by the program.

Data Analysis with Pivot Tables

Pivot tables are so very versatile because they enable you to easily analyze summaries of large amounts of data by using a variety of summary functions (although totals created with the SUM function will probably remain your old standby). When setting up the original pivot table (as described in the following section), you make several decisions: what summary function to use, which columns (fields) the summary function is applied to, and which columns (fields) these computations are tabulated with.

REMEMBER

Pivot tables are perfect for cross-tabulating one set of data in your data list with another. For example, you can create a pivot table from an employee database table that totals the salaries for each job category cross-tabulated (arranged) by department or job site.

Pivot tables via the Quick Analysis tool

Excel 2019 makes creating a new pivot table a snap with the Quick Analysis tool. To preview various types of pivot tables that Excel can create for you on the spot using the entries in a data table or list that you have open in an Excel worksheet, simply follow these steps:

1. **Select the data (including the column headings) in your table or list as a cell range in the worksheet.**

2. **Click the Quick Analysis tool that appears right below the lower-right corner of the current cell selection.**

   Doing this opens the palette of Quick Analysis options with the initial Formatting tab selected and its various conditional formatting options displayed.

3. **Click the Tables tab at the top of the Quick Analysis options palette.**

   Excel selects the Tables tab and displays its Table and PivotTable option buttons. The Table button previews how the selected data would appear formatted as a table (see Chapter 3 for details). The other PivotTable buttons preview the various types of pivot tables that can be created from the selected data.

4. **To preview each pivot table that Excel 2019 can create for your data, highlight its PivotTable button in the Quick Analysis palette.**

   As you highlight each PivotTable button in the options palette, Excel's Live Preview feature displays a thumbnail of a pivot table that can be created using your table data. This thumbnail appears above the Quick Analysis options palette for as long as the mouse or Touch pointer is over its corresponding button.

5. **When a preview of the pivot table you want to create appears, click its button in the Quick Analysis options palette to create it.**

Excel 2019 then creates the previewed pivot table on a new worksheet that is inserted at the beginning of the current workbook. This new worksheet containing the pivot table is active so that you can immediately rename and relocate the sheet as well as edit the new pivot table, if you wish.

Figures 9-1 and 9-2 show you how this procedure works. In Figure 9-1, I've highlighted the third suggested PivotTable button in the Quick Analysis tool's option palette. The previewed table in the thumbnail displayed above the palette shows subtotals and grand totals for company sales for each of the three months of the first quarter organized by their sector (Retail or Service).

Figure 9-2 shows you the pivot table that Excel created when I clicked the highlighted button in the options palette in Figure 9-1. Note this pivot table is selected on its own worksheet (Sheet1) that's been inserted in front of the Q1 Sales worksheet. Because the new pivot table is selected, the PivotTable Fields task pane is displayed on the right side of the Excel worksheet window, and the PivotTable Tools contextual tab is displayed on the Ribbon. You can use the options on this task pane and contextual tab to then customize your new pivot table, as described in the "Formatting Pivot Tables" and "Modifying Pivot Tables" sections later in this chapter.

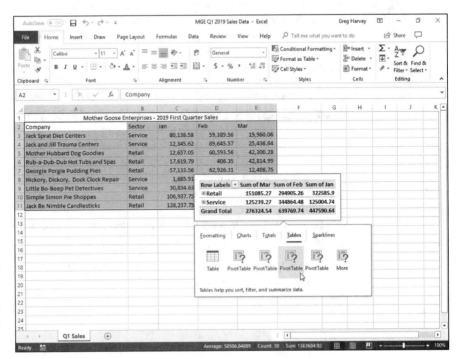

FIGURE 9-1:
Previewing the pivot table to create from the selected data in the Quick Analysis options palette.

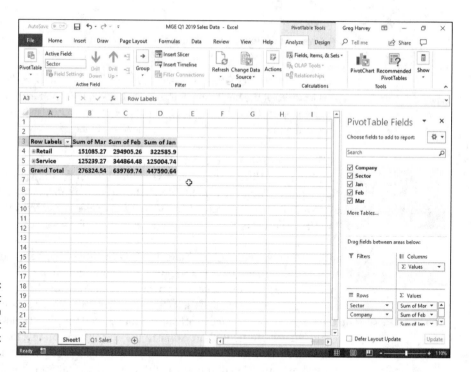

FIGURE 9-2:
Previewed pivot
table created on
a new worksheet
with the Quick
Analysis tool.

REMEMBER

Note that if Excel can't suggest various pivot tables to create from the selected data in the worksheet, a single Blank PivotTable button is displayed after the Table button in the Quick Analysis tool's options on the Tables tab. You can select this button to manually create a new pivot table for the data, as described later in this chapter.

Pivot tables by recommendation

If creating a new pivot table with the Quick Analysis tool (described in the previous section) is too much work for you, you generate them in a snap with the Recommended Pivot Tables command button. To use this method, follow these easy steps:

1. **Select a cell in the data list for which you want to create the new pivot table.**

Provided that your data list has a row of column headings with contiguous rows of data as described in Chapter 11, this can be any cell in the table.

2. **Select the Recommended PivotTables command button on the Insert tab of the Ribbon or press Alt+NSP.**

Excel displays a Recommended PivotTables dialog box similar to the one shown in Figure 9-3. This dialog box contains a list box on the left side that shows samples of all the suggested pivot tables that Excel 2019 can create from the data in your list.

3. **Select the sample of the pivot table you want to create in the list box on the left and then click OK.**

FIGURE 9-3:
Creating a new
pivot table from
the sample
pivot tables
displayed in the
Recommended
PivotTables
dialog box.

As soon as you click OK, Excel creates a new pivot table following the selected sample on its own worksheet (Sheet1) inserted in front of the others in your workbook. This pivot table is selected on the new sheet so that the Pivot Table Fields task pane is displayed on the right side of the Excel worksheet window and the PivotTable Tools contextual tab is displayed on the Ribbon. You can use the options on this task pane and contextual tab to then customize your new pivot table as described in the "Formatting Pivot Tables" and "Modifying Pivot Tables" sections later in this chapter.

Manually producing pivot tables

Sometimes, none of the pivot tables that Excel 2019 suggests when creating a new table with the Quick Analysis tool or the Recommended PivotTables command button fit the type of data summary you have in mind. In such cases, you can either select the suggested pivot table whose layout is closest to what you have in mind, or you can choose to create the pivot table from scratch (a process that isn't all that difficult or time consuming).

To manually create a new pivot table from the worksheet with the data to be analyzed, position the cell pointer somewhere in the cells of this list and then click the PivotTable command button on the Ribbon's Insert tab or press Alt+NV.

Excel then opens the Create PivotTable dialog box and selects all the data in the list containing the cell cursor (indicated by a marquee around the cell range). You can then adjust the cell range in the Table/Range text box under the Select a Table or Range button if the marquee does not include all the data to summarize in the pivot table. By default, Excel builds the new pivot table on a new worksheet it adds to the workbook. If, however, you want the pivot table to appear on the same worksheet, click the Existing Worksheet button and then indicate the location of the first cell of the new table in the Location text box, as shown in Figure 9-4. (Just be sure that this new pivot table isn't going to overlap any existing tables of data.)

FIGURE 9-4:
Indicate the data source and pivot table location in the Create PivotTable dialog box.

TIP

If the data source for your pivot table is an external database table created with a separate database management program, such as Access, you need to click the Use an External Data Source button, click the Choose Connection button, and then click the name of the connection in the Existing Connections dialog box. (See

Chapter 11 for information on establishing a connection with an external file and importing its data through a query.) Also, Excel 2019 supports analyzing data from multiple related tables on a worksheet (referred to as a Data Model). If the data in new pivot table you're creating is to be analyzed along with another existing pivot table, be sure to select the Add This Data to the Data Model check box.

If you indicate a new worksheet as the location for the new pivot table in the Create PivotTable dialog box, when you click OK, the program inserts a new worksheet at the front of the workbook with a blank grid for the new pivot table. It also opens the PivotTable Fields task pane on the right side of the Worksheet area and adds the PivotTable Tools contextual tab to the Ribbon (see Figure 9-5). The PivotTable Fields task pane is divided into two areas: the Choose Fields to Add to Report list box with the names of all the fields in the data list you can select as the source of the table preceded by empty check boxes, and a Drag Fields between Areas Below section divided into four drop zones (FILTERS, COLUMNS, ROWS, and VALUES).

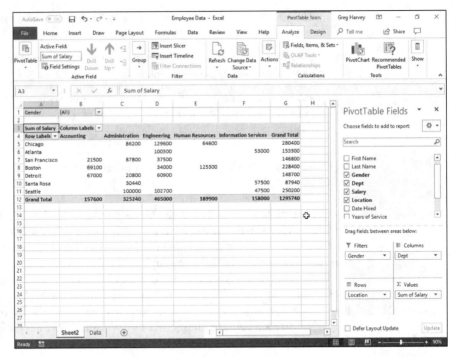

FIGURE 9-5:
Completed pivot table after adding the fields from the employee data list to the various drop zones.

REMEMBER

You can also insert a new worksheet with the blank pivot table grid like the one shown in Figure 9-5 by selecting the Blank PivotTable button in the Recommended PivotTable dialog box (shown in Figure 9-3) or the Quick Analysis tool's options palette (displayed only when Quick Analysis can't suggest pivot tables for your data). Just be aware that when you select the Blank PivotTable button in this dialog box or palette, Excel 2019 does not first open the Create PivotTable dialog box shown in Figure 9-4. If you need to use any of the options offered in this dialog box in creating your new pivot table, you need to create the pivot table with the PivotTable command button rather than the Recommended PivotTables command button on the Insert Tab.

To complete the new pivot table, all you have to do is assign the fields in the PivotTable Fields task pane to the various parts of the table. You do this by dragging a field name from the Choose Fields to Add to Report list box and dropping it in one of the four areas below, called drop zones:

>> **FILTERS:** This area contains the fields that enable you to page through the data summaries shown in the actual pivot table by filtering out sets of data — they act as the filters for the report. For example, if you designate the Year field from a data list as a report filter, you can display data summaries in the pivot table for individual years or for all years represented in the data list.

>> **COLUMNS:** This area contains the fields that determine the arrangement of data shown in the columns of the pivot table.

>> **ROWS:** This area contains the fields that determine the arrangement of data shown in the rows of the pivot table.

>> **VALUES:** This area contains the fields that determine which data are presented in the cells of the pivot table — they are the values that are summarized in its last column (totaled by default).

To understand how these various zones relate to a pivot table, look at the completed pivot table shown in Figure 9-5.

For this pivot table, I assigned the Gender field from the data list (a field that contains F (for female) or M (for male) to indicate the employee's gender in the FILTERS drop zone. I also assigned the Dept field (that contains the names of the various departments in the company) to the COLUMNS drop zone, the Location field (that contains the names of the various cities with corporate offices) to the ROWS drop zone, and the Salary field to the VALUES drop zone. As a result, this pivot table now displays the sum of the salaries for both the male and female employees in each department (across the columns) and then presents these sums by their corporate location (in each row).

As soon as you add fields to a new pivot table (or select the cell of an existing table in a worksheet), Excel selects the Analyze tab of the PivotTable Tools contextual tab that automatically appears in the Ribbon. Among the many groups on this tab, you find the Show group at the end that contains the following useful command buttons:

>> **Field List** to hide and redisplay the PivotTable Field List task pane on the right side of the Worksheet area

>> **+/− Buttons** to hide and redisplay the expand (+) and collapse (-) buttons in front of particular column fields or row fields that enable you to temporarily remove and then redisplay their particular summarized values in the pivot table

>> **Field Headers** to hide and redisplay the fields assigned to the Column Labels and Row Labels in the pivot table

Formatting Pivot Tables

Excel 2019 makes formatting a new pivot table you've added to a worksheet as quick and easy as formatting any other table of data or list of data. All you need to do is click a cell of the pivot table to add the PivotTable Tools contextual tab to the Ribbon and then click its Design tab to display its command buttons.

The Design tab is divided into three groups:

>> **Layout** group that enables you to add subtotals and grand totals to the pivot table and modify its basic layout

>> **PivotTable Style Options** group that enables you to refine the pivot table style you select for the table using the PivotTable Styles gallery to the immediate right

>> **PivotTable Styles** group that contains the gallery of styles you can apply to the active pivot table by clicking the desired style thumbnail

Refining the Pivot Table style

When selecting a new formatting style for your new pivot table from the Pivot-Table Styles drop-down gallery, you can use Excel's Live Preview feature to see how the pivot table would look in any style that you highlight in the gallery with your mouse or Touch pointer.

After selecting a style from the gallery in the PivotTable Styles group on the Design tab, you can then refine the style using the check box command buttons in the PivotTable Style Options group. For example, you can add banding to the columns or rows of a style that doesn't already use alternate shading to add more contrast to the table data by putting a check mark in the Banded Rows or Banded Columns check box, or you can remove this banding by clearing these check boxes.

Formatting values in the pivot table

To format the summed values entered as the data items of the pivot table with an Excel number format, you follow these steps:

1. **Click the field in the table that contains the words "Sum of" and the name of the field whose values are summarized there, click the Active Field command button on the Analyze tab under the PivotTable Tools contextual tab, and then click the Fields Settings option on its pop-up menu.**

   Excel opens the Value Field Settings dialog box.

2. **Click the Number Format command button in the Value Field Settings dialog box to open the Format Cells dialog box with its sole Number tab.**

3. **Click the type of number format you want to assign to the values in the pivot table on the Category list box of the Number tab.**

4. **(Optional) Modify any other options for the selected number format, such as Decimal Places, Symbol, and Negative Numbers, that are available for that format.**

5. **Click OK twice, the first time to close the Format Cells dialog box, and the second to close the Value Field Settings dialog box.**

Sorting and Filtering Pivot Table Data

When you create a new pivot table, you'll notice that Excel automatically adds drop-down buttons to the Report Filter field, as well as the labels for the column and row fields. These drop-down buttons, known officially as *filter buttons* (see Chapter 11 for details), enable you to filter all but certain entries in any of these fields, and in the case of the column and row fields, to sort their entries in the table.

If you've added more than one column or row field to your pivot table, Excel adds collapse buttons (–) that you can use to temporarily hide subtotal values for a particular secondary field. After clicking a collapse button in the table, it immediately becomes an expand button (+) that you can click to redisplay the subtotals for that one secondary field.

Filtering the report

Perhaps the most important filter buttons in a pivot table are the ones added to the field(s) designated as the pivot table FILTERS. By selecting a particular option on the drop-down lists attached to one of these filter buttons, only the summary data for that subset you select displays in the pivot table.

For example, in the sample pivot table (refer to Figure 9-5) that uses the Gender field from the Employee Data list as the Report Filter field, you can display the sum of just the men's or women's salaries by department and location in the body of the pivot table doing either of the following:

>> Click the Gender field's filter button and then click M on the drop-down list before you click OK to see only the totals of the men's salaries by department.

>> Click the Gender field's filter button and then click F on the drop-down list before you click OK to see only the totals of the women's salaries by department.

When you later want to redisplay the summary of the salaries for all the employees, you then reselect the (All) option on the Gender field's drop-down filter list before you click OK.

REMEMBER

When you filter the Gender Report Filter field in this manner, Excel then displays M or F in the Gender Report Filter field instead of the default (All). The program also replaces the standard drop-down button with a cone-shaped filter icon, indicating that the field is filtered and showing only some of the values in the data source.

Filtering column and row fields

The filter buttons on the column and row fields attached to their labels enable you to filter out entries for particular groups and, in some cases, individual entries in the data source. To filter the summary data in the columns or rows of a pivot table, click the column or row field's filter button and start by clicking the check box for the (Select All) option at the top of the drop-down list to clear this box of its check mark. Then, click the check boxes for all the groups or individual entries whose summed values you still want displayed in the pivot table to put back check marks in each of their check boxes. Then click OK.

As with filtering a Report Filter field, Excel replaces the standard drop-down button for that column or row field with a cone-shaped filter icon, indicating that the field is filtered and displaying only some of its summary values in the pivot table. To redisplay all the values for a filtered column or row field, you need to click its filter button and then click (Select All) at the top of its drop-down list. Then click OK.

Figure 9-6 shows the sample pivot table after filtering its Gender Report Filter field to women (by selecting F in the Gender drop-down list) and its Dept Column field to Accounting, Administration, and Human Resources.

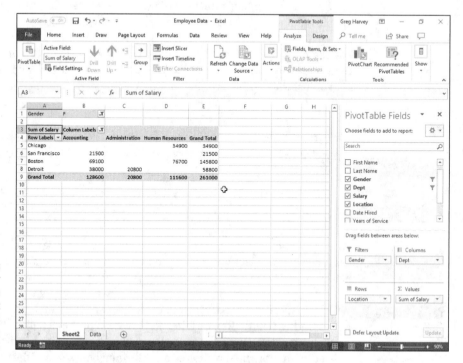

FIGURE 9-6:
Pivot table after
filtering the
Gender Report
Filter field and
the Dept Column
field.

REMEMBER

In addition to filtering out individual entries in a pivot table, you can also use the options on the Label Filters and Value Filters continuation menus to filter groups of entries that don't meet certain criteria, such as company locations that don't start with a particular letter or salaries between $45,000 and $65,000. For more on using these types of filtering options, see the section about filtering the records in a data list in Chapter 11.

Filtering with slicers

Slicers in Excel 2019 make it a snap to filter the contents of your pivot table on more than one field. (They even allow you to connect with fields of other pivot tables that you've created in the workbook.)

To add slicers to your pivot table, you follow just two steps:

1. **Click one of the cells in your pivot table to select it and then click the Insert Slicer button located in the Filter group of the Analyze tab under the PivotTable Tools contextual tab.**

   Excel opens the Insert Slicers dialog box with a list of all the fields in the active pivot table.

2. **Select the check boxes for all the fields that you want to use in filtering the pivot table and for which you want slicers created and then click OK.**

   Excel then adds slicers (as graphic objects — see Chapter 10 for details) for each pivot table field you select and automatically closes the PivotTable Fields task pane if it's open at the time.

After you create slicers for the pivot table, you can use them to filter its data simply by selecting the items you want displayed in each slicer. You select items in a slicer by clicking them just as you do cells in a worksheet — hold down Ctrl as you click nonconsecutive items and Shift to select a series of sequential items.

Figure 9-7 shows you the sample pivot table after using slicers created for the Gender, Dept, and Location fields to filter the data so that only salaries for the men in the Human Resources and Administration departments in the Boston, Chicago, and San Francisco offices display.

REMEMBER

Because slicers are Excel graphic objects (albeit some pretty fancy ones), you can move, resize, and delete them just as you would any other Excel graphic; see Chapter 10 for details. To remove a slicer from your pivot table, click it to select it and then press the Delete key.

Filtering with timelines

Excel 2019 offers another fast and easy way to filter your data with its timeline feature. You can think of timelines as slicers designed specifically for date fields that enable you to filter data out of your pivot table that doesn't fall within a particular period, thereby allowing you to see timing of trends in your data.

To create a timeline for your pivot table, select a cell in your pivot table and then click the Insert Timeline button in the Filter group on the Analyze contextual tab under the PivotTable Tools tab on the Ribbon. Excel then displays an Insert Timelines dialog box displaying a list of pivot table fields that you can use in creating the new timeline. After selecting the check box for the date field you want to use in this dialog box, click OK.

FIGURE 9-7:
Sample pivot
table filtered
with slicers
created for the
Gender, Dept,
and Location
fields.

Figure 9-8 shows you the timeline I created for the sample Employee Data list by selecting its Date Hired field in the Insert Timelines dialog box. As you can see, Excel created a floating Date Hired timeline with the years and months demarcated and a bar that indicates the time period selected. By default, the timeline uses months as its units, but you can change this to years, quarters, or even days by clicking the MONTHS drop-down button and selecting the desired time unit.

I then literally use the timeline to select the period for which I want my pivot table data displayed. In Figure 9-8, I have filtered the sample pivot table so that it shows the salaries by department and location for only employees hired in the year 2000. I did this simply by dragging the timeline bar in the Date Hired timeline graphic so that it begins at Jan, 2000 and extends just up to and including Dec, 2000. And to filter the pivot table salary data for other hiring periods, I simply modify the start and stop times by dragging the timeline bar in the Date Hired timeline.

Sorting the pivot table

You can instantly reorder the summary values in a pivot table by sorting the table on one or more of its column or row fields. To re-sort a pivot table, click the filter button for the column or row field you want to use in the sorting and then click the Sort A to Z option or the Sort Z to A option at the top of the field's drop-down list.

FIGURE 9-8:
Sample pivot table filtered with a timeline created for the Date Hired field.

Click the Sort A to Z option when you want the table re-ordered by sorting the labels in the selected field alphabetically or, in the case of values, from the smallest to largest value or, in the case of dates, from the oldest to newest date. Click the Sort Z to A option when you want the table re-ordered by sorting the labels in reverse alphabetical order, values from the highest to smallest, and dates from the newest to oldest.

Modifying Pivot Tables

Pivot tables are much more dynamic than standard Excel data tables because they remain so easy to manipulate and modify. Excel makes it just as easy to change which fields from the original data source display in the table as it did adding them when the table was created. Additionally, you can instantly restructure the pivot table by dragging its existing fields to new positions on the table. Add the ability to select a new summary function using any of Excel's basic Statistical functions, and you have yourself the very model of a flexible data table!

Modifying the pivot table fields

To modify the fields used in your pivot table, first you display the PivotTable Fields task pane by simply clicking one of the cells in your pivot table. The Pivot-Table Fields task pane shows the fields that are currently in the pivot table, as well as the areas to which they're currently assigned. This task pane is usually displayed automatically when creating or selecting a Pivot Table, but if you do not see the task pane, click the Field List button on the Analyze contextual tab.

After displaying the PivotTable Fields task pane, you can make any of the following modifications to the table's fields:

» To remove a field, drag its field name out of any of its drop zones (FILTERS, COLUMNS, ROWS, and VALUES) and, when the mouse pointer changes to an x, release the mouse button or click its check box in the Choose Fields to Add to Report list to remove its check mark.

» To move an existing field to a new place in the table, drag its field name from its current drop zone to a new zone at the bottom of the task pane.

» To add a field to the table, drag its field name from the Choose Fields to Add to Report list and drop the field in the desired drop zone. If all you want to do is add a field to the pivot table as an additional row field, you can do this by selecting the field's check box in the Choose Fields to Add to Report list to add a check mark (you don't have to drag it to the ROWS drop zone).

Pivoting the table's fields

As *pivot* implies, the fun of pivot tables is being able to restructure the table simply by rotating the column and row fields. For example, suppose that after making the Dept field the column field and the Location field the row field in the example pivot table, I now decide I want to see what the table looks like with the Location field as the column field and the Dept field as the row field.

No problem at all: In the PivotTable Fields task pane, I simply drag the Dept field label from the COLUMNS drop zone to the ROWS drop zone and the Location field from the ROWS drop zone to the COLUMNS drop zone.

Voilà — Excel rearranges the totaled salaries so that the rows of the pivot table show the departmental grand totals and the columns now show the location grand totals.

TIP

You can switch column and row fields by dragging their labels to their new locations directly in the pivot table itself. Before you can do that, however, you must select the Classic PivotTable Layout (Enables Dragging of Fields in the Grid) check box on the Display tab of the PivotTable Options dialog box. To open this dialog box, you select the Options item on the PivotTable button's drop-down menu. This button is located at the very beginning of the Analyze tab beneath the Pivot-Table Tools contextual tab.

Modifying the table's summary function

By default, Excel uses the good old SUM function to create subtotals and grand totals for the numeric field(s) that you assign as the Data Items in the pivot table.

Some pivot tables, however, require the use of another summary function, such as AVERAGE or COUNT. To change the summary function that Excel uses, simply click the Sum Of field label that's located at the cell intersection of the first column field and row field in a pivot table. Next, click the Field Settings command button on the Analyze tab to open the Value Field Settings dialog box for that field, similar to the one shown in Figure 9-9.

FIGURE 9-9:
Selecting a new summary function in the Value Field Settings dialog box.

After you open the Value Field Settings dialog box, you can change its summary function from the default Sum to any of the following functions by selecting it in the Summarize Value Field By list box:

>> **Count** to show the count of the records for a particular category (Count is the default setting for any text fields that you use as Data Items in a pivot table)

» **Average** to calculate the average (that is, the arithmetic mean) for the values in the field for the current category and page filter

» **Max** to display the largest numeric value in that field for the current category and page filter

» **Min** to display the smallest numeric value in that field for the current category and page filter

» **Product** to display the product of the numeric values in that field for the current category and page filter (all non-numeric entries are ignored)

» **Count Numbers** to display the number of numeric values in that field for the current category and page filter (all non-numeric entries are ignored)

» **StdDev** to display the standard deviation for the sample in that field for the current category and page filter

» **StdDevp** to display the standard deviation for the population in that field for the current category and page filter

» **Var** to display the variance for the sample in that field for the current category and page filter

» **Varp** to display the variance for the population in that field for the current category and page filter

After you select the new summary function to use in the Summarize Value Field By list box on the Summarize Values By tab of the Value Field Settings dialog box, click OK to have Excel apply the new function to the data present in the body of the pivot table.

Creating Pivot Charts

After creating a pivot table, you can create a pivot chart to display its summary values graphically in two simple steps:

1. **Click the PivotChart command button in the Tools group on the Analyze tab under the PivotTable Tools contextual tab to open the Insert Chart dialog box.**

   Remember that the PivotTable Tools contextual tab with its two tabs — Analyze and Design — automatically appears whenever you click any cell in an existing pivot table.

2. **Click the thumbnail of the type of chart you want to create in the Insert Chart dialog box and then click OK.**

As soon you click OK after selecting the chart type, Excel displays two things in the worksheet with the pivot table:

>> **Pivot chart** using the type of chart you selected that you can move and resize as needed (officially known as an *embedded chart* — see Chapter 10 for details)

>> **PivotChart Tools with** three contextual tabs — Analyze, Design, and Format — each with its own set of buttons for customizing and refining the pivot chart

REMEMBER

You can also create a pivot chart from scratch by building it in a similar manner to manually creating a pivot table. Simply select a cell in the data table or list to be charted and then select the PivotChart option on the PivotChart button's drop-down menu on the Insert tab of the Ribbon (select the PivotChart & PivotTable option on this drop-down menu instead if you want to build a pivot table as well as a pivot chart). Excel then displays a Create PivotChart dialog box with the same options as the Create PivotTable dialog box (refer to Figure 9-4). After selecting your options and closing this dialog box, Excel displays a blank chart grid and a PivotChart Fields task pane along with the PivotChart Tools contextual tab on the Ribbon. You can then build your new pivot chart by dragging and dropping desired fields into the appropriate zones.

TIP

Excel 2019's new Insights feature is a great way to gain new perspectives on your data by creating instant pivot charts illustrating some of their more interesting and, often, non-evident aspects. To use the Insights feature, all you do is position the cell cursor in one of the cells of your data table before selecting Insert ⇨ Insights or pressing Alt+NDI. Excel then opens an Insights task pane containing thumbnails of suggested pivot charts (and sometimes regular charts) designed to high-light particular aspects of the data that may not be otherwise evident. To create one of the pivot chart suggested in the Insights task pane, all you have to do is click the Insert PivotChart link in the lower left of its thumbnail. Excel then inserts a new worksheet into the current workbook containing the embedded pivot chart complete with its supporting pivot table!

Moving pivot charts to separate sheets

Although Excel automatically creates all new pivot charts on the same worksheet as the pivot table, you may find it easier to customize and work with it if you move the chart to its own chart sheet in the workbook. To move a new pivot chart to its own chart sheet in the workbook, you follow these steps:

1. **Click the Analyze tab under the PivotChart Tools contextual tab to bring its tools to the Ribbon.**

   If the PivotChart Tools contextual tab doesn't appear at the end of your Ribbon, click anywhere on the new pivot chart to make this tab reappear.

2. **Click the Move Chart button in the Actions group.**

   Excel opens a Move Chart dialog box.

3. **Click the New Sheet button in the Move Chart dialog box.**

4. **(Optional) Rename the generic Chart1 sheet name in the accompanying text box by entering a more descriptive name there.**

5. **Click OK to close the Move Chart dialog box and open the new chart sheet with your pivot chart.**

Figure 9-10 shows a clustered column pivot chart after moving the chart to its own chart sheet in the workbook.

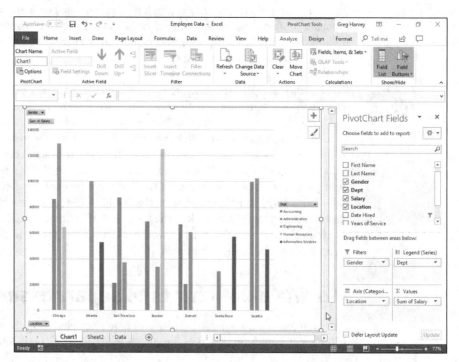

FIGURE 9-10:
Clustered column pivot chart moved to its own chart sheet.

Filtering pivot charts

When you graph the data in a pivot table using a typical chart type, such as column, bar, or line, that uses both an x- and y-axis, the Row labels in the pivot table appear along the x- (or category) axis at the bottom of the chart and the Column labels in the pivot table become the data series that are delineated in the chart's legend. The numbers in the Values field are represented on the y- (or value) axis that goes up the left side of the chart.

You can use the drop-down buttons that appear after the Filter, Legend fields, Axis fields, and Values field in the PivotChart to filter the charted data represented in this fashion like you do the values in the pivot table. As with the pivot table, remove the check mark from the (Select All) or (All) option and then add a check mark to each of the fields you still want represented in the filtered pivot chart.

Click the following drop-down buttons to filter a different part of the pivot chart:

>> **Axis Fields (Categories)** to filter the categories that are charted along the x-axis at the bottom of the chart

>> **Legend Fields (Series)** to filter the data series shown in columns, bars, or lines in the chart body and identified by the chart legend

>> **Filter** to filter the data charted along the y-axis on the left side of the chart

>> **Values** to filter the values represented in the PivotChart

Formatting pivot charts

The command buttons on the Design and Format tabs attached to the PivotChart Tools contextual tab make it easy to further format and customize your pivot chart. Use the Design tab buttons to select a new chart style for your pivot chart or even a brand-new chart type. Use the Format tab buttons to add graphics to the chart as well as refine their look.

REMEMBER

To get specific information on using the buttons on these tabs, see Chapter 10, which covers creating charts from regular worksheet data. The Chart Tools contextual tab that appears when you select a chart you've created contains its own Design and Format tabs with comparable command buttons.

5
Life Beyond the Spreadsheet

Create charts and add graphics.

Create, sort, and filter data lists.

Load and use add-in programs.

Link sheets with hyperlinks.

Record routine command sequences as macros so that they can be played back at lightning speed.

Discover different ways to edit and share your workbooks online.

Visit www.dummies.com/extras/excel2019 for great Dummies content online.

Chapter **10**

Charming Charts and Gorgeous Graphics

As the Chinese sage Confucius was reported to have once observed, "A picture is worth a thousand words" (or, in our case, numbers). By adding charts to worksheets, you not only heighten interest in the otherwise boring numbers, but also illustrate trends and anomalies that may not be apparent from just looking at the values alone. Because Excel 2019 makes it so easy to chart the numbers in a worksheet, you can also experiment with different types of charts until you find the one that best represents the data — in other words, the picture that best tells the particular story.

Making Professional-Looking Charts

I just want to say a few words about charts in general before taking you through the steps for making them in Excel 2019. Remember your high school algebra teacher valiantly trying to teach you how to graph equations by plotting different values on an x-axis and a y-axis on graph paper? Of course, you were probably too busy with more important things like cool cars and rap music to pay too much attention to an old algebra teacher. Besides, you probably told yourself, "I'll never need this junk when I'm out on my own and get a job!"

Well, see, you just never know. It turns out that even though Excel automates almost the entire process of charting worksheet data, you may need to be able to tell the x-axis from the y-axis, just in case Excel doesn't draw the chart the way you had in mind. To refresh your memory and make your algebra teacher proud, the x-axis is the horizontal axis, usually located along the bottom of the chart; the y-axis is the vertical one, usually located on the left side of the chart.

In most charts that use these two axes, Excel plots the categories along the x-axis at the bottom and their relative values along the y-axis on the left. The x-axis is referred to as the *Category* axis, while the y-axis is referred to as the *Value* axis. Often, the x-axis can be thought of as the *time axis* because the chart often depicts values along this axis in time periods, such as months, quarters, years, and so on.

REMEMBER

Worksheet values represented graphically in the chart remain dynamically linked to the chart so that, should you make a change to one or more of the charted values in the worksheet, Excel automatically updates the affected part of the chart to suit.

Excel 2019 offers you many quick and easy ways to chart your data. Before you use any of these methods, you need to indicate the data you want graphed. To do this, you simply position the cell pointer somewhere within the data table to select one of its cells. If, however, you want to chart only a part of the data within a larger table, in that case, you must select the values and headings you want included in the new chart.

Charts thanks to Recommendation

My personal favorite way to create a new chart in Excel 2019 is with the Recommended Charts command button on the Insert tab of the Ribbon (Alt+NR). When you use this method, Excel opens the Insert Chart dialog box with the Recommended Charts tab selected, similar to the one shown in Figure 10-1. Here, you can preview how your data will appear in different types of charts by simply clicking its thumbnail in the list box on the left. When you find the type of chart you want to create, you then simply click the OK button to have it embedded into the current worksheet.

FIGURE 10-1:
Insert Chart
dialog
box with the
Recommended
Charts tab
selected.

Charts from the Ribbon

To the right of the Recommended Charts button in the Charts group of the Ribbon's Insert tab, you find particular command buttons with drop-down galleries for creating the following types and styles of charts:

» **Insert Column or Bar Chart** to preview your data as a 2-D or 3-D vertical column chart or horizontal bar chart

» **Insert Hierarchy Chart** to preview your data as a 2-D Treemap or Sunburst chart

» **Insert Waterfall, Funnel, Stock, Surface or Radar Chart** to preview your data as a 2-D waterfall, funnel, or stock chart (using typical stock symbols), 2-D or 3-D surface chart, or 3-D radar chart

» **Insert Line or Area Chart** to preview your data as a 2-D or 3-D line or area chart

» **Insert Statistic Chart** to preview a statistical analysis of your data as a 2-D histogram or box and whisker chart

» **Insert Combo Chart** to preview your data as a 2-D combo clustered column and line chart or clustered column and stacked area chart

>> **Insert Pie or Doughnut Chart** to preview your data as a 2-D or 3-D pie chart or 2-D doughnut chart

>> **Insert Scatter (X,Y) or Bubble Chart** to preview your data as a 2-D scatter (X,Y) or bubble chart

>> **Insert Map Chart** to preview categories across regions in your data as a 2-D filled map chart

>> **PivotChart** to preview your data as a PivotChart (see Chapter 9 for more on creating this special type of interactive summary chart)

When using the galleries attached to these chart command buttons on the Insert tab to preview your data as a particular chart style, you can embed the chart in your worksheet by simply clicking its chart icon.

If you're not sure what type of chart best represents your data, rather than go through the different chart type buttons on the Ribbon's Insert tab, you can use the All Charts tab of the Insert Chart dialog box shown in Figure 10-2 to try out your data in different chart types and styles. You can open the Insert Chart dialog box by clicking the Dialog Box launcher in the lower-right corner of the Charts group on the Insert tab and then display the complete list of chart types by clicking the All Charts tab in this dialog box.

FIGURE 10-2:
Insert Chart dialog box with the All Charts tab selected where you can preview and select from a wide variety of chart types and styles.

Charts via the Quick Analysis tool

For those times when you need to select a subset of a data table as the range to be charted (as opposed to selecting a single cell within a data table), you can use the Quick Analysis tool to create your chart. Just follow these steps:

1. **Click the Quick Analysis tool that appears right below the lower-right corner of the current cell selection.**

Doing this opens the palette of Quick Analysis options with the initial Formatting tab selected and its various conditional formatting options displayed.

2. **Click the Charts option at the top of the Quick Analysis options palette.**

Excel selects the Charts tab and displays a number of recommended charts (such as Clustered Bar, Stacked Bar, Clustered Column, Scatter, and Stacked Column) followed by the More Charts option button. The recommended chart type buttons preview how the selected data in a different type of chart will look. The final More Charts button opens the Insert Chart dialog box with the Recommended Charts tab selected. Here you can preview and select a chart from an even wider range of chart types.

3. **In order to preview each type of chart that Excel 2019 can create using the selected data, highlight its chart type button in the Quick Analysis palette.**

As you highlight each chart type button in the options palette, Excel's Live Preview feature displays a large thumbnail of the chart that will be created from your table data. This thumbnail appears above the Quick Analysis options palette for as long as the mouse or Touch pointer is over its corresponding button.

4. **When a preview of the chart you actually want to create appears, click its button in the Quick Analysis options palette to create it.**

Excel 2019 then creates a free-floating chart (called an embedded chart) within the current worksheet. This embedded chart is active so that you can immediately move it and edit it as you wish.

Figures 10-3 and 10-4 show you how this procedure works. In Figure 10-3, I've selected only the first quarter sales figures (with their column headings) in the much larger YTD spreadsheet. After selecting the range and clicking the Quick Analysis tool that appears in the lower-right corner of the cell selection, I clicked the Charts tab and then highlighted the Clustered Column chart type button in the Quick Analysis tool's option palette. The previewed clustered column chart then appears in the thumbnail displayed above the palette.

FIGURE 10-3:
Previewing the clustered column chart to be created from the selected data via the Quick Analysis tool.

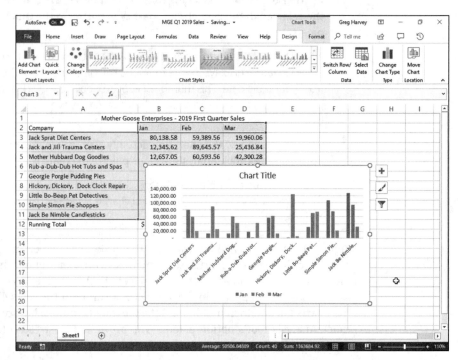

FIGURE 10-4:
Embedded clustered column chart after creating it in the worksheet with the Quick Analysis tool.

Figure 10-4 shows you the embedded chart created by clicking the Clustered Column chart type button in the Quick Analysis tool's palette. When first created, the new chart is active and its chart area is automatically selected. When this is the case, you can move the entire chart to a new part of the worksheet by dragging it. While the chart area is selected, Excel outlines and highlights the data represented in the chart in red for the headings used in the chart legend; in purple for the headings used as labels along the horizontal, Category, or x-axis; and in blue for the values represented graphically by the bars in the chart and in the vertical, Value, or y-axis. In addition, the Chart Tools contextual tab with its Design and Format tabs are added to the Ribbon, and the Design tab, with its options for making further design changes, is selected.

Charts on their own chart sheets

Sometimes you know you want your new chart to appear on its own separate sheet in the workbook and you don't have time to fool around with moving an embedded chart created with the Quick Analysis tool or the various chart command buttons on the Insert tab of the Ribbon to its own sheet. In such a situation, simply position the cell pointer somewhere in the table of data to be graphed (or select the specific cell range in a larger table) and then just press F11.

Excel then creates a clustered column chart using the table's data or cell selection on its own chart sheet (Chart1) that precedes all the other sheets in the workbook (see Figure 10-5). You can then customize the chart on the new chart sheet as you would an embedded chart that's described later in the chapter.

Moving and resizing embedded charts

Right after you create a new embedded chart in a worksheet, you can easily move or resize the chart because the chart is still selected. You can always tell when an embedded chart is selected because the chart is outlined with a thin double-line and you see *sizing handles* — those squares at the four corners and midpoints of the outline that appears around the perimeter of the chart. In addition, the following three buttons appear in the upper-right corner of the outlined chart:

>> **Chart Elements** button with the plus sign icon to modify chart elements such as the chart titles, legends, gridlines, error bars, and trendlines

>> **Chart Styles** button with the paintbrush icon to modify the chart layout and color scheme

>> **Chart Filters** with the cone filter icon to modify the data series represented in the chart or the labels displayed in the legend or along the Category axis

FIGURE 10-5:
New clustered column chart on its own chart sheet instantly created from selected data by pressing F11.

Whenever an embedded chart is selected (as it is automatically immediately after creating it or after clicking any part of it), the Chart Tools contextual tab with its Design, Layout, and Format tabs appears on the Ribbon, and Excel outlines each group of cells represented in the selected chart in a different color in the worksheet.

When an embedded chart is selected in a worksheet, you can move or resize it as follows:

» To move the chart, position the mouse pointer in a blank area inside the chart and drag the chart to a new location.

» To resize the chart (you may want to make it bigger if it seems distorted in any way), position the mouse pointer or Touch pointer on one of the sizing handles. When the pointer changes from the arrowhead to a double-headed arrow, drag the side or corner (depending on which handle you select) to enlarge or reduce the chart.

When the chart is properly sized and positioned in the worksheet, set the chart in place by deselecting it (simply click any cell outside the chart). As soon as you deselect the chart, the sizing handles disappear, as do the Chart Elements, Chart Styles, and Chart Filters buttons along with the Chart Tools contextual tab from the Ribbon.

To reselect the chart later to edit, size, or move it again, just click anywhere on the chart with the mouse pointer. The moment you do, the sizing handles return to the embedded chart and the Chart Tools contextual tab appears on the Ribbon.

Moving embedded charts to chart sheets

Although Excel automatically embeds all new charts on the same worksheet as the data they graph (unless you create the chart by using my F11 trick), you may find it easier to customize and work with it if you move the chart to its own chart sheet in the workbook. To move an embedded chart to its own chart sheet in the workbook, follow these steps:

1. **Select the chart and then click the Move Chart button above Location on the Design tab under the Chart Tools contextual tab to open the Move Chart dialog box.**

2. **Click the New Sheet button in the Move Chart dialog box.**

3. **(Optional) Rename the generic Chart1 sheet name in the accompanying text box by entering a more descriptive name.**

4. **Click OK to close the Move Chart dialog box and open the new chart sheet with your chart.**

If, after customizing the chart on its own sheet, you decide you want the finished chart to appear on the same worksheet as the data it represents, click the Move Chart button on the Design tab again. This time, click the Object In button and then select the name of the worksheet in its associated drop-down list box before you click OK.

Customizing charts from the Design tab

You can use the command buttons on the Design tab of the Chart Tools contextual tab to make all kinds of changes to your new chart. The Design tab contains the following groups of buttons to use:

>> **Chart Layouts:** Click the Add Chart Element button to modify particular elements in the chart such as the titles, data labels, legend, and so on (note that most of the chart element options on this drop-down menu are duplicated on the chart elements palette that appears when you click the Chart Elements button in the worksheet to the right of a selected embedded chart). Click the Quick Layout button to select a new layout for the selected chart.

>> **Chart Styles:** Click the Change Colors button to display a pop-up palette with different colorful and monochromatic color schemes that you can apply to your chart. Highlight the various chart styles in the Chart Styles gallery to preview and select a style for the current type of chart.

>> **Data:** Click the Switch Row/Column button to interchange the worksheet data used for the Legend Entries (series) with that used for the Axis Labels (Categories) in the selected chart. Click the Select Data button to open the Select Data Source dialog box where you can not only interchange the Legend Entries (series) with the Axis Labels (Categories), but also edit out or add particular entries to either category.

>> **Type:** Click the Change Chart Type button to open the All Charts tab of the Change Chart Type dialog box where you can preview and select a new type of chart to represent your data.

>> **Location:** Click the Move Chart button to move the chart to a new chart sheet or another worksheet.

Customizing chart elements

The Chart Elements button (with the plus sign icon) that appears to the right of an embedded chart when it's selected contains a list of the major chart elements that you can add to your chart. To add an element to your chart, click the Chart Elements button to display an alphabetical list of all the elements, Axes through Trendline. To add a particular element missing from the chart, select the element's check box in the list to put a check mark in it. To remove a particular element currently displayed in the chart, select the element's check box to remove its check mark.

To add or remove just part of a particular chart element or, in some cases as with the Chart Title, Data Labels, Data Table, Error Bars, Legend, and Trendline, to also specify its layout, you select the desired option on the element's continuation menu.

So, for example, to reposition a chart's title, you click the continuation button attached to Chart Title on the Chart Elements menu to display and select from among the following options on its continuation menu:

>> **Above Chart** to add or reposition the chart title so that it appears centered above the plot area

>> **Centered Overlay Title** to add or reposition the chart title so that it appears centered at the top of the plot area

>> **More Options** to open the Format Chart Title task pane on the right side of the Excel window where you can use the options that appear when you select the Fill & Line, Effects, and Size and Properties buttons under Title Options and the Text Fill & Outline, Text Effects, and the Textbox buttons under Text Options in this task pane to modify almost any aspect of the title's formatting

Adding data labels

Data labels identify the data points in your chart (that is, the columns, lines, and so forth used to graph your data) by displaying values from the cells of the worksheet represented next to them. To add data labels to your selected chart and position them, click the Chart Elements button next to the chart and then select the Data Labels check box before you select one of the following options on its continuation menu:

>> **Center** to position the data labels in the middle of each data point

>> **Inside End** to position the data labels inside each data point near the end

>> **Inside Base** to position the data labels at the base of each data point

>> **Outside End** to position the data labels outside of the end of each data point

>> **Data Callout** to add text labels and values that appear within text boxes that point to each data point

>> **More Options** to open the Format Data Labels task pane on the right side, where you can use the options that appear when you select the Fill & Line, Effects, Size & Properties, and Label Options buttons under Label Options and the Text Fill & Outline, Text Effects, and Textbox buttons under Text Options in the task pane to customize almost any aspect of the appearance and position of the data labels

Adding data tables

Sometimes, instead of data labels that can easily obscure the data points in the chart, you'll want Excel to draw a data table beneath the chart showing the worksheet data it represents in graphic form.

To add a data table to your selected chart and position and format it, click the Chart Elements button next to the chart and then select the Data Table check box before you select one of the following options on its continuation menu:

>> **With Legend Keys** to have Excel draw the table at the bottom of the chart, including the color keys used in the legend to differentiate the data series in the first column

>> **No Legend Keys** to have Excel draw the table at the bottom of the chart without any legend

>> **More Options** to open the Format Data Table task pane on the right side, where you can use the options that appear when you select the Fill & Line, Effects, Size & Properties, and Table Options buttons under Table Options and the Text Fill & Outline, Text Effects, and Textbox buttons under Text Options in the task pane to customize almost any aspect of the data table

Figure 10-6 illustrates how the sample clustered column chart looks with a data table added to it. This data table includes the legend keys as its first column.

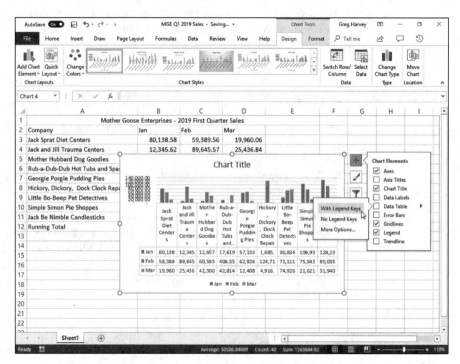

FIGURE 10-6:
Embedded
clustered column
chart with data
table with
legend keys.

REMEMBER

If you decide that displaying the worksheet data in a data table at the bottom of the chart is no longer necessary, simply click the chart to select it, then click the Chart Elements button to display its pop-up menu. Finally, click the Data Table check box to remove its check mark. You can also remove a data table from the selected chart by selecting Design⇨Add Chart Element⇨Data Table⇨None on the Excel Ribbon or pressing Alt+JCABN.

Editing the generic titles in a chart

When Excel first adds titles to a new chart, it gives them generic names, such as Chart Title and Axis Title (for both the x- and y-axis title). To replace these generic titles with the actual chart titles, click the title in the chart or click the name of the title on the Chart Elements drop-down list. (Chart Elements is the drop-down button at the top of the Current Selection group on the Format tab under Chart Tools. Its text box displays the name of the element currently selected in the chart.) Excel lets you know that a particular chart title is selected by placing selection handles around its perimeter.

After you select a title, you can click the insertion point in the text and then edit as you would any worksheet text or you can click to select the title, type the new title, and press Enter to completely replace it with the text you type. To force part of the title onto a new line, click the insertion point at the place in the text where the line break is to occur. After the insertion point is positioned in the title, press Enter to start a new line.

After you finish editing the title, click somewhere else on the chart area to deselect it (or a worksheet cell if you've finished formatting and editing the chart).

REMEMBER

Formatting the chart titles

When you add titles to your chart, Excel uses the Calibri (Body) font for the chart title (in 14-point size) and the x- and y-axis (in 10-point size). To change the font used in a title or any of its attributes, select the title and then use the appropriate command buttons in the mini-toolbar that appears next to the selected title or from the Font group on the Home tab.

Use Live Preview to see how a particular font or font size for the selected chart title looks in the chart before you select it. Simply click the Font or Font Size drop-down buttons and then highlight different font names or sizes to have the selected chart title appear in them.

REMEMBER

If you need to change other formatting options for the titles in the chart, you can do so using the command buttons on the Format tab of the Chart Tools contextual tab. To format the entire text box that contains the title, click one of the following buttons in the Shape Styles group:

>> **Shape Styles** thumbnail in its drop-down gallery to format both the text and text box for the selected chart title

>> **Shape Fill** button to select a new color for the text box containing the selected chart title from its drop-down palette

>> **Shape Outline** button to select a new color for the outline of the text box for the selected chart text from its drop-down palette

>> **Shape Effects** button to apply a new effect (Shadow, Reflection, Glow, Soft Edges, and so on) to the text box containing the selected chart title from its drop-down list

To format just the text in chart titles, click one of the buttons in the WordArt Styles group:

>> **WordArt Styles** thumbnail in its drop-down gallery to apply a new WordArt style to the text of the selected chart title

>> **Text Fill** button to select a new fill color for the text in the selected chart title from its gallery

>> **Text Outline** button (immediately below the Text Fill button) to select a new outline color for the text in the selected chart title from its drop-down palette

>> **Text Effects** button (immediately below the Text Outline button) to apply a text effect (Shadow, Reflection, Glow, Bevel, and so on) to the text of the selected chart title from its drop-down list

Formatting the x- and y-axis

When charting a bunch of values, Excel isn't too careful how it formats the values that appear on the y-axis (or the x-axis when using some chart types, such as the 3-D Column chart or an XY Scatter chart).

If you're not happy with the way the values appear on either the x-axis or y-axis, you can easily change the formatting as follows:

1. **Click the x-axis or y-axis directly in the chart or click the Chart Elements button (the first button in the Current Selection group of the Format tab) and then click Horizontal (Category) Axis (for the x-axis) or Vertical (Value) Axis (for the y-axis) on its drop-down list.**

   Excel surrounds the axis you select with selection handles.

2. **Click the Format Selection button in the Current Selection group of the Format tab.**

   Excel opens the Format Axis task pane with Axis Options under the Axis Options group selected.

3. **To change the scale of the axis, the appearance of its tick marks, and where it crosses the other axis, change the appropriate options under Axis Options (automatically selected when you first open the Format Axis task pane) as needed.**

   These options include those that fix the maximum and minimum amount for the first and last tick mark on the axis, display the values in reverse order (highest to lowest), and apply a logarithmic scale. You can display units on the axis (hundreds, thousands, millions, and so forth) and divide the values by those units, reposition the tick marks on the axis, and modify the value at which the other axis (y-axis when modifying the x-axis and x-axis when modifying the y-axis) crosses.

4. **To change the number formatting for all values on the selected axis, click the Number option and then select the number format you want to apply in the Category drop-down list box followed by the appropriate options associated with that format. To assign the same number formatting to the values on the selected axis as assigned to the values in their worksheet cells, simply select the Linked To Source check box.**

   For example, to select the number format with the comma as the thousands separator and no decimal places, you select Number on the Category drop-down list box; then leave the Use 1000 Separator (,) check box selected and enter 0 in the Decimal Places text box.

5. **To change the alignment and orientation of the labels on the selected axis, click the Size & Properties button under Axis Options on the Format Axis task pane. Then, indicate the new orientation by clicking the desired vertical alignment in the Vertical Alignment drop-down list box and desired text direction in the Text Direction drop-down list.**

6. **Click the Close button to close the Format Axis task pane.**

REMEMBER

As you choose new options for the selected axis, Excel 2019 shows you the change in the chart. However, these changes are set in the chart only when you click Close in the Format Axis dialog box.

TIP

To change the default font, font size, or other text attributes for entries along the selected x- or y-axis, click the appropriate command buttons in the Font group on the Home tab (see Chapter 3 for details).

Adding Great-Looking Graphics

Charts are not the only kind of graphic objects you can add to a worksheet. Indeed, Excel lets you spruce up a worksheet with a whole bevy of graphics, including sparklines (tiny charts that fit right inside worksheet cells), graphic shapes, commonly used icons, text boxes, as well as standard 2-D and 3-D graphic images imported from other sources, such as digital photos, scanned images, and pictures downloaded from the Internet.

In addition to these graphics, Excel 2019 supports the creation of fancy graphic text called WordArt as well as a whole bevy of organizational and process diagrams known collectively as SmartArt graphics.

Sparking up the data with sparklines

Excel 2019 supports a special type of information graphic called a *sparkline* that represents trends or variations in collected data. Sparklines are tiny graphs generally about the size of the text that surrounds them. In Excel 2019, sparklines are the height of the worksheet cells whose data they represent and can be any of the following chart types:

>> **Line** that represents the relative value of the selected worksheet data

>> **Column** where the selected worksheet data is represented by tiny columns

>> **Win/Loss** where the selected worksheet data appears as a win/loss chart; wins are represented by blue squares that appear above red squares (representing the losses)

Sparklines via the Quick Analysis tool

In Excel 2019, you can use its Quick Analysis tool to quickly add sparklines to your data. All you have to do is select the cells in the worksheet to be visually represented and click the Quick Analysis tool followed by Sparklines on its options palette. This displays buttons for the three types of sparklines: Line, Column, and Win/Loss. To preview how your data looks with each type, highlight the button in the palette with the mouse pointer or Touch pointer. Then, to add the previewed sparklines to your worksheet, simply click the appropriate Sparklines button.

Figure 10-7 shows the sample Mother Goose Enterprises worksheet with the first quarter sales for 2019 after I selected the cell range B3:D11 and then opened the Sparklines tab in the Quick Analysis tool's palette. Excel immediately previews line-type trendlines in the cell range E3:E11 of the worksheet. To add these trendlines, all you have to do is click the Line option in the tool's palette.

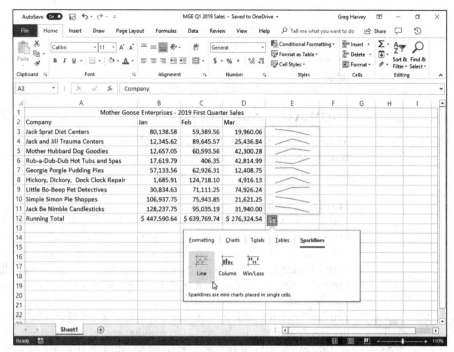

FIGURE 10-7:
Previewing sparklines to visually represent the trends in the three-month sales for each company in the Quick Analysis tool's Sparklines palette.

Sparklines from the Ribbon

You can also add sparklines with the Sparklines command buttons on the Insert tab of the Ribbon. To manually add sparklines to the cells of your worksheet:

1. Select the cells in the worksheet with the data you want to represent with sparklines.

2. Select the chart type you want for your sparklines (Line, Column, or Win/Loss) in the Sparklines group of the Insert tab or press Alt+NSL for Line, Alt+NSO for Column, or Alt+NSW for Win/Loss.

Excel opens the Create Sparklines dialog box containing two text boxes:

- *Data Range:* Shows the cells you select with the data you want to graph.

- *Location Range:* Lets you designate the cell or cell range where you want the sparklines to appear.

3. Select the cell or cell range where you want your sparklines to appear in the Location Range text box and then click OK.

When creating sparklines that span more than a single cell, the number of rows and columns in the location range must match the number of rows and columns in the data range. (That is, the cell range needs to be of equal size and shape.)

TIP

Because sparklines are so small, you can easily add them to the cells in the final column of a table. That way, the sparkline graphics (as shown in Figure 10-7) can depict the data visually and enhance meaning while being an integral part of the table.

Formatting sparklines

After you add sparklines to your worksheet, Excel 2019 adds a Sparkline Tools contextual tab with its own Design tab to the Ribbon that appears when the cell or range with the sparklines is selected.

This Design tab contains buttons that you can use to edit the type, style, and format of the sparklines. The final group (called Group) on this tab enables you to band a range of sparklines into a single group that can share the same axis and/or minimum or maximum values (selected using the options on the Axis drop-down button). This is very useful when you want a collection of sparklines to share the same charting parameters so that they represent the trends in the data equally.

REMEMBER

You can't delete sparklines from a cell range by selecting the cells and then pressing the Delete button. Instead, to remove sparklines, right-click their cell range and choose Sparklines ⇨ Clear Selected Sparklines from its context menu. If you've selected a grouped collection of sparklines to remove, select the Clear Selected Sparkline Groups option instead.

Telling all with a text box

Text boxes, as their name implies, are boxes to which you can add commentary or explanatory text for the charts you create in Excel. They're like Excel comments (see Chapter 6) that you add to worksheet cells except that you have to add the arrow if you want the text box to point to something in the chart.

In Figure 10-8, you see a clustered column chart for the MGE (Mother Goose Enterprises) 2019 First Quarter Sales. I added a text box with an arrow that points out how extraordinary the sales were for the Hickory, Dickory, Doc Clock Shops in this quarter and formatted the values on the y-axis with the Currency number format with zero decimal places.

Adding and formatting a text box

To add a text box like the one shown in Figure 10-8 to the chart when a chart is selected, select the Format tab under the Chart Tools contextual tab. Then, click the Insert Shapes drop-down button to open its palette where you select the Text Box button (the very first button in the Basic Shapes section).

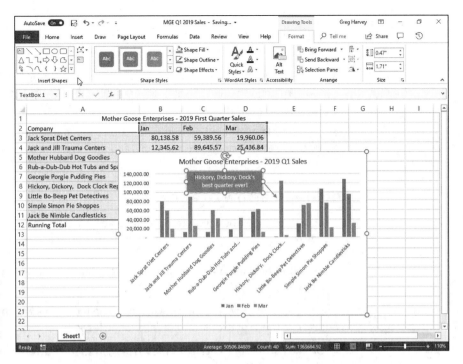

FIGURE 10-8:
Clustered column
chart, with added
text box and
formatted y-axis
values.

TIP

To insert a text box in a worksheet when a chart or some other type of graphic isn't selected, you can open the Insert tab on the Ribbon and then click the Text Box option on the Text button's drop-down palette.

Excel then changes the mouse pointer to a narrow vertical line with a short cross near the bottom. Click the location where you want to draw the text box and then draw the box by dragging its outline. When you release the mouse button after dragging this pointer, Excel draws a text box in the shape and size of the outline.

After creating a horizontal text box, the program positions the insertion point at the top left, and you can then type the text you want to appear within it. The text you type appears in the text box and will wrap to a new line should you reach the right edge of the text box. You can press Enter when you want to force text to appear on a new line. When you finish entering the message for your text box, click anywhere outside the box to deselect it.

After adding a text box to a chart or worksheet while it's still selected, you can edit it as follows:

» Move the text box to a new location in the chart by dragging it.

» Resize the text box by dragging the appropriate sizing handle.

» Rotate the text box by dragging its rotation handle (the white circular arrow at the top) in a clockwise or counterclockwise direction.

» Modify the formatting and appearance of the text box using the various command buttons in the Shape Styles group on the Format tab under the Drawing Tools contextual tab.

» Delete the text box by clicking its perimeter so that the dotted lines connecting the selection handles become solid and then pressing the Delete key.

Adding an arrow to a text box

When creating a text box, you may want to add an arrow to point directly to the object or part of the chart you're referencing. To add an arrow, follow these steps:

1. **Click the text box to which you want to attach the arrow in the chart or worksheet.**

Sizing handles appear around the text box, and the Format tab under the Drawing Tools contextual tab is added to the Ribbon.

2. **On the Format tab, click the Line Arrow command button in the Shapes drop-down gallery.**

The Line Arrow command button is the second from the left in the row in the Lines section (with the picture of an arrow) of the gallery. When you click this button, the mouse pointer or Touch pointer assumes the crosshair shape.

3. **Drag the crosshair pointer from the place on the text box where the end of the arrow (the one *without* the arrowhead) is to appear to the place where the arrow starts (and the arrowhead will appear) and release the mouse button or remove your finger or stylus from the touchscreen.**

As soon as you do this, Excel draws two points, one at the base of the arrow (attached to the text box) and another at the arrowhead. At the same time, the contents of the Shape Styles drop-down gallery changes to line styles.

4. **Click the More button in the lower-right corner of the Shape Styles drop-down gallery to display the thumbnails of all its line styles and then highlight the thumbnails to see how the arrow would look in each.**

As you move through the different line styles in this gallery, Excel draws the arrow between the two selected points in the text box using the highlighted style.

5. **Click the thumbnail of the line style you want the new arrow to use in the Shape Styles gallery.**

Excel then draws a new arrow using the selected shape style, which remains selected (with selection handles at the beginning and end of the arrow). You can then edit the arrow as follows:

» Move the arrow by dragging its outline into position.

» Change the length of the arrow by dragging the sizing handle at the arrowhead.

» Change the direction of the arrow by pivoting the crosshair pointer around a stationary sizing handle.

» Change the shape of the arrowhead or the thickness of the arrow's shaft by clicking a thumbnail on the Shape Styles drop-down gallery. Click a new option on the Shape Outline and Shape Effects buttons on the Format tab of the Drawing Tools contextual tab or open the Format Shape task pane (Ctrl+1) and then select the appropriate options on its Line Color, Line Style, Shadow, Reflection, Glow and Soft Edges, 3-D Format, 3-D Rotation, Size, and Text Box tabs.

» Delete the selected arrow by pressing the Delete key.

Inserting online images

Excel 2019 makes it easy to insert online 2-D and 3-D graphic images into your worksheet. The Online Pictures dialog box enables you to use Microsoft's Bing search engine to search the entire web for 2-D images to use. If that's not enough, you can also download images that you've saved in the cloud on your Windows OneDrive.

To download an image into your worksheet from any of these sources, you click the Online Pictures button in the Illustrations group on the Insert tab of the Ribbon (Alt+NF). Excel opens the Online Pictures dialog box similar to the one shown in Figure 10-9. When you first open the Online Pictures dialog box, it contains a number of sample Bing searches arranged alphabetically by category with a sample image representing that category displayed.

To display the photos and line art available for a particular category, such as Books or Money, click the sample image in its category. If none of the pictures in that or any of the other available categories fit the bill, you can use the search text box in the Online Pictures dialog box to try to locate a more suitable image.

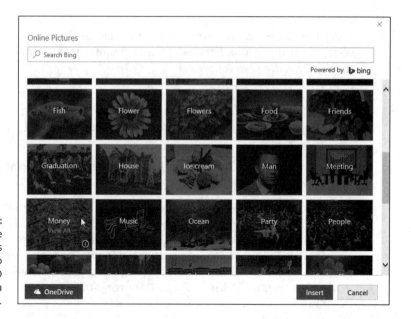

FIGURE 10-9:
Opening the
Online Pictures
dialog box to
insert a 2-D
graphic into a
worksheet.

The search text box in the Online Pictures dialog box contains a drop-down button to the immediate left with the following search options:

>> **Bing** (default) to use the Bing search engine to locate images on the web of a particular type that you want to add to your worksheet

>> **OneDrive** to locate images saved on your SkyDrive to add to your worksheet

After you click a category in the opening Online Pictures dialog box or perform a Bing search by clicking the dialog box's Search button (the magnifying glass icon), the Online Pictures dialog box displays a scrollable list of thumbnails of the photos or line art that you can insert into your current worksheet, as shown in Figure 10-10.

Above the thumbnails, the Online Pictures dialog box displays a selected Creative Commons Only check box. When this check box is selected, Excel filters the thumbnail images shown to just those that are covered by Creative Commons licensing. *Creative Commons licensing* grants free distribution of what is otherwise copyrighted material under certain conditions (often noncommercial or educational use). Select the Creative Commons Only check box to remove its check mark only if you're sure that you are comfortable using images in your worksheets not covered by Creative Commons licensing.

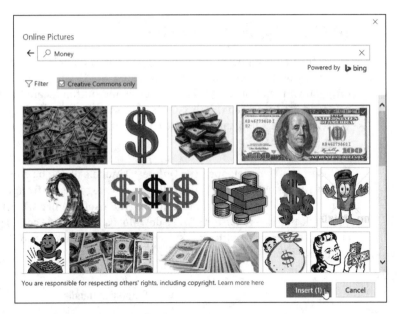

FIGURE 10-10:
Selecting the thumbnail of a line art image of dollar signs in the Money category to download into the current worksheet.

To the immediate left of the Creative Commons Only check box, the Online Pictures dialog box contains a Filter button (see Figure 10-10). When you click the Filter button, Excel displays a pop-up menu that enables you to filter the thumbnails displayed below in the Online Pictures dialog box by the image's size, type, layout, and/or color.

At the bottom of the dialog box below the area with the thumbnails, the Online Pictures dialog box displays the message, "You are responsible for respecting others' rights, including copyright" followed by a Learn More Here hyperlink. Clicking this link opens a Microsoft Copyright web page in your default web browser that gives you basic information on copyright law, including information about what type of creative works are covered by copyright and the doctrine of fair use.

To insert one of the located images into the current worksheet, click its thumbnail to select it (shown by the check mark in the box in the upper-left corner and then click the Insert button (or you can simply double-click the thumbnail). If you want to insert more than one of the displayed images into your worksheet, click their thumbnails to select them before you click the Insert button.

When you click the Insert button, Excel closes the Online Pictures dialog box and downloads into the active worksheet both the graphic image(s) you've selected along with a text box, containing a caption containing author credits for the downloaded picture(s). This caption text box contains two hyperlinks: the first takes you to a web page with more information about the picture and its author, and the second takes you to a web page with more specific information about the picture's licensing.

Inserting 3-D images

Excel 2019 also supports the use of 3-D images downloaded from the Microsoft Remix 3D online community website using the From Online Sources option on drop-down menu of the 3D Models command button located in the Illustrations group on the Insert tab (Alt+NS3O). When you insert one of these 3-D images into your worksheet, you can rotate it so that it can be viewed from any angle you want.

To insert a 3-D model, open the Online 3D Models dialog box and select a thumbnail of the model from one of its displayed categories or from a search you perform of the 3-D images uploaded to the Microsoft Remix 3D website. As soon as you click the Insert button, Excel downloads a copy of the 3-D model into the current worksheet with its selection and rotation handles displayed (see Figure 10-11).

FIGURE 10-11: A 3-D model of a laptop computer downloaded from the Electronics and Gadgets of category in the 3D Models dialog box to download into the current worksheet.

Inserting local images

If the 2-D image you want to use in a worksheet is saved on your computer in one of the local or network drives, you can insert it by selecting the Pictures command button on the Insert tab of the Ribbon (Alt+NP). Doing this opens the Insert Picture dialog box (which works just like opening an Excel workbook file in the Open dialog box) where you open the folder and select the local graphics file and then import it into the worksheet by clicking the Insert button.

If you have an image of a 3-D model saved on a local or network drive, you can locate, select, and insert it in your worksheet from the Insert 3D Model dialog box opened by selecting the From a File option on the drop-down menu on the 3D Models command button located in the Illustrations group on the Insert tab (Alt+NS3F).

TIP

If you want to bring in a graphic image created in another graphics program that isn't saved in its own file, select the graphic in that program and then copy it to the Clipboard (press Ctrl+C). When you get back to your worksheet, place the cursor where you want the picture to appear and then paste the image (press Ctrl+V or click the Paste command button at the beginning of the Home tab).

Editing inserted pictures

When you first insert any new graphic image into the worksheet, both the graphic image and its caption text box are selected automatically, indicated by the sizing handles around the perimeter and a 2-D rotation handle at the top of each (as shown in Figure 10-12).

TIP

If you want to remove the caption text box from the worksheet and just work with the downloaded image, you first need to click a cell in the worksheet outside the borders of the selected image and caption text box to deselect them both. Then, click only the caption text box and once its selected, press the Del key. If you want to make the caption in the text box a part of the image as you work with the graphic, select Format ➪ Group Objects ➪ Group on the Excel Ribbon while both the image and its text box are selected. After that, the caption becomes an integral part of the picture that automatically moves, rotates, and resizes whenever you adjust the graphic image itself.

If your image is a 3D model, the selected image will also display a 3-D Rotation handle in the center. To deselect the image and set it in the worksheet, click anywhere in the worksheet outside of the image.

2-D Rotation Handle   Sizing Handle

FIGURE 10-12:
Clip-art image
with caption text
box ready for
editing in the new
worksheet.

While a clip-art image or a picture that you've inserted into your worksheet is selected, however, you can make any of the following changes:

>> Move the selected image to a new location in the chart by dragging it.

>> Resize the selected image by dragging the appropriate sizing handle.

>> Rotate the selected image a number of degrees in flat circle by dragging its 2-D Rotation handle (the white rotation arrow at the top) in a clockwise or counterclockwise direction. Rotate a selected 3-D model to any angle in three dimensions by dragging its 3-D Rotation handle (see Figure 10-11) in the center of the graphic.

>> Delete the image by pressing the Delete key.

Formatting inserted 2-D images

When an inserted 2-D graphic image is selected in the worksheet, Excel adds the Drawing Tools contextual tab to the Ribbon with a Format tab (refer to Figure 10-12). The Format tab under the Picture Tools contextual tab is divided into four groups: Adjust, Picture Styles, Accessibility, Arrange, and Size.

The Adjust group contains the following important command buttons:

» **Remove Background** opens the Background Removal tab and makes a best guess about what parts of the picture to remove. You have the option to mark areas of the picture to keep or further remove, and the shaded areas automatically update as you isolate what areas of the picture you want to keep. Click Keep Changes when you are finished or Discard All Changes to revert back to the original picture.

» **Corrections** to open a drop-down menu with a palette of presets you can choose for sharpening or softening the image and/or increasing or decreasing its brightness. Or select the Picture Corrections Options item to open the Format Picture dialog box with the Picture Corrections tab selected. There, you can sharpen or soften the image or modify its brightness or contrast by selecting a new preset thumbnail on the appropriate Presets palette or by entering a new positive percentage (to increase) or negative percentage (to decrease) where 0% is normal in the appropriate combo box or dragging its slider.

» **Color** to open a drop-down menu with a palette of Color Saturation, Color Tone, or Recolor presets you can apply to the image, set a transparent color (usually the background color you want to remove from the image), or select the Picture Color Options item to open the Picture Color tab of the Format Picture dialog box. There, you can adjust the image's colors using Color Saturation, Color Tone, or Recolor presets or by setting a new saturation level or color tone temperature by entering a new percentage in the appropriate combo box or selecting it with a slider.

» **Artistic Effects** to open a drop-down menu with special effect presets you can apply to the image or select the Artistic Effects Options item to open the Artistic Effects options in the Format Picture task pane where you can apply a special effect by selecting its preset thumbnail from the palette that appears when you click the Artistic Effect drop-down button.

» **Compress Pictures** to open the Compress Pictures dialog box to compress all images in the worksheet or just the selected graphic image to make them more compact and thus make the Excel workbook somewhat smaller when you save the images as part of its file.

» **Change Picture** where you click the From a File, From Online Sources, From Icons, or From Clipboard to find and select a new image to replace the current picture. Note that the replacement image inherits the settings and formatting applied to the image it's replacing.

» **Reset Picture** button to select the Reset Picture option to remove all formatting changes made and return the picture to the state it was in when you originally inserted it into the worksheet or the Reset Picture & Size to reset all its formatting as well as restore the image to its original size in the worksheet.

REMEMBER

You can also format a selected image by opening the Format Picture task pane (Ctrl+1) and then selecting the appropriate options attached to the Fill & Line, Effects, Size & Properties, and Picture buttons, which cover almost all aspects of formatting any image you use.

In addition to the command buttons in the Adjust group, you can use the command buttons in the Picture Styles group. Click a thumbnail on the Picture Styles drop-down gallery to select a new orientation and style for the selected picture. You can also modify any of the following:

>> Border width, line style, and color on the Picture Border button's drop-down palette

>> Shadow, glow, reflection, or 3-D rotation effect on the Picture Effects button's drop-down menus

>> Convert the image to a SmartArt Graphic so that you resize, crop, and caption one of the SmartArt styles on the Layout on the Picture Layout button's drop-down palette (see "Make mine SmartArt" later in this chapter for details)

Formatting inserted 3-D images

When you select a 3-D image that you've inserted into your worksheet, Excel adds a 3D Model Tools contextual tab to the ribbon with its own Format tab. This Format tab is divided into the following groups:

>> **Adjust** to replace the selected image with another online or local 3-D model or to reset the image to its original rotation and/or size

>> **3D Model Views** to select a preset three-dimensional rotation

>> **Accessibility** with its sole Alt Text button to open the Alt Text task pane where you can enter a description of the graphic that the computer can read aloud to a visually-impaired user

>> **Arrange** to modify the selected image's layer or to group or align it with other images (see "Controlling How Graphic Objects Overlap" later in this chapter for details)

>> **Size** to enter a new width or height (in inches, if that is the default unit in Excel) for the selected image

TIP

You can also format a selected 3-D image with the options in the Format 3D Model task pane opened by pressing Ctrl+1 or clicking the Format 3D Model button on the right side of the 3D Model Views group or the Size and Position button on the right side of the Size group on the Format tab under the 3D Model Tools contextual tab.

This task pane contains four buttons, Fill & Line, Effects, Size & Options, and 3D Model, with all sorts of options for formatting the appearance of the selected 3-D image.

Adding graphic shapes

In addition to icons and online and local 2-D and 3-D images, you can insert pre-set graphic shapes (officially known as Microsoft Office drawing objects) in your chart or worksheet by selecting their thumbnails on the Shapes drop-down gallery on the Insert tab of the Ribbon (see Figure 10-13).

FIGURE 10-13:
Click the shape's thumbnail on the Shapes drop-down gallery and then drag the mouse pointer or Touch pointer to draw it out in the chart or sheet.

When you open the Shapes gallery by clicking the Shapes button in the Illustrations group on the Insert tab of the Ribbon, you see that it's divided into nine sections: Recently Used Shapes, Lines, Rectangles, Basic Shapes, Block Arrows, Equation Shapes, Flowchart, Stars and Banners, and Callouts.

After you click the thumbnail of a preset shape in this drop-down gallery, the mouse pointer becomes a crosshair you use to draw the graphic by dragging it to the size you want.

REMEMBER

After you release the mouse button, the shape you've drawn in the worksheet is still selected. This is indicated by the selection handles around its perimeter and the rotation handle at the top, which you can use to reposition, resize, and rotate the shape, if need be. Additionally, the program activates the Format tab on the Drawing Tools contextual tab, and you can use the Shape Styles gallery or other command buttons to further format the shape to the way you want it. To set the shape and remove the selection and rotation handles, click anywhere in the worksheet outside of the shape.

Adding Icons

Excel 2019 makes it easy to add black-and-white iconic images to your worksheet to boldly and quickly visually communicate the meaning and implications of the data entered into your worksheet. To add an icon, click the Icons command button on the Insert tab of the ribbon or press Alt+NY.

Excel then opens the Insert Icons dialog box similar to the one shown in Figure 10-14. This dialog box enables you to select different categories of iconic images to choose from by clicking their description on the left side or by scrolling to it on the right side.

FIGURE 10-14:
Selecting the paperclip icon in the Business category of the Insert Icons dialog box to add to your worksheet.

As with other adding online graphic images, you can select more than one icon to insert into the worksheet by clicking its image (indicated by a check mark in the upper-left corner) before selecting the Insert button to download them.

When you click the Insert button after selecting one or more iconic images in the Insert Icons dialog box, Excel adds them to the worksheet. Excel also adds a Graphic Tools contextual tab with its Format tab below that contains command buttons for formatting the selected icons with tools very similar to those found on the Format tab under the Drawing Tools contextual tab that appears when an inserted graphic shape is selected.

TIP

You can use the Convert to Shape command button on the Graphic Tools's Format tab to convert the selected icons to graphic shapes (as though you had added them from the Shapes drop-down menu (as described in the previous section). When you select this command button, Excel displays an alert dialog box reminding you that this is an imported picture and not a group (of graphic objects) and asking you to confirm this conversion to Microsoft Office drawing object by selecting the Yes button. By converting an icon into a drawing object you are able to format individual parts of the graphic as you like using the options on the Drawing Tools' Format tab.

Working with WordArt

If selecting gazillions of preset symbols and shapes available from the Shapes gallery and Insert Icons dialog box doesn't provide enough variety for jazzing up your worksheet, you may want to try adding some fancy text using the WordArt gallery, opened by clicking the WordArt command button in the Text group of the Insert tab.

You can add this type of "graphic" text to your worksheet by following these steps:

1. **Click the WordArt command button on the Text button's drop-down menu found on the Insert tab or simply press Alt+NW.**

   Excel displays the WordArt drop-down gallery.

2. **Click a thumbnail in the WordArt style you want to use in the WordArt drop-down gallery.**

   Excel inserts a selected text box containing Your Text Here in the center of the worksheet in the WordArt style you selected in the gallery.

3. **Type the text you want to display in the worksheet in the Your Text Here text box.**

   As soon as you start typing, Excel replaces Your Text Here with the characters you enter.

4. **(Optional) To format the background of the text box, use Live Preview in the Shape Styles drop-down gallery on the Format tab to find the style to use and then set it by clicking its thumbnail.**

   The Format tab under the Drawing Tools contextual tab is added and activated automatically when WordArt text is selected in the worksheet.

5. **After making any final adjustments to the size, shape, or orientation of the WordArt text with the selection and rotation handles, click a cell somewhere outside of the text to deselect the graphic.**

When you click outside of the WordArt text, Excel deselects the graphic, and the Drawing Tools contextual tab disappears from the Ribbon. (If you ever want this tab to reappear, all you have to do is click somewhere on the WordArt text to select the graphic.)

REMEMBER

You can change the size of WordArt text and the font it uses after creating it by dragging through the WordArt text to select it and then using the Font and Font Size command buttons on the mini-toolbar that appears next to the selected WordArt to make your desired changes.

Make mine SmartArt

SmartArt in Excel 2019 is a special type of graphic object that gives you the ability to construct fancy graphical lists, diagrams, and captioned pictures in your worksheet quickly and easily. SmartArt lists, diagrams, and pictures come in a wide array of configurations (including a bunch of organizational charts and various process and flow diagrams) that enable you to combine your own text with the predefined graphic shapes.

To insert a SmartArt list, diagram, or picture to caption into the worksheet, click the Insert a SmartArt Graphic button in the Illustrations group on the Insert tab or press Alt+NM1 to open the Choose a SmartArt Graphic dialog box (shown in Figure 10-15). Then click a category in the navigation pane on the left followed by the list's, diagram's, or picture's thumbnail in the center section before you click OK.

Excel then inserts the basic structure of the selected object into your worksheet displaying [Text] in the shapes in the diagram (as shown in Figure 10-16) where you can enter the text for the various parts of the list, diagram, or captions in the case of SmartArt pictures. At the same time, the Design tab of the SmartArt Tools contextual tab with Layouts and SmartArt Styles galleries for the particular type of SmartArt list or diagram you originally selected appears on the Ribbon.

FIGURE 10-15:
Select the
SmartArt list or
diagram to insert
in the worksheet
in this dialog box.

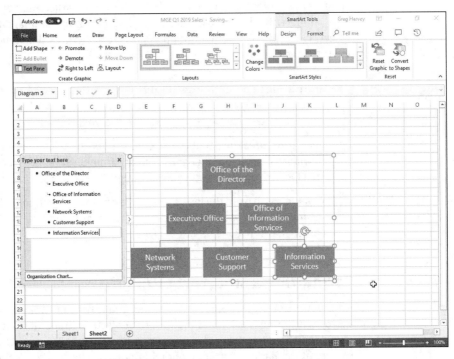

FIGURE 10-16:
Adding text
to a new
organizational
chart.

Filling in the text for a new SmartArt graphic

To fill in the text for the first for your new SmartArt graphic, click its [Text] place-holder and then simply type in the text. When you finish entering the text for your new diagram, click outside the graphic to deselect it.

You can also add to specific shape in your SmartArt graphic using the Text Pane (with the title "Type Your Text Here" as shown in Figure 10-16). To open this pane, you simply click the Text Pane button on the Design tab when the SmartArt graphic is selected.

If the style of the SmartArt list or diagram you select comes with more sections than you need, you can delete the unused graphics by clicking them to select them (indicated by the selection and rotation handles around it) and then pressing the Delete key.

Adding an image to a SmartArt picture graphic

If the SmartArt graphic object you've added to your worksheet is one of those from the Picture group of the Choose a SmartArt Graphic dialog box, your selected SmartArt graphic contains Insert Picture button (marked only by a small picture icon) along with the [Text] indicators. To add a graphic image to the SmartArt object, click this picture icon to open an Insert Pictures dialog box with the following three options:

>> **From a File** to open the Insert Picture dialog box where you can select a local photo or other graphic image saved in a local or networked drive on your computer (see "Inserting local images" earlier in this chapter)

>> **Online Pictures** to open the Online Pictures dialog box where you can download a photo or other graphic image from online source such as Flickr or your OneDrive (see "Inserting online images" earlier in this chapter)

>> **From Icons** to open the Insert Icons dialog box where you can select one of the many categories of black and white images to insert (see "Adding Icons" earlier in this chapter)

Formatting a SmartArt graphic

After you deselect your SmartArt graphic, you can still format its text and format. To format the text, select all the graphic objects in the SmartArt list or diagram that need the same type of text formatting. (Remember you can select several objects in the list or diagram by holding down Ctrl as you click them.) Then click the appropriate command buttons in the Font group on the Home tab of the Ribbon.

To refine or change the default formatting of the SmartArt graphic, you can use the Layouts, Change Colors, and SmartArt Styles drop-down galleries available on the Design tab of the SmartArt Tools contextual tab:

» Click the More button in the Layouts group and then click a thumbnail on the Layouts drop-down gallery to select an entirely new layout for your SmartArt list or diagram.

» Click the Change Colors button in the SmartArt Styles group and then click a thumbnail in the drop-down gallery to change the colors for the current layout.

» Click the More button in the SmartArt Styles group and then click a thumbnail on the SmartArt Styles drop-down gallery to select a new style for the current layout using the selected colors.

Screenshots, anyone?

Excel 2019 supports the creation of screenshot graphics of objects on your Windows 10 desktop that you can automatically insert into your worksheet. To take a picture of a window open on the desktop or any other object on it, select the Screenshot drop-down button in the Illustrations group of the Ribbon's Insert tab (Alt+NSC).

Excel then opens a drop-down menu that displays a thumbnail of available screen shots (ones currently available) followed by the Screen Clipping item. To take a picture of any portion of your Windows desktop, click the Screen Clipping option (or press Alt+NSCC). Excel then automatically minimizes the Excel program window on the Windows taskbar and then brightens the screen and changes the mouse pointer to a thick black cross. You can then use this pointer to drag an out-line around the objects on the Windows desktop you want to include in the screen-shot graphic.

The moment you release the mouse button or remove your finger or stylus from the touchscreen, Excel 2019 then automatically reopens the program window to its previous size displaying the selected graphic containing the Windows screen-shot. You can then resize, move, and adjust this screenshot graphic as you would any other that you add to the worksheet.

TIP

Excel automatically saves the screenshot graphic that you add to a worksheet when you save its workbook. However, the program does not provide you with a means by which to save the screenshot graphic in a separate graphics file for use in other programs. If you need to do this, you should select the screenshot graphic in the Excel worksheet, copy it to the Windows Clipboard, and then paste it into another open graphics program where you can use its Save command to store it in a favorite graphics file format for use in other documents.

Theme for a day

Through the use of its themes, Excel 2019 supports a way to format uniformly all the text and graphics you add to a worksheet. You can do this by simply clicking the thumbnail of the new theme you want to use in the Themes drop-down gallery opened by clicking the Themes button on the Page Layout tab of the Ribbon or by pressing Alt+PTH.

Use Live Preview to see how the text and graphics you've added to your worksheet appear in the new theme before you click its thumbnail.

Excel Themes combine three default elements: the color scheme applied to the graphics, the font (body and heading) used in the text and graphics, and the graphic effects applied. If you prefer, you can change any or all of these elements in the worksheet by clicking their command buttons in the Themes group at the start of the Page Layout tab:

>> **Colors** to select a new color scheme by clicking its thumbnail on the drop-down palette. Click Customize Colors at the bottom of this palette to open the Create New Theme Colors dialog box where you can customize each element of the color scheme and save it with a new descriptive name.

>> **Fonts** to select a new font by clicking its thumbnail on the drop-down list. Click Customize Fonts at the bottom of this list to open the Create New Theme Fonts dialog box where you can customize the body and heading fonts and save it with a new descriptive name.

>> **Effects** to select a new set of graphic effects by clicking its thumbnail in the drop-down gallery.

To save your newly selected color scheme, font, and graphic effects as a custom theme that you can reuse in other workbooks, click the Themes command button and then click Save Current Theme at the bottom of the gallery to open the Save Current Theme dialog box. Edit the generic Theme1 filename in the File Name text box (without deleting the `.thmx` filename extension) and then click the Save button. Excel then adds the custom theme to a Custom Themes section in the Themes drop-down gallery, and you can apply it to any active worksheet by simply clicking its thumbnail.

Controlling How Graphic Objects Overlap

In case you haven't noticed, graphic objects float on top of the cells of the worksheet. Most of the objects (including charts) are opaque, meaning that they hide (*without* replacing) information in the cells beneath. If you move one opaque graphic so that it overlaps part of another, the one on top hides the one below, just as putting one sheet of paper partially on top of another hides some of the information on the one below. Most of the time, you should make sure that graphic objects don't overlap one another or overlap cells with worksheet information that you want to display.

Reordering the layering of graphic objects

When graphic objects (including charts, text boxes, inserted line art and photos, drawn shapes, icons, and SmartArt graphics) overlap each other, you can change how they overlay each other by sending the objects back or forward so that they reside on different (invisible) layers.

Excel 2019 enables you to move a selected graphic object to a new layer in one of two ways:

>> To move the selected object up toward or to the top layer, select the Bring Forward or Bring to Front option on the Bring Forward button's drop-down menu in the Arrange group on the object's Drawing, Pictures, Graphic, or SmartArt Tools contextual tab. To move the selected object down toward or to the bottom layer, select the Send Backward or Send to Back option on the Send Backward button's drop-down menu in the Arrange group on object's Drawing, Pictures, Graphics, or SmartArt Tools contextual tab. You can also access these commands by pressing Alt+PAFF for Bring Forward, Alt+PAFR for Bring to Front, Alt+PAEB for Send Backward, and Alt+PAEK for Send to Back.

>> Click the Selection Pane command button in the Arrange group on the Format tab under the Drawing, Pictures, Graphic, or SmartArt Tools contextual tab to display the Selection task pane or simply press Alt+PAP. Then, click the Bring Forward button (with the triangle pointing up) or Send Backward button (with the triangle pointing down) at the top of the task pane to the immediate right of the Show All and Hide All buttons. You click the Bring Forward or Send Backward button until the selected graphic object appears on the desired layer in the task pane (where the graphic at the top of the list is on the topmost graphic layer and the one at the bottom of the list is on the bottommost graphic layer).

Figure 10-17 illustrates how the Selection task pane works. Here I have a combination of a downloaded web hundred dollar bill photo, Surface Pro 3-D model, and thumbs up icon on the same worksheet but on different layers. As you can see in the Selection task pane, the Surface Pro graphic labeled 3D Model 11 in the task pane is on the topmost layer so that it would obscure any of the other three graphic objects on layers below that it happens to overlap. Next comes the picture of the thumbs up icon labeled Graphic 10 on the second graphics layer so that it obscures part of the hundred dollar bill photo with its caption labeled Textbox 14 and Picture 13 that are placed on the third and fourth (and last) graphics layers, respectively. To move any of these graphic objects to a new layer, I have only to select them in the Selection pane followed by the Bring Forward or Send Backward buttons.

REMEMBER

Excel gives generic names (such as Picture1, Graphic 2, Diagram3, and so forth) to every graphic object you add to your worksheet. To give these objects more descriptive names, double-click the generic graphic name in the Selection task pane, type a new name, and then press Enter to replace it.

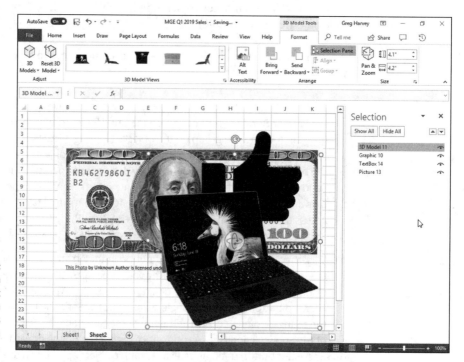

FIGURE 10-17:
Worksheet with various graphic objects on different layers of the Selection task pane.

Grouping graphic objects

Sometimes you may find that you need to group several graphic objects so that they act as one unit (like a text box with its arrow). That way, you can move these objects or size them in one operation.

To group objects, Ctrl+click each object you want to group to select them all. Next, click the Group Objects button in the Arrange group (the one with the picture of two entwined squares) on the Format tab under the appropriate Tools tab and then click Group on its drop-down menu.

After grouping several graphic objects, whenever you click any part of the mega-object, every part is selected (and selection handles appear only around the perimeter of the combined object).

REMEMBER

If you need to independently move or size grouped objects, you can ungroup them by right-clicking an object and then choosing Group⇨Ungroup on the object's shortcut menu or by selecting Group⇨Ungroup on the Format tab under the appropriate Tools contextual tabs.

Hiding graphic objects

The Selection task pane enables you not only to change the layering of various graphic objects in the worksheet, but also to control whether they are hidden or displayed. To open the Selection task pane, select one of the graphic objects on the worksheet and then click the Format button under the respective Tools contextual tab. Then click the Selection Pane button found in the Arrange group of the object's Format tab.

After you open the Selection task pane, you can temporarily hide any of the graphic objects listed by clicking its eye check box (to remove the eye icon). To remove the display of all the charts and graphics in the worksheet, click the Hide All button at the top task pane instead.

To redisplay a hidden graphic object, simply click its empty eye check box to put the eye icon back into it. To redisplay all graphic objects after hiding them all, click the Show All button at the top of the task pane.

WARNING

If you hide all the charts and graphics in a worksheet by clicking the Hide All button and then close the Selection task pane by clicking its Close button, you'll have no way of redisplaying this task pane so that you can bring back their display by clicking the Show All button. That's because you have no visible graphic objects left to select in the worksheet and, therefore, no way to get the contextual tabs with their Selection Pane buttons to appear on the Ribbon.

TIP

In this dire case, you have to select Page Layout⇨Arrange⇨Selection Pane on the Excel Ribbon (Alt+PZAAP) to redisplay the Selection task pane. With the Selection task pane open, click the Show All button to bring back the display of all the charts and graphics you want to keep.

Printing Just the Charts

Sometimes, you may want to print only a particular chart embedded in the worksheet (independent of the worksheet data it represents or any of the other stuff you've added). To do this, open the Selection task pane (as described in the preceding section) and make sure that any hidden charts are displayed in the worksheet by putting the eye icons back in their check boxes.

Next, click the chart to select it in the worksheet and then choose File ⇨ Print or press Ctrl+P to open the Print screen in Backstage view, where you see the chart now displayed in the print preview area.

If you need to change the printed chart size or the orientation of the printing (or both), click the Page Setup link on the Print screen in the Backstage view (Ctrl+P) or click the Page Setup Dialog Box launcher on the Page Layout tab of the Ribbon to open the Page Setup dialog box. To change the orientation of the printing (or the paper size), change the appropriate options on the Page tab in the Page Setup dialog box. To change the print quality or print a color chart in black and white, click the Chart tab and change these options. You can then return to the print preview area in the Print screen in Backstage view by clicking the Print Preview button at the bottom of the Page Setup dialog box. If everything looks good in the print preview area, start printing the chart by clicking the Print button.

IN THIS CHAPTER

» Setting up a data list in Excel

» Entering and editing records in the data list

» Sorting records in the data list

» Filtering records in the data list

» Importing external data into the worksheet

Chapter **11**

Getting on the Data List

The purpose of all the worksheet tables that I discuss elsewhere in this book has been to perform essential calculations (such as to sum monthly or quarterly sales figures) and then present the information in an understand-able form. However, you can create another kind of worksheet table in Excel: a *data list* (less accurately and more colloquially known as a *database table*). The pur-pose of a data list is not so much to calculate new values but rather to store lots and lots of information in a consistent manner. For example, you can create a data list that contains the names and addresses of all your clients, or you can create a list that contains all the essential facts about your employees.

Creating Data Lists

Creating a new data list in a worksheet is much like creating a worksheet table except that it has only column headings and no row headings. To set up a new data list, follow these steps:

1. Click the blank cell where you want to start the new data list and then enter the column headings (technically known as *field names* in database parlance) that identify the different kinds of items you need to keep

track of (such as First Name, Last Name, Street, City, State, and so on) in the columns to the right.

After creating the fields of the data list by entering their headings, you're ready to enter the first row of data.

2. Make the first entries in the appropriate columns of the row immediately following the one containing the field names.

These entries in the first row beneath the one with the field names constitute the first *record* of the data list.

3. Click the Format as Table button in the Styles group of the Ribbon's Home tab and then click a thumbnail of one of the table styles in the drop-down gallery.

Excel puts a marquee around all the cells in the new data list, including the top row of field names. As soon as you click a table style in the drop-down gallery, the Format As Table dialog box appears listing the address of the cell range enclosed in the marquee in the Where Is the Data for Your Table text box.

4. Click the My Table Has Headers check box to select it, if necessary.

5. Click the OK button to close the Format As Table dialog box.

Excel formats your new data list in the selected table format and adds filters (drop-down buttons) to each of the field names in the top row (see Figure 11-1).

FIGURE 11-1:
Create a new data list by formatting the field names and the first record as a table.

Adding records to data lists

After creating the field names and one record of the data list and formatting them as a table, you're ready to start entering the rest of its data as records in subsequent rows of the list. The most direct way to do this is to press the Tab key when the cell cursor is in the last cell of the first record. Doing this causes Excel to add an extra row to the data list where you can enter the appropriate information for the next record.

CALCULATED FIELD ENTRIES

When you want Excel to calculate the entries for a particular field by formula, you need to enter that formula in the correct field in the first record of the data list. In the sample Employee Data list, for example, the Years of Service field in cell I2 of the first record shown in Figure 11-1 is calculated by the formula =YEAR(TODAY())-YEAR(H2). Cell H2 contains the date of hire that this formula uses to compute the number of years that an employee has worked at the company. Excel then inserts the result of this calculation into the cell as the field entry to which you can then assign the appropriate Number format.

TIP

When doing data entry directly in a data list table, press the Tab key to proceed to the next field in the new record rather than the → key. That way, when you complete the entry in the last field of the record, you automatically extend the data list, add a new record, and position the cell cursor in the first field of that record. If you press → to complete the entry, Excel simply moves the cell cursor to the next cell outside the data list table.

Using the Form button

Instead of entering the records of a data list directly in the table, you can use Excel's data form to make the entries. The only problem with using the data form is that the command to display the form in a worksheet with a data list is not part of the Ribbon commands. You can access the data form only by adding its command button to the Quick Access toolbar or a custom Ribbon tab.

To add this command button to the Quick Access toolbar, follow these steps:

1. Click the Customize Quick Access Toolbar button at the end of the Quick Access toolbar and then click the More Commands item at the bottom of its drop-down menu.

Excel opens the Excel Options dialog box with the Quick Access Toolbar tab selected.

The Form command button you want to add to the Quick Access toolbar is only available when you click the Commands Not in the Ribbon option on the Choose Commands From drop-down list.

2. Click the Commands Not in the Ribbon option near the top of the Choose Commands From drop-down list.

3. **Click Form in the Choose Commands From list box and then click the Add button.**

Excel adds the Form button to the very end of the Quick Access toolbar. If you so desire, you can click the Move Up and Move Down buttons to reposition the Form button on this toolbar.

4. **Click OK to close the Excel Options dialog box and return to the worksheet with the data list.**

Adding records via the data form

The first time you click the custom Form button you added to the Quick Access toolbar, Excel analyzes the row of field names and entries for the first record and creates a data form. This data form lists the field names down the left side of the form with the entries for the first record in the appropriate text boxes next to them. In Figure 11-2, you can see the data form for the new Employee Data database; it looks kind of like a customized dialog box.

Form button

FIGURE 11-2:
Enter the second record of the data list in its data form.

The data form Excel creates includes the entries you made in the first record. The data form also contains a series of buttons (on the right side) that you use to add, delete, or find specific records in the database. Right above the first button (New), the data form lists the number of the record you're looking at followed by the total number of records (1 of 1 when you first create the data form). When creating new entries it will display New Record above this button instead of the record number.

TIP

All the formatting that you assign to the particular entries in the first record is applied automatically to those fields in subsequent records you enter and is used in the data form. For example, if your data list contains a telephone field, you need to enter only the ten digits of the phone number in the Telephone field of the data form if the initial telephone number entry is formatted in the first record with the Special Phone Number format. (See Chapter 3 for details on sorting number formats.) That way, Excel takes a new entry in the Telephone file, such as 3075550045, for example, and automatically formats it so that it appears as (307) 555-0045 in the appropriate cell of the data list.

The process for adding records to a data list with the data form is simple. When you click the New button, Excel displays a blank data form (marked New Record at the right side of the data form), which you get to fill in.

After you enter the information for the first field, press the Tab key to advance to the next field in the record.

WARNING

Whoa! Don't press the Enter key to advance to the next field in a record. If you do, you'll insert the new, incomplete record into the database.

Continue entering information for each field and pressing Tab to go to the next field in the database.

>> If you notice that you've made an error and want to edit an entry in a field you already passed, press Shift+Tab to return to that field.

>> To replace the entry, just start typing.

>> To edit some of the characters in the field, press ← or click the I-beam pointer in the entry to locate the insertion point; then edit the entry from there.

When entering information in a particular field, you can copy the entry made in that field from the previous record by pressing Ctrl+' (apostrophe). Press Ctrl+', for example, to carry forward the same entry in the State field of each new record when entering a series of records for people who all live in the same state.

When entering dates in a date field, use a consistent date format that Excel knows. (For example, enter something like **7/21/98**.) When entering zip codes that sometimes use leading zeros that you don't want to disappear from the entry (such as zip code 00102), format the first field entry with the Special Zip Code number format (refer to Chapter 3 for details on sorting number formats). In the case of other numbers that use leading zeros, you can format it by using the Text format or put an ' (apostrophe) before the first 0. The apostrophe tells Excel to treat the number like a text label but doesn't show up in the database itself. (The only place you can see the apostrophe is on the Formula bar when the cell cursor is in the cell with the numeric entry.)

Press the ↓ key when you've entered all the information for the new record. Or, instead of the ↓ key, you can press Enter or click the New button (refer to Figure 11-2). Excel inserts the new record as the last record in the database in the worksheet and displays a blank data form in which you can enter the next record (see Figure 11-3).

When you finish adding records to the database, press the Esc key or click the Close button at the bottom of the dialog box to close the data form.

FIGURE 11-3:
When you advance to a new record in the data form, Excel inserts the record just completed as the last row of the list.

Editing records in the data form

After the database is under way and you're caught up with entering new records, you can start using the data form to perform routine maintenance on the database. For example, you can use the data form to locate a record you want to change and then make the edits to the particular fields. You can also use the data form to find a specific record you want to remove and then delete it from the database.

» Locate the record you want to edit in the database by bringing up its data form. See the following two sections ("Moving through records in the data form" and "Finding records with the data form") and Table 11-1 for hints on locating records.

» To edit the fields of the current record, move to that field by pressing Tab or Shift+Tab and replace the entry by typing a new one.

Alternatively, press ← or → or click the I-beam cursor to reposition the insertion point, and then make your edits.

» To clear a field entirely, select it and then press the Delete key.

TABLE 11-1   **Ways to Get to a Particular Record**

Keystrokes or Scroll Bar Technique	Result
Press ↓ or Enter or click the down scroll arrow or the Find Next button	Moves to the next record in the data list and leaves the same field selected
Press ↑ or Shift+Enter or click the up scroll arrow or the Find Prev button	Moves to the previous record in the data list and leaves the same field selected
Press PgDn	Moves forward ten records in the data list
Press PgUp	Moves backward ten records in the data list
Press Ctrl+↑ or Ctrl+PgUp or drag the scroll box to the top of the scroll bar	Moves to the first record in the data list
Drag the scroll box to almost the bottom of the scroll bar	Moves to the last record in the data list

To delete the entire record from the database, click the Delete button in the data form. Excel displays an alert box with the following dire warning:

```
Displayed record will be permanently deleted
```

To delete the record displayed in the data form, click OK. To play it safe and keep the record intact, click the Cancel button.

WARNING

You cannot use the Undo feature to bring back a record you removed with the Delete button! Excel is definitely not kidding when it warns *permanently deleted*. As a precaution, always save a back-up version of the worksheet with the database before you start removing old records.

Moving through records in the data form

In the data form, you can use the scroll bar to the right of the list of field names or various keystrokes (both summarized in Table 11-1) to move through the records in the database until you find the one you want to edit or delete.

>> **To move to the next record in the data list:** Press ↓, press Enter, or click the down scroll arrow at the bottom of the scroll bar.

>> **To move to the previous record in the data list:** Press ↑, press Shift+Enter, or click the up scroll arrow at the top of the scroll bar.

>> **To move to the first record in the data list:** Press Ctrl+↑, press Ctrl+PgUp, or drag the scroll box to the very top of the scroll bar.

>> **To move to a new record in the data form immediately following the last record in the database:** Press Ctrl+↓, press Ctrl+PgDn, or drag the scroll box to the very bottom of the scroll bar.

Finding records with the data form

In a large data list, trying to find a particular record by moving from record to record — or even moving ten records at a time with the scroll bar — can take all day. Rather than waste time trying to manually search for a record, you can use the Criteria button in the data form to look it up.

When you click the Criteria button, Excel clears all the field entries in the data form (and replaces the record number with the word *Criteria*) so that you can enter the criteria to search for in the blank text boxes.

For example, suppose that you need to edit Sherry Caulfield's profit sharing status. Unfortunately, her paperwork doesn't include her ID number. All you know is that she works in the Boston office and spells her last name with a *C* instead of a *K*.

To find her record, you can use the information you have to narrow the search to all the records where the last name begins with the letter *C* and the Location field contains Boston. To limit your search in this way, open the data form for the Employee Data database, click the Criteria button, and then type **C*** in the text box for the Last Name field. Also enter **Boston** in the text box for the Location field.

When you enter search criteria for records in the blank text boxes of the data form, you can use the ? (for single) and * (for multiple) wild-card characters.

Now click the Find Next button. Excel displays in the data form the first record in the database where the last name begins with the letter C and the Location field contains Boston. The first record in this data list that meets these criteria is for William Cobb. To find Sherry's record, click the Find Next button again. Sherry Caulfield's record then shows up. Having located Caulfield's record, you can then edit her profit sharing status from No to Yes in the text box for the Profit Sharing field. When you click the Close button, Excel records her new profit sharing status in the data list.

When you use the Criteria button in the data form to find records, you can include the following operators in the search criteria you enter to locate a specific record in the database:

Operator	Meaning
=	Equal to
>	Greater than
>=	Greater than or equal to
<	Less than
<=	Less than or equal to
<>	Not equal to

For example, to display only those records where an employee's salary is greater than or equal to $50,000, enter **>=50000** in the text box for the Salary field and then click the Find Next button.

When specifying search criteria that fit a number of records, you may have to click the Find Next or Find Prev button several times to locate the record you want. If no record fits the search criteria you enter, the computer beeps at you when you click these buttons.

To change the search criteria, first clear the data form by clicking the Criteria button again and then clicking the Clear button.

To switch back to the current record without using the search criteria you enter, click the Form button. (This button replaces the Criteria button as soon as you click the Criteria button.)

Sorting Data Lists

Every data list you put together in Excel will have some kind of preferred order for maintaining and viewing the records. Depending on the list, you may want to see the records in alphabetical order by last name. In the case of a client data table, you may want to see the records arranged alphabetically by company name. In the case of the Employee Data list, the preferred order is in numerical order by the ID number assigned to each employee when he or she is hired.

When you initially enter records for a new data list, you no doubt enter them in either the preferred order or the order in which you retrieve their records. However you start out, as you will soon discover, you don't have the option of adding subsequent records in that preferred order. Whenever you add a new record, Excel tacks that record onto the bottom of the database by adding a new row.

Suppose you originally enter all the records in a client data list in alphabetical order by company (from Acme Pet Supplies to Zastrow and Sons), and then you add the record for a new client: Pammy's Pasta Palace. Excel puts the new record at the bottom of the barrel — in the last row right after Zastrow and Sons — instead of inserting it in its proper position, which is somewhere after Acme Pet Supplies but definitely well ahead of Zastrow and his wonderful boys!

This isn't the only problem you can have with the original record order. Even if the records in the data list remain stable, the preferred order merely represents the order you use *most* of the time. What about those times when you need to see the records in another, special order?

For example, if you usually work with a client data list in numerical order by case number, you might instead need to see the records in alphabetical order by the client's last name to quickly locate a client and look up his or her balance due in a printout. When using records to generate mailing labels for a mass mailing, you want the records in zip code order. When generating a report for your account representatives showing which clients are in whose territory, you need the records in alphabetical order by state and maybe even by city.

To have Excel correctly sort the records in a data list, you must specify which field's values determine the new order of the records. (Such fields are technically known as the *sorting keys* in the parlance of the database enthusiast.) Further, you must specify what type of order you want to create using the information in these fields. Choose from two possible orders:

UP AND DOWN THE ASCENDING AND DESCENDING SORT ORDERS

When you use the ascending sort order on a field in the data list that contains many different kinds of entries, Excel places numbers (from smallest to largest) before text entries (in alphabetical order), followed by any logical values (FALSE and TRUE), error values, and finally, blank cells. When you use the descending sort order, Excel arranges the different entries in reverse: numbers are still first, arranged from largest to smallest; text entries go from Z to A; and the TRUE logical value precedes the FALSE logical value.

>> **Ascending order:** Text entries are placed in alphabetical order from A to Z, values are placed in numerical order from smallest to largest, and dates are placed in order from oldest to newest.

>> **Descending order:** This is the reverse of alphabetical order from Z to A, numerical order from largest to smallest, and dates from newest to oldest.

Sorting on a single field

When you need to sort the data list on only one particular field (such as the Record Number, Last Name, or Company field), you simply click that field's AutoFilter button and then click the appropriate sort option on its drop-down list:

>> **Sort A to Z** or **Sort Z to A** in a text field

>> **Sort Smallest to Largest** or **Sort Largest to Smallest** in a number field

>> **Sort Oldest to Newest** or **Sort Newest to Oldest** in a date field

Excel then re-orders all the records in the data list in accordance with the new ascending or descending order in the selected field. If you find that you've sorted the list in error, simply click the Undo button on the Quick Access toolbar or press Ctrl+Z right away to return the list to its order before you selected one of these sort options.

TIP Excel shows when a field has been used to sort the data list by adding an up or down arrow to its AutoFilter button. An arrow pointing up indicates that the ascending sort order was used and an arrow pointing down indicates that the descending sort order was used.

Sorting on multiple fields

You need to use more than one field in sorting when the first field you use contains duplicate values and you want a say in how the records with duplicates are arranged. (If you don't specify another field to sort on, Excel just puts the records in the order in which you entered them.)

The best and most common example of when you need more than one field is when sorting a large database alphabetically by last name. Suppose that you have a database that contains several people with the last name Smith, Jones, or Zastrow (as is the case when you work at Zastrow and Sons). If you specify the Last Name field as the only field to sort on (using the default ascending order), all the duplicate Smiths, Joneses, and Zastrows are placed in the order in which their records were originally entered. To better sort these duplicates, you can specify the First Name field as the second field to sort on (again using the default ascending order), making the second field the tie-breaker, so that Ian Smith's record precedes that of Sandra Smith, and Vladimir Zastrow's record comes after that of Mikhail Zastrow.

To sort records in a data list on multiple fields, follow these steps:

1. **Position the cell cursor in one of the cells in the data list table.**

2. **If the Home tab on the Ribbon is selected, click Custom Sort on the Sort & Filter button's drop-down list (Alt+HSU). If the Data tab is selected, click the Sort command button.**

   Excel selects all the records of the database (without including the first row of field names) and opens the Sort dialog box, shown in Figure 11-4.

3. **Click the name of the field you first want the records sorted by in the Sort By drop-down list.**

   If you want the records arranged in descending order, remember also to select the descending sort option (Z to A, Largest to Smallest, or Newest to Oldest) in the Order drop-down list to the right.

4. **(Optional) If the first field contains duplicates and you want to specify how the records in this field are sorted, click the Add Level button to insert another sort level. Select a second field to sort on in the Then By drop-down list and select either the ascending or descending option in its Order drop-down list to its right.**

5. **(Optional) If necessary, repeat Step 4, adding as many additional sort levels as required.**

6. Click OK or press Enter.

Excel closes the Sort dialog box and sorts the records in the data list using the sorting fields in the order of their levels in this dialog box. If you see that you sorted the database on the wrong fields or in the wrong order, click the Undo button on the Quick Access toolbar or press Ctrl+Z to restore the database records to their previous order.

FIGURE 11-4:
Set up to sort records alphabetically by last name and then first name.

Check out how I set up my search in the Sort dialog box in Figure 11-4. In the Employee Data List, I chose the Last Name field as the first field to sort on (Sort By) and the First Name field as the second field (Then By) — the second field sorts records with duplicate entries in the first field. I also chose to sort the records in the Employee Data List in alphabetical (A to Z) order by last name and then first name. See the Employee Data List right after sorting (in Figure 11-5). Note how the Edwards — Cindy and Jack — are now arranged in the proper first name/last name alphabetical order.

FIGURE 11-5:
The Employee
Data List sorted
in alphabetical
order by last
name and then
by first name.

SORTING SOMETHING BESIDES A DATA LIST

The Sort command is not just for sorting records in the data list. You can use it to sort financial data or text headings in the spreadsheet tables you build as well. When sorting regular worksheet tables, just be sure to select all the cells with the data to be sorted (and only those with the data to be sorted) before you open the Sort dialog box by clicking Custom Sort on the Sort & Filter button's drop-down list on the Ribbon's Home tab or the Sort button on the Data tab.

Excel automatically excludes the first row of the cell selection from the sort (on the assumption that this row is a header row containing field names that shouldn't be included). To include the first row of the cell selection in the sort, be sure to deselect the My Data Has Headers check box before you click OK to begin sorting.

If you want to sort worksheet data by columns, click the Options button in the Sort dialog box. Click the Sort Left to Right button in the Sort Options dialog box and then click OK. Now you can designate the number of the row (or rows) to sort the data on in the Sort dialog box.

Filtering Data Lists

Excel's Filter feature makes it a breeze to hide everything in a data list except the records you want to see. To filter the data list to just those records that contain a particular value, you then click the appropriate field's AutoFilter button to display a drop-down list containing all the entries made in that field and select the one you want to use as a filter. Excel then displays only those records that contain the value you selected in that field. (All other records are hidden temporarily.)

TIP

If the column headings of your data list table don't currently have filter drop-down buttons displayed in their cells after the field names, you can add them simply by clicking Home ⇨ Sort & Filter ⇨ Filter or pressing Alt+HSF.

For example, in Figure 11-6, I filtered the Employee Data List to display only those records in which the Location is either Boston or San Francisco by clicking the Location field's AutoFilter button and then clicking the (Select All) check box to remove its check mark. I then clicked the Boston and San Francisco check boxes to add check marks to them before clicking OK. (It's as simple as that.)

FIGURE 11-6:
The Employee Data List after filtering out all records except those with Boston or San Francisco in the Location field.

TIP

After you filter a data list so that only the records you want to work with are displayed, you can copy those records to another part of the worksheet to the right of the database (or better yet, another worksheet in the workbook). Simply select the cells, then click the Copy button on the Home tab or press Ctrl+C, move the cell cursor to the first cell where the copied records are to appear, and then press Enter. After copying the filtered records, you can then redisplay all the records in the database or apply a slightly different filter.

If you find that filtering the data list by selecting a single value in a field drop-down list box gives you more records than you really want to contend with, you can further filter the database by selecting another value in a second field's drop-down list. For example, suppose that you select Boston as the filter value in the Location field's drop-down list and end up with hundreds of Boston records displayed in the worksheet. To reduce the number of Boston records to a more manageable number, you could then select a value (such as Human Resources) in the Dept field's drop-down list to further filter the database and reduce the records you have to work with onscreen. When you finish working with the Boston Human Resources employee records, you can display another set by displaying the Dept field's drop-down list again and changing the filter value from Human Resources to some other department, such as Accounting.

When you're ready to display all the records in the database again, click the filtered field's AutoFilter button (indicated by the appearance of a cone filter on its drop-down button) and then click the Clear Filter from (followed by the name of the field in parentheses) option near the middle of its drop-down list.

REMEMBER

You can temporarily remove the AutoFilter buttons from the cells in the top row of the data list containing the field names and later redisplay them by clicking the Filter button on the Data tab or by pressing Alt+AT or Ctrl+Shift+L. You can also use Slicer and Timeline filters on your data lists as described in Chapter 9.

Using ready-made number filters

Excel contains a number filter option called Top 10. You can use this option on a number field to show only a certain number of records (like the ones with the ten highest or lowest values in that field or those in the ten highest or lowest percent in that field or just those that are above or below average of that field).

To use the Top 10 option to filter a database, follow these steps:

1. **Click the AutoFilter button on the numeric field you want to filter with the Top 10 option. Then highlight Number Filters in the drop-down list and click Top 10 on its submenu.**

   Excel opens the Top 10 AutoFilter dialog box. By default, the Top 10 AutoFilter chooses to show the top ten items in the selected field. However, you can change these default settings before filtering the database.

2. **To show only the bottom ten records, change Top to Bottom in the left-most drop-down list box.**

3. **To show more or fewer than the top or bottom ten records, enter the new value in the middle text box (that currently holds 10) or select a new value by using the spinner buttons.**

4. To show those records that fall into the Top 10 or Bottom 10 (or whatever) percent, change Items to Percent in the right-most drop-down list box.

5. Click OK or press Enter to filter the database by using your Top 10 settings.

In Figure 11-7, you can see the Employee Data List after using the Top 10 option (with all its default settings) to show only those records with salaries that are in the top ten. David Letterman would be proud!

FIGURE 11-7: The Employee Data List after using the Top 10 AutoFilter to filter out all records except for those with the ten highest salaries.

Using ready-made date filters

When filtering a data list by the entries in a date field, Excel makes available a variety of date filters that you can apply to the list. These ready-made filters include Equals, Before, After, and Between as well as Tomorrow, Today, Yesterday, as well as Next, This, and Last for the Week, Month, Quarter, and Year. Additionally, Excel offers Year to Date and All Dates in the Period filters. When you select the All Dates in the Period filter, Excel enables you to choose between Quarter 1 through 4 or any of the 12 months, January through December, as the period to use in filtering the records.

To select any of these date filters, you click the date field's AutoFilter button, then highlight Date Filters on the drop-down list and click the appropriate date filter option on the continuation menu(s).

Using custom filters

In addition to filtering a data list to records that contain a particular field entry (such as Newark as the City or CA as the State), you can create custom AutoFilters that enable you to filter the list to records that meet less-exacting criteria (such as last names starting with the letter M) or ranges of values (such as salaries between $25,000 and $75,000 a year).

To create a custom filter for a field, you click the field's AutoFilter button and then highlight Text Filters, Number Filters, or Date Filters (depending on the type of field) on the drop-down list and then click the Custom Filter option at the bottom of the continuation list. When you select the Custom Filter option, Excel displays a Custom AutoFilter dialog box, similar to the one shown in Figure 11-8.

FIGURE 11-8:
Use a custom
AutoFilter to
display records
with entries in the
Salary field
between $25,000
and $75,000.

TIP

You can also open the Custom AutoFilter dialog box by clicking the initial operator (Equals, Does Not Equal, Greater Than, and so on) on the field's Text Filters, Number Filters, or Date Filters submenus.

In this dialog box, you select the operator that you want to use in the first drop-down list box. (See Table 11-2 for operator names and what they locate.) Then enter the value (text or numbers) that should be met, exceeded, fallen below, or not found in the records of the database in the text box to the right.

If you want to filter records in which only a particular field entry matches, exceeds, falls below, or simply is not the same as the one you enter in the text box, you then click OK or press Enter to apply this filter to the database. However, you can use the Custom AutoFilter dialog box to filter the database to records with field entries that fall within a range of values or meet either one of two criteria.

TABLE 11-2   **Operators Used in Custom AutoFilters**

Operator	Example	What It Locates in the Database
Equals	Salary equals 35000	Records where the value in the Salary field is equal to $35,000
Does not equal	State does not equal NY	Records where the entry in the State field is not NY (New York)
Is greater than	Zip is greater than 42500	Records where the number in the Zip field comes after 42500
Is greater than or equal to	Zip is greater than or equal to 42500	Records where the number in the Zip field is equal to 42500 or comes after it
Is less than	Salary is less than 25000	Records where the value in the Salary field is less than $25,000 a year
Is less than or equal to	Salary is less than or equal to 25000	Records where the value in the Salary field is equal to $25,000 or less than $25,000
Begins with	Begins with d	Records with specified fields have entries that start with the letter *d*
Does not begin with	Does not begin with d	Records with specified fields have entries that do not start with the letter *d*
Ends with	Ends with ey	Records whose specified fields have entries that end with the letters *ey*
Does not end with	Does not end with ey	Records with specified fields have entries that do not end with the letters *ey*
Contains	Contains Harvey	Records with specified fields have entries that contain the name Harvey
Does not contain	Does not contain Harvey	Records with specified fields have entries that don't contain the name Harvey

To set up a range of values, you select the "is greater than" or "is greater than or equal to" operator for the top operator and then enter or select the lowest (or first) value in the range. Then, make sure that the And option is selected, select "is less than" or "is less than or equal to" as the bottom operator, and enter the highest (or last) value in the range.

Check out Figures 11-8 and 11-9 to see how I filter the records in the Employee Data List so that only those records where Salary amounts are between $25,000 and $75,000 are displayed. As shown in Figure 11-8, you set up this range of values as the filter by selecting "is greater than or equal to" as the operator and 25,000 as the lower value of the range. Then, with the And option selected, you select "is less than or equal to" as the operator and 75,000 as the upper value of the range. The results of applying this filter to the Employee Data List are shown in Figure 11-9.

FIGURE 11-9: The Employee Data List after applying the custom AutoFilter.

To set up an either/or condition in the Custom AutoFilter dialog box, you normally choose between the "equals" and "does not equal" operators (whichever is appropriate) and then enter or select the first value that must be met or must not be equaled. Then you select the Or option and select whichever operator is appropriate and enter or select the second value that must be met or must not be equaled.

For example, if you want to filter the data list so that only records for the Accounting or Human Resources departments in the Employee Data List appear, you select "equals" as the first operator and then select or enter Accounting as the first entry. Next, you click the Or option, select "equals" as the second operator, and then select or enter Human Resources as the second entry. When you then filter the database by clicking OK or pressing Enter, Excel displays only those records with either Accounting or Human Resources as the entry in the Dept field.

Importing External Data

Excel 2019 makes it easy to import data into a worksheet from other database tables created with stand-alone database management systems (such as Microsoft Access), a process known as making an *external data query.*

You can also use web queries to import data directly from various web pages containing financial and other types of statistical data that you need to work with in the Excel worksheet.

Querying Access database tables

To make an external data query to an Access database table, you click Data⇨ Get Data⇨ From Database⇨ From Microsoft Access Database on the Ribbon or press Alt+APNDC. Excel opens the Import Data box where you select the filename of the Access database and then click Import.

The Navigator dialog box then appears from which you can preview and select the data table(s) and/or queries that you want to import into the worksheet. To select more than one data table or query in the database, click the Select Multiple Items check box and then select each item under Display Options on the left side to import.

When you are ready to import the selected table and/or queries selected in the Navigator dialog box, you can choose among the following options:

>> **Transform Data** to open the Power Query Editor dialog box where you can further refine the Access data before importing into your Excel workbook with the Close & Load or the Close & Load To option on its Close and Load command button (these options work just like the Load and Load To options described in next two bullet points)

>> **Load** to have the data in the Access data table and/or query imported into a new worksheet in the current workbook

>> **Load To** (on the Load button's drop-down menu) to open an Import Data dialog box where you can choose to have the Access data imported as a new Excel data table, pivot table, or pivot chart (see Chapter 9) or just create a link to the data without bringing it into Excel (Only Create Connection option) as well as specify where to import the data in your workbook and whether or not to add it to your Data Model when you click OK.

Figure 11-10 shows you an Excel worksheet after importing the Invoices data table from the sample Northwind Access database as a new data table in Excel. After importing the data, you can then use the AutoFilter buttons attached to the various fields to sort and filter the data (as described earlier in this chapter).

TIP

Excel keeps a list of all the external data queries you make so that you can reuse them to import updated data from another database or web page. To reuse a query, click the Existing Connections button on the Data tab (Alt+AX) to open the Existing Connections dialog box to access this list and then click the name of the query to repeat.

TECHNICAL
STUFF

Databases created and maintained with Microsoft Access are not, of course, the only external data sources on which you can perform external data queries. When you select the Get Data button on the Data tab, in addition to the From Database option, the Get Data continuation menu gives a choice of these other data sources:

>> **From File** to import data from local files that can include data lists in Excel workbooks and text files

>> **From Azure** to import data from Microsoft Azure online services, including Azure SQL databases, analytics, and storage

- **From Online Services** to import data from online services to which you subscribe, such as Facebook

- **From Other Sources** to import data from a variety of different data sources including a table or range of data in an Excel workbook, the web, as well as from existing data queries and data feeds

When you select the From Database option on the Get Data continuation menu, in addition to From Microsoft Access Database, you have a choice of data sources, including but not limited to

- **From SQL Server Database** to import data from an SQL Server table

- **From Analysis Services** to import data from an SQL Server Analysis cube

- **From SQL Server Analysis Services Database (Import)** to import a database or MDX or DAX query from an SQL SAS database)

TIP

For specific help with importing data using these various sources, see my *Excel 2019 All-in-One For Dummies*.

Performing web queries

To make a web page query, you click the From Web command button on the Data tab of the Ribbon or press Alt+AFW. Excel then opens the From Web dialog box containing an URL text box where you enter the web address of the web page whose data you want to bring into Excel before clicking the OK button. Excel then connects to website and opens a Navigator dialog box where you can preview and preview the tables of data to bring into a worksheet in your current workbook.

When you click a table in the Display Options pane of the Navigator dialog box, Excel displays the column headings and data the table will appear in your worksheet in the area on the right (see Figure 11-11). To import more than one table from a web page, click the Select Multiple Items check box before clicking the check box before each table's description on the left side.

After you finish checking all the tables you want to import on the page, in the Navigator dialog box, you can choose among the following options:

- **Transform Data** to open the Power Query Editor dialog box where you can further refine the table data before importing into your Excel workbook with the Close & Load or the Close & Load To option on its Close and Load command button (these options work just like the Load and Load To options described in next two bullet points)

FIGURE 11-11:
Selecting a table
of data showing
an overview of
stock market
trading to import
from home page
of the Nasdaq
website in the
Navigator
dialog box.

>> **Load** to have the data in the selected data table(s) imported into a new worksheet in the current workbook

>> **Load To** (on the Load button's drop-down menu) to open an Import Data dialog box where you can choose have the table data imported as a new Excel data table, pivot table or pivot chart (see Chapter 9) or just create a link to the data without bringing it into Excel (Only Create Connection option) as well as specify where to import the data in your workbook and whether or not to add it to your Data Model when you click OK

REMEMBER

Excel brings this data from a web query into the worksheet as an Excel table so that you can use its AutoFilter buttons to sort or filter this imported financial data as you desire.

WARNING

You can make web queries only when your computer has Internet access. Therefore, if you're using Excel 2019 on a portable device that can't currently connect to the web, you won't be able to perform a new web query until you're in a place where you can connect.

IN THIS CHAPTER

» **Using Office and Excel Add-ins to automate and enhance Excel 2019**

» **Adding hyperlinks to other workbooks, worksheets, Office documents, web pages, or e-mail**

» **Creating and using macros to automate common spreadsheet tasks**

» **Sharing your worksheets on the web**

» **Editing your worksheets in a web browser with Excel Online**

Chapter **12**

Linking, Automating, and Sharing Spreadsheets

t your first reading of the chapter title, you might have the impression that this is just a catch-all, potpourri chapter, containing the last bits of program information that don't fit anywhere else in the book. Actually, this is not the case because this chapter has a very definite theme, and that theme is how you go about extending the power of Excel 2019.

It just so happens that Office and Excel Add-ins, hyperlinks, and macros represent major ways to make Excel worksheets more vigorous and versatile: add-ins through the extra features they give Excel 2019; hyperlinks through links to other worksheets, Office documents, and web pages; and macros through complex automated command sequences that you can play back whenever needed. And sharing your worksheets by attaching them to e-mail messages or publishing them to the web as well as being able to edit them anywhere in the world using the Excel Online web application are all part of the new collaboration features that enable you to both communicate and collaborate more quickly and effectively.

Using Office Add-ins

Office Add-ins are small programs (sometimes called apps) that run inside various Microsoft Office 2019 programs to extend their functionality. There are Office Add-ins to help you learn about Excel's features, look up words in the Merriam-Webster dictionary, and even enter dates into your spreadsheet by selecting them on a calendar.

Most of the Office Add-ins are available free of charge, whereas others offer a limited free trial. To use any of these Office Add-ins in Excel 2019, you first need to install them:

1. **Click the My Add-ins button on the Insert tab of the Ribbon followed by the See All option on its drop-down menu (Alt+NAPS) and then click the Store tab at the top.**

   When the Office Add-ins dialog box first opens, it shows all the add-in programs available in Excel when you installed Office 2019. When you click the Store tab, this dialog box then displays all the available Office Add-ins arranged in categories that you can add to Excel 2019.

   The Office Add-ins dialog box displays thumbnails of all available Office add-ins for Excel arranged in various categories ranging from CRM (Customer Relationship Management) to Visualization (see Figure 12-1).

2. **To display Office Add-ins for a particular category, such as Financial Management or Data, click its link in the Category list to the left.**

3. **When you find an Office Add-in that you may want to install in any one of the categories, click its thumbnail.**

   The Office Add-ins dialog box displays information about the Office Add-in you selected, including the name of the add-in's creator, its rating, and how it works with your Excel data and whether or not it can send data over the Internet.

4. **To install the add-in, click the Add button. To return to the list of suggested add-ins in the Office Add-ins Store, click the Back button above it.**

   Once you click the Add button for a free Office Add-in, Excel closes the Office Add-ins dialog box and downloads the add-in in the current worksheet for you to use. It also adds the Office add-in to the list of installed Office Add-ins on the My Add-ins tab of the Office Add-ins dialog box.

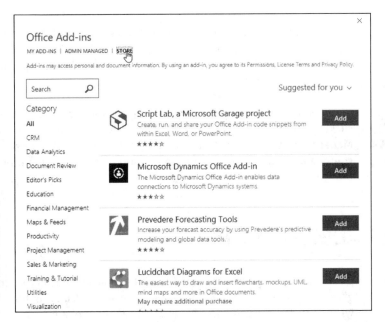

Once installed, the add-in appears in its own task pane in the current worksheet where you can start learning about its features and begin using it. Thereafter, you can then insert the Office Add-in you want to use into any open worksheet. To do this, follow these steps:

1. **If the Office Add-ins dialog box is not currently open in Excel, open it by clicking Insert ➪ Add-ins ➪ My Add-ins ➪ See All or press Alt+NAPS.**

   Excel displays all the Office Add-ins currently installed in Excel 2019 in the My Add-ins tab of the Office Add-ins dialog box.

2. **Click the Office Add-in you want to use in your worksheet to select it and then click the Add button or press Enter.**

Excel then inserts the Office Add-in into your current worksheet and displays its task pane so that you can start using its features. Some Office Add-ins such as the Merriam-Webster Dictionary app and QuickHelp Starter open in task panes docked on the right side of the worksheet window. Others, such as Bing Maps and the Mini Calendar and Date Picker, open as graphic objects that float above the worksheet.

To close Office Add-ins that open in docked task panes, you simply click the task pane's Close button. To close Office Add-ins that open as floating graphic objects, you need to select the graphic and then press the Delete key (don't worry — doing this only closes the app without uninstalling it).

Note that after you start using various Office Add-ins in Excel, they're added to the Recently Used Add-ins section of the My Add-ins button's drop-down menu. You can then quickly reopen any closed Office add-in that appears on this menu simply by clicking it.

TIP

If you don't see any of your installed apps in the Office Add-ins dialog box after clicking the My Add-ins link, click the Refresh link to refresh the list. Use the Manage My Apps link in this dialog box to keep tabs on all the Office Add-ins you've installed for Office 2019 and SharePoint as well as uninstall any add-in that you're no longer using.

Using Excel Add-Ins

Excel add-in programs are small modules that extend the program's power by giving you access to a wide array of features and calculating functions not otherwise offered in the program. There are three types of add-ins:

>> Built-in add-ins available when you install Excel 2019

>> Add-ins that you can download for Excel 2019 from Microsoft's Office Online website (www.office.microsoft.com)

>> Add-ins developed by third-party vendors for Excel 2019 that often must be purchased

When you first install Excel 2019, the built-in add-in programs included with Excel are fully loaded and ready to use. To load any other add-in programs, you follow these steps:

1. **Click File ⇨ Options to open the Excel Options dialog box and then click the Add-Ins tab or press Alt+FTAA.**

   The Add-Ins tab lists the name, location, and type of add-ins you have access to.

2. **Click the Go button while Excel Add-Ins is selected in the Manage drop-down list box.**

   Excel opens the Add-Ins dialog box (similar to the one shown in Figure 12-2) showing all the names of the built-in add-in programs you can load.

3. **Select the check boxes for each add-in program that you want loaded in the Add-Ins Available list box.**

   Click the name of the add-in in the Add-Ins Available list box to display a brief description of its function at the bottom of this dialog box.

4. **Click the OK button to close the Add-Ins dialog box.**

An alert dialog box may appear, asking whether you want to install each selected add-in.

5. **Click the OK button in each alert dialog box to install its add-in.**

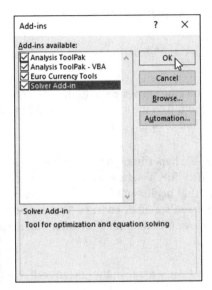

FIGURE 12-2:
Activate built-in add-ins in the Add-Ins dialog box.

Excel automatically places command buttons for the activated add-ins in either an Analysis group on the Ribbon's Data tab or in a Solutions group on the Formulas tab, depending on the type of add-in. For example, Excel places the command buttons for the Analysis ToolPak or Solver add-in in the Analysis group on the Data tab. For the Euro Currency Tools, Excel places its command buttons in the Solutions group on the Formulas tab.

TIP

If you end up never using a particular add-in you've loaded, you can unload it (and thereby free up some computer memory) by following the previously outlined procedure to open the Add-Ins dialog box and then clicking the name of the add-in to remove the check mark from its check box. Then click OK.

Adding Hyperlinks to a Worksheet

Hyperlinks automate Excel worksheets by making the opening of other Office documents and Excel workbooks and worksheets just a mouse click away. It doesn't matter whether these documents are located on your hard drive, a server on your LAN (Local Area Network), or web pages on the Internet or a company's intranet. You can also set up e-mail hyperlinks that automatically address messages to coworkers with whom you routinely correspond, and you can attach Excel workbooks or other types of Office files to these messages.

The hyperlinks that you add to your Excel worksheets can be of the following types:

>> Text entries in cells (known as hypertext, normally formatted as underlined blue text)

>> Imported graphics from files you've inserted into the worksheet (see Chapter 10)

>> Graphics you've created from the Shapes drop-down gallery or downloaded with the Icons command button on the Insert tab (see also Chapter 10) — in effect, turning the graphic images into buttons

When creating a text or graphic hyperlink, you can make a link to another Excel workbook or other type of Office file, a website address (using the URL address — you know, that monstrosity that begins with http://), a named location in the same workbook, or even a person's e-mail address. The named location can be a cell reference or named cell range (see Chapter 6 for details on naming cell ranges) in a particular worksheet.

To add the hyperlink to the text entry made in the current cell or a selected graphic object (see Chapter 10) in your worksheet, follow these steps:

1. **Click the Link button on the Insert tab of the Ribbon or press Alt+NI2I, or simply press Ctrl+K.**

   Excel opens the Insert Hyperlink dialog box (similar to the one shown in Figure 12-3) in which you indicate the file, the web address (URL), or the named location in the workbook.

2a. **To have the hyperlink open another document, a web page on a company's intranet, or a website on the Internet, click the Existing File or Web Page button if it isn't already selected and then enter the file's directory path or web page's URL in the Address text box.**

   If the document you want to link to is located on your hard drive or a hard drive that is mapped on your computer, click the Look In drop-down button, select the folder, and then select the file in the list box. If you've recently opened the document you want to link to, you can click the Recent Files button and then select it from the list box.

   If the document you want to link to is located on a website and you know its web address (the www.dummies.com-like thing), you can type it into the Address text box. If you recently browsed the web page you want to link to, you can click the Browsed Pages button and then select the address of the page from the list box.

2b. **To have the hyperlink move the cell pointer to another cell or cell range in the same workbook, click the Place in This Document button. Next, type the address of the cell or cell range in the Type the Cell Reference text box or select the desired sheet name or range name from the Or Select a Place in This Document list box.**

2c. **To open a new e-mail message addressed to a particular recipient, click the e-mail Address button and then enter the recipient's e-mail address in the e-mail Address text box.**

As soon as you begin typing the e-mail address in the e-mail Address text box, Excel inserts the text mailto: in front of whatever you've typed. (mailto: is the HTML tag that tells Excel to open your e-mail program when you click the hyperlink.)

If you want the hyperlink to add the subject of the e-mail message when it opens a new message in your e-mail program, enter this text in the Subject text box.

If the recipient's address is displayed in the Recently Used e-mail Addresses list box, you can enter it into the e-mail Address text box simply by clicking the address.

3. **(Optional) To change the hyperlink text that appears in the cell of the worksheet (underlined and in blue) or add text if the cell is blank, type the desired label in the Text to Display text box.**

4. **(Optional) To add a ScreenTip to the hyperlink that appears when you position the mouse pointer over the hyperlink, click the ScreenTip button, type the text that you want to appear next to the mouse pointer in the ScreenTip box, and then click OK.**

5. **Click OK to close the Insert Hyperlink dialog box.**

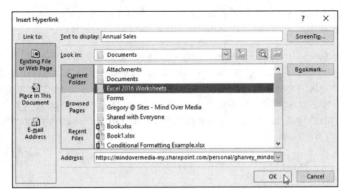

FIGURE 12-3:
Linking a downloaded icon to a web page in the Insert Hyperlink dialog box.

After you create a hyperlink in a worksheet, you can follow it to whatever destination you associated with the hyperlink. To follow a hyperlink, position the mouse pointer over the underlined blue text (if you assigned the hyperlink to text in a cell) or the graphic image (if you assigned the hyperlink to a graphic inserted in the worksheet). When the pointer changes to a hand with the index finger pointing upward, click the hypertext or graphic image, and Excel makes the jump to the designated external document, web page, cell within the workbook, or e-mail message.

TIP

The drop-down menu on the Links command button on the Insert tab (Alt+NI2) keeps a list of recently opened worksheets stored in the cloud on your OneDrive or SharePoint website. You can quickly create a hyperlink to one of these recently opened online items by first selecting the cell with the text entry or the graphic object to which it's to be linked and then simply clicking the Link drop-down button followed by the name of the worksheet on this list.

REMEMBER

After you follow a hypertext link to its destination, the color of its text changes from the traditional blue to a dark shade of purple (without affecting its underlining). This color change indicates that the hyperlink has been used. (Note, however, that graphic hyperlinks do not show any change in color after you follow them.) Additionally, Excel restores this underlined text to its original (unfollowed) blue color the next time that you open the workbook file.

WARNING

If you need to edit a hyperlink attached to a worksheet cell or graphic object, you must be careful that, when getting Excel into Edit mode so that you can change the text, you don't inadvertently follow the link. When dealing with hypertext in a cell or assigned to a graphic object, you're best off right-clicking the cell or image and then clicking the appropriate editing command (Edit Hyperlink or Remove Hyperlink) on its shortcut menu.

Automating Commands with Macros

Macros automate Excel worksheets by enabling you to record complex command sequences. By using macros that perform routine tasks, you not only speed up the procedure considerably (because Excel can play back your keystrokes and mouse actions much faster than you can perform them manually), but you are also assured that each step in the task is carried out the same way every time you perform the task.

REMEMBER

The Excel macro recorder records all the commands and keystrokes that you make in a language called Visual Basic for Applications (VBA), which is a special version of the BASIC programming language developed and refined by the good folks at Microsoft for use with all their Office application programs. You can then later learn how to use Excel's Visual Basic Editor to display and make changes to the macro's VBA code.

Recording new macros

Excel 2019 enables you to add an optional Developer tab to the Ribbon that contains its own Record Macro command button (among other command buttons that are very useful when doing more advanced work with macros). To add the Developer tab to the Excel 2019 Ribbon, follow these two steps:

1. **Click File ⇨ Options or press Alt+FT to open the Excel Options dialog box.**

2. **Click Customize Ribbon, then select the Developer check box under Main Tabs in the Customize the Ribbon list box on the right side of the dialog box, and then click OK.**

Even if you don't add the Developer tab to the Ribbon, the Excel 2019 Status bar contains a Record Macro (to the immediate right of the Ready status indicator), and the View tab of the Ribbon contains a Macros command button with a drop-down menu containing a Record Macro option.

When you turn on the macro recorder in the Record Macro dialog box — opened by clicking the Record Macro button on the Status bar (automatically added once you record your first macro), the Record Macro option on the Macros button's drop-down menu (Alt+WMR), or even the Record Macro button on the Developer tab (Alt+LR) — the macro recorder records all your actions in the active worksheet or chart sheet when you make them.

REMEMBER

The macro recorder doesn't record the keystrokes or mouse actions that you take to accomplish an action — only the VBA code required to perform the action itself. This means that mistakes that you make while taking an action that you rectify won't be recorded as part of the macro; for example, if you make a typing error and then edit it while the macro recorder is on, only the corrected entry shows up in the macro without the original mistakes and steps taken to remedy them.

The macros that you create with the macro recorder can be stored as part of the current workbook, in a new workbook, or in a special, globally available Personal Macro Workbook named PERSONAL.XLSB that's stored in a folder called XLSTART on your hard drive. When you record a macro as part of your Personal Macro Workbook, you can run that macro from any workbook that you have open. (This is because the PERSONAL.XLSB workbook is secretly opened whenever you launch

Excel, and although it remains hidden, its macros are always available.) When you record macros as part of the current workbook or a new workbook, you can run those macros only when the workbook in which they were recorded is open in Excel.

When you create a macro with the macro recorder, you decide not only the workbook in which to store the macro but also what name and shortcut keystrokes to assign to the macro that you are creating. When assigning a name for your macro, use the same guidelines that you use when you assign a standard range name to a cell range in your worksheet. When assigning a shortcut keystroke to run the macro, you can assign

» The Ctrl key plus a letter from A to Z, as in Ctrl+Q

» Ctrl+Shift and a letter from A to Z, as in Ctrl+Shift+Q

You can't, however, assign the Ctrl key plus a punctuation or number key (such as Ctrl+1 or Ctrl+/) to your macro.

To see how easy it is to create a macro with the macro recorder, follow these steps for creating a macro that enters the company name in 12-point, bold type and centers the company name across rows A through E with the Merge and Center feature:

1. **Open the Excel workbook that contains the worksheet data or chart you want your macro to work with.**

    If you're building a macro that adds new data to a worksheet (as in this example), open a worksheet with plenty of blank cells in which to add the data. If you're building a macro that needs to be in a particular cell when its steps are played back, put the cell pointer in that cell.

2. **Click Record Macro button on the Status bar or Alt+WMR or Alt+LR if you have added the Developer tab to the Ribbon.**

    The Record Macro dialog box opens, similar to the one shown in Figure 12-4, where you enter the macro name, define any keystroke shortcut, select the workbook in which to store the macro, and enter a description of the macro's function.

3. **Replace the Macro1 temporary macro name by entering your name for the macro in the Macro Name text box.**

    Remember that when naming a macro, you must not use spaces in the macro name and it must begin with a letter and not some number or punctuation symbol. For this example macro, you replace Macro1 in the Macro Name text box with the name Company_Name.

REMEMBER

Next, you can enter a letter between A and Z that acts like a shortcut key for running the macro when you press Ctrl followed by that letter key. Just remember that Excel has already assigned a number of Ctrl+letter keystroke shortcuts for doing common tasks, such as Ctrl+C for copying an item to the Clipboard and Ctrl+V for pasting an item from the Clipboard into the worksheet (see the Cheat Sheet online at www.dummies.com/cheatsheet/excel2019 for a complete list). If you assign the same keystrokes to the macro you're building, your macro's shortcut keys override and, therefore, disable Excel's ready-made shortcut keystrokes.

4. **(Optional) Click the Shortcut key text box and then enter the letter of the alphabet that you want to assign to the macro.**

For this example macro, press Shift+C to assign Ctrl+Shift+C as the shortcut keystroke (so as not to disable the ready-made Ctrl+C shortcut).

Next, you need to decide where to save the new macro that you're building. Select Personal Macro Workbook on the Store Macro In drop-down list box to be able to run the macro anytime you like. Select This Workbook (the default) when you need to run the macro only when the current workbook is open. Select New Workbook if you want to open a new workbook in which to record and save the new macro.

5. **Click the Personal Macro Workbook, New Workbook, or This Workbook option on the Store Macro In drop-down list to indicate where to store the new macro.**

For this example macro, select the Personal Macro Workbook so that you can use it to enter the company name in any Excel workbook that you create or edit.

TIP

Next, you should document the purpose and function of your macro in the Description list box. Although this step is purely optional, it is a good idea to get in the habit of recording this information every time you build a new macro so that you and your coworkers can always know what to expect from the macro when it's run.

6. **(Optional) Click the Description list box and then insert a brief description of the macro's purpose in front of the information indicating the date and who recorded the macro.**

Now you're ready to close the Record Macro dialog box and start recording your macro.

7. **Click OK to close the Record Macro dialog box.**

The Record Macro dialog box closes, the square Stop Recording button appears on the Status bar, and the Record Macro option becomes Stop Recording on the Macros button's drop-down menu and in the Code group on the Developer tab.

On the Macros button's drop-down menu on the Ribbon's View tab and Code group on the Developer tab, you find a Use Relative References option. You click this drop-down menu item or command button when you want the macro recorder to record the macro relative to the position of the current cell. For this example macro, which enters the company name and formats it in the worksheet, you definitely need to click the Use Relative References button before you start recording commands. Otherwise, you can use the macro only to enter the company name starting in cell A1 of a worksheet.

8. **(Optional) Click the Use Relative References option on the Macros button's drop-down menu on the View tab or click the Use Relative References button on the Developer tab if you want to be able to play back the macro anywhere in the worksheet.**

9. **Select the cells, enter the data, and choose the Excel commands required to perform the tasks that you want recorded just as you normally would in creating or editing the current worksheet, using the keyboard, the mouse, or a combination of the two.**

For the example macro, type the company name and click the Enter button on the Formula bar to complete the entry in the current cell. Next, click the Bold button and then click 12 on the Font Size drop-down list in the Font group on the Home tab. Finally, drag through cells A1:E1 to select this range and then click the Merge and Center command button, again on the Home tab.

After you finish taking all the actions in Excel that you want recorded, you're ready to shut off the macro recorder.

10. **Click the Stop Recording button on the Status bar or select Stop Recording option on the View or Developer tab on the Ribbon.**

The square Stop Recording button on the Status bar turns into a Record Macro button (with an icon showing a tiny worksheet with a circle in the left corner). This lets you know that the macro recorder is now turned off and no further actions will be recorded.

FIGURE 12-4:
Defining the new macro to record in the Record Macro dialog box.

TIP

After you finish recording your first macro in Excel 2019, the Record Macro button continues to appear on the Status bar whenever you use the program. This means that you can click or tap this button to open the Record Macro dialog box whenever you need to create new macros rather than having to select the Record Macro option on the View or Developer tab of the Ribbon, as described in the previous steps.

Running macros

After you record a macro, you can run it by clicking the View Macros option on the Macros button's drop-down menu on the View tab, the Macros button on the Developer tab of the Ribbon, or by pressing Alt+F8 to open the Macro dialog box (see Figure 12-5). As this figure shows, Excel lists the names of all the macros in the current workbook and in your Personal Macro Workbook (provided you've created one) in the Macro Name list box. Simply click the name of the macro that you want to run and then click the Run button or press Enter to play back all its commands.

FIGURE 12-5:
Select a macro to play back in the Macro dialog box.

TIP

If you assigned a shortcut keystroke to the macro, you don't have to bother opening the Macro dialog box to run the macro: Simply press Ctrl plus the letter key or Ctrl+Shift plus the letter key that you assigned and Excel immediately plays back all the commands that you recorded.

WARNING

The reason that macros you record in the Personal Macro Workbook are always available in any Excel workbook is because the PERSONAL.XLSB workbook is also open — you just don't know it because Excel hides this workbook immediately after opening it each time you launch the program. As a result, if you try to edit or delete a macro in the Macro dialog box saved in the Personal Macro Workbook, Excel displays an alert dialog box telling you that you can't edit a hidden workbook.

To unhide the Personal Macro Workbook, first clear the alert dialog box and close the Macro dialog box; then click the Unhide button on the View tab (Alt+WU) and click the OK button in the Unhide dialog box while PERSONAL.XLSB is selected. Excel then makes the Personal Macro Workbook active, and you can open the Macro dialog box and edit or delete any macros you've saved in it. After you finish, close the Macro dialog box and then click the Hide button on the View tab (or press Alt+WH) to hide the Personal Macro Workbook once more.

Assigning macros to the Ribbon and the Quick Access toolbar

If you prefer, instead of running a macro by selecting it in the Macro dialog box or by pressing shortcut keys you assign to it, you can assign it to a custom tab on the Ribbon or a custom button on the Quick Access toolbar and then run it by clicking that custom button.

To assign a macro to a custom group on a custom Ribbon tab, you follow these steps:

1. **Click File ⇨ Options and then click the Customize Ribbon tab in the Excel Options dialog box (or press Alt+FTC).**

   Excel displays the Customize Ribbon pane in the Excel Options dialog box.

2. **Click Macros in the Choose Commands From drop-down list box on the left.**

   Excel lists the names of all the macros created, both those in the current workbook and those that are saved in the PERSONAL.XLSB workbook, in the Choose Commands From list box.

3. **Click the name of the custom group on the custom tab to which you want to add the macro in the Main Tabs list box on the right.**

   If you haven't already created a custom tab and group for the macro or need to create a new one, follow these steps:

a. Click the New Tab button at the bottom of the Main Tabs list.

Excel adds both a New Tab (Custom) and New Group (Custom) item to the Main Tabs list while at the same time selecting the New Group (Custom) item.

b. Click the New Tab (Custom) item you just added to the Main Tabs.

c. Click the Rename button at the bottom of the Main Tabs list box and then type a display name for the new custom tab before you click OK.

d. Click the New Group (Custom) item right below the custom tab you just renamed.

e. Click the Rename button and then type a display name for the new custom group before you click OK.

4. **In the Choose Commands From list box on the left, click the name of the macro you want to add to the custom group now selected in the Main Tabs list box on the right.**

5. **Click the Add button to add the selected macro to the selected custom group on your custom tab. If you want to rename the macro and/or assign it a new icon, click the Rename button and make these changes in the Rename dialog box before you click the OK button to close the Excel Options dialog box.**

After you add a macro to the custom group of a custom tab, the name of the macro appears on a button on the custom tab of the Ribbon. Then, all you have to do to run the macro is click this command button.

To assign a macro to a custom button on the Quick Access toolbar, follow these steps:

1. **Click the Customize Quick Access Toolbar button at the end of the Quick Access toolbar and then click More Commands on its drop-down menu.**

Excel opens the Excel Options dialog box with the Quick Access Toolbar tab selected.

2. **Click Macros in the Choose Commands From drop-down list box.**

Excel lists the names of all the macros you created, both those in the current workbook and those that are saved in the PERSONAL.XLSB workbook, in the Choose Commands From list box.

3. **Click the name of the macro to add to a custom button on the Quick Access toolbar in the Choose Commands From list box and then click the Add button.**

4. **Click the Modify button to open the Modify Button dialog box if you want to change the display name and assign a different icon to the macro button.**

5. **Click OK to close the Excel Options dialog box.**

After you close the Excel Options dialog box, a custom button sporting its associated macro icon (the default with a standard command flowchart unless you changed it) appears on the Quick Access toolbar. To see the name of the macro assigned to this custom macro button as a ScreenTip, position the mouse pointer over the button. To run the macro, click the button.

Sharing Your Worksheets

Excel 2019 makes it easy to share your spreadsheets with trusted clients and coworkers. You can use the Share button to the right of the Ribbon tabs or the Share screen in the Backstage view to save your workbook files in the cloud on your Windows OneDrive or a SharePoint site and then easily share their worksheets by inviting coworkers and clients to open them in Excel on their own devices or, if they don't have access to Excel 2019, in their web browser using the Microsoft Excel Online web app.

You can also use the options on the Share screen in Backstage view (File ⇨ Share) to e-mail workbooks or to first convert them into Adobe PDF (Portable Document Format) files and then send them out as e-mail attachments, which can then be reviewed and commented on the Adobe Acrobat software on the recipient's device.

Additionally, you can review or edit the workbooks you save on your OneDrive when you're away from your office and the computer to which you have access doesn't have a compatible version of Excel installed on it. You simply use that computer's Internet access to log on to the My Documents folder of your OneDrive containing uploaded copies of your spreadsheets, and then use Excel Online (that runs on most modern web browsers) to open and then review and edit them.

Sharing workbooks saved on OneDrive

Before you can share your Excel workbook, you must save a copy of it in the cloud in a folder on your OneDrive or SharePoint site. The easiest way to do this is to first open the workbook to share in Excel and click the Share button that appears on the right side of the Ribbon tabs. Excel then opens a Share dialog box containing links to OneDrive and SharePoint sites to which you have access. After you click the online drive to which to save a copy of the workbook in the cloud, the

Send Link dialog box then opens where you can enter a name of a coworker or client from your contacts list or their e-mail address to send them a link to workbook (or you can use the Send a Copy drop-down list at the bottom to send them a copy of the original workbook file or a PDF attached to a new e-mail message).

You can also save your workbook to a OneDrive location by clicking File ⇨ Share and then clicking the Save to Cloud button on the Share screen in the Backstage (Alt+FZ). When you click the Save to Cloud button, Excel opens the Save As screen in the Backstage view where you can save the workbook in a folder on your OneDrive (see Chapter 2 for details). Once you've saved the workbook on your OneDrive in the Backstage, the Share screen displaying the name and location of the workbook file saved in the cloud appears. On the Share screen, click the Share with People button to open the Send Link dialog box shown in Figure 12-6. (If you used the Share button in the worksheet to save the workbook on OneDrive, this Send Link dialog box automatically opens as soon as the file is finished saving.)

With the Send Link dialog box open, you can set the options for sharing the workbook by following these steps:

1. **Begin typing the e-mail address of the first person with whom you want to share the workbook.**

    As you type, Excel matches the letters with the names and e-mail addresses entered in your Address Book. When it finds possible matches, they are displayed in a drop-down menu, and you can select the person with whom you want to share the workbook file by clicking his or her name to add to the list of recipients. To add additional people with whom the file is to be shared, click the Add Another text box and then type their e-mail address and click their name.

2. **(Optional) Click the Anyone with the Link Can Edit button to open the Link Settings dialog box and modify the people for whom the link works, deny editing privileges to those with whom you share the file, and/or set an expiration date after which the link is no longer operational and then click the Apply button.**

    By default, Excel 2019 creates a sharing link that enables anyone who can access the workbook file online access to the file even when they are not logged into Office 365 or OneDrive. However, you can make modifications:

    - *To restrict access to only coworkers in your company who are logged into Office 365,* click the People in <*organization*> option (where *organization* is the name of your company as in People in Mind Over Media, the name of my company).

    - *To restrict the file sharing to only those to whom you've given prior access to the workbook file or its folder on your SharePoint site,* click the People with Existing Access option.

- *To create a sharing link that only particular people can use,* click the Specific People option before you click the Apply button, Then, in the Send Link dialog box, click the ellipses (. . .) to the right of the Send Link title and click Manage Access on the drop-menu to open the Permissions dialog box where you select the names of the people with whom to share the workbook file before you click the back arrow button (←) to return to the Send Link dialog box.

TIP

By default, Excel allows the people with whom you share your workbooks to make editing changes to the workbook that are automatically saved on your OneDrive. You can also modify these editing privileges:

- *To restrict your recipients to reviewing the data without being able to make changes,* click the Allow Editing check box to remove its check mark before you click Apply.

  To set an expiration date after which the sharing link is no longer operational, click the Set Expiration Date button to open the pop-up calendar where you select an expiration date by clicking it in the calendar. After selecting the expiration date, click somewhere in the dialog box to close the pop-up calendar and enter the date in the Link Settings dialog box.

3. **(Optional) Click the Add a Message (Optional) text box and type any personal message that you want to incorporate as part of the e-mail with the generic invitation to share the file.**

   By default, Excel creates a generic invitation.

4. **Click the Send button.**

   As soon as you click the Send button, Excel displays a Sending Mail message. Once the e-mail(s) with the invitation to share the workbook to each of the recipients entered in the Send Link dialog box has been sent, Excel display a confirmation dialog box that you can close by clicking its Close (with an X) button.

All the people with whom you share a workbook receive an e-mail message containing a link to the workbook attached to an Open button. When they click the Open button to follow the link, a copy of the workbook opens on a new page in their default web browser using the Excel Online app (if the web app is not compatible with the type of browser in use on their device, the browser opens it with the web viewer). If you've given the user permission to edit the file, the web app contains an Edit Workbook button.

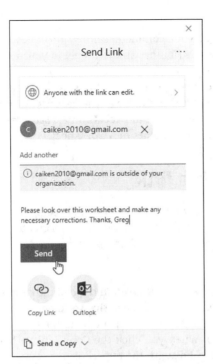

FIGURE 12-6:
Inviting coworkers or clients to share an Excel workbook saved on your OneDrive in the Send Link dialog box.

When users open the workbook file in Excel Online, if they've been granted editing privileges with the default Anyone with Link Can Edit setting for sharing files, they can go ahead and make simple editing changes to the workbook in Excel Online, using the command buttons on the Home, Insert, Data, Review, and View tabs of the Excel Online Ribbon. All changes they make to the workbook are automatically saved in the file on OneDrive.

If you have the shared workbook open in Excel 2019 at the same time the users with whom you're sharing the file are making their editing changes in Excel Online, the Share button in Excel changes into a Guest Contributor button (marked GC). When you click this GC button, a drop-down list with the names of all the contributors making editing changes are displayed. All the editing changes made to the sheets of the shared workbook in Excel Online are automatically updated in workbook in Excel 2019 (in as close to real time as the speed of your device's Internet access provides). Likewise, all the editing changes that you make to the workbook in Excel 2019 are automatically updated in their workbooks in Excel Online.

TIP

If a questionable editing change made by a guest contributor working on the same file in Excel Online appears in your worksheet, add a comment to the cell containing the edit-in-question (Review ⇨ New Comment) that communicates your reservations about the change they made and then click the Post button. A small balloon then appears above the cell where you made the comment in the contributor's worksheet in Excel Online. When the contributor clicks this balloon, Excel

Online displays the text of your comment calling into question their edit in a Comments task pane. The contributor can then reply to your reservations by typing their explanation for the change in the same Reply text box under the comment in this task pane and then updating it in your workbook by clicking the Post button, or they can just go ahead and make any necessary updates reflecting your reservations directly in the worksheet in Excel Online. (See Chapter 6 for more on adding and viewing threaded comments in a worksheet.)

Getting a sharing link

Instead of sending e-mail invitations to individual recipients with links to the workbooks you want to share on your OneDrive, you can create hyperlinks to them that you can then make available to all the people who need online editing or review access.

To create a link to an Excel workbook saved in the cloud that enables anyone you share it with to edit the file, you need to open the workbook in Excel 2019 and then click the Copy Link option at the bottom of the Send Link dialog box (opened by clicking the Share button). When you click the Copy Link, a Link To dialog box then opens containing a text box with the hyperlink.

REMEMBER

After creating the edit link for your workbook in the Send Link dialog box, you can select the entire hyperlink by simply clicking the Copy button that appears to the immediate right of its text box. When you do this, Excel copies the long and complex hyperlink to the Office Clipboard. After copying it to the Clipboard, you can insert it into a new e-mail message (Ctrl+V) that you send to all the people with whom you want to share the Excel workbook to which it refers.

E-mailing workbooks

To e-mail a copy of a workbook you have open in Excel to a client or coworker, select File⇨Share⇨e-mail (Alt+FZE). When you do this, a Send Using e-mail panel appears with the following five options:

» **Send as Attachment** to create a new e-mail message using your default e-mail program with a copy of the workbook file as its attachment file.

» **Send a Link** to create a new e-mail message using your default e-mail program that contains a hyperlink to the workbook file.

>> **Send as Adobe PDF** or **Send as PDF** to convert the Excel workbook to the Adobe PDF (Portable Document File) format and make this new PDF the attachment file in a new e-mail message. (Your e-mail recipient must have a copy of the Adobe Reader installed on his or her computer in order to open the attachment.)

>> **Send as XPS** to convert the Excel workbook to a Microsoft XPS (XML Paper Specification) file and make this new XPS file the attachment in a new e-mail message. (Your e-mail recipient must have an XPS Reader installed on his or her computer in order to open the attachment; this reader is installed automatically on computers running Windows 10.)

>> **Send as Internet Fax** to send the workbook as a fax through an online fax service provider. You will need an account with a service provider as well as the Windows Fax and Scan Windows feature installed.

After selecting the e-mail option you want to use, Windows opens a new e-mail message in your e-mail program with a link to the workbook file or the file attached to it. To send the link or file, fill in the recipient's e-mail address in the To text box and any comments you want to make about the spreadsheet in the body of the message before you click the Send button.

Editing Worksheets in Excel Online

Microsoft offers several Office Online Web apps for Word, Excel, PowerPoint, and OneNote as part of your Windows account and OneDrive storage in the cloud. You can use Excel Online to edit worksheets saved on your OneDrive online right within your web browser.

This comes in real handy for those occasions when you need to make last-minute edits to an Excel worksheet but don't have access to a device on which Excel 2019 is installed. As long as the device has an Internet connection and runs a web browser that supports Excel Online (such as Internet Explorer on a Surface Pro tablet or even Safari on a MacBook Pro), you can make eleventh-hour edits to the data, formulas, and even charts that are automatically saved in the workbook file on your OneDrive.

REMEMBER

The great part about using Excel Online to edit a copy of your online workbook is that it runs successfully under the latest versions of Microsoft's Edge Explorer as well as under the latest versions of many other popular web browsers, including Mozilla Firefox for Windows, Mac, and Linux as well as Macintosh's Safari web browser on the iMac and iPad.

To edit a workbook saved on your OneDrive with the Excel Online, you follow these simple steps:

1. Launch the web browser on your device that supports the Excel web app and then go to www.office.live.com and sign in to your Windows account.

The Microsoft Office Home web page welcomes you to your Office 365 account. Under Apps on this page, you see a bunch of buttons for each of the online apps.

2. Click the Excel button under Apps.

Excel Online display a Welcome to Excel screen in your web browser. This screen is somewhat similar to the Open screen in Excel 2019 (see Figure 12-7). Across the top of this screen, beneath the label New, a bunch of template thumbnails appear in a single row, starting with New Blank Workbook. Below the row of Excel templates, you see the following options for selecting the file you want to edit:

- *Recent* (the default) to list all the workbooks that have recently been uploaded to your OneDrive.

- *Pinned* to list just the workbook files that you've pinned (to pin a file, mouse over the name of the file in the Recent list and then click the push pin icon that appears after its filename).

- *Shared with Me* to list only those workbook files that have been shared with you.

- *Discover* to list shared workbooks that others are currently working on.

- *Upload and Open* to display a dialog box where you can select a local workbook file to upload and save on OneDrive for editing with Excel Online. Note that if the device on which you're using Excel Online has Excel installed on it, the Excel Open dialog box will appear. Otherwise, the file management dialog box for the device's operating system will appear (as in, File Explorer on a Windows machine and Finder on a Mac).

If you can't locate the workbook file you want to edit using these options, click the Search Apps, Documents, People, and Sites text box at the top of the Welcome to Excel screen and start typing its filename here. As you type, Excel Online will display a list of results matching the characters that you've entered.

3. Locate the Excel workbook file you want to edit and then click its filename.

As soon as you select the name of the workbook file to edit, Excel Online opens the workbook in a new tab in your web browser, in the Editing view complete with a File button and the Home, Insert, Data, Review, and View Ribbon tabs (see Figure 12-8).

You can then use the option buttons on the Home and Insert tabs (most of which are identical to those found on the Home and Insert tabs on the Excel 2019 Ribbon) to modify the layout or formatting of the data and charts on any of its sheets. You can use the options on the Data tab to recalculate your workbook and sort data in ascending or descending order on its worksheets. You can also use the options on the Review add and display comments in the cells of the worksheets as well as options on the View tab to turn off Headings and Gridlines and switch back to Reading view. You can also add new data to the worksheets as well as edit existing data just as you do in Excel 2019.

WARNING

Note that if you open a workbook file in Excel Online that contains features that can't be displayed in your browser, the file will open in a new tab without the Ribbon and a "There are some features in your workbook that we can't show in the browser" alert will appear above the Worksheet area. To continue and edit a copy of the workbook file with Excel Online without the features that can't be displayed, click the Edit Workbook drop-down button and then click the Edit in Browser option on the drop-down menu (if Excel is installed on your device and you want access to all the workbook's features, click the Edit in Excel option instead). When you select the Edit in Browser option, an Edit a Copy dialog box appears. When you click the Edit a Copy button, a Save As dialog box appears and shows Editable appended to the original filename. After you click Save in this dialog box, the copy of the original workbook file opens in Excel Online in Editing view.

4. **When you're finished editing the workbook, click the Close button on your web browser's tab to save your changes. If you want to save a copy under a new filename in the same folder on the OneDrive, click File ⇨ Save As and then click the Save As option to open a Save As dialog box where you can edit the filename that appears in the text box before you click its Save button. (Or select the Overwrite Existing Files check box if you want to save the changes under the same filename.)**

The Excel Online app is a whiz at making simple editing, formatting, and layout changes to your spreadsheet data and charts using common commands on its Home, Insert, and even Chart Tools tab (when a chart is selected). However, Excel Online has no support for graphic objects other than shapes and pictures saved to disk that you can insert with very limited formatting and editing options.

For those times when you need more editing choices, you can open the workbook in a local copy of Excel (assuming that the device you're using has some compatible version of Excel installed on it) by clicking the Edit in Excel command button on the Ribbon. Or, you can download a copy of the workbook to your local office computer (where you do have Excel 2019 installed) by selecting File ⇨ Save As ⇨ Download a Copy and make the more advanced edits to this downloaded copy of the file after you get back to the office.

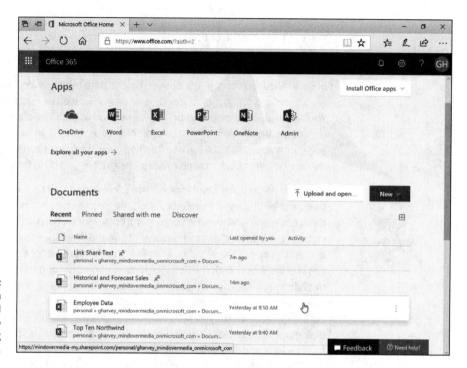

FIGURE 12-7:
Selecting a workbook saved on OneDrive to open for editing in Excel Online.

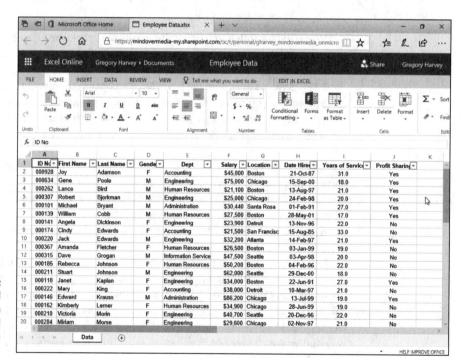

FIGURE 12-8:
Using Excel Online to edit a workbook saved on OneDrive in my web browser.

6

The Part of Tens

Discover the top ten fundamental skills required to use Excel 2019 successfully.

Explore the do's and don'ts that can make any Excel 2019 experience heavenly.

Survey the top ten features for managing and maintaining loads of data in Excel 2019.

Examine the top ten features for identifying trends and vital indicators in your Excel data.

Enjoy an additional Excel 2019 Part of Tens chapter online at www.dummies.com.

Chapter **13**

Top Ten Beginner Basics

f these ten items are all you master in Excel 2019, you'll still be way ahead of the competition. When all is said and done, this top ten list lays out all the fundamental skills required to use Excel 2019 successfully.

10. **To start Excel 2019 from the Windows Start screen,** simply click the Start menu and then click Excel 2019 under the Most Used section of the Windows menu or click its tile if you pinned Excel 2019 to the Start menu. If Excel 2019 isn't yet one of your Most Used apps and isn't pinned to the Start menu, type **exc** in the Search the Web and Windows text box to the immediate right of the Start button and then click Excel 2019 on its pop-up menu.

9. **To launch Excel 2019 automatically when you open an Excel workbook that needs editing,** simply locate the folder containing the Excel workbook you want to edit in Windows Explorer and double-click its file icon.

8. **To locate a part of the worksheet that is not currently displayed in the Excel Worksheet area,** click the scroll bars at the right and bottom of the Workbook window to bring new parts of the worksheet into view.

7. **To start a new workbook containing a blank worksheet using the Excel default template,** simply press Ctrl+N. To open a new workbook based on another template, select File ⇨ New or press Alt+FN and then select the template to use on the New screen in the Backstage view, where you can select a template or download one from Office.com. To add a new worksheet to a workbook (should you need more than one), click the New Sheet button (with a plus sign in a circle) to the immediate right of the last tab at the bottom of the Worksheet area.

6. **To activate an open workbook and display it onscreen** (in front of any others you have open), click the Ribbon's View tab and then click the window to activate the Switch Windows button's drop-down menu (or press Alt+WW followed by the window's number). To locate a particular worksheet in the active workbook, click that worksheet's sheet tab at the bottom of the workbook document window. To display more sheet tabs, click the Sheet Tab scroll buttons on the left side of the bottom of the Workbook window.

5. **To enter stuff in a worksheet,** select the cell where the information should appear; then begin typing. When you finish, click the Enter button on the Formula bar (the one with the check mark) or press Tab, Enter, or one of the arrow keys.

4. **To edit the stuff you entered into a cell already,** double-click the cell or position the cell pointer in the cell and press F2. Excel then positions the insertion point at the end of the cell entry and goes into Edit mode (see Chapter 2 for details). When you finish correcting the entry, click the Enter button on the Formula bar or press the Tab or Enter key.

3. **To choose one of the many Excel commands on the Ribbon,** click the Ribbon tab, locate the group containing the command button, and then click the button. (Or press the Alt key to display the hot keys on the Ribbon and then type the letter of the tab you want to select followed by the letter[s] of the command button to use.) To choose a command in the Backstage view, select File and then click its menu option or press Alt+F followed by the option's hot key letter. To choose a command on the Quick Access toolbar, click its command button.

2. **To save a copy of your workbook on disk the first time around,** click the Save button on the Quick Access toolbar or press Ctrl+S. Next, designate the place to save the new workbook file on the Save As screen of the Backstage view. If the drive and folder in which you want to save the file is not displayed on this screen, click the Browse button to open the Save As dialog box and select the drive and folder there. After designating the place where the file is to be saved, replace the temporary Book1.xlsx filename in the File Name text box with your own filename (up to 255 characters long, including spaces) and then click the Save button. To save a workbook so that older versions of Excel can open it, click the Excel 97-2003 Workbook option in the Save as Type drop-down menu before you click the Save button.

1. **To exit Excel when you're done working with the program,** right-click the Excel icon on the Windows taskbar and then click Close Window or Close All Window on the pop-up menu. If you have only one workbook file open in Excel, you can also click the Excel window's Close button (the one with the *x* in the upper-right corner of the Excel program window) to close both the file and Excel (or press Alt+F4 or Alt+FX). If the open workbook contains unsaved changes, Excel 2019 asks whether you want to save the workbook before closing Excel and returning to Windows.

Chapter **14**

The Ten Commandments of Excel 2019

When working with Excel 2019, you discover certain do's and don'ts that, if followed religiously, can make using this program just heavenly. Lo and behold, the following Excel Ten Commandments contain just such precepts for eternal Excel bliss.

10. **Whensoever the AutoSave feature functioneth not thou shalt commit thy work to disk** by saving thy changes often (clicketh or tappeth the Save button on the Quick Access toolbar or presseth Ctrl+S). To saveth thy file in the almighty cloud so that thou may easily access thy workbook from any of thy computing devices, selecteth a folder on thy OneDrive.

9. **Thou shalt nameth thy workbooks** when saving them the first time with filenames of no more than 12 score and 15 characters (255), including spaces and all manner of weird signs and symbols. So, too, thou shalt mark well into which folder thou savest thy file lest thou thinkest in error that thy workbook be lost when next thou hast need of it.

8. **Thou shalt not spread wide the data in thy worksheet,** but rather thou shalt gather together thy tables and avoideth skipping columns and rows unless this is necessary to make thy data intelligible. All this thou shalt do in order that thou may conserve the memory of thy computer.

7. **Thou shalt begin all thy Excel 2019 formulas with = (equal)** as the sign of computation. If, however, ye be formerly of the Lotus 1-2-3 tribe, thou shalt haveth special dispensation and can commence thy formulas with the + sign and thy functions with the @ sign.

6. **Thou shalt select thy cells before thou bringeth any Excel command to bear upon them,** just as surely as thou doth sow before thou reapeth.

5. **Thou shalt useth the Undo feature (clicketh or tappeth the Undo button on the Quick Access toolbar or presseth Ctrl+Z)** immediately upon committing any transgression in thy worksheet so that thou mayest clean up thy mess. Should thou forgeteth to useth thy Undo feature straightaway, thou must select the action that thou wouldst undo from the pop-up menu attached to the Undo command button on the Quick Access toolbar. Note well that any action that thou selectest from this drop-down list will undo not only that action, but also the actions that precedeth it on this menu.

4. **Thou shalt not delete, nor insert, columns and rows in a worksheet** lest thou hath first verified that no part yet undisplayed of thy worksheet will thereby be wiped out or otherwise displaced.

3. **Thou shalt not print thy spreadsheet report lest thou hath first previewed its pages by clicking the Page Layout View button** (the middle button of the three to the immediate left of the Zoom slider on the Status bar) and art satisfied that all thy pages are upright in the sight of the printer. If thou art still unsure of how thy pages break, clicketh the Page Break Preview button to its immediate right on the Status bar to seeth how Excel doth divide thy pages.

2. **Thou shalt changeth the manner of recalculation of thy workbooks from automatic to manual** (clicketh Formulas ⇨ Calculation Options ⇨ Manual or presseth Alt+MXM) when thy workbook groweth so great in size that Excel sloweth down to a camel crawl whenever thou doeth anything in any one of its worksheets. Woe to thee, should thou then ignoreth the Calculate message on the Status bar and not presseth the Calculate Now key (F9) or clicketh Formulas ⇨ Calculate Now before such time as thou mayest print any of thy workbook data.

1. **Thou shalt protecteth thy completed workbook and all its worksheets from corruption and iniquities** at the hands of others (clicketh Review ⇨ Protect Sheet or Protect Workbook). And if thou be brazen enough to addeth a password to thy workbook protection, beware lest thou forgeteth thy password in any part. For verily I say unto thee, on the day that thou knowest not thy password, that day shalt be the last upon which thou lookest upon thy workbook in any guise.

Chapter **15**

Top Ten Ways to Manage Your Data

For a great many business people, the Excel worksheet provides the ideal place for managing and manipulating the vast amount of data that your particular job entails. Unlike dedicated database management programs that require a whole lot of specialized knowledge in order to set up and maintain data tables, data management in Excel 2019 requires mastery of only a few special features, all of which function within the confines of the new familiar worksheet grid. Here's my list of the top ten features for helping you manage large amounts of data in Excel:

10. **Format as Table.** Don't forget about the power of formatting the data list you create in a worksheet as a table (Alt+HT). When you do this, Excel formats all the records in your data list according to the table style you select. It also identifies the cell range in the worksheet containing the entire data list as well as the headings in the first line of the list as field names. The program also automatically adds AutoFilter buttons to each field name.

Selecting the right type of banded table style can make the records in a data list easier to read just as the AutoFilter buttons make it easy to quickly sort and filter your data. On top of this, as you enter new records to a data list formatted as a table, Excel instantly applies the appropriate formatting to the new records as the program extends the cell range containing your entire data table.

See Chapter 3 for more on formatting your data list as a table.

9. **Data Form.** As old-fashioned as the Excel Data Form may seem to be, it still provides a really efficient means for not only entering new records into a data list you've created in a worksheet but also for quickly finding any records that need updating.

The only problem is that in order to use the Data Form in Excel 2019, you first have to add the Form command button from among the Commands Not in the Ribbon to either a custom Ribbon tab or to the Quick Access toolbar. Once added, you can use the commands in the Form dialog box to add new records, delete unneeded ones, as well as locate records in the data list that need checking and editing.

See "Adding records to data lists" in Chapter 11 for more on adding the Form button to the Quick Access toolbar and using its features to maintain your data list.

8. **Freeze Panes.** Most, if not all, of the data lists you create and maintain in an Excel worksheet will end up having more records than your computer monitor can possibly display all at one time. If you use the Freeze Panes feature to freeze the first row of the data list with the field names, these labels will always remain visible on the screen as you scroll through any part of the data list.

To freeze the row with the field names of a data list, simply position the cell cursor in any one of the data list's cells and then select View ⇨ Freeze Panes ⇨ Freeze Top Row (Alt+WFR). After that, you will always be able to see the field names to identify the columns of data as you scroll through the list as well as use their AutoFilter buttons to sort and/or select the data.

See Chapter 6 for more on Freeze Panes.

7. **Sort.** Being able to instantly arrange the records in a data list with the various Sort command options in Excel is a key component in maintaining a data list in an Excel worksheet. Sorting enables you to reorder the records of a data list in whatever way to you need to see them, whenever the need arises.

The easiest way to sort an entire data list in ascending order (A to Z alphabetical and lowest to highest numeric), according to the entries in a single field, is to position the cell cursor in one of the cells in that column of the data list and then select Home ⇨ Sort ⇨ Sort A to Z (Alt+HSS). To sort the list in descending order (Z to A alphabetical and highest to lowest numeric), you simply select Home ⇨ Sort ⇨ Sort Z to A (Alt+HSO) instead.

When you need to sort the records in the data list on more than one field to get the desired order, use the Sort A to Z or Sort Z to A option on each of the field's AutoFilter drop-down menus.

If you want to be able to display the records in your data list in the original order in which they were entered, you need to add a Records Number field as the first column of the data list before you do any sorting. Simply insert a new column at the beginning of the data list (Alt+HIC), label its first cell Record No. (or something like that), manually enter the first record number in the cell below, and then use AutoFill to extend the records numbers down the column to the last row of the list (remembering to hold the Ctrl key down as you drag the fill handle). Use the Convert to Range command on the Table's Design tab under Table Tools to temporarily convert your data list back into a regular cell range and then use the Format as Table command on the Home tab to format the data list, including the new Record No. field, as table. Once you do this, no matter how the records are sorted, you can always restore the data list to its original data entry order by sorting list on the Record No. in ascending order.

See Chapter 11 for more on using Excel's various sorting options.

6. **Flash Fill.** Some lists of data come to you as text entered in other programs, such as Microsoft Word 2019. When you copy these data into Excel, the text entries are copied into the rows of a single, very wide column of the worksheet. You then need to split the long text entries up into individual components, such as First Name, Middle Initial, and Last Name, so that you can then effectively sort and filter the data list using their separate columns.

TIP

The fastest way to split up text entries entered into a single worksheet column where the individual components are separated by a single space, such as First Name, Middle Initial, and Last Name, is with the Flash Fill feature. In a separate column to the immediate right of the one with the long text entry, type the first entry that should be extracted from the first long text entry (such as the first name). Then, in the cell in the row immediately below this, start entering the second entry that should be extracted from the second of the long text entries. Excel 2019 will then detect the pattern and extract the same components from all the subsequent long text entries and then into separate cells of the new column as soon as you press Enter.

See Chapter 2 for more examples on how to use Flash Fill to split up a list of full names into their individual components.

5. **Text to Columns.** Some lists of text data that copy into a worksheet in a single column are separated by other delimiting characters, such as commas, semicolons, or even full colons. When this is the case, you need to use the Text to Columns command on the Data tab rather than Flash Fill to split the entries up into individual columns.

To use this feature, select the range of cells with the long text entries and then select Data ⇨ Text to Columns (Alt+AE). Excel opens the Convert Text to Columns Wizard where you specify the type of character or characters that separate the components of the long entry. When you click the Finish button after specifying these character(s), Excel splits the long text entries up by entering their delimited components into as many columns of the worksheet as required.

4. **Web Query.** Rather than making you manually enter all the data you need to follow in your data list, Excel provides several ways to import the data from external sources. If the data you need to track in a worksheet data list is available online in a website, you may be able to import the data directly from a web page into your Excel worksheet using the From Web option on the Get External Data menu.

Before you can do such a Web Query, you need to know the URL address of the website that contains the data you want to import. The easiest way to do this is first use your computer's web browser to go the desired website. Then, copy the URL address from browser's address text box into the Office Clipboard (Ctrl+C). Next, switch back to Excel 2019 and select Data ⇨ Get Data ⇨ From Web (Alt+AFW). Click the Address text box and then paste the URL address into it (Ctrl+V) before you click the OK command button.

Excel then connects to the web page. Excel opens the Navigator with a list of the tables of data on that page that you can download. Click a table name to preview its data on the Table View tab of the Navigator. To select more than one table, click the Select Multiple Tables check box before clicking the check box in front of each table name to select them. Once you select the table or tables of data you want to import into the Excel worksheet, click the Load button in the Navigator to import the selected web data table(s) into an existing or new worksheet at the cell cursor. To import the table(s) into a new worksheet, select the Load To option on the Load button's drop-down menu. To further filter and refine the web data to be imported, click the Transform Data button to open the table(s) in the Power Query Editor (see Transform Data that follows).

See Chapter 11 for more on importing data from the web.

3. **Get Data.** Many businesses maintain their corporate data in tables created and managed by stand-alone database programs, such as Microsoft Access or Microsoft SQL Server. If you have access to these types of corporate databases, you can directly import data from their tables into your Excel worksheet using the appropriate option (From File, From Database, From Online Services, or From Other Services) on the Get Data command button's drop-down menu located on the Data tab of the Ribbon (Alt+APN).

If you're importing data from an Access database, select the From Database option followed by From Microsoft Access Database option. If you're importing data from an SQL Server or other data feed, such Windows Azure Marketplace, select the From Other Sources option followed by the particular type of database program or feed.

After selecting the source of the external data, you need to select the database file followed by the table or tables in that database file that contain the data you want to import into Excel in the Navigator dialog box that appears. Finally, click the Load button in the Navigator if you want to import the selected external data into the current worksheet starting at the cell cursor's position. To import the table(s) into a new worksheet, select the Load To option on the Load button's drop-down menu. To further filter and refine the web data to be imported, click the Transform Data button to open the table(s) in the Power Query Editor (see Transform Data that follows).

See Chapter 11 for more on importing external data into your worksheet.

2. **Transform Data.** Sometimes you don't need to import all the records stored in the tables of an external database or web page into the Excel worksheet. Before downloading the data, you can use the Power Query Editor to sort, filter, and otherwise refine the data records before loading them into your worksheet. To open the Power Query Editor, click the Transform Data button in the Navigator dialog box when setting the external data import. Excel then opens a new query in the Power Query Editor (whose interface greatly resembles that of Excel 2019). After editing the query in the Power Query Editor, you can save the query and download the remaining external data by selecting the Close & Load button to import the data into the current worksheet starting at the cell cursor's position. Select the Close & Load To option on the Close & Load button's drop-down menu to import the data to a new worksheet.

1. **Relationships.** When you import data maintained in database programs such as Microsoft Access, you can import more than one table into the different sheets of your workbook. Often these data tables are related to one another by the occurrence of a duplicate field known as the table's *key field*. When such relationships occur between imported tables in an Excel workbook, it is known as a *data model,* and Excel enables you to create pivot tables and pivot charts using fields from any of the related tables.

To see all the key fields in the imported data tables and how they're related to one another, select Data ➪ Relationships on the Ribbon (Alt+AA). Excel 2019 then displays a Manage Relationships dialog box that shows all the related data tables in the data model in the current workbook. This dialog box also displays the name of the key field in each of the related tables. If there are other relationships between fields of the imported data tables that you want Excel to recognize, you can select the Edit button and manually specify the key fields to be used.

See Chapter 9 for more on building pivot tables using fields from a data model.

Chapter **16**

Top Ten Ways to Analyze Your Data

When working with really large data lists in your Excel worksheets, it's all too easy to lose sight of the developing trends in that data indicating new business opportunities, let alone warning of possible dangers. Fortunately, Excel 2019 offers several easy-to-use features designed to help you summarize and visualize directions and movements inherent in the vast quantities of data you deal with.

Here are my top ten favorite features in Excel 2019 for evaluating the data and drawing out the prevailing trends and vital indicators:

10. **Pivot Tables.** The PivotTable feature offers one of the most efficient and flexible ways to summarize and analyze large amounts of data in the data lists you maintain or import into your Excel worksheets. Pivot tables are extremely easy to create as well as to modify.

Pivot tables provide you with an easy way to cross-tabulate your data using any of the most common statistical functions (Sum, Count, Average, Max, Min, and so forth). They also provide you with the means for adding "filtering" fields from the data list or model that enable you to instantly refine the summarized data.

See Chapter 9 for more on creating and using pivot tables to analyze large amounts of data.

9. **Pivot Charts.** As the visual companion to pivot tables, Excel's PivotChart feature allows you to graph the data summarized in your pivot tables using any of the types of charts supported by Excel 2019. As with pivot tables, pivot charts are highly flexible, enabling you to filter the graphed data on the fly and instantly see the effect in your pivot chart.

   See Chapter 9 for more on creating and using pivot charts to graphically highlight the data summarized by your pivot tables.

8. **Slicers.** Slicers provide a highly efficient way to refine the summarized data in your pivot tables using criteria from as many fields as needed. Moreover, as graphic objects, you can easily position slicers so that they're displayed just as you need them on the screen and quickly modify their criteria.

   See Chapter 9 for more on creating and using slicers to quickly refine the data displayed in your pivot tables using multiple criteria from several fields.

7. **Timelines.** Timelines are slicers specifically for the date fields used in your pivot tables. They enable you to filter the summarized table data using specific time-related criteria based on any of a number of time intervals (days, months, quarters, or years). Timelines make it possible to see the summaries of your pivot table data for any time period you care to track.

   See Chapter 9 for more on creating and using timelines to refine the data displayed in your pivot tables using time-sensitive criteria from date fields in your pivot tables.

6. **AutoFilters.** Excel offers a variety of AutoFilter controls that you can use to instantly refine the data you track in the data lists you maintain in your Excel worksheets. As soon as you format your data list as an Excel table (Alt+HT), Excel automatically adds AutoFilter buttons to the header row of the data list containing the list's field names.

   At the most basic level, you can filter the data list by setting the criteria to particular entries in certain fields of the data list. In addition, Excel offers a set of Text, Date, and Number Filters (depending upon the type of entries in a field) that make it easy to refine the list using a wide variety of field-type specific criteria. If none of these readymade filters will do, you can always use the Custom Filter option in order to set up a range for the criteria that can include multiple fields using And or Or conditions.

   See Chapter 11 for more on using the various AutoFilter controls to refine the data displayed in your Excel data list.

5. **Advanced Filter.** In addition to filtering the data list in place as do the AutoFilter options attached to the specific fields of an Excel data list, the Advanced Filter feature (available by selecting Data ⇨ Advanced on the Ribbon or pressing Alt+AQ) also enables you to copy the records from the data list that meet your criteria to a new location in the worksheet.

Before you use the Advanced Filter feature, you need to set up a Criteria Range somewhere on the worksheet outside (usually to the side) of the data list you're going to filter. This Criteria Range consists of a copy of the row of field names from the top row of the data list. Beneath the particular fields' names that are to be used in the filtering, you place the actual criteria. So, for example, if you wanted to work only with records where the zip code is 94102, you enter **94102** in the blank cell right below the field name Zip Code. So too, if you want to work with records where the zip code is 94102 or 94103, you enter **94103** in the blank cell below the one containing 94102. When filtering the data list on criteria in numeric fields, you can use number operators such as =, >, <, <>, and so forth. Just keep in mind that criteria under different fields in the same row of the criteria range create an And condition (as in City is Chicago and Order Total is >100.00) just as criteria in different rows of the criteria range create an Or condition (as in City is Chicago or New York) and that the Criteria Range needs to include the row with the copied data list field names as well as all the rows that contain criteria you want used in filtering the data list.

TIP

The Advanced Filter feature is great when you need to work with a subset of the data list that meets certain criteria (such as the records in an orders data list where the order total greater than or equal to $500.00) without affecting the original data list itself.

4. **Goal Seeking.** Goal Seeking provides a simple way to analyze simple goals that need to be set in order to meet important milestones in your business. Goal Seeking works by attempting to find the particular value you designate for a Set Cell by changing the value that's entered in the so-called Changing Cell.

   So, for example, with Goal Seeking, you can immediately see how much you have to make in gross sales in order to meet a particular net sales amount. You do this by designating the cell with gross sales as the Changing Cell and the cell with the net sales as the Set Cell in a worksheet table containing the formulas the calculate the net sales by deducting all the expected costs of doing business from the gross sales.

   See Chapter 8 for more on forecasting with the Goal Seeking feature.

3. **Scenario Manager.** Excel's Scenario Manager takes what-if data analysis to a whole new level by making it easy for you to create a whole series of possible financial scenarios, such as Most Likely, Best, and Worst case, based on various assumptions that indicate different levels of confidence. Perhaps the best part of the Scenario Manager is the Summary feature that enables you to create a summary table or pivot table on a separate worksheet that immediately shows the effect of the various scenario assumptions on the bottom line side by side.

   See Chapter 8 for more on using the Scenario Manager.

2. **Recommended Charts.** Never underestimate the power of the chart to help you immediately see trends that would otherwise go unnoticed in your worksheet data. And, a lot of times, choosing just the right type of chart for the type of data you're graphing is the key to bringing a developing trend to light. That's where Excel's Recommended Charts feature (Insert ⇨ Recommended Charts or Alt+NR) comes in so handy.

   When you choose this command, Excel previews the range of data currently selected in your worksheet, depicting the data in several different chart types that the program assumes best suit that data. You can then scroll through these chart previews to see which one does the best job in telling the data's story. If none of Excel's recommended charts seem to do the trick, you can then switch over to the All Charts tab where you can preview the data in any type of chart that Excel 2019 supports.

   See Chapter 10 for more on creating great-looking charts using the Recommended Charts feature.

1. **Insights.** The new Insights feature in Excel 2019 enables you to instantly build pivot charts and regular charts that highlight otherwise unnoticed aspects of your data.

   To use the Insights feature, you simply position the cell cursor in one of the cells in your data list before you select Data ⇨ Insights on the Ribbon or press Alt+NDI. Excel then opens an Insights task pane that contains thumbnails of pivot charts and sometimes regular charts based on a particular aspect of the data.

   Then, all that remains to do is for you to create any or all of the suggested charts appearing in the Insights task pane is to click the Insert PivotChart or Insert Chart link that appears in the lower-left corner of its thumbnail. Excel 2019 then creates an embedded chart on a new worksheet. In the case of a pivot chart, the program also creates a supporting pivot table on the new worksheet

   See Chapter 9 for more on creating and using pivot tables and pivot charts in a worksheet.

Index

Symbols and Numerics

K

Keep Source Column Widths option (Paste options palette), 165

Keep Source Formatting option (Paste options palette), 165

keyboard

cell selection with

AutoSelect feature, 104–105

extending cell selection, 104

Go To feature, 106

nonadjacent cell selections, 105–106

Shift+click method, 104

selecting commands with, 19

Touch keyboard

arrow keys, 31

Backspace key, 30

Ctrl key, 31

Dock Keyboard option, 30

Emoticon key, 31

Enter key, 30

Expanded Keyboard option, 30

Float Keyboard option, 30

Inking Keyboard option, 30

Keyboard Tips option, 30

Language Preferences option, 30

Mobile Keyboard option, 29

Numeric key, 30

overview, 28–29

Shift keys, 30

Split-Keyboard option, 29

Standard Keyboard option, 29

Typing Settings option, 30

Worksheet area, 28–31

keystroke shortcuts

assigning to macros, 368–369

for correcting errors, 63–64

inserting manual page breaks, 200–201

moving between worksheets with, 237

moving cell cursor, 27–28

navigating to records, 341–342

Office Clipboard, 369

opening Format Cells dialog box, 115

recalculation modes, 229

replacing cell entries, 226

toggling between normal cell display and formula cell display, 202

undo, 152–153

L

labels

columns, 25

positioning data labels, 305

text entries, 48–49

landscape orientation, 187–188

Language Preferences option (Touch keyboard), 30

launching Excel

when opening workbook, 385

from Windows 10

Metro view in tablet mode, 36–37

Search text box, 36

Start menu, 35

layering graphics

grouping graphic objects, 332–333

hiding graphic objects, 332–333

overview, 330–331

reordering graphic objects, 331–332

Layout selector (Status bar), 34

Line sparklines, 310

Linked Picture option (Paste options palette), 165

links

adding to worksheet, 363–366, 378

deleting, 170

sharing workbooks saved on OneDrive, 374–378

local images, inserting, 319

locking worksheets, 230–232

M

macros

automating commands with

assigning macros to Ribbon, 372–373

assigning to Quick Access toolbar, 373–374

overview, 366–367

recording new macros, 367–371

running macros, 371–372

defined, 234

maintaining worksheets

electronic sticky notes, 213–217

adding comments, 214

displaying comments, 215

editing comments, 216

overview, 213

printing comments, 216

finding data, 222–225

fixed headings, 210–213

multiple worksheets

adding worksheets, 238

color-coding, 240

comparing worksheets, 247–248

summary worksheet
  overview, 252–254
  scenarios, 269
Symbol dialog box, 76
synchronous scrolling, 247–248

T

tables
  data tables
    adding to charts, 305–306
    one-variable data table, 258–261
    overview, 257
    two-variable data table, 261–263
    what-if analysis with, 258–264
  database tables
    adding records to, 336–340
    editing records with data form, 341–342
    external data queries, 355–358
    filtering, 349–354
    finding records in, 342–343
    navigating records in, 342
    overview, 335–336
    sorting, 344–348
  formatting
    Banded Columns option, 109
    Banded Rows option, 109
    customizing table style, 110–111
    data list as table, 389
    Filter Button option, 109
    First Column option, 109
    Header Row option, 109
    Last Column option, 109
    overview, 106–109
    Total Row option, 109

pivot tables
  creating manually, 276–279
  creating with Quick Analysis tool, 272–274
  creating with Recommended Pivot Tables command, 274–275
  data analysis, 395
  defined, 271
  filtering, 280–284
  formatting, 279–280
  modifying, 285–288
Technical Stuff icon, 6
Tell Me help feature, 39–40
templates
  Blank Workbook template, 12–13, 43–44
  Welcome to Excel template, 43
ten-key entry method, values, 53–54
text boxes
  adding arrow to, 314–315
  adding to graphic, 312–313
  formatting, 313–314
text entries
  overview, 48–49
  text wraps, 131–132
Text to Columns command, 391
Text to Speech feature, 174–176
themes, graphics, 330
thesaurus, 174
3-D images
  formatting, 322–323
  inserting, 318, 319
Tiled option (Arrange Windows dialog box), 243

timelines
  data analysis, 396
  filtering pivot table data with, 283–284
Tip icon, 7
Touch keyboard
  arrow keys, 31
  Backspace key, 30
  Ctrl key, 31
  Dock Keyboard option, 30
  Emoticon key, 31
  Enter key, 30
  Expanded Keyboard option, 30
  Float Keyboard option, 30
  Inking Keyboard option, 30
  Keyboard Tips option, 30
  Language Preferences option, 30
  Mobile Keyboard option, 29
  Numeric key, 30
  overview, 28–29
  Shift keys, 30
  Split-Keyboard option, 29
  Standard Keyboard option, 29
  Typing Settings option, 30
  Worksheet area, 28–31
Touch mode
  Quick Access toolbar, 22
  selecting commands in, 20
touchscreen
  cell selection, 101
  cut and paste on, 156
  using AutoFill feature on, 72–73
transforming data, 393
Transpose option (Paste options palette), 165
Transpose option (Paste Special dialog box), 169

About the Author

Greg Harvey has authored tons of computer books, the most recent and most popular being *Excel 2016 For Dummies* and *Excel 2019 All-in-One Desk Reference For Dummies*. He started out training business users on how to use IBM personal computers and their attendant computer software in the rough and tumble days of DOS, WordStar, and Lotus 1-2-3 in the mid-'80s of the last century. After working for a number of independent training firms, Greg went on to teach semester-long courses in spreadsheet and database management software at Golden Gate University in San Francisco.

His love of teaching has translated into an equal love of writing. *For Dummies* books are, of course, his all-time favorites to write because they enable him to write to his favorite audience: the beginner. They also enable him to use humor (a key element to success in the training room) and, most delightful of all, to express an opinion or two about the subject matter at hand.

Greg received his doctorate degree in Humanities in Philosophy and Religion with a concentration in Asian Studies and Comparative Religion in May 2004. Everyone is glad that Greg was finally able to get out of school before he retired.

Dedication

To my great supports who keep me going: Chris and Riley

Author's Acknowledgments

Let me take this opportunity to thank all the people, both at John Wiley & Sons, Inc., and at Mind over Media, whose dedication and talent combined to get this book out and into your hands in such great shape.

At Wiley, I want to thank Katie Mohr for her encouragement and help in getting this project underway and her ongoing support every step of the way. She made sure that the project stayed on course and made it into production so that all the talented folks, especially Guy Hart-Davis as technical editor and Kelly Ewing as project editor, on the production team could create this great final product.

At Mind over Media, I want to thank Christopher Aiken for his review of the updated manuscript and invaluable input and suggestions on how best to restructure the book to accommodate all the wonderful new features in Excel 2019 and, more importantly, lay out the exciting new "anytime, anywhere" story to Excel users.

Publisher's Acknowledgments

Senior Acquisitions Editor: Katie Mohr
Project Editor: Kelly Ewing
Technical Editor: Guy Hart-Davis
Editorial Assistant: Matthew Lowe
Sr. Editorial Assistant: Cherie Case

Production Editor: Mohammed Zafar Ali
Cover Image: © dim4ik-69/Shutterstock